SPECIAL EDITION USI

KEYBOARD SHORTCUTS FOR QUICKBOOKS TASKS

To produce dates...	Press these keys...
Increase date by one day	+
Decrease date by one day	–
Today	t
First day of week	w
Last day of week	k
First day of month	m
Last day of month	h
First day of year	y
Last day of year	r
Display date calendar	Alt+down arrow

To edit text...	Press these keys...
Copy selected characters	Ctrl+C
Cut selected characters	Ctrl+X
Decrease check or form number by one	–
Delete character to left of insertion point	Backspace
Delete character to right of insertion point	Delete
Delete line	Ctrl+Delete
Edit current transaction in register	Ctrl+E
Increase check or form number by one	+
Insert line	Ctrl+Insert
Paste cut or copied characters	Ctrl+V
Undo changes made	Ctrl+Z

While using dialog boxes or forms...	Press these keys...
Close window	Esc
Display help	F1
Move across one word at a time in field	Ctrl+right arrow
Move across report columns to left	Left arrow
Move across report columns to right	Right arrow
Move back to previous word in field	Ctrl+left arrow

continues

KEYBOARD SHORTCUTS FOR QUICKBOOKS TASKS CONTINUED

While using dialog boxes or forms...	Press these keys...
Move down one line on form or report	Down arrow
Move down one screen in report	Page down
Move to beginning of current field or row	Home
Move to end of current field or row	End
Move to first item on list or previous month in register	Ctrl+page up
Move to last item on list or next month in register	Ctrl+page down
Move to next option or topic	Tab
Move to previous option or topic	Shift+Tab
Move up one line on form or report	Up arrow
Move up one screen in report	Page up

To perform QuickBooks activities...	Press these keys...
Quickfill and Recall (type first few letters of name and press Tab—rest of name fills in)	*abc* Tab
Display account list	Ctrl+A
Delete current check, invoice, transaction, or item from list	Ctrl+D
Edit list or register	Ctrl+E
Find transaction	Ctrl+F
Hide/show Qcards	Ctrl+F1
Go to register of transfer account	Ctrl+G
Show history of accounts receivable or accounts payable transaction	Ctrl+H
Create invoice	Ctrl+I
Display Customer:Job list	Ctrl+J
Display list for current field	Ctrl+L
Memorize transaction or report	Ctrl+M
Create new invoice, bill, check, or list item	Ctrl+N
Copy transaction in register	Ctrl+O
Print	Ctrl+P
QuickReport of transaction or list item	Ctrl+Q
Display memorized transaction list	Ctrl+T
Display register, or use list item	Ctrl+U
Paste copied transaction in register	Ctrl+V
Write check	Ctrl+W
QuickZoom on report	Enter
Display QuickBooks overview	F2

Special Edition Using QuickBooks® and QuickBooks Pro 99

Gail Perry, CPA

que

A Division of Macmillan Computer Publishing, USA
201 W. 103rd Street
Indianapolis, Indiana 46290

Contents at a Glance

Introduction

I Getting Started in QuickBooks
1. QuickBooks Overview 9
2. Getting Help 21
3. Periodic QuickBook Activities 31
4. Setting Up a Company in QuickBooks 39
5. Setting up Accounts, Inventory, Fixed Assets, and Payroll 63
6. Entering Historical Information 87
7. Chart of Accounts 105
8. Setting Up Services, Customers, and Suppliers 121
9. Separating Your Company into Logical Divisions 159

II Taking Care of Business
10. Job-cost Estimating and Tracking 169
11. Invoicing, Monthly Statements, and Accounts Receivable 183
12. Recording Income 197
13. Reporting Sales Tax 205
14. Using Inventory Features 217
15. Purchase Orders, Accounts Payable, and Paying Bills 233
16. Managing Fixed Assets 253
17. Entering Cash Transactions 263

III Paying Employees and Contractors
18. Paying Employees and Contractors 273
19. QuickBooks and Payroll Taxes 307

V Making QuickBooks Work for You
20. Customizing QuickBook Forms 337
21. QuickBooks Reports and Graphs 361
22. Setting Preferences 383

V QuickBooks Meets and 21st Century
23. Going Online with QuickBooks 409
24. Online Web Information 431

VI Getting the Most from QuickBooks
25. QuickBooks Pro and Time Tracking 443
26. Budgeting 463
27. Forecasting Your Financial Future with QuickBooks 471
28. Security 481
29. Income Taxes 489

VII Appendixes
A. Installation of QuickBooks 501
B. Sharing QuickBooks on a Network 505
C. Transferring Data Between QuickBooks and Other Applications 507
D. State Revenue Agencies 513

Glossary 521
Index 525

SPECIAL EDITION USING QUICKBOOKS® AND QUICKBOOKS PRO 99

Copyright ©1999 by Que®

All rights reserved. No part of this book shall be reproduced, stored in a retrieval system, or transmitted by any means, electronic, mechanical, photocopying, recording, or otherwise, without written permission from the publisher. No patent liability is assumed with respect to the use of the information contained herein. Although every precaution has been taken in the preparation of this book, the publisher and author assume no responsibility for errors or omissions. Neither is any liability assumed for damages resulting from the use of the information contained herein.

International Standard Book Number: 0-7897-1965-7

Library of Congress Catalog Card Number: 99-60354

Printed in the United States of America

First Printing: March 1999

00 99 01   4 3 2 1

TRADEMARKS

All terms mentioned in this book that are known to be trademarks or service marks have been appropriately capitalized. Que cannot attest to the accuracy of this information. Use of a term in this book should not be regarded as affecting the validity of any trademark or service mark.

QuickBooks is a registered trademark of Intuit.

WARNING AND DISCLAIMER

Every effort has been made to make this book as complete and as accurate as possible, but no warranty or fitness is implied. The information provided is on an "as is" basis. The authors and the publisher shall have neither liability nor responsibility to any person or entity with respect to any loss or damages arising from the information contained in this book.

Publisher
John Pierce

Executive Editor
Angela Wethington

Acquisitions Editor
Jamie Milazzo

Development Editor
Faithe Wempen

Managing Editor
Thomas F. Hayes

Project Editor
Sara Bosin

Copy Editor
JoAnna Kremer

Proofreader
Benjamin Berg

Technical Editor
Karen L. Boor

Interior and Cover Designs
Ruth Lewis
Dan Armstrong

Layout Technicians
Susan Geiselman
Amy Parker

Contents

Introduction 1

Using QuickBooks Every Day 2

Conventions Used in This Book 3
   Chapter Roadmaps 3
   Stepped Procedures 3
   Notes 4
   See Alsos 4
   Inline Index Entries 5
   Troubleshooting 5
   Underlined Hot Keys, or Mnemonics 5
   Shortcut Key Combinations 5
   Menu Commands 5

I Getting Started in QuickBooks

1 QuickBooks Overview 9

QuickBooks and QuickBooks Pro 10

Changes in QuickBooks Version 6 11

Changes in QuickBooks 99 12

Starting QuickBooks 12
   Running QuickBooks from the CD-ROM 13
   Running QuickBooks from Your Hard Drive 14

Backing Up Your Data 14
   How to Back Up 15
   How to Restore 16

QuickBooks Reminders 16

Troubleshooting 19

2 Getting Help 21

Using This Book for Help 22

Using the QuickBooks Help Index 23

Using the Help Find Feature 24

Using QCards 25

Using the How Do I? Button 26

Getting Help on the CD-ROM 26

Using Online Help 27

Intuit Technical Support 28
   Using the Automated Expert 28
   Telephone Technical Support 28
   QuickFax System 29

QuickBooks and Your Industry 29

Troubleshooting 29

3 Periodic QuickBooks Activities 31

Keeping QuickBooks Up-to-Date 32

Performing Daily Activities 32
   Understanding Types of Activities 33
   Creating a Checklist 33

Performing Weekly Activities 34

Working with Payroll 35

Performing Monthly Activities 35

Performing Quarterly Activities 36

Completing Annual Activities 37

Troubleshooting 38

4 Setting Up a Company in QuickBooks 39

The Start Date 40

The EasyStep Interview 42
   Stopping and Restarting the Interview 43
   Moving Around in the Interview 43

The General Section 44
    Upgrading from Earlier Versions of QuickBooks and Quicken 44
    New Users of QuickBooks 45
    Entering Company Information 46
    Setting Up Your Company Address 47
    Federal Identification Number 48
    First Month of the Year 48
    Choose a Tax Return 49
    Type of Business 50
    Save Your Work 51
    The QuickBooks Standard (Customized) Chart of Accounts 51
    Who Has Access to the Company File? 52
    Do You Have Inventory? 53
    Do You Want to Keep Track of Inventory in QuickBooks? 53
    Do You Collect Sales Tax from Customers? 54
    Selecting a Stylish Invoice 56
    Using QuickBooks for Your Payroll 57
    Making Estimates on Jobs 58
    Tracking Time in QuickBooks Pro 59
    Using Classes to Separate Your Business 59
    Bill Paying: Now or Later 60
    Displaying the Reminders List 60

Troubleshooting 61

5 Setting Up Accounts, Inventory, Fixed Assets, and Payroll 63

Setting Up Income Accounts 64

Setting Up Expense Accounts 65

General Information About Your Company's Income 66

Setting Up Items 67
    Creating a Service Item 67
    Creating a Non-Inventory Part Item 69
    Creating an Other Charge Item 70
    Creating Inventory Items 71

Entering Opening Balances 72
    Entering Customers 74
    Entering Vendors 74
    Credit Card Accounts 75
    Lines of Credit 76
    Setting Up Loans and Other Liabilities 76
    Set Up Your Bank Account 78
    Setting Up Asset Accounts 78
    Your Equity Accounts 79

Setting Up Payroll 80
    Setting Up Payroll Items 80
    Entering Starting Balances for Payroll 83

Finishing the Interview 85

Troubleshooting 86

6 Entering Historical Information 87

Changing Your Start Date 88

Checklist of Items Before You Begin 88

Entering Historical Bills Received 90

Entering Historical Invoices 92

Entering Money Received 94
    Entering Payments Against Invoices 94
    Reflecting Credits and Discounts 95
    Entering Cash Payments 97

Entering Bills Paid 99

Entering Deposits Made 99

Entering Payroll Transactions 100

Entering All Other Payments Made 102

Troubleshooting 103

7 Chart of Accounts 105

Understanding the Importance of Accounting 106

What Is an Account? 106

Types of Accounts 107
    Debits and Credits 107
    Assets and Why You Care About Them 108

Your Company's Liabilities 109

Equity: What Your Company Is Worth 109
    Understanding Equity Accounts 110
    Understanding the Type of Business 111

Income: Your Company's Bread and Butter 112

Expenses Reduce Business Income 112

QuickBooks Gives You a Standard List of Accounts 112
    Adding Accounts 113
    Deleting Accounts 114
    Deactivating an Account that Has Seen Some Action 115
    Deleting (Merging) an Account that Has Seen Some Action 116

Numbering Your Chart of Accounts 117
    Assigning Account Numbers with QuickBooks 117
    Assigning Account Numbers Yourself 118

Printing a Chart of Accounts List 119

Troubleshooting 119

8 Setting Up Services, Customers, and Suppliers 121

Understanding Items 122
    Types of Items 124
    Creating Subitems 126

Locating Information with Lists 127
    Updating Lists 128
    Merging Two List Entries 129
    Viewing an Entire List Entry 129

Working With Lists 130
    Features Common to All Lists 130
    Moving an Item in a List 130
    Listing Subitems 131
    Finding a List Entry 131

Quick Access to Editing 132
    Creating a New Item 133
    Using the Items List 134
    Generating Sales, Invoices, and Price Changes 134
    Calculating New Prices 136
    Receiving Items, Bills, and Credit from a Vendor 137
    Acknowledging Received Merchandise 139
    Changing the Receipt Into a Bill 140
    Entering Receipts and Credit from a Vendor 140
    Adjusting Quantity/Value of Inventory on Hand 140
    Adjusting Value Rather than Quantity 142

Making Reports Based on Items 142

Creating Reports from the Item List 142
    Generating a QuickReport 143
    Using Available Item List Reports 144
    Project 147
    Graphs 147

Customer, Vendor, and Employee Lists 149
    Customer:Job List 149
    Vendors List 151
    Employee List 153

Customer, Job, and Vendor Type Lists 154

Terms, Customer Messages, and Payment Method Lists 154
  Editing and Creating Payment Terms 154
  Printing, Deactivating, and Locating Terms in Use 156

Troubleshooting 157

9 Separating Your Company into Logical Divisions 159

What's a Class? 160

Setting Up Classes 160
  Creating a List of Classes 161
  Other Features of the Class List Window 162
  Creating Classes On-the-Fly 163

Reporting on Classes 164

Troubleshooting 165

II Taking Care of Business

10 Job-cost Estimating and Tracking 169

Setting Up Jobs 170

Optional Job Information 171
  Job Status 171
  Job Dates 173
  Job Description 173
  Job Type 174

Creating an Estimate 174

Invoicing Against an Estimate 176

Revising Estimates 179

Reporting on Work in Progress 180

Troubleshooting 181

11 Invoicing, Monthly Statements, and Accounts Receivable 183

Creating an Invoice 184

Creating a Monthly Statement 188

Tracking Accounts Receivable 191
  Viewing the Accounts Receivable Register 191
  Accounts Receivable Reports 192

Troubleshooting 194

12 Recording Income 197

Receiving Payments for Your Invoices 198

Receiving Cash 199

Making Deposits 201

Receiving Advances and Down Payments 203

Troubleshooting 204

13 Reporting Sales Tax 205

Understanding How Sales Tax Works 206

Getting Ready to Collect Sales Tax 206

Creating a Sales Tax Item 207
  Setting Up a Sales Tax Item 208
  Telling QuickBooks to Charge Sales Tax 209

Charging Sales Tax to Customers 210

Taxable Versus Non-Taxable Sales 212

Tax-Exempt Sales 212

Monthly Sales Tax Reports 213

Paying Sales Tax 214

Troubleshooting 215

14 Keeping Track of Your Inventory 217

What is Inventory? 218

Raw Materials, Work in Progress, and Finished Goods 218

Determining the Average Cost of Inventory Items 219

Using the QuickBooks Inventory Features 220

Setting Up Inventory Items On-the-Fly 221

Setting Up Inventory Items in General 223

Editing Items 224

Adding to Your Inventory 224
    Receiving Items Without a Bill 224
    Receiving Items with a Bill 226

Reports About Inventory 226

Taking a Physical Inventory Count 227

Adjusting Quantity and Value of Inventory Account 228

Alternatives to the QuickBooks Inventory Feature 229
    The Spreadsheet Alternative 230
    The Database Alternative 231
    Other Software Alternatives 231

Troubleshooting 232

15 Purchase Orders, Accounts Payable, and Paying Bills 233

Using Purchase Orders 234

What's on Order? 238

Tax-Exempt Purchases 238

Receiving Goods 239
    Goods Received Without a Bill 239
    Goods Received With a Bill 241

Paying Bills 241

Writing Checks in QuickBooks 243

Printing Checks 245

The QuickBooks Check Register 247

Voiding Checks 248

The Monthly Ritual of Bank Account Reconciliation 248

Troubleshooting 251

16 Managing Fixed Assets 253

Why Do We Have to Use Depreciation? 254

Accounting for Fixed Assets 254

Calculating Depreciation 255
    Straight-Line Depreciation 256
    MACRS Depreciation 256
    MACRS Depreciation Tables 257

Recording Depreciation 258
    Creating a General Journal Entry 259

Following the Audit Trail 260

Selling Depreciable Assets 260

Alternatives to QuickBooks for Fixed Asset Tracking 261

Troubleshooting 262

17 Entering Cash Transactions 263

Forms of Cash 264

Quick Cash Entry 264

Daily Cash Summaries 265

Cash Over or Short 266

Depositing Cash 268

Credit Card Payments from
Customers 268

Troubleshooting 269

III Paying Employees and Contractors

18 Paying Employees and Contractors 273

Determining Employees and Independent
Contractors 274

Gathering Payroll Information 275
  Your Personal Experience With
  Payroll 275
  Planning Payroll 276

Paying Employees Versus Paying
Independent Contractors 277

QuickBooks Payroll and Employee
Setup 278
  Payroll Expense and Liability
  Accounts 278
  Understanding Payroll Expenses and
  Payroll Liabilities 278

Setting Up Employees 279
  Specifying Earnings 280
  Applying New Payroll Items 281
  Additions, Deductions, and Company
  Contributions 283
  Setting up Payroll Taxes 283
  Establishing Sick and Vacation
  Time 284

Updating Year-to-Date Amounts 284
  Entering Year-to-Date Paycheck
  Amounts 285
  Entering Prior Payments of Taxes and
  Liabilities 287

Updating Payroll Tax Tables 288

Payday 291
  Preparing Paychecks 291
  Previewing Your Checks 292
  Special Payroll Reports 296
  Working with W-2s 298
  Paying Independent Contractors 301

Troubleshooting 305

19 QuickBooks and Payroll Taxes 307

Creating Checks To Pay Your Taxes 309
  Writing Two Tax Liability Checks to
  the Same Vendor 311
  Setting Up Employee Tax Status,
  Withholding, and Allowances 312
  Supplying Wage Base Information for
  State Taxes 315
  Setting Up Payroll Items to Collect
  State Taxes 316
  Creating a New Tax Payroll Item 317
  Creating a Report of State Payroll
  Taxes 320
  Preparing, Reviewing, and Printing
  Form 941 322
  Making Adjustments 322
  Creating Form 940 323

Reports That Help with Tax
Corrections 326
  Employee Earnings Summary 326
  Payroll Summary by Item 327
  Searching For More Specific
  Information 327

Common Problems With Tax
Figures 329
  Federal Unemployment Tax Seems
  High 329
  Liability Amounts Seem Incorrect 330
  Correcting Liability Amount
  Errors 331

Setting Up Advance Earned Income
Credit 332

Troubleshooting 333

IV Making QuickBooks Work for You

20 Customizing QuickBooks Forms 337

Customizing a Form 338
  Determining Which Template to Change 339
  Adding and Removing Fields 340
  Customizing a Form Header 342
  Customizing Individual Fields 342
  Adding, Removing, and Reordering Columns 342
  Customizing a Progressive Estimate Invoice 344
  Customizing a Form Footer 345
  Customizing Company Info and Adding a Logo 346
  Making a Template Inactive 348

Moving and Resizing Fields 348
  Creating a Common Height or Width 349
  Resizing and Changing Text in a Form 350
  Adding a Border to a Form Element 351
  Changing Your View of Your Form 352
  The Layout Designer Grid 352
  Layout Designer Margins 352
  Show Envelope Window 353
  Previewing Your Form 353
  Creating Custom Fields 354
  When to Use Custom Fields 354
  Reviewing a Custom Field Example 354
  Applying Your New Fields 355
  Creating Forms That Use Your New Field 355

Customizing Tips 357
  Special Considerations for Statements 358
  Adding a Form to the Iconbar 358

Troubleshooting 359

21 QuickBooks Reports and Graphs 361

Standard Reports 363

Commonly Used QuickBooks Reports 363
  Profit and Loss Statement 364
  Balance Sheet 365
  Accounts Receivable Aging Reports 366
  Collections Report 367
  General Ledger 368

Customizing Reports 368
  Changing the Report Date 369
  Changing the Report Columns 369
  Changing Report Headers and Footers 370
  Collapsing Subaccounts 371
  Using the Customize Button 371
  Applying Filters 372
  Formatting a Report 373
  Memorizing the Report Format and Setting 373
  Editing and Deleting Memorized Reports 374

Printing Reports 374

QuickBooks's Graphs 376

Troubleshooting 381

22 Setting Preferences 383

Accounting Preferences 384

Checking Preferences 385

Finance Charge Preferences 386

General Preferences 388

Iconbar Preferences 390

Jobs & Estimates Preferences 392

Menus Preferences 393

Payroll and Employees Preferences 394

Purchases & Vendors Preferences 396

Reminders Preferences 398

Reports and Graphs Preferences 399

Sales & Customers Preferences 402

Sales Tax Preferences 403

Tax 1099 Preferences 404

Time Tracking Preferences 405

Troubleshooting 406

V QuickBooks Meets the 21st Century

23 Going Online with QuickBooks 409

Common Questions About QuickBooks and Online Banking 410

Preliminary and Precautionary Steps 411

After Your Account is Activated 412

Setting Up QuickBooks's Internet Connection 413

Using QuickBooks Online Interview 414
    If You've Received Your Bank Info Through The Mail 416
    If You Are Still Exploring Your Options 417

Going Online with A New Account 418
    Retrieving your QuickStatements 419
    Matching QuickBooks Accounts with Online Bank Statements 419
    Looking Up An Account's Identification 421

Making an Online Payment 422
    Sending and Editing a Payment 423
    Highlighting Items You Want to Send 423

Sending an Online Message 423

Sending a Payment Inquiry 425

Transferring Money Between Accounts Online 425

Obtaining a Report on Online Transactions 426

QuickBooks Online Payroll Service 427

QuickBooks's Online Resources 427
    QuickBooks.com 427
    Find an Advisor 428
    www.cashfinder.com 428
    Small Business by Quicken.com 429

Troubleshooting 430

24 Online Web Information 431

Poking Around on the Web 432

Visiting the QuickBooks Home Page on the Web 432

Useful Business Resources 433

Taxes and Accounting 435

Laws and Regulations 435

What's in the News? 436

Odds and Ends 438

Troubleshooting 439

VI Getting the Most from QuickBooks

25 QuickBooks Pro and Time Tracking 443

QuickBooks Timer Overview 444

What You Need To Run the QuickBooks Timer 446

Getting Ready to Use the Timer 446
    Exporting a List for the Timer 447
    Installing the Timer 448

Learning Your Way Around The
Timer 449
Using the Timer 451
Creating a New Timed Activity 452
Using an Activity Template 453

Exporting Timer Data To
QuickBooks 454

Opening Timer Data in QuickBooks 455

Creating Install Disks for the Timer 457

Getting Your Employees Up to Speed
With the Timer 458

Backed Up and Condensed Timer
Data 458
Condensing and Backing Up Timer
Data 459
Restoring Backed Up Timer
Data 460

Viewing and Editing Timer Data
in Detail 460

Troubleshooting 461

26 Budgeting 463

What is a Budget? 464

Creating a Budget 464

The First Year of Business 465

Creating Budget Reports 467
The Budget Overview Report 467
The Budget Versus Actual Report 467
The Budget by Job Overview
Report 468
The Budget by Job Comparison
Report 469
The Budget Balance Sheet Overview
Report 469
The Budget Balance Sheet
Comparison Report 470

Troubleshooting 470

27 Forecasting Your Financial Future with QuickBooks 471

Understanding the Types of
Forecasting 472

Utilizing a Sales Forecast 472
Preparing a Sales Forecast 473
Printing a Sales Report 474

Preparing Forecasts 475
Cash Receipts Forecast 475
Cash Outflow for Inventory
Forecast 476
Cash Outflow Forecast 477
Cash Flow Forecast 477

Troubleshooting 479

28 Security 481

Backing Up Your Company Files 482

Working With Passwords and User
Access 482
Setting Up the Administrator
First 483
Setting Up Access for Other
Users 485
Assigning Access to Areas of
QuickBooks 486

Year-End Protection: Closing Your
Books 487

Troubleshooting 488

29 Income Taxes 489

Preparing Quarterly Estimated Taxes 490
Estimated Payments for
Corporations 490
Estimated Payments for
Individuals 491

Assigning Tax Lines 491

Tax Reports **492**
  Income Tax Preparation Report **492**
  Income Tax Summary Report **493**
  Income Tax Detail Report **494**

Tax Forms **495**

Tax Software Programs **496**

Non–Tax-Related Transactions **497**

Hiring a Pro **498**

Troubleshooting **498**

VII Appendixes

A Installation of QuickBooks **501**

Hardware and Software Requirements **501**

Performing the Installation **502**

Installing from Floppy Disks **503**

B Sharing QuickBooks on a Network **505**

Network Requirements **505**

Performing the Installation **505**
  Setting Up Your Users **506**
  Multiuser and Single-User Mode **506**

C Transferring Data Between QuickBooks and Other Applications **507**

Using QuickBooks with Quicken **507**

Using QuickBooks with Your Favorite Program **508**

Exporting Lists **510**

Using Microsoft Word with QuickBooks **511**

Troubleshooting **512**

D State Revenue Agencies **513**

Glossary **521**

Index **525**

About the Author

Gail Perry is a CPA and a graduate of Indiana University. She has worked in public accounting for more than 20 years and has spent that time helping her clients make the best use of the tax laws and accounting rules that benefit them. Gail is a former senior tax consultant with the international CPA firm of Deloitte and Touche, where she specialized in provided tax planning services and advice to small businesses.

Gail is the author of over a dozen books, including *Using QuickBooks and QuickBooks Pro 6.0*, *The Complete Idiot's Guide to Doing Your Income Taxes*, and *Using Quicken 5 for Windows*. She is a columnist for the *Indianapolis Star*, where she fields tax questions on a weekly basis.

In addition, Gail has been an instructor of adult computer education since 1985 and currently teaches classes in QuickBooks for the Indiana CPA Society.

Dedication

To Katherine and Georgia, who constantly remind me that I have a life beyond the computer keyboard.

Acknowledgments

Special thanks to the great crew at Macmillan Computer Publishing who worked long hours, including weekends and nights, to get this book out on time. I particularly want to thank Jamie Milazzo, Faithe Wempen, and Karen Boor, who worked so hard to make sure this book would be the excellent resource that it is. I also want to thank Rick Pranitis, who continuously makes sure that my computer can keep pace with my flying fingers, and whose perpetual encouragement keeps me going.

Tell Us What You Think!

As the reader of this book, *you* are our most important critic and commentator. We value your opinion and want to know what we're doing right, what we could do better, what areas you'd like to see us publish in, and any other words of wisdom you're willing to pass our way.

As an executive editor at Macmillan Computer Publishing, I welcome your comments. You can fax, email, or write me directly to let me know what you did or didn't like about this book—as well as what we can do to make our books stronger.

Please note that I cannot help you with technical problems related to the topic of this book, and that due to the high volume of mail I receive, I might not be able to reply to every message.

When you write, please be sure to include this book's title and author as well as your name and phone or fax number. I will carefully review your comments and share them with the author and editors who worked on the book.

Fax: 317.581.4663

Email: office_que@mcp.com

Mail: Executive Editor
Macmillan Computer Publishing
201 West 103rd Street
Indianapolis, IN 46290 USA

INTRODUCTION

INTRODUCTION

Welcome to *Special Edition Using QuickBooks & QuickBooks Pro 99!*

This book is the most comprehensive and useful reference available for QuickBooks 99, an Intuit program. With this book you will learn how to put the nation's number one selling business accounting software program to work for you, how to keep track of all the financial activity of your business, and how to produce useful information that will help you with budgeting, planning for the future, and meeting important deadlines such as tax return filing dates, financial statement reporting dates, and so on.

Having learned to do bookkeeping on a manual system—using large ledger pages and lots of erasers—I have a vast appreciation for many of the important time-saving elements of this program.

With QuickBooks you can

- Produce professional-looking financial statements and reports and be assured of their accuracy.
- Quickly customize and revise reports to include just the information you need.
- Produce reports for any time period you want.
- Easily compare data from one year to the next.
- Prepare tax forms.
- Create a budget and monitor your performance.
- Cross-reference numbers on reports to the documents in which the original numbers were entered.

This is just a short list of the major changes you will see when moving to a computerized program. The following section presents you with a sample of all the day-to-day transactions you can perform, effortlessly, with QuickBooks.

Using QuickBooks Every Day

Whether you enter your business transactions daily or catch up on a weekly or less-frequent basis depends on many factors. These factors include how many transactions you have, how organized you are, how much time you have to devote to computer data entry, and how important it is to you to have up to the minute reports at your fingertips.

Just look what you can do, as frequently as you want, with QuickBooks at your side:

- **Create and maintain a Customer list**—You can keep an up-to-date list of all your customers: name, address, shipping address, phone, email, fax, contact name, favorite color (really! You can save any type of information you want!), not to mention accounting information such as the terms you usually apply to a particular customer's order and whether the customer is subject to sales tax.

- **Create and maintain a Vendor list**—Keep information handy on all your vendors: name, address, phone, fax, email, contact name, your account number, hours of business, and items you normally order from each vendor.

- **Write and print checks**—Enter checks on an onscreen form that look just like your own checks, and then print the checks on actual check forms. All you have to do is sign the check! Check amounts are automatically deducted from your bank account balance and charged to the appropriate expense account.

- **Write and print invoices**—Prepare invoices for your customers on an onscreen form that looks just like a real invoice. If you prepare estimates in QuickBooks Pro, you can generate invoices right from the estimates. Print the invoice on a form that you design yourself—one that conforms to your own business needs.

- **Write and print purchase orders**—Fill out a purchase order onscreen, entering the items that you want to purchase. Choose a vendor name, and the address fills in automatically. Print the purchase order on a form that you design yourself (or use one of the standard forms that come with QuickBooks).

- **Reconcile your checking account**—All right, so you probably won't do this one every day—but when you're ready to reconcile, the process is easier than you can imagine. Just check off every check and deposit that appears on your bank statement, and you're finished!

- **Record payments from your customers**—Enter amounts received from your customers by simply checking off items from a list of amounts owed to you. Your accounts receivable balance is updated automatically.

- **Enter and pay bills from vendors**—Update your accounts payable immediately as you enter each bill you receive. Cross-check bills against purchase orders and records of merchandise received. Then make bill payments by checking off which bills you want to pay. Checks are prepared automatically.

- **Create and print numerous reports**—Use the standard reports that come with QuickBooks—reports for nearly every situation—or customize your own reports to reflect just the activity you want to show. Prepare Quick Reports with a simple mouse click, displaying the details behind the numbers on your reports or showing all the activity for any one of your customers or vendors.

- **Create a budget**—Use QuickBooks to style a budget that helps you stay in touch with your company's potential. Know how to plan the future performance of your company.
- **Generate payroll tax forms**—Prepare all your federal payroll tax forms in QuickBooks: Form 941, Form 940, W-2, W-3, and W-4.
- **Prepare income tax reports**—Create quarterly and annual reports to help you in the preparation of your business income tax returns. Export tax information to TurboTax software for computerized tax return preparation.
- **Use QuickBooks for more than one company**—You can keep records for as many companies as you want with a single copy of QuickBooks software.
- **Record separate financial activity for different locations of your business**—Use the Class feature of QuickBooks to identify separate divisions or locations of the same business. Then you can generate reports for each class individually or for the company as a whole.
- **Produce sales tax reports**—Always know how much you owe in sales tax by preparing a sales tax payable report.
- **Generate aging reports**—Find out how much is owed by your customers, and find out how much of that is overdue, by producing an aging report.

Conventions Used in This Book

With more than a decade of experience writing and developing the most successful computer books available, Que has learned what special features help users the most. Look for the following special features throughout *Special Edition Using QuickBooks and QuickBooks Pro 99*.

Chapter Roadmaps

Each chapter begins with a roadmap, a list of topics that are covered in the chapter. This way you can tell at a glance what you will find in each chapter.

Stepped Procedures

When learning a new computer program, many features are most easily explained in a step-by-step process. The procedures explained in this book are presented with numbered steps that don't leave out any instructions. Follow along with the steps as you perform tasks at your own keyboard. Following is an example of a numbered procedure.

To set up a new income account, complete the following steps:

1. Make sure that Yes is selected, and then click on Next. The Adding an Income Account screen appears.

2. Enter the name of an income account that you want to add (for example, Catering or Lumber Sales or Machine Rental).
3. Choose a tax line for the account if you plan to use QuickBooks to help you summarize information for your income tax return.
4. Click Next, and you see that your new income account has been added to the list of income accounts for the company.

NOTES

Notes point out key features, warnings, and real-world examples, as well as technical, non-essential, or interesting information that you might not otherwise pick up from using the program. You can learn the program without reading the notes, but you'll find that they can greatly enhance your experience with QuickBooks. Following are a few examples of Notes:

> **Note**
> You can print a report to a file instead of a printer. By doing so, you have the capability to open the file in another program (such as a spreadsheet program) and further manipulate the numbers. Choose File, Print, and then click on File. Enter the name that you want to give the file, and then click Print.

> **Tip #1001 from Gail Perry**
> Keep a copy of last year's tax return nearby to use as a reference for assigning tax lines. If this is the first year that your company will file a tax return, use a blank tax form as a reference.

> Warning! Credit Card Statement Date Must Fall On or Before Start Date! You get an error message if you try to enter a credit card statement date that falls after your start date. The implication is that there was a balance due on your start date that is not being properly reflected. If there was no balance due on your start date, go ahead and set up the credit card, entering zero in the Statement Ending Balance area. If you can't find the credit card statement from just prior to your start date, you can back into the amount that was on that statement by looking at the beginning balance on the first statement from after the start date.

SEE ALSOS

Throughout the book you will find See Alsos, which are cross-references designed to take you to other places in the book that include information that might be helpful to the topic at hand. A See Also looks like this:

→ To memorize a report, **see p. 373**.

In addition to the features listed previously, there are several other conventions designed to help you find your way through the program.

Inline Index Entries

These entries are a convenient way for the reader to find a definition or explanation of a term, without having to look it up in the index. Look for entries that direct you to the page number where the definition of a term appears.

Troubleshooting

This section appears at the end of each chapter, providing you with a quick question and answer session for problems that arise frequently among QuickBooks users.

Underlined Hot Keys, or Mnemonics

Just like an onscreen menu that contains underlined letters as keyboard alternatives to the mouse, the menu and screen references in this book contain underlined letters. To activate a feature using an underlined letter, press the Alt key, and then press the underlined letter. You do not need to (and often should not) hold down the Alt key while pressing the underlined letter. For instance, to choose the Next button, press Alt, and then press the letter N. The N does not need to be capitalized.

Shortcut Key Combinations

Shortcut key combinations are presented with plus signs joining the keys. For example, Ctrl+Z means hold down the Ctrl key while you press the Z key.

Menu Commands

Instructions for choosing menu commands are presented as follows:

> Choose Activities, Lists

This example means open the Activities menu and select Lists, which in this case opens the box displaying all the types of lists for your company.

This book also has the following typeface enhancements to indicate special text, as indicated in the following mini-table:

Typeface	Description
Italics	Italics is used to indicate new terminology.
`Computer Type`	This type is used to indicate things that you type in.
MYFILE.DOC	Filenames and directories are set in all capital letters to distinguish them from regular text.

PART I

GETTING STARTED IN QUICKBOOKS

1 QuickBooks Overview 9

2 Getting Help 21

3 Periodic QuickBooks Activities 31

4 Setting Up a Company in QuickBooks 39

5 Setting Up Accounts, Inventory, Fixed Assets, and Payroll 63

6 Entering Historical Information 87

7 Chart of Accounts 105

8 Setting Up Services, Customers, and Suppliers 121

9 Separating Your Company into Logical Divisions 159

CHAPTER 1

QUICKBOOKS OVERVIEW

In this chapter

QuickBooks and QuickBooks Pro   10

Changes in QuickBooks Version 6   11

Changes in QuickBooks 99   12

Starting QuickBooks   12

Backing Up Your Data   14

QuickBooks Reminders   16

Welcome to Intuit's QuickBooks, a program designed for you and your business. QuickBooks is an accounting program that has been specially created for people who don't have a background in accounting. The program contains very little accounting jargon, and the data entry screens have been created with actual business forms in mind. You'll find that you don't have to learn new accounting or data entry techniques to take advantage of this program.

Many aspects of operating a business can be simplified and better understood with the help of QuickBooks and your computer. For example, QuickBooks can help you perform the following tasks:

- Keep records for your business
- Track sales activity
- Pay the people who work for you
- Produce reports about financial aspects of your business
- Learn more about your business
- Prepare and use budgets
- Plan for the future
- Prepare payroll tax forms
- Prepare job costing and estimates (QuickBooks Pro only)
- Prepare income tax forms
- Reconcile your bank and credit card accounts
- Keep lists of customers and vendors
- Prepare form letters and mailing labels
- Keep track of separate locations and departments of the same company
- Bank and pay bills online

With this book, you will learn how to make all the preceding tasks part of your regular routine.

QuickBooks and QuickBooks Pro

Which program should you purchase, QuickBooks or QuickBooks Pro? Both programs offer nearly the same features. The following features are unique to QuickBooks Pro:

- **Time tracking**—Use timesheets right on your computer to enter employee time and have it automatically flow to the payroll features. You can also associate time with jobs automatically, and bill that time on your invoices. Create reports to help analyze how employees use their time by displaying employee time organized by job and type of activity.

- **Estimates and bids**—Use QuickBooks Pro to keep track of bids you make on jobs, to compare actual job costs to your estimates, to revise estimates as the job progresses, and to prepare various reports incorporating job estimates. Create invoices from your estimates; this can be billing for the entire estimate, particular items from the estimate, or a percentage of completion.
- **Advanced job costing**—Produce reports that display job progress and profitability, and classify the information on these reports by job, by type of service you provide, or by type of item you sell.
- **Multiuser environment**—Up to five users can work with your QuickBooks Pro company file at one time. Levels of password protection are available so that each user can have rights to various parts of the file.

If you don't keep track of separate jobs in your business, or if the time tracking features aren't important to you, then QuickBooks is the program you need. If the preceding features will be of use to you, you need to consider QuickBooks Pro.

Changes in QuickBooks Version 6

QuickBooks and QuickBooks Pro version 6 offer several new features:

- Multiple users can access information in QuickBooks Pro version 6 at the same time.
- Users of the program can have master preferences (see Chapter 22, "Setting Preferences") and individual preferences at the same time.
- Options for protecting sensitive data from prying eyes have been improved in this latest version (see Chapter 28, "Security").
- Adding new users is easier than before using the Setup Wizard (see Appendix B, "Sharing QuickBooks on a Network").
- You can keep track of who is making what changes to the company data by following the trail (see Chapter 28).
- Entering dates is easier and faster (see Chapter 11, "Invoicing, Monthly Statements, and Accounts Receivable").
- Improved sorting options are available in the registers (see Chapter 15, "Purchase Orders, Accounts Payable, and Paying Bills").
- Pop-up menus open with a right-click (mentioned throughout the book).
- More Web services, such as online banking and bill-paying, are available (see Part V, "QuickBooks Meets the 21st Century").
- You can set up online direct deposit for employees (see Chapter 18, "Paying Employees and Contractors").
- Handling of state and local payroll taxes has been improved (see Chapter 18).
- You can track withholding for Advance Earned Income Credit (see Chapter 18).
- Various reports throughout the program are new (see Chapter 21, "QuickBooks Reports and Graphs").

Changes in QuickBooks 99

The latest version of QuickBooks and QuickBooks Pro offers the following new features:

- **Expanded date field**—All forms and registers now include a four-digit year field.
- **Deposit slips**—You can print a deposit slip to accompany your deposit at the bank.
- **Purchase orders**—The new QuickBooks enables you to open purchase orders by job reports and track customer jobs right on your purchase order forms.
- **Cash Flow report**—QuickBooks has added a Cash Flow report to its group of standard reports.
- **Improved reports**—Printed reports are more professional looking than ever before.
- **Enhanced time tracking**—You can use the new stopwatch timer and use QuickBooks's timer to pay owners, contractors, and employees.
- **Total Y2K compliance**—QuickBooks is completely ready for the year 2000.
- **Mailing improvements**—Use the new nine-digit zip code for more precise sorting, and you can choose mailing labels by zip code.
- **Greater integration with other software programs**—New integration features mean ease of import and export of reports and data to and from Microsoft Word and Microsoft Excel.

As you can see, plenty of changes and improvements have been made in the program. If you are already a user of QuickBooks, you will surely find something of interest in the preceding list. If you are new to QuickBooks, everything you see here will just seem like the most natural thing to you because you don't need to know how the program ran before these features were added.

Starting QuickBooks

If this is the first time you are using QuickBooks, you need to know how to get things started. After installing your program (see Appendix A, "Installation of QuickBooks," for information about installation), you have the choice of running QuickBooks from the CD-ROM or from your hard drive.

> **Note** If you are running QuickBooks on a network, see Appendix B for special network considerations.

Running QuickBooks from the CD-ROM

Starting your program when you have a QuickBooks CD-ROM is as simple as turning on the computer and placing the CD-ROM in the appropriate drive. The program starts automatically, and you will see the screen shown in Figure 1.1.

Note

If your computer does not automatically recognize a CD-ROM when it is inserted in the drive, the CD-ROM notification feature might be turned off. To turn on CD-ROM notification (or turn it off if you don't want to use this feature), click the Start button on your Windows taskbar. Then choose Settings, Control Panel, and double-click on the System icon. Choose the Device Manager tab, and click the plus sign next to CD-ROM. Click on your CD-ROM, and then click the Properties button. Click the Settings tab, and then check (or uncheck, if you are turning off this feature) the box labeled Auto Insert Notification. Click OK to save your settings and exit the box. Click OK again to close the System Properties box. By the way, you will find that some older CD-ROMs do not automatically turn on, even when this notification is enabled.

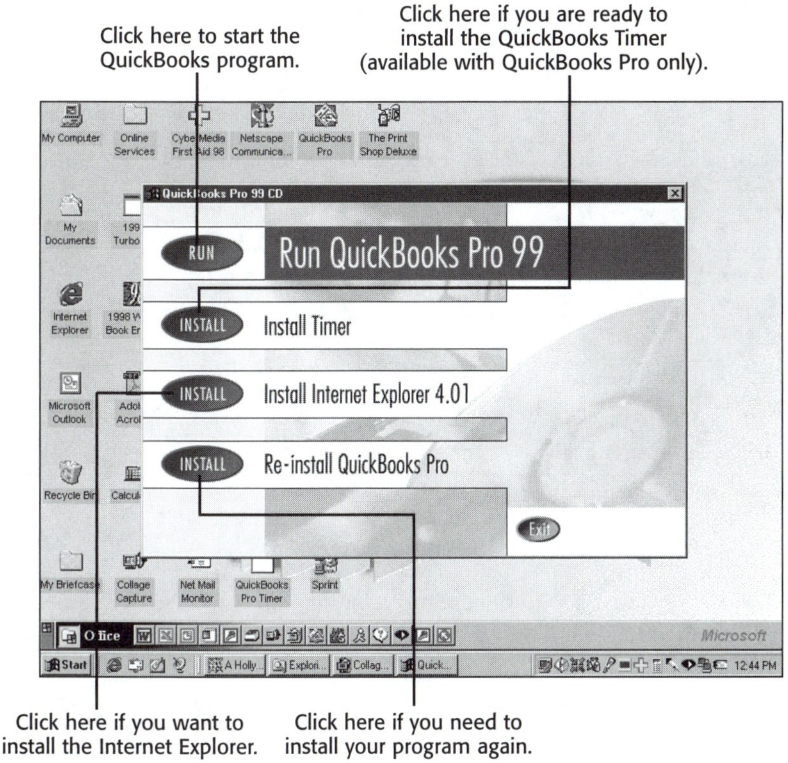
Click here to start the QuickBooks program.
Click here if you are ready to install the QuickBooks Timer (available with QuickBooks Pro only).
QuickBooks Pro 99 CD
RUN
Run QuickBooks Pro 99
INSTALL
Install Timer
INSTALL
Install Internet Explorer 4.01
INSTALL
Re-install QuickBooks Pro
Exit
Click here if you want to install the Internet Explorer.
Click here if you need to install your program again.

Figure 1.1
Inserting your QuickBooks CD-ROM in its drive produces this introductory screen.

From the introductory QuickBooks screen, click the Run QuickBooks (or Run QuickBooks Pro) button to start the program.

RUNNING QUICKBOOKS FROM YOUR HARD DRIVE

CD-ROM not available? You can still run your QuickBooks program. When you installed the program, a QuickBooks icon probably appeared on your desktop. Double-click the QuickBooks icon to start the program.

Alternatively, click the Start button on the Windows 95 taskbar, and then choose Programs, QuickBooks (Pro). When the QuickBooks program group appears, you can choose QuickBooks (see Figure 1.2), QuickBooks Help, or the QuickBooks Timer (if you have it installed) to start the QuickBooks program.

Figure 1.2
Use the Start menu to get to your QuickBooks program.

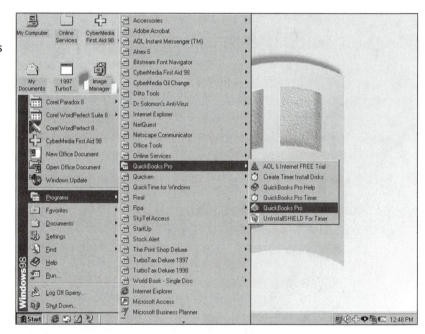

BACKING UP YOUR DATA

No doubt, you are eager to get started with QuickBooks—setting up your company, entering your data, and taking advantage of all the useful forms and reports that QuickBooks can produce for you.

Before you begin, plan a backup schedule. When you're ready to enter your company's precious financial data in a computer program, nothing is more important than keeping backups of the information.

A wise person once said, "A computer that hasn't crashed is a computer that hasn't crashed *yet*." Computers break down, lightning sends its messengers into electrical circuitry, employees betray employers, viruses send ripples through your system, magnets erase or corrupt data stored on disks, and even unexplainable events occur causing computer or software failure. The advent of the paperless office might have eased up on storage needs, but it has caused a new array of problems in the form of vulnerability of data.

Use some sort of backup device, and use it frequently—at least every week. After all your data is entered in QuickBooks, store a backup of your complete data file somewhere away from your business, in a safe place in case a fire or some other serious damage occurs to your place of business.

You can back up your data in many ways. Choose the one that is the easiest for you to use so that backing up won't be a burden. Following are just a few of the various backup techniques you might want to consider:

- Tape backup system
- Floppy disks
- External hard drive
- ZIP drive

How to Back Up

After you create a company file in QuickBooks, you need to put yourself on a regular backup schedule. Open your QuickBooks program when you're ready to back up your information; then follow these instructions:

1. To back up your company data to a disk, ZIP drive, or another hard drive, choose File, Back Up. The Back Up Company To box appears.
2. Choose a filename to use to store your backed-up information, and indicate the disk drive on which you want to place the data (see Figure 1.3).
3. Click the Save button. QuickBooks begins the backup process. Note that if you are backing up to a file you used previously, QuickBooks asks you whether you want to write over this file. Answering No prompts QuickBooks to ask you for a different filename for the backup. QuickBooks backs up your data to the designated file. You are returned to your data screen when the process is complete.

Figure 1.3
Not backing up at all is the only wrong method for backing up. Use this window to choose a drive location and filename for your backup.

The backup feature on the menu is dim if you try to back up without any company file open.

Note that you can back up only one company file at a time using the QuickBooks backup feature. If you are using QuickBooks to keep records for more than one company, you must open each company file individually and then perform the backup steps.

The first time you use the File, Back Up feature, you see a notice about Online-Backup. If you click Yes in the box that appears onscreen you are taken to the QuickBooks Web site where you can read more information about backing up to remote locations.

To back up your data using a tape backup system, follow the instructions that accompany the tape system. You do not need to use the backup command found in QuickBooks.

How to Restore

To restore your data from a disk, follow these steps:

1. From within QuickBooks, choose File, Restore. The Restore From dialog box appears (see Figure 1.4).
2. Choose the filename that you used to store your backed-up data, and then click OK.
3. When a second dialog box, Restore To, opens defaulting to the QuickBooks directory on your hard drive, click the Open button, and your data is restored.

Figure 1.4
Restoring your data returns you to the last data you backed up. Transactions entered since the last backup must be reentered.

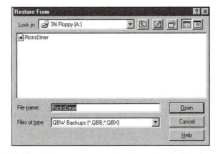

To restore your data from a tape backup system, follow the instructions that accompany the tape system. You do not need to use the restore command found in QuickBooks.

QuickBooks Reminders

Forget about keeping lists and slips of paper all over your desk. The QuickBooks Reminders feature keeps the lists for you and tells you what you need to do each day by starting your QuickBooks sessions with a Reminders dialog box (see Figure 1.5).

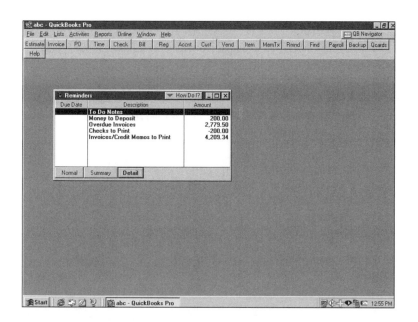

Figure 1.5
Let QuickBooks do your thinking for you. Double-click on any item to see the related details, or click the Detail button to see the details of all items.

QuickBooks can remind you of almost anything, including

- Invoices that are past due for which you haven't received payment
- Bills that you need to pay
- Checks and other forms that you have completed in QuickBooks but have yet to print
- Purchase orders that have yet to be filled
- Money waiting to be deposited
- Memorized transactions that need to be entered
- Personal notes such as your anniversary or your brother's birthday
- Whatever else you ask the program to tell you about on your personal To Do list

Tell QuickBooks what items you want to be reminded about by following these steps:

1. Choose File, Preferences. The Preferences window appears.
2. Scroll down through the icons that appear on the left side of the screen and click on the Reminders icon when it appears. The Reminders window appears.
3. On the My Preferences tab, check the box to have QuickBooks show you the Reminders window each time you start the program.
4. Click on the Company Preferences tab to view the screen shown in Figure 1.6.

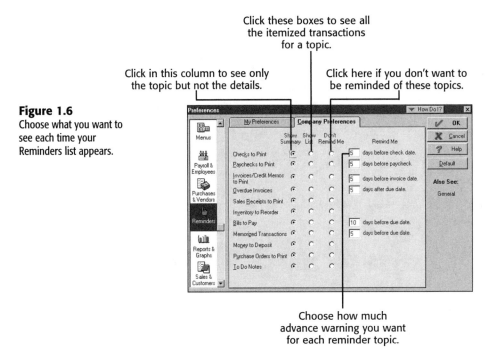

Figure 1.6
Choose what you want to see each time your Reminders list appears.

5. Choose one of the following three options for each task:
    - **Show Summary**—Display the item in the Reminders window when something comes due, but do not display the related details unless the user requests it.
    - **Show List**—Show the details about tasks and other items that have come due; don't wait to be asked. You might want all the items on your To Do list to show automatically whenever the Reminders window opens so you won't forget an important engagement.
    - **Don't Remind Me**—Don't include this type of item on the Reminders list. For example, perhaps you don't want to include the Money to Deposit item on your Reminders list. People using the program might not need to know that undeposited funds are hiding in your desk drawer.
6. Examine the Remind Me section of the screen and choose how close to the deadline you want to have these items appear in your Reminders list. If your electric bill isn't due until next Tuesday, do you want to wait to be reminded on Tuesday, or do you want a few days notice so that you can write the check and get it in the mail before the due date?
7. Click OK when you are finished making your choices.

If you choose not to display your Reminders list each time you start QuickBooks, or if you have closed the list and want to view it again, click on the Reminders button on your iconbar or choose Lists, Reminders.

Troubleshooting

Opening a Company File

When I start my program, I see a message indicating that there is no company file open.

Choose File, Open Company, and then select the name of the company file you want to open. Click the Open button and your company data will be available for your use.

Restoring Your Data

I backed up my data, but when I tried to restore it I was unable to find the file.

Make sure that the File Name section of your Restore From window reads `.QBB, .QBX`. Then, make sure the proper disk or directory shows in the Look In field at the top of the window.

Using the Reminders

I'm sure there are bills that need to be paid, but my Reminders list doesn't display any outstanding bills.

Choose File, Preferences, and then click the Reminders button. Choose Company Preferences and indicate that you want to show Bills to Pay. Verify the number of days of advance notice that you want to receive for bill payments, and then click OK to save your changes.

CHAPTER 2

GETTING HELP

In this chapter

Using This Book for Help   22

Using the QuickBooks Help Index   23

Using the Help Find Feature   24

Using QCards   25

Using the How Do I? Button   26

Getting Help on the CD-ROM   26

Using Online Help   27

Intuit Technical Support   28

QuickBooks and Your Industry   29

Using This Book for Help

One of the greatest frustrations about using any computer program occurs when you have a question and can't find the answer. You set aside time for computer tasks, and then you get stuck, unable to proceed without a solution to a problem. Not only does your admiration for the computer program, its manufacturer, and the computer itself decline, but you find yourself wasting valuable time trying to solve what you're certain is a simple problem. Then you have to reschedule time to get back on the computer while other jobs get pushed aside, and you find yourself behind schedule, missing deadlines, and wishing you had stuck to pencil and paper and never messed with the computer.

Before you turn to other resources, spend some time familiarizing yourself with the layout of this book. Read through the Table of Contents and you will see that the book is broken into seven useful parts:

- **Part I: Getting Started in QuickBooks**—In Part I, new users learn how to set up a company in QuickBooks and how to enter transactions that have already occurred. Learn how to organize your data to produce the reports and other information that will help your business operate efficiently.

- **Part II: Taking Care of Business**—This part covers the ongoing accounting tasks that you will perform in QuickBooks on a regular basis. Learn how to record revenue and expense transactions, how to report sales tax, and how to manage your inventory and fixed assets.

- **Part III: Paying Employees and Contractors**—Most businesses rely on the help of others to get the job done. Learn the difference between an employee and a contractor, set up payroll records for employees, learn which tax forms you are responsible for filing, and generate those tax forms.

- **Part IV: Making QuickBooks Work for You**—Make QuickBooks change to meet your needs, rather than change yourself to accommodate the program. In this part, learn how to change the input screens so that they look the way you want them to look, to create the reports that will give you the results that you need, and to customize the program so that it performs in ways that make sense to you.

- **Part V: QuickBooks Meets the 21st Century**—If you are interested in the online features of QuickBooks, online banking and online bill-paying, this part of the book provides you with all the information you need to get up and running with your modem. You also get an introduction to the Web services that are available to you.

- **Part VI: Getting the Most from QuickBooks**—Learn budgeting and forecasting techniques that really work, learn how to protect your QuickBooks data, find out how the QuickBooks time tracking feature can help you, and learn what you need to prepare your income tax return using QuickBooks.

- **Part VII: Appendixes**—Get instructions for the installation of QuickBooks, learn how to use QuickBooks on a network, explore new techniques for transferring data between QuickBooks and Microsoft Word and Excel, and check out the complete listing of state revenue agencies.

General topics are listed in the Table of Contents. For more detailed digging, try finding the topic you need in the index found at the end of this book. Still over a barrel regarding an answer you can't find? Try some of the other sources listed in the remaining sections of this chapter.

USING THE QUICKBOOKS HELP INDEX

The Help index that accompanies your QuickBooks program provides you with a lengthy alphabetical listing of all the topics covered in the onscreen help file. You can access the QuickBooks Help index by choosing Help, Help Index, or by clicking the Index button whenever a Help window is displayed.

When the Help index appears (see Figure 2.1), you can enter the first few letters of any subject with which you need help. As you type, QuickBooks finds its way to the subject. Double-click on the subject in the list of Help index subjects and you see a list of additional subjects that provide details about the general subject you chose.

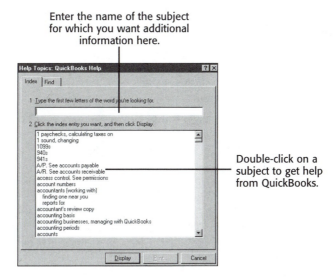

Figure 2.1
The QuickBooks Help index gives you onscreen instructions and descriptions of all facets of the program.

After the help information is displayed, you can proceed in several directions:

- Choose Options, Print Topic if you want a printed copy of this help screen.
- The green help topics are hyperlinks and require only a single click to get you to further information.
- Keep the help information on the top of your screen while you work by choosing Options, Keep Help on Top, On Top.

- Add your own notations to the help screen (as a reminder to you when you open this screen again, or to provide useful comments for the next user) by choosing <u>O</u>ptions, <u>A</u>nnotate. A window opens in which you can enter information. Click on <u>S</u>ave when you are finished. A paper clip appears on the help screen indicating annotations are available (see Figure 2.2). Clicking on the paper clip displays the annotations.

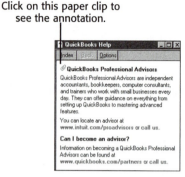

Figure 2.2
Personalize the help screens with your own comments as you get to know QuickBooks.

Click on this paper clip to see the annotation.

- Close the help window by clicking the X in the upper-right corner of the window.

USING THE HELP FIND FEATURE

The Find part of the QuickBooks Help system goes a step further than the Help index. With the Find feature you can search the text of all QuickBooks help screens for a particular word. QuickBooks displays a list of all help screens that contain the word for which you are searching. In this way, you can discover help screens that contain references to your topic even when your topic isn't the main topic on the help screen.

For example, perhaps you want to find out how to record the sale of an asset you are depreciating. If you look up "depreciation" in the Help Index, you won't find any information about selling assets. If you enter "depreciation" using the Find feature, however, you will discover that several help topics include a discussion of depreciation, including one called "Selling a Fixed Asset."

To use the Find feature in QuickBooks, follow these steps:

1. Choose <u>H</u>elp, <u>H</u>elp Index. The Help Topics window appears.
2. Click the Find tab at the top of the Help Topics window. If you have not used this feature previously, QuickBooks leads you through two setup screens on which you can click <u>N</u>ext and <u>F</u>inish, respectively, to set up Find for first-time use.
3. In the box labeled 1 (<u>T</u>ype the Words You Want to Find), enter a word describing the topic you want to find (for my example, I entered depreciation).

Variations on the word you entered (plural, past tense, and so on) appear in the area labeled 2 (Select Some Matching Words to Narrow Your Search). By default, all the choices in area 2 are selected. If you want, you can click on one or more choices instead of leaving them all selected.

4. Area 3 (Click a Topic, Then Click Display) shows all the help topics that include the word you entered in area 1. Double-click on any topic to see a help screen about that topic.

USING QCARDS

QCards are pop-up boxes that appear onscreen as you move from one task to another in QuickBooks. The cards provide descriptive information about the specific place in the program on which you are working.

For example, when you prepare an invoice in QuickBooks, the first area, or *field*, in which you enter information on the form is the Customer:Job area in the upper-left corner. When you are ready to enter a customer name in this field, a QCard appears onscreen describing exactly how to enter information in this field, and what to do when you're finished (see Figure 2.3). As you move from one field to the next on this form, a new QCard appears for each field.

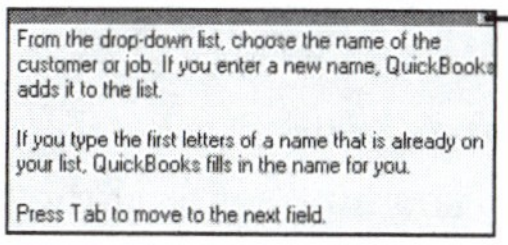
From the drop-down list, choose the name of the customer or job. If you enter a new name, QuickBooks adds it to the list.

If you type the first letters of a name that is already on your list, QuickBooks fills in the name for you.

Press Tab to move to the next field.

Figure 2.3 QCards provide explanations and instructions as you use QuickBooks.

If QCards do not appear on your screen and you want to see them, choose Help, Hide/Show QCards or press Ctrl+F1. If QCards were previously turned off, they are turned on. If they were on (even if you had temporarily turned off the display by clicking the X close box in the corner of a QCard box), they are turned off.

If the QuickBooks iconbar is displayed on your screen, you can click the QCard icon button off and on to quickly turn the view of QCards off and on.

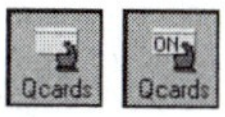

→ To find more information about the iconbar, including information about how to view the iconbar if it is not visible, **see p. 390.**

To move a QCard out of the way but keep it visible, drag the colored bar on the top of the QCard box.

Using the How Do I? Button

Every window in QuickBooks includes a How Do I? button in the upper-right corner; it provides you with a quick list of the questions you are most likely to ask while using that particular window. Click once on the button and a drop-down list appears (see Figure 2.4). Click on any question on the list and a help screen opens, displaying information relating to the question.

Figure 2.4
Click the How Do I? button for fast answers to common questions. Click on any question to see the answer, or click anywhere off the list to remove the list from your screen.

The last item on each How Do I? list is Search the Help Index. Clicking on this item opens the main Help index, where you can enter a topic with which you need help (see the earlier section, "Using the QuickBooks Help Index").

Getting Help on the CD-ROM

Use your QuickBooks CD-ROM to familiarize yourself with the operation of the program. You can view video presentations that show you how some of the QuickBooks features operate, providing you with a visual display of the QuickBooks program at work.

When you open the QuickBooks program, you see a box in which you are asked if you want to create a new company or open an existing one. Unless you have already set up a company file, you must indicate that you want to create a new company.

If you have opened QuickBooks previously and examined the sample company file, return to QuickBooks; you see the screen shown in Figure 2.5. (Note: This screen disappears after you have set up your own file in QuickBooks.)

Choose See the Introduction to QuickBooks (or QuickBooks Pro) from the opening screen, click OK, and then sit back (pop some popcorn if you want) and watch the videos tell you all about your program.

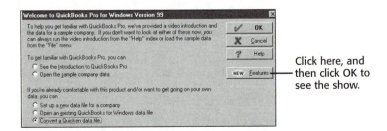

Figure 2.5
View the video display when you ask to see the Introduction to QuickBooks.

Click here, and then click OK to see the show.

You can choose from five videos, each displaying a different part of QuickBooks. The videos are not interactive in that you can't make choices to control screen display, but they are educational, graphically interesting (see Figure 2.6), and provide you with a good introduction to the way the software works.

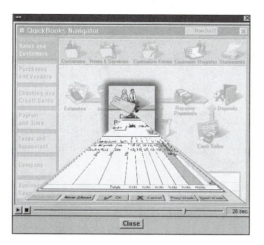

Figure 2.6
The graphic artists at Intuit make QuickBooks approachable and easy to understand.

USING ONLINE HELP

Head for the Internet if you want to connect with Intuit and the people who brought you QuickBooks. The QuickBooks Web site is located at www.quickbooks.com. There you can find answers to *frequently asked questions* (*FAQ*s). Just click on Frequently Asked Questions under the Support Resources heading (see Figure 2.7).

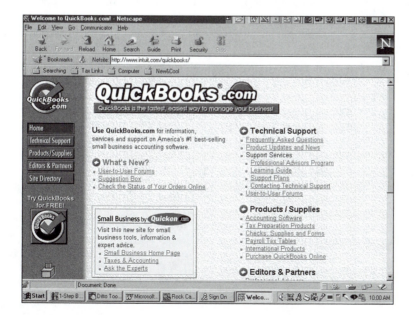

Figure 2.7
You can find plenty of interesting help, guidance, new product information, and advice at the QuickBooks Web site. Because this site is being constantly upgraded, your screen might not look exactly like this.

In addition, you can visit the User-to-User forums—places where QuickBooks users post and answer questions. If you're having a problem, you might find that others share your situation and have either posted a question about that problem or comments on how to solve it. You can post your own question and receive answers from experienced QuickBooks users who might have worked through a similar problem.

Click on User-to-User Forums under the Support Resources heading on the QuickBooks Web site. You are asked to register by giving your name, address, and some other basic information (none of which appear when you post your inquiry); you can then enter the forums.

Even if you're not having a problem with QuickBooks you'll find valuable information in the FAQs and User-to-User forums, including shortcuts and techniques for using the program that you might not have considered. Furthermore, if you have figured out a clever way to perform a task or save time in QuickBooks you can share your expertise with other users in the forums.

INTUIT TECHNICAL SUPPORT

You might find the answers to your questions by placing a phone call to Intuit's technical support group.

USING THE AUTOMATED EXPERT

You can call Intuit for recorded answers to questions about the way QuickBooks works. The answers are thorough and easy to understand. You can choose from many categories of information by pressing buttons, as directed, on your touch-tone phone.

The topics covered are standard topics such as printing concerns, installation problems, and information about entering basic transactions.

Call 888-322-7276 to use the Automated Expert. This service is available 24 hours a day.

TELEPHONE TECHNICAL SUPPORT

If you are still having difficulty, you can try to reach a real person at Intuit who will help you work through your problem. Intuit offers free telephone technical support for problems related to installation, data conversion, and product defects.

You can purchase technical support from Intuit at a rate of $2 per incident. Note, however, that there is a $35 minimum charge for each incident. You also can purchase a support plan. The Premiere Plus plan costs $129 and gives you the right to make an unlimited number of calls for technical support in a 12-month period. You pay long distance charges for the calls. This plan provides you with a secret phone number that puts you in a short line for technical support, so presumably your hold time will not be excessive.

The number for contacting Intuit's technical support service is 888-320-7276. The hours of operation are Monday through Friday, 5 a.m. to 5 p.m., Pacific time, for the $2 standard per incident technical support. For Premiere Plus plan participants, the hours are Monday through Friday, 5 a.m. to 9 p.m., Pacific time, and 7 a.m. to 4 p.m. on Saturday and Sunday.

QuickFax System

You can request, by fax, documents that provide answers to the top 30 common questions about performing various QuickBooks tasks. The questions available by fax are very similar to the Frequently Asked Questions on the QuickBooks Web site.

Call 800-858-6090 from your fax machine to request an index of available documents that will provide you with the documents' numbers for the individual answers to questions. Then, you can call back and request specific documents. This service is available 24 hours per day.

QuickBooks and Your Industry

The people at Intuit have compiled useful information about 22 industries. Many familiar business types and industries are included, such as law firms, manufacturing companies, construction contractors, real estate brokers, and so on. This information is designed to help you understand how other people in your line of business keep accounting records. The information is presented in an easy-to-understand format and is extremely informative.

View the information for your industry by choosing Help, QuickBooks and Your Industry. A help screen appears, showing a variety of topics relating to various aspects of record-keeping for your industry. Clicking on any individual topic provides you with detailed information about that topic.

There's a lot of reading here, so you might want to take the time to print the topics that interest you and read them on paper rather than onscreen. Print a topic by choosing Options, Print topic when the information you want to print is onscreen.

Troubleshooting

Finding Your Registration Number

QuickBooks telephone technical support asks for my registration number when I call with a problem.

Choose Help, About QuickBooks (Pro) from your QuickBooks menu. The registration number appears in a box onscreen.

Using QCards

These little QCard windows keep getting in my way.

Choose Help, Hide/Show QCards to either turn off or turn on the display of QCards. Or, if your iconbar is displayed, clicking the QCard button turns the display on or off.

Displaying the Help Window

When I open the QuickBooks Help window, it continues to stay on top of my screen for as long as the window is open. I want to keep the window open, but not on top of my other windows.

From within the Help window, choose Options, Keep Help on Top, and then click on Not on Top.

CHAPTER 3

PERIODIC QUICKBOOKS ACTIVITIES

In this chapter

Keeping QuickBooks Up-to-Date   32

Performing Daily Activities   32

Performing Weekly Activities   34

Working with Payroll   35

Performing Monthly Activities   35

Performing Quarterly Activities   36

Completing Annual Activities   37

Keeping QuickBooks Up-to-Date

Any kind of accounting system works best when you are organized and you stay on top of the record-keeping process. If you fall behind at entering data, many of the quick reports that QuickBooks can produce will be wasted because the information they contain will be dated. In fact, one of the greatest benefits of using QuickBooks is being able to produce, at a moment's notice, up-to-the-minute reports giving the status of important balances such as

- Accounts receivable
- Accounts payable
- Inventory on hand
- Money in the bank
- Orders pending
- Year-to-date earnings
- Amount due on loans

To stay abreast of how your business is doing, you must perform some activities on a regular basis. In this chapter, you learn which QuickBooks tasks need to be accomplished regularly, and with what frequency. You learn how to create checklists that help remind you when to perform certain tasks.

Each time you have a question about how a certain aspect of the business is doing, you'll be grateful that you read this chapter because all the information you need will be right at your fingertips.

Tip #1 from

Some of the tasks mentioned in this chapter might not apply to you. For example, if you are a business owner with no employees, the information about due dates of payroll tax forms (mentioned in the Monthly, Quarterly, and Annual sections) might be of little interest to you. When you make your checklists, just leave off the items that don't pertain to you or your business.

Performing Daily Activities

The easiest way to stay on top of the day-to-day transactions of your business is to enter those transactions each day. The more you allow data entry to pile up, the more time you have to set aside to enter transactions, the more difficult it is to find that time, and the more out of date the information in your QuickBooks reports becomes.

If your business has very few transactions on a daily basis, or if there aren't any transactions at all on some days, you might find it more convenient to skip a few days before performing the tasks listed in this part of the chapter. I strongly recommend, however, that you not allow more than a week to go by without doing what I call the *daily activities*.

Understanding Types of Activities

The following list includes activities that you can perform on a daily basis (the chapters in this book that discuss these activities in depth are noted):

- **Enter all cash sales transactions**—Include all cash sales if your business allows cash sales, and all charge transactions if you accept credit card sales (Chapter 11, "Invoicing, Monthly Statements, and Accounts Receivable").
- **Enter all bills and shipments received**—Keeping on top of bills and shipments means your accounts payable is always current, and your inventory records are up-to-date (Chapter 14, "Keeping Track of Your Inventory").
- **Enter any checks you write by hand and all cash payments made**—Chapter 15, "Purchase Orders, Accounts Payable, and Paying Bills."
- **Enter all bank deposits made**—Chapter 12, "Recording Income."
- **Enter name, address, phone number, and other pertinent information for all new customers and vendors**—Chapter 8, "Setting Up Services, Customers, and Suppliers."
- **Enter all estimates issued**—(Some companies don't use this feature; you must use QuickBooks Pro to produce estimates.) Enter estimates as you create them. They can be revised later if changes in the project occur (Chapter 10, "Job-cost Estimating and Tracking").
- **Record all hourly time in the time tracking feature**—If you use time tracking, updating your payroll records and related jobs on a daily basis is useful (Chapter 25, "QuickBooks Pro and Time Tracking").

Creating a Checklist

Prepare a checklist that can be copied and made available to whomever is entering data. The checklist needs to have a place for today's date and the name of the person entering data. List each of the preceding items that apply to your business (and any others that you can think of that might not be included on this list but that you want to have performed each day). Next to each item will be a check box and a place to enter additional information, such as the following:

- Quantity of each item entered (such as 12 checks or 2 estimates)
- Reference numbers of the items entered (such as check numbers 2165–2176)
- Comments (such as "Did not enter estimate #263 because this is for a new customer who is not yet in the system—need customer information such as address, contact name, and so on")

Your checklist might look something like the one pictured in Figure 3.1.

Figure 3.1
A daily checklist helps you remember what needs to be entered into QuickBooks each day. It also provides a record of who did the data entry, and what was entered.

Rick's Construction Co-op
Daily Checklist of QuickBooks Activities

Date: _____ Name: _____

✓	Item	Quantity Entered	Reference Numbers	Comments
	Payments received			
	Cash sales			
	Bills received			
	Shipments received			
	Purchase orders issued			
	Payments made			
	Estimates issued			
	Time on jobs			
	New customers			
	New vendors			
	Other (describe below)			

File your completed checklists in a file drawer or a three-ring binder in case you ever need to trace or confirm some information that was entered, or determine who made the entries. Preparing and saving checklists might seem like extra work, especially in an office where only one or two people work; you will find, however, that this is an excellent way of providing a trail that helps you verify if, when, and by whom certain jobs were accomplished. You will have no doubts if you have the checklists.

Performing Weekly Activities

As mentioned previously, some of the items in the Daily Activities section might find their way onto a weekly checklist if their daily occurrence is minimal. In fact, you might find that issuing all your payments or invoices on one day of the week is easier than performing those tasks on a daily basis.

Following are some additional tasks that need to be completed weekly:

- Enter all invoices issued (Chapter 11).
- Enter purchase orders for all items you need to purchase (Chapter 15).
- Perform a full backup of your QuickBooks data files (Chapter 1, "QuickBooks Overview").

> **Tip #2 from Gail Perry**
>
> Your company might issue invoices and purchase orders more or less frequently than weekly. The preceding are just general guidelines.

Working with Payroll

Every company is different when it comes to payroll. Your company might issue paychecks weekly, every two weeks, semi-monthly, or monthly. Perhaps you issue weekly paychecks to hourly employees and semi-monthly paychecks to salaried employees. Or you might issue daily paychecks if you have employees who perform piece-meal work for you.

QuickBooks can accommodate any combination of pay periods that fits your needs. No matter when you issue paychecks, do so in an organized fashion. Choose the same time each week (or every two weeks, or however often you issue checks), and enter your payroll in the same order each time. Not only does a regular payroll entry schedule make the process go more smoothly for you, it also serves to build expectations in employees so that they don't look for checks ahead of schedule.

Include the following steps in your payroll checklist. These steps need to be performed each time the payroll is entered:

- Determine which employees to pay.
- Enter hours for hourly employees, and verify salaries for salaried employees.
- Verify sick time and vacation time usage, if you use these features.
- Verify that all benefits are correct.
- Print payroll.

→ To find information about entering your payroll, **see p. 273**.

Performing Monthly Activities

Once a month, you need to spend more time than usual with QuickBooks because many activities are only performed monthly. In addition, many of the reports you generate that tell you how your business is doing are based on monthly totals, so keeping on top of the monthly record-keeping requirements is very important.

Activities that you need to perform monthly include the following:

- **Pay monthly bills**—Some bills come due every month like clockwork—the rent, utilities, loan payments, and so on (Chapter 15).
- **Make payroll tax deposits**—Chapter 19, "QuickBooks and Payroll Taxes."

- **Reconcile your checkbook**—Your bank statement probably arrives monthly, but the bank might not necessarily issue the statement on the last day of each month. For individuals, this is often not a problem, but when you're trying to run a business you need to be able to confirm your bank balance as of the last day of each month. If your bank statement is issued on some day other than the last day of each month, contact your bank and ask to change the closing date of your statement (Chapter 15).
- **Reconcile your credit card transactions**—Checkbooks aren't the only thing you need to reconcile monthly (Chapter 17, "Entering Cash Transactions").
- **Fund your retirement plan**—You can wait until year-end to make contributions to your retirement plan, or you might find that making regular monthly payments is easier on your cash flow (Chapter 29, "Income Taxes").
- **Produce monthly reports**—Chapter 21, "QuickBooks Reports and Graphs." The reports you need to produce and examine each month include the following:
  - Profit and Loss statement for the month
  - Profit and Loss statement for the year-to-date comparing current year to prior year
  - Balance sheet for the year-to-date
  - Monthly payroll summary
  - Accounts receivable aging summary
  - Accounts payable detail
  - Monthly budget report
  - Inventory stock status report

You might find additional reports useful for the operation and understanding of your company. The discussion of reports in Chapters 20, "Customizing QuickBooks Forms," and 21 will help you decipher the reports and determine what they tell you about how your company is doing.

Performing Quarterly Activities

You need to perform a few QuickBooks activities at the end of each quarter. Their infrequency, however, does nothing to diminish their importance. Quarterly tax deposits, for example, must be paid. Your company's lenders and investors might require quarterly reports of your business progress. Overall business performance can often be more easily judged when examining a quarter instead of a month at a time. You can spot trends, for example, which might not show up on monthly reports but might become evident during a quarter.

The following list includes many of the quarterly activities you will perform. Your own business might dictate that other activities be added to this list:

- Pay quarterly deposits of income taxes (Chapter 29).
- Pay quarterly deposits of payroll taxes, especially unemployment tax (Chapter 19).
- Prepare quarterly reports including the following (Chapter 21):
    - Profit and Loss statement for the quarter
    - Profit and Loss statement for the year-to-date comparing current year to prior year
    - Quarterly payroll summary
    - Quarterly budget report
    - Income tax summary report for the quarter
    - Income tax detail report for the quarter

Completing Annual Activities

The end of the year is the time to finalize your records for the year, make any necessary corrections, assemble year-end statements, and assess the performance of your business. In addition to the end-of-month and end-of-quarter activities that you must complete at the end of the year, you need to accomplish some jobs only once a year.

The year-end tasks include the following:

- Prepare W-2 forms for your employees (Chapter 18).
- Prepare 1099 forms for contractors and others with whom you do business (Chapter 18).
- Prepare end-of-year payroll tax reports (Chapter 18). These reports include the following:
    - W-3 form (submitted to the Social Security Administration with your W-2 forms) (Chapter 18)
    - State equivalent of Federal W-3 form (actual form number and name vary by state) (Chapter 18)
    - 1096 form (submitted to the IRS as the cover sheet with 1099 forms) (Chapter 18)
    - State equivalent of Federal 1096 form (actual form number and name vary by state) (Chapter 18)
    - Federal Form 940 for unemployment tax (Chapter 19)
    - State unemployment compensation report (Chapter 19)
- Prepare federal and state income tax returns (Chapter 29).
- Take a physical inventory count (Chapter 14).
- Prepare and print hard copies of the following reports:

- Income statement for the year (Chapter 21)
- Comparative income statement for the year (Chapter 21)
- Income tax summary report for the year (Chapter 29)
- Income tax detail report for the year (Chapter 29)
- Budget report for the year (Chapter 26, "Budgeting")

■ Review and adjust depreciation expense for the year (Chapter 16, "Managing Fixed Assets").

■ Safeguard your QuickBooks information so that no one can make unauthorized adjustments to your year-end numbers (Chapter 28, "Security").

These year-end tasks cannot all be performed at midnight, December 31 (in fact, you might have much more fun things to do at midnight, December 31!), and they cannot all be performed at once. You might not prepare your income tax returns, for example, until later in the spring when the filing date approaches.

Nevertheless, the preceding are all considered to be year-end activities, so you must plan for them on an annual basis. That planning includes preparation of the list that you will use when you actually check off all these tasks.

Troubleshooting

Making Corrections

I entered all of last month's transactions with today's date.

Open the documents (invoices, purchase orders, and so on) for last month's transactions and change the date to the correct date.

I used the company checkbook to write a check for a purchase, but I can't remember what I bought.

Enter the check directly in the register (choose Lists, Chart of Accounts, and then double-click on the cash account from which you wrote the check). Enter the check, using an account such as Miscellaneous to categorize the expenditure. When the cancelled check comes back from the bank, you can go back to the register entry and change any incorrect information such as the category or the amount.

CHAPTER 4

SETTING UP A COMPANY IN QUICKBOOKS

In this chapter

The Start Date   40

The EasyStep Interview   42

The General Section   44

The Start Date

Before you can use QuickBooks, you must set aside time to get some basic company information into the program. You have to tell QuickBooks a few things about your company so that the program will be ready for you to enter transactions and prepare reports.

When you're ready to start entering information into QuickBooks, you need to take a few minutes to consider your company's *start date*. The start date is not necessarily today's date, but rather the date on which you want to begin tracking information in QuickBooks. When you set up a company in QuickBooks, you need to enter all transactions that have occurred in the company from the start date to today.

If possible, your start date will be the first day of the current year (usually January 1, but see the accompanying note about fiscal years). Or, if the business you are setting up is a new business that didn't get started until sometime after January 1, your start date will be the first day that you started doing business.

 To make a change in your start date, **see** "Troubleshooting" at the end of this chapter.

If you start on the first day of the year (or the first day that the company had any activity), the reports and financial statements that you produce include information for the entire year. Having this information is particularly important when you're gathering information at the end of the year for tax return preparation.

> **Note**
>
> Most companies begin their fiscal year on January 1, just like the calendar year. The *fiscal year* is one complete 12-month cycle; sometimes companies have a fiscal year that is different from a calendar year, if it is more appropriate for reporting the activity of the business. For example, the company's fiscal year might go from October 1 to September 30. If you want to change your fiscal year to something other than the calendar year, you must request permission from the IRS.

If your business was in operation all year but you chose a start date other than the first day of the year, the statements you produce cover only part of this year. Next year and in future years, of course, your statements will cover the entire year. The advantage of choosing a start date that falls sometime during the year—rather than going back to the first day of the year—is that you won't have as many transactions to enter at setup.

If it's close to the end of the year (November or December, for example) and you don't have a lot of spare time on your hands for tediously entering checks and deposits for the entire year, you might want to sit tight and wait until January 1 to start fresh with a new year. When you start really depends on how many transactions and how much time you have.

Alternatively, you might want to consider using QuickBooks for a couple of months while still using your old system, so that you can get used to the program. You can make mistakes and learn and still keep your other records updated. Practicing with your own records instead of with the QuickBooks sample company will give you a much better sense of how the program really works.

> **Tip #3 from Gail Perry**
>
> If you feel truly ambitious, and if your business has been around long enough, you might want to designate January 1 of *last year* as your start date. Naturally, you will have to spend more time entering information into QuickBooks if you plan to enter all of last year's transactions in addition to the current year's information, but the result will be the opportunity to produce reports that compare your business activity from one year to the next—an extremely useful tool for planning and projecting.

This initial setup procedure might take one or two hours or it might take several hours, depending on how organized your information is before you start and how much information you have to enter.

Use the accompanying checklist as a guide to help you assemble the information you need to have by your side before you begin setting up your company. Some of the items on the checklist might not be applicable to your company.

Have the following items on hand before starting the New Company Interview:

- Company name, address, type of business
- Federal Identification Number
- Bank statements and cancelled checks from the start date forward, including your bank balances as of the start date
- Chart of accounts, if you have one
- Customer list of all the people and companies you sell to regularly, including name, address, telephone number, fax number, personal contact, ship-to address, sales tax status, terms you typically apply to this customer, and current jobs you are working on for this customer
- Inventory list of all the items you sell, including a description of inventory items, cost of items, standard sales price of items, preferred supplier of items, quantity of items on hand, and number of items at which a reorder request needs to be issued
- Details of all amounts you owe as of the start date
- Details of all amounts owed to you as of the start date
- The rate at which you charge sales tax, the name and address of the taxing agency, and amount of sales tax owed as of the start date
- Vendor list of all your regular suppliers and creditors, including name, address, telephone and fax numbers, personal contact, your account number with each vendor, and whether the vendors require a 1099 form
- Any existing budget information
- List of employees, including names and addresses, Social Security numbers, rates of pay, withholding allowances and other deductions, and year-to-date information (if setting up the company after January 1)
- Payroll tax information including state unemployment compensation rate, local tax rates, information regarding payroll taxes due as of the start date

- Current value of all assets including original cost, date purchased, methods used for calculating depreciation, accumulated depreciation to date
- Credit card statements you have received since the start date
- Details of all transactions since the start date, including checks written, amounts deposited, credit card transactions, and so on

THE EASYSTEP INTERVIEW

The QuickBooks interview is called EasyStep because it leads you through the setup process in a step-by-step fashion, and it is relatively easy. Easy, that is, if you have gathered all the information you were told to get earlier in this chapter. If you skipped over the setup checklist thinking you'd just plow ahead and see what QuickBooks requests of you in the interview, go back and try it again. You'll thank me when the setup process is finished.

When you start the QuickBooks program, you are faced with a screen that gives you an option to set up a new data file for a company (see Figure 4.1). Choose that option and click OK, and you'll be off and running.

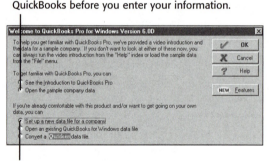

Choose this option if you want to play around in QuickBooks before you enter your information.

Figure 4.1
The opening screen in QuickBooks gives you the opportunity to open some sample data or to get started entering your own company data.

Click here, and then click OK to begin your own QuickBooks experience.

If you've experimented with the sample data or have used QuickBooks in another way and you don't want to see the welcome screen, you can get to the EasyStep interview by choosing File, New Company.

The first screen of the EasyStep interview appears, telling you to click Next to begin. The interview features seven tabs along the right side:

- General—In this section, you are asked for your company name, address, Federal Identification Number, what tax form your company files, the type of business, whether you want to use the QuickBooks standard chart of accounts, the start date for when your company will begin using QuickBooks, and some general information about your anticipated usage of some of the QuickBooks features. The information you provide in this section will trigger certain input screens in the later interview sections.

- **Income & Expenses**—Here you create names of accounts that will help you classify your income and expenses.
- **Income Details**—On this tab, you set up a list of the services that your company offers and the goods it sells. If you plan to keep track of your *inventory (page 53)* in QuickBooks, you list the types of inventory items that your company sells here.
- **Opening Balances**—Here you enter all the bills you owe and all the amounts that customers owe you as of the start date (see "The Start Date" section earlier in this chapter for more information).
- **Payroll**—If you plan to use QuickBooks to keep track of your payroll, enter your employees' names and vital statistics here, as well as all the payroll taxes you owe and what types of things you pay and withhold from pay for your employees. You can skip this section if you don't have a payroll or if you have another way of paying employees.
- **Menu Items**—On this tab, you find just a few questions about the way your menus will be arranged.
- **What's Next**—This section includes general recommendations for how you will proceed after the interview is completed, information about setting up passwords to protect your data, advice on setting up tracking for vendors who will need 1099 forms at the end of the year, and a general advertisement for the QuickBooks Web site.

Answer all the questions that are presented to you in the General tab first. After you complete the general questions you can proceed through the interview, clicking the tabs at the right out of order instead of from top to bottom. Most people, though, move through the entire interview in order, so that is how the interview is explained in this chapter.

Stopping and Restarting the Interview

At any time (dinner time, fingers getting tired…), you can leave the interview. When you return, QuickBooks remembers just where you left off and takes you right back. However, be sure that you get at least as far as the screen in the General section that asks you to save your QuickBooks file and that you give it a filename.

To leave the QuickBooks interview before you have finished answering all the questions, click on the Leave button.

To get back to work in the interview, choose File, EasyStep Interview.

Moving Around in the Interview

You can click your way through the interview, or you can use the following keyboard shortcuts to get from screen to screen:

- Pressing Enter generally activates the Next button at the bottom of the interview screen.
- Alt+N also activates Next.
- Alt+V activates the Previous button (Prev).

- The Tab key moves you from one field to another on each screen.
- After you tab to a particular check box or selection circle, pressing the Spacebar places an x in a check box (or removes one if it is already there) or makes a selection in a selection circle.
- After you tab to a scroll list, the up- and down-arrow keys move you through the list. Move to the item you want to select, and then press Tab or Enter to make the selection.

THE GENERAL SECTION

Use the General section to enter preliminary information about your company; the actual numbers come later.

The first screen you encounter in the General section of the EasyStep interview asks whether you want to upgrade from another Intuit product (see Figure 4.2). In other words, have you been using Quicken or QuickBooks to record your data previously? You can upgrade from any prior version of QuickBooks for Windows or Macintosh as well as nearly all versions of Quicken.

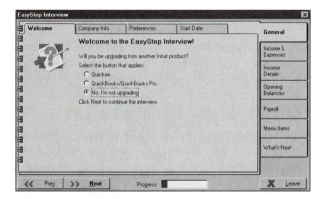

Figure 4.2
This screen is for prior Quicken or QuickBooks users. If that's not you, click Next and move on.

UPGRADING FROM EARLIER VERSIONS OF QUICKBOOKS AND QUICKEN

If you have been using an earlier version of QuickBooks, you really don't need to go through the interview process. Click the Leave button to leave the interview, and then choose File, Open. Request that QuickBooks open your data file from the earlier version; you are then asked whether you want to convert that data to the new version of QuickBooks.

When you agree to convert your old data to the new version, QuickBooks makes your old data inaccessible to the earlier version of QuickBooks. To be safe, back up your old data before converting in case something goes wrong with the conversion, or in case you want to view the old data in the earlier version (if you have the earlier version of QuickBooks on another computer, for example). You cannot go back and forth between the two versions with the same data.

If you plan to use QuickBooks for data that was previously tracked in Quicken, follow the onscreen instructions that advise you about how to separate business items from any personal items that might be in your Quicken file. You are then prompted to back up your Quicken file before proceeding with the upgrade.

New Users of QuickBooks

If you have not been using Quicken or QuickBooks to track your company's financial information, or if you are ready to begin tracking information for a new company, choose No, I'm Not Upgrading on the first interview screen; then click Next.

Skipping the interview is not recommended (see Figure 4.3). Skipping it is kind of like buying a piece of equipment that you have to put together yourself and throwing out the step-by-step instructions before you begin. The Skip Interview button looms at you like a dare; this is one dare you shouldn't take. There are many parts to setting up a company in QuickBooks, and the interview covers nearly all of them. Click the Next button and continue with the interview.

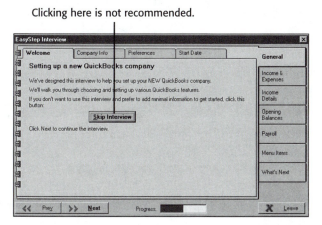

Figure 4.3
Set up your own company using the EasyStep interview.

The next interview screen simply gives you some basic information about how the interview works: The Next button moves you forward, Prev puts you in reverse, and Leave closes shop for the day.

A couple of clicks on Next and you see a cheerful reminder that you can always go back and change answers in the interview (see Figure 4.4). Don't believe this message! Although you can back up, revisit a screen, and make some changes many times during the interview, in many places you can't make changes until the interview is through with you. The moral of this story: Take the interview slowly and answer all interview questions carefully, checking spelling as you type.

Figure 4.4
While you're working your way through the interview, keep a laundry list of items you forgot to enter or want to change nearby.

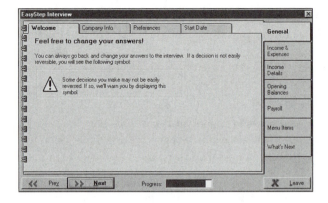

Tip #4 from

If you make mistakes (spelling an inventory item incorrectly, for example) during the EasyStep interview, and clicking the Prev button doesn't take you to a screen where you can correct your mistakes, keep a list of all the things you want to do when the interview is finished. That way, you won't forget the chores that need to be completed later.

When you complete a section of the interview, the related tab is checked off (see Figure 4.5).

Entering Company Information

It's finally time to limber up your fingers and tell QuickBooks all about your company. On the first input screen of the company information section, shown in Figure 4.5, you are asked for your company name and the legal name of your company. "What's the difference," you ask?

Figure 4.5
Enter your company name (for example, Rick's Diner), followed by your legal business name (for example, Olive Another Restaurant, Inc.).

This check mark means you've graduated to the next section.

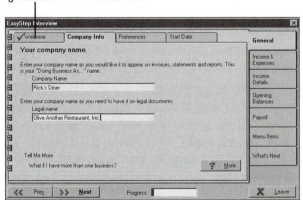

The company name is the name by which your customers know and love you. Your legal name is the name under which your company is registered with the state authorities. The company name is the name that will appear on nearly every statement and report that QuickBooks produces (notable exceptions include tax reports—the IRS wants to know who you really are).

If your company is just you and you don't have any fancy names, legal or otherwise, just enter your own name in both sections of the screen.

More Than One Company

If you are trying to enter information for more than one company into QuickBooks, stop trying. Enter all the information for one company at one time, completing the entire interview. Then, if you have another company to set up, choose File, New Company, and start all over for the other company.

One Company: Many Locations

If you have multiple locations of the same company (for example, a restaurant company might operate two or more restaurants, or a store owner might have stores in several locations), you can enter all the information for all your company locations into one QuickBooks file.

Tip #5 from Gail Perry

If your company operates in multiple locations, I recommend setting up classes (see an introductory section on classes later in this chapter and read all about classes in Chapter 9, "Separating Your Company into Logical Divisions"). Classes enable you to keep different parts of your business separate, while still enabling you to create reports about the entire business.

Setting Up Your Company Address

Enter your company address on the screen shown in Figure 4.6. Entering the address probably seems like a simple matter, unless, of course, you have more than one address.

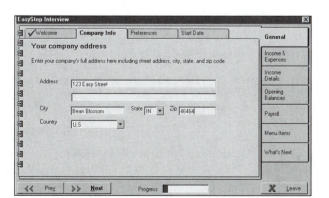

Figure 4.6
The address you enter will appear on statements and reports.

For companies with more than one address (such as a company with a store in one location and an office in another), enter the address that you want to appear most often on the forms you will use, such as invoices and purchase orders.

You always have the opportunity to override the address when preparing forms and reports in QuickBooks.

FEDERAL IDENTIFICATION NUMBER

Sounds serious, doesn't it? The *Federal Identification Number*, or *FEIN*, is the number by which the IRS and other state and federal authorities know you. For most sole proprietors, the FEIN is the Social Security number; if your business is not a corporation, this might be the only number you have.

Corporations always have a separate FEIN, and many individuals who own a business sign up for a business FEIN just to keep business tax records separate from their personal records.

Enter the number you use to identify your business; this number will appear on all tax forms you prepare in QuickBooks.

FIRST MONTH OF THE YEAR

Usually, but not always, a business's fiscal year and tax year are the same.

The QuickBooks interview requests that you enter the first month of both your fiscal year and your tax year (see Figure 4.7). The fiscal year is the 12-month period you use for reporting your business activity on yearly financial statements. If your business is like most other businesses, you track your financial activity on a calendar-year basis (January to December), so January is the first month of your fiscal year.

Figure 4.7
The setup continues with identification number and fiscal and tax years.

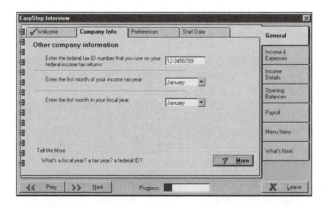

You might find, however, that a different 12-month period more naturally expresses the way in which you do business. For example, imagine a gift store that does a lot of business in late December each year. Revenue is always very high in December, but come January, many people bring in gifts to return or exchange. A better reflection of year-end sales can be accomplished by waiting until the end of January to prepare annual financial statements. This company can benefit from having a fiscal year that goes from February to January.

Tip #6 from *Gail Perry*	Corporations (other than S Corporations and personal service corporations, described later in this chapter) do not have to beg the IRS to allow them to use a tax year that is different from the calendar year. Corporations simply file their first tax return for the year they want to use as a tax year.

CHOOSE A TAX RETURN

The QuickBooks request for you to choose a tax return (see Figure 4.8) is a not-so-subtle way of asking what kind of business you have. The type of business determines the type of tax return you file. Choose from the following forms:

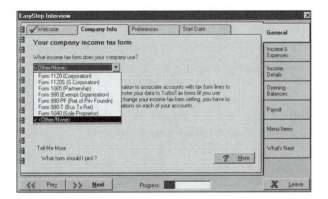

Figure 4.8
Indicate the form your company uses (or will use) to file its tax return with the IRS.

- **Form 1120**—Use this form if you are a corporation. Corporations are entities unto themselves, taxed at their own rates, and liable for their own debts.
- **Form 1120S**—Use this form if you are an S corporation. An *S corporation* is a business that behaves like a corporation, except that it is not taxed like a corporation. Income of the business is passed through to the corporation's owners and taxed on their personal tax returns at their personal rates of income tax.
- **Form 1065**—Use this form if you are a partnership. Partnerships are a lot like S corporations. Income is passed through to the partners and taxed on their tax returns.
- **Form 1040**—This form is for sole proprietors. *Sole proprietors* are people who haven't turned their business into a corporation or a partnership. The 1040 is the tax return that individuals file, and your business income will most likely show up on Schedule C of your 1040.
- **Form 990**—Use this form if you are an exempt organization. Exempt organizations are usually those that are in the business of helping others. The IRS must give your exempt status approval; then, the only income that is taxed is income not related to your reason for exempt status.

- **Form 990-PF**—Use this form if you are a private foundation. A private foundation is usually a tax exempt organization, but one that must meet stricter rules than an average tax exempt organization.
- **Form 990-T**—This is the form you use if you are a tax exempt organization with a little profitable business on the side (a business that is not related to your exempt purpose). Only the activity of this unrelated business is shown on Form 990-T.

If you know which tax return is the right one for you, make your choice and move on. If you are just now trying to decide how to report your business income and what type of entity you want to become, spend a little time with a lawyer or an accountant and talk through all the advantages and disadvantages of the different business types.

*To change the tax return type you chose in the EasyStep Interview, **see** "Troubleshooting" at the end of this chapter.*

Find a professional who has experience in helping people set up new businesses. You can ask other business owners for a referral, check the yellow pages, or try calling your state CPA society and bar association to ask for referrals. A little time spent up front discussing your business goals and your business financing options with an experienced professional will help you structure the business in the way that best suits your long-range needs.

Type of Business

QuickBooks provides you with a listing of many business types (see Figure 4.9) and hopes you will find one that matches, or is similar to, your own.

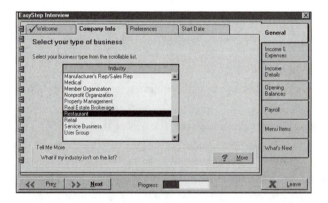

Figure 4.9
Clicking on a business type that is similar but not identical to your business won't cause any problems for you.

Your choice of one of the business types from this list aids QuickBooks in setting up your business by enabling it to determine some standard account names that are appropriate to your business (see "The QuickBooks Standard (Customized) Chart of Accounts," later in this chapter). Also, QuickBooks gears some of its questions to your type of business. Choose Other if you don't see anything that comes close to describing your business.

Save Your Work

By now, you might be wondering why you've never been asked to name the file that contains the data for your company. What if your computer suddenly shuts down on you? Nothing you have entered up to this point has been saved, so you're back to the drawing board.

At this point in the interview, QuickBooks gets around to asking for a filename (see Figure 4.10). QuickBooks uses the business name you entered previously as a filename, but you can change this name if you feel something else is more appropriate.

Figure 4.10
It's official! Your QuickBooks company file has been established.

The QuickBooks Standard (Customized) Chart of Accounts

A *chart of accounts* is a group of categories into which you classify your company's income, expenses, debts, and assets so that you can make some sense of all your business transactions in the form of professional-looking financial statements.

→ To learn how to set up asset and liability accounts, **see p. 63**. For more detailed information about asset and liability accounts and how they are used in your business, **see p. 105**.

Without a chart of accounts, your company's financial statements might look like this:

Revenue	$xx,xxx.xx
- Expense	xx,xxx.xx
= Income (Loss)	$xx,xxx.xx

Some say the bottom line is everything, but without the details that accounts provide, you won't know what kind of expenses you spent money on, and you might not know the source of your income. Without knowing any detailed information about how the money comes in and where it goes, you cannot make intelligent decisions about how your business will be run.

When you chose a type of business, QuickBooks decided on a list of account names that might be useful to you (see Figure 4.11). The accounts are divided into categories, and the first accounts you see listed are income accounts and expense accounts.

Figure 4.11
You can choose not to use the standard accounts, but you'll have a lot more work ahead of you.

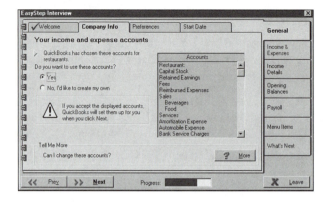

Income accounts are accounts that reflect the earnings of your company. You might have only one type of income, such as fees for your services, or you might have many types of income, such as sales of inventory, equipment rental, and service fees. By separating your income into different accounts you can produce reports that show more clearly the source of your income.

Expense accounts are accounts into which you categorize the expenses paid that keep your business running. Examples of expenses might include purchases of inventory, utilities, rent, supplies, repairs, office expense, telephone, and so on. Just as with income, a detailed breakdown of where your money goes helps you to analyze your business performance.

If yours is a new business, I highly recommend that you use the accounts that QuickBooks has chosen for you. You can add accounts to this list during the interview, and after the interview has ended you can delete accounts that you don't intend to use.

Tip #7 from
Gail Perry

An established business might already have a chart of accounts in place. Abandoning an existing chart of accounts in favor of the accounts that QuickBooks has chosen for you doesn't make sense. You might end up having some additional data entry, but if your company is already using a group of account names, you probably need to reject the QuickBooks chart of accounts and enter all your own account names.

Tip #8 from
Gail Perry

You might find it useful to use account numbers in addition to naming your accounts. Although the interview has no provision for numbering accounts, you can see Chapter 7 for instructions on adding account numbers after the interview is finished.

Who Has Access to the Company File?

The QuickBooks interview asks you how many people have access to your QuickBooks company. This is a security question. You do not have an opportunity in the interview to establish levels of security for yourself and others; after the interview has ended, however, you can add some password protection to the program to prevent nonauthorized people from viewing the company data (see Figure 4.12).

THE GENERAL SECTION | 53

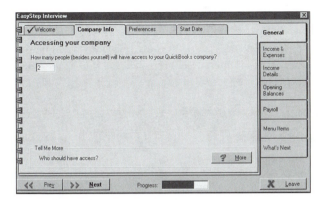

Figure 4.12
You can change the number of authorized users after the interview has ended.

→ To learn more about security issues, **see p. 480**.

DO YOU HAVE INVENTORY?

Inventory is the stock of items that you sell to earn money in your business. You might sell machine parts, books, or groceries that you purchase somewhere and offer for sale to others; or you might produce your own inventory, such as clothing that you make, ships that you build, or pottery that you throw. These items in total make up your inventory, and you might have a variety of inventory accounts to describe all the items that you keep in stock.

Some businesses don't have inventory at all. A business that provides a service, such as a law firm or a doctor's office, might not have anything tangible to sell, making inventory accounts unnecessary.

When QuickBooks asks whether you maintain an inventory (see Figure 4.13), it is getting ready to set up inventory and related cost of sales accounts for you.

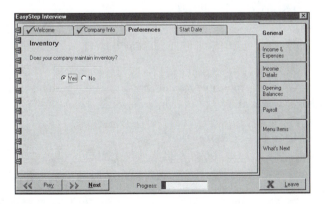

Figure 4.13
Choosing Yes here triggers some additional inventory questions in the interview.

DO YOU WANT TO KEEP TRACK OF INVENTORY IN QUICKBOOKS?

You might think that because you have inventory, you naturally want to keep track of it in QuickBooks. Your choice in doing so depends on how complicated a process you use (or plan to use) for valuing your inventory.

QuickBooks is a great program when it comes to keeping track of how many inventory items you have in stock and giving you reminders about when it is time to reorder (see Figure 4.14, which appears only if you selected Yes at the screen shown in Figure 4.13). However, QuickBooks has limited skills when it comes to helping you value your inventory and report on your inventory to the IRS.

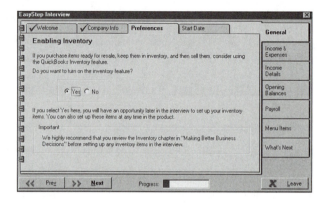

Figure 4.14
Let QuickBooks help you keep track of how many items you have in stock.

Chapter 14, "Keeping Track of Your Inventory," provides you with insight into using the QuickBooks inventory features and into the valuation expectations of the IRS. It also provides you with alternatives to QuickBooks for calculating the value of your inventory.

If you maintain an inventory, I recommend that you use QuickBooks as a means of keeping track of all your inventory items. I also strongly recommend that you read Chapter 14 to find out how various IRS rules apply to your situation and what you can do about accommodating those rules.

Do You Collect Sales Tax from Customers?

Chapter 13, "Reporting Sales Tax," provides you with detailed information about who is responsible for collecting and paying sales tax, and about how the process works in QuickBooks.

If you have determined that you are responsible for collecting sales tax from your customers, choose Yes when asked about sales tax in the interview (see Figure 4.15).

Do You Pay Sales Tax to More Than One Agency?

Your company might have to pay sales tax to multiple taxing agencies if, for example, you have more than one location and each location is situated in a different sales tax jurisdiction.

If you must pay sales tax to more than one agency, choose the multiple tax agencies option in the interview. (See Figure 4.16, which appears only if you selected Yes at the screen shown in Figure 4.15). You need to enter information for each agency to which you pay tax. However, this information will not be requested during the interview. See "Creating a Sales Tax Item" in Chapter 13 for instructions on setting up your sales tax agencies.

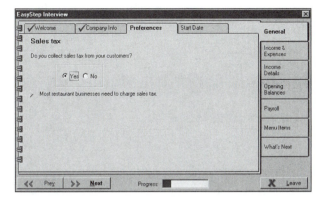

Figure 4.15
Collecting sales tax might not be fun, but somebody's got to do it…

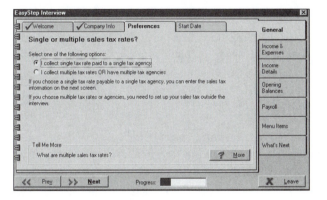

Figure 4.16
A little extra setup work is involved outside the interview if you have to pay tax to more than one agency.

Setting Up a Sales Tax Item

As you use QuickBooks more, you'll get used to hearing about items. An *item* is the QuickBooks way of describing any piece of information that has an amount associated with it, and that can appear on a form (an invoice, a purchase order, a paycheck, and so on).

Sales tax is an item because an amount is associated with the sales tax you charge, and the sales tax amount can appear on invoices that you prepare for your customers.

In the interview (unless you pay sales tax to more than one agency), you are asked to set up your sales tax item by describing how you want the item to appear on your forms, the rate at which tax is charged, and the name of the agency to which you ultimately pay the tax (see Figure 4.17, which appears only if you indicated that you collect sales tax).

Figure 4.17
If you don't know all this information during the interview, you can set up your sales tax item later (see Chapter 13).

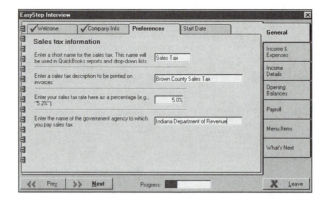

Selecting a Stylish Invoice

QuickBooks provides three standard invoice formats, or styles. You can choose the one that you think will work best in your business or the one that most closely resembles forms you have used previously in your business, or you can choose to create your own form.

During the interview (see Figure 4.18), QuickBooks asks if you want one of the following styles of invoice:

- **Product**—The product invoice is the most detailed, with sections for product description, purchase order number, shipping terms, ship-to address, project name, sales representative code, and more. Use this invoice if you sell and track inventory.

- **Professional**—This invoice includes places for a description and an amount. Use this invoice if you charge for professional fees and plan to enter a description of what your fees cover.

- **Service**—You can enter a quantity, a description, a rate, and an amount on this invoice. If you charge by the hour and plan to break out those charges on the invoice (three hours for radiator repair, two hours to repaint the hood, and so on), choose this invoice.

- **Custom**—Making this choice tells QuickBooks that you plan to create your own invoice after the interview is finished.

Figure 4.18
Choose the invoice style that best fits your business. You have the option of later changing the style that you use.

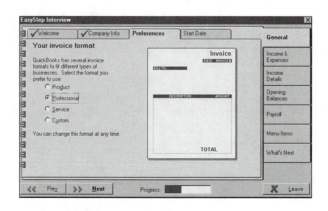

Using QuickBooks for Your Payroll

The QuickBooks interview asks you how many employees you have on your payroll (see Figure 4.19). This general, nosy question has nothing to do with whether you use QuickBooks for preparing paychecks.

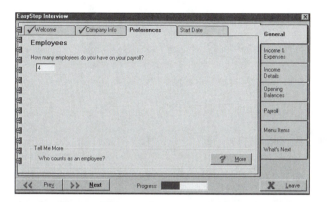

Figure 4.19
Enter the number of employees your company has. This number can change later.

Unless you have a giant payroll and don't want to be bothered to do it yourself, you will probably use the QuickBooks Payroll feature (see Figure 4.20). It is a thorough payroll program that anticipates the payroll needs for nearly every type of business.

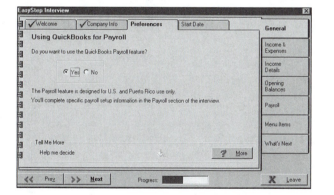

Figure 4.20
If you plan to use the QuickBooks Payroll feature, choose Yes here. You actually set up payroll later in the interview.

If you indicate that you plan to use QuickBooks to calculate your payroll, you might be interested to know that QuickBooks tries its best to stay on top of the latest tax withholding tables.

The screen that appears in Figure 4.21 (which appears only if you chose to activate the Payroll feature as shown in Figure 4.20) tells you the version of the payroll tables you have installed with your program. You can call a phone number on this screen to verify that your version is the most current. You don't have to call now, but you'll want to call every few months to make sure that all the tax tables you use are up-to-date. (Chapter 18, "Paying Employees and Contractors," discusses the process for checking on and obtaining payroll tax updates.)

Figure 4.21
You don't have to call right this minute, and you don't have to memorize this phone number.

MAKING ESTIMATES ON JOBS

If your company typically prepares estimates for jobs that you perform, you have the option of recording those estimates in QuickBooks Pro (see Figure 4.22). This feature is available only in the Pro version.

Figure 4.22
Choose Yes if you want to track estimates in QuickBooks Pro.

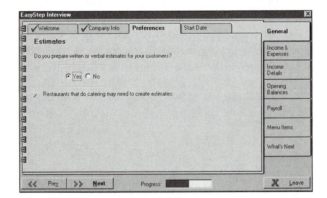

When you track estimates in QuickBooks Pro, you can bill from those estimates, you can prepare progress reports showing how much of the estimates have been completed, and you can prepare comparative reports that show estimates versus actual costs on jobs.

If you choose to use QuickBooks Pro for creating and monitoring estimates, you have an option to bill for portions of your estimates instead of waiting for a job to be completed (see Figure 4.23). For example, you can prepare an invoice for 30 percent of the estimated price of a job, or you can charge your customer for the cost of materials as indicated on the estimate, holding off on billing for your time until later.

THE GENERAL SECTION | 59

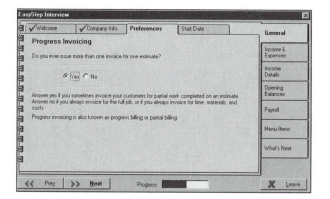

Figure 4.23
Choose Yes if you think you might want to use the QuickBooks partial billing feature.

→ To find detailed information about preparing and using estimates for pricing your jobs, **see p. 169**.

TRACKING TIME IN QUICKBOOKS PRO

QuickBooks Pro offers a time tracking feature that enables you and your coworkers to fill out timesheets that feed directly onto jobs for easy invoicing (see Figure 4.24).

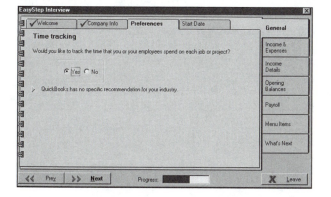

Figure 4.24
You can always change your mind later, but check Yes if you think you want to use the time tracking feature available in QuickBooks Pro.

→ To find more information on the time tracking feature, **see p. 443**.

USING CLASSES TO SEPARATE YOUR BUSINESS

Chapter 9 provides detailed information about the QuickBooks Classes feature and how you can report on different segments of the same business as if they were separate businesses. If you think that you want to use this feature, choose Yes on the screen shown in Figure 4.25.

Figure 4.25
Classes enable you to prepare reports on different sections of the same company.

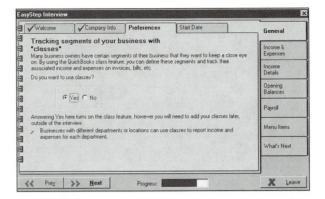

BILL PAYING: NOW OR LATER

In Figure 4.26, you are asked whether your company plans to pay its bills at the same time that they are entered in the computer (in other words, not enter the bills until they are paid), or if you will enter the bills when they arrive and plan on paying them later. This approach is a nontechnical way of asking whether you want to establish an account for your payables, an account that keeps track of how much your company owes at any given time.

Figure 4.26
If you enter bills when you receive them rather than waiting until they are due, QuickBooks gives you nice little reminders so that you won't forget to pay your bills on time.

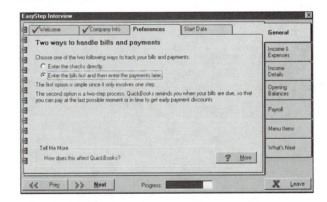

If you choose to enter bills before paying them, the QuickBooks menus are set up in a way that makes this process more intuitive.

DISPLAYING THE REMINDERS LIST

If you plan to use the QuickBooks Reminders list to keep yourself on top of important due dates and To Do lists, choose At Start Up from the screen shown in Figure 4.27. This way, you see the Reminders list each time you start the program.

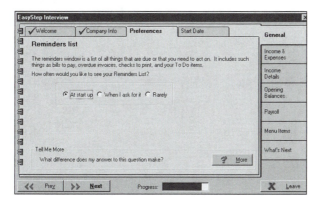

Figure 4.27
View reminders at startup, and you have no one to blame but yourself if your tasks don't get done!

And that wraps up the General section of your interview. The other sections aren't nearly so daunting. You've made all the decisions in the General section; now just sit back and fill in the blanks when asked questions about those decisions.

TROUBLESHOOTING

CHANGING THE START DATE

I chose a start date during the interview. But now the interview is over, and I find that I need to use a different date for my start date.

You can open the register for any balance sheet account and change the opening balance information. Access the registers by choosing Lists, Chart of Accounts, and then double-clicking on any account whose opening balance information needs to be changed.

CHANGING COMPANY TYPE

My company used to be a sole proprietorship, but I just incorporated. Now I need to tell this to QuickBooks.

Change your company type by choosing File, Company Info. Change the information at Income Tax Form Used.

CHAPTER 5

SETTING UP ACCOUNTS, INVENTORY, FIXED ASSETS, AND PAYROLL

In this chapter

Setting Up Income Accounts   64

Setting Up Expense Accounts   65

General Information About Your Company's Income   66

Setting Up Items   67

Entering Opening Balances   72

Setting Up Payroll   80

Finishing the Interview   85

SETTING UP INCOME ACCOUNTS

After you've gotten through the General section of the EasyStep Interview, it's time to set up the actual accounts that you plan to use to keep track of income and expenses for your company. In this chapter, you will also set up your inventory items, fixed assets, loans, and payroll.

By the time you finish this chapter you'll be ready to start using QuickBooks on a regular basis.

The next section of the QuickBooks setup procedure addresses identifying income accounts. *Income accounts* are the categories you use to keep track of your various forms of income. If all your revenue comes from only one source, you might have only one income account (Rent, for example, or Contracting).

Alternatively, you might want more detailed income records that provide more specific sources of income (Apartment Rent, Commercial Rent, Home Repair, Room Additions, House Painting).

In the setup process of Chapter 4, "Setting Up a Company in QuickBooks," you chose whether to accept a standard chart of accounts for your company. The standard chart of accounts includes some income and expense accounts for tracking your business activity.

If you chose the standard accounts assigned by QuickBooks, examine all the standard income accounts and set up additional accounts to describe each type of income you want to track. Use the following steps to do so:

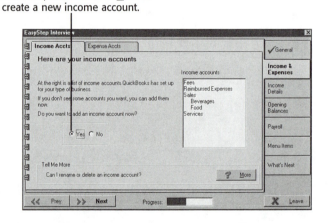

Figure 5.1
QuickBooks chooses income accounts based on the type of business you described earlier in the setup.

1. Choose Yes when you are asked if you want to add an income account (see Figure 5.1), and then click Next. The Adding an Income Account screen appears.

2. Enter the name of an income account that you want to add (for example, Catering, Lumber Sales, Machine Rental, and so on).

3. Choose a tax line for the account if you plan to use QuickBooks to help you summarize information for your income tax return (as discussed in Chapter 29, "Income Taxes").

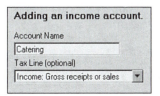

Figure 5.2

Type carefully when you enter account name information in the EasyStep Interview. This is one area where you can't go back and make corrections. If you misspell an account name or decide you want to call the account by another name, you have to wait until the interview is over, and then edit the account name (see Chapter 8, "Setting Up Services, Customers, and Suppliers").

Tip #9 from

Keep a copy of last year's tax return nearby to use as a reference for assigning tax lines. If this is the first year your company will file a tax return, use a blank tax form as a reference.

4. Click Next, and you see that your new income account has been added to the list of income accounts for the company.

Repeat steps 1–4 until you have added all the income accounts that you plan to use. Choose No for step 1 when you have finished entering income accounts.

You can add income accounts at any time after you have finished the EasyStep Interview. See Chapter 7, "Chart of Accounts," for more information about adding accounts.

SETTING UP EXPENSE ACCOUNTS

The process for setting up expense accounts is nearly identical to that of setting up income accounts. The main difference is that you have an opportunity to designate whether an account is a *parent* or a *subaccount* for your expense accounts.

A parent account is a major category of expense account. You can provide more details of the components of a parent account by creating subaccounts. The total value of all the subaccounts of one parent make up the total amount in the parent account.

When presented on financial statements, the subaccounts are indented beneath their related parent account (see Figure 5.3).

Figure 5.3
A partial chart of accounts listing shows subaccounts indented beneath their parents.

Subaccounts can be broken down into additional subaccounts, thus making the first-level subaccount the parent of lower-level subaccounts. You can have up to five levels of parent/subaccounts. For example, under a parent account of Remodeling you might include subaccounts of Painting, Drywall, and Hardware. The Hardware subaccount might be broken down further into such subaccounts as Lighting Fixtures, Electrical Supplies, and Window/Door Hardware. Use the following steps to add an expense account:

1. Choose Yes when asked if you want to add an expense account. The Adding an Expense Account screen appears.
2. Enter the name that you want to give your new expense account in the box indicated.
3. Choose a tax line for the account if you plan to use QuickBooks to help you summarize information for your income tax return (as discussed in Chapter 29).
4. Check the Subaccount Of box if this account is to be a subaccount of another expense account.
5. Choose the parent account of which this account is to be a subaccount, if applicable.
6. Click Next and notice that this expense account has been added to your list of other expense accounts.

Repeat steps 1–6 for as many expense accounts as you want to add at this time. When you have finished entering expense accounts, choose No for step 1.

GENERAL INFORMATION ABOUT YOUR COMPANY'S INCOME

The Income Details section of the EasyStep Interview asks for information about the way your company reports its income. Your answers in this section help QuickBooks further customize your company setup.

The next screen asks if you receive full payment at the time you provide a service or sell a product. A business such as a retail store will probably answer Always to this question (unless the store provides an opportunity for favored customers to open store charge accounts, in which case the appropriate choice is Sometimes). A manufacturing company that ships its finished goods, and then bills for the product, will probably answer Never when asked if full payment is received at the time of sale. The answer you give depends on your own circumstances.

QuickBooks is trying to find out if you need to keep track of *accounts receivable*—without overloading you with accounting jargon. Accounts receivable is the total of the amounts owed to you by your customers.

If you answer Sometimes or Never to the question about receiving full payment at the time of sale, you are asked if you charge a fee to your customers for late payments. If you answer Yes to the question about receiving full payment, you will be set up to produce optional monthly statements in QuickBooks wherein you assess a fee for late payments.

SETTING UP ITEMS

The word *item* is used extensively throughout the QuickBooks program. This term refers to any amount that you list on an invoice or other sales form. Each item you set up takes one of the following forms:

- **Service Item**—A service you perform, such as teaching, writing, manual labor, carpet laying, or child care.
- **Inventory Part Item**—Something that you keep in stock and subsequently sell, such as lumber, T-shirts, or seeds.
- **Non-Inventory Part Item**—Something that you sell but do not hold in inventory. A contractor, for example, might purchase some hardware items specifically for the home improvement job he is performing, and then resell those items to his customer. These hardware items are not considered part of his inventory. A farmer raises livestock for resale or grows crops—the livestock and crops that he raises are considered non-inventory items.
- **Other Charge Item**—Other amounts that you charge your customers, such as delivery or packaging fees, go into this category.

In the next section of the EasyStep Interview, you establish the items for which you bill your customers.

Creating a Service Item

The first type of item you are asked to create is a service item. If your company doesn't have any service items (if, for example, you sell merchandise but don't charge for your time), choose No and continue to the next section. Use the following steps to create a service item:

1. Choose Yes on the screen provided, and then click Next. The Service Item: Name screen appears.
2. Enter a short name for the service (see Figure 5.4). You are limited to 13 characters and spaces. This name is for your reference and is the name you use to request this item on a sales form.

Figure 5.4
The sales description appears on forms that you give to your customers.

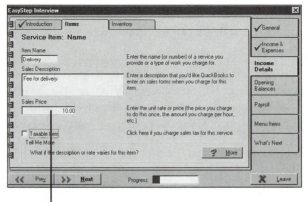

Enter the standard price for which you will sell this item.

3. Enter a description for the service. This is the description that appears on the sales forms you give to your customers. (See Figure 5.4.)

4. Enter the normal price that you charge for this service. This can be entered as a flat fee or as an hourly rate. If you anticipate that the price will change from one customer to the next, you can leave the amount blank.

5. Indicate if this service is normally subject to sales tax. Most personal services are not subject to sales tax. To be certain, however, check the sales tax laws applicable in your state.

Tip #10 from Gail Perry

It's easy to find out if a service is subject to sales tax in your state. Contact the taxing agency for your state and ask to speak to someone in the sales tax division. Explain what service your company performs, and ask if that service is subject to sales tax in the state. State taxing agencies and their phone numbers are listed at the back of this book in Appendix D, "State Revenue Agencies."

---

6. Click Next to proceed to the Service Item: Income Account screen.

7. Indicate the income account that relates to this service item. For example, the items Flooring Installation, Drywall Repair, and Finishing might be associated with the income account Remodeling.

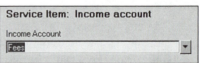

Figure 5.5

> **Note**
> Some of the screens described throughout this chapter might not appear when you work your way through the interview. Screens are triggered to appear depending on the choices you make. Also, some screens (such as any screens relating to preparing estimates) appear only in the Pro version of the QuickBooks software.

8. Click <u>N</u>ext. The Subcontracted Expenses screen appears. If you ever expect to hire someone else to perform this job and then bill your client for the subcontracted work, choose Yes. You then see the screens mentioned in steps 9–11. Otherwise, choose No.

9. Click <u>N</u>ext. The Service Items: Purchase Description screen appears. On this screen, indicate a description of the item. This description is for your purposes. It appears on your company check stubs and the bills that you enter in your system when you pay for the item.

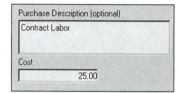

Figure 5.6

10. Enter your normal cost for this item and click <u>N</u>ext.

11. On the Service Item: Expense Account screen that appears, indicate the expense account in which you will normally categorize the cost of this item when you purchase it. An account such as Contract Labor, Fees, or Commissions is a typical account to charge for service for which you are subcontracting (and subsequently charging to your customers).

Repeat steps 1–11 for each service item you want to add.

CREATING A NON-INVENTORY PART ITEM

The next type of item that you are asked to create is a non-inventory part item. If your company doesn't have any such items, choose No and continue to the next section. To create a non-inventory part item, follow these steps:

1. Choose Yes on the screen provided, and then click <u>N</u>ext. The Non-Inventory Parts: Sales Information screen appears.

2. Enter a short name for the item. You are limited to 13 characters and spaces. This name is for your reference and is the name you will use to request this item on a sales form.

3. Enter a description of the item. This is the description that appears on the sales forms that you give to your customers.

4. Enter the price that you normally charge for this item. You always have the capability to override this amount on your sales forms.

5. Indicate if this item is normally subject to sales tax. You always have the capability to override this choice on your sales forms.

6. Click <u>N</u>ext to proceed to the Non-Inventory Parts: Income Account screen.

7. Click the down arrow to drop down a list of choices for the income account that relates to this item. For example, the item Lumber might be associated with the income account Building Materials. If the income account that you want to use is not listed, you can add it quickly by clicking Add New. You are prompted to give a name and description for the new account, and to note if it is a subaccount of some other income account.

8. Click Next. You are asked if this is an item that you purchase for a specific customer. If you answer Yes, you see the screens described in steps 9 and 10. If this is a product you raise (such as crops) or produce yourself, answer No to this question, and then click Next. (Don't worry if you don't see this screen or those described in steps 9 and 10—the appearance of these screens depends on answers you gave to questions earlier in the interview.)

9. If you selected Yes in step 8, the next screen asks you for a purchase description and a cost. The purchase description is a specific description of the item that will appear on your purchase orders and the bills that you receive. If the cost of the item varies each time you make a purchase, leave the cost section blank. Click Next when you have finished entering this information.

10. Indicate the expense account in which you normally categorize the cost of this item when you purchase it.

Repeat steps 1–10 for each non-inventory part item you want to add.

CREATING AN OTHER CHARGE ITEM

Other charge items include such things as delivery charges, shipping and postage costs, packaging, photocopying, and reimbursable expenses that you incur on behalf of your customer. Use the following steps to create an other charge item:

1. Choose Yes on the screen provided, and then click Next. The Other Charges: Name and Sales Information screen appears.

2. Enter a short name for the item. You are limited to 13 characters and spaces. This name is for your reference and is the name you will use to request this item on a sales form.

3. Enter a description of the item. This is the description that appears on the sales forms that you give to your customers.

4. Enter the price that you normally charge for this item. If the price varies from one occurrence of this charge to another, leave the amount blank.

5. Indicate if this item is normally subject to sales tax.

6. Click Next to proceed to the Other Charges: Income Account screen.

7. Click the down arrow to drop down a list of choices for the income account that relates to this item. Choose the account in which you will record income received for this item, or select Add New if you need to create a new account.

8. Click Next. You are asked if this is an item that you pay for, and for which you seek reimbursement. Sometimes you might acquire supplies or job parts on behalf of your customers, and then pass the cost of these items through to your customer. If you choose Yes, you are asked for information relating to your purchase of the items. (Don't worry if you don't see this screen or those described in steps 9 and 10—the appearance of these screens depends on answers you gave to questions earlier in the interview.)

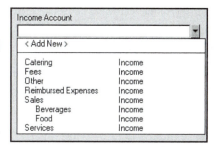

Figure 5.7

9. If you select Yes in step 8, the next screen asks you for a purchase description and cost. The purchase description is a specific description of the item that will appear on your purchase orders and other documents. If the cost of the item varies each time you make a purchase, leave the cost section blank. Click Next when you have finished entering this information.

10. Indicate the expense account in which you will normally categorize the cost of this item when you purchase it. A Cost of Sales account is a typical account to charge for items that you are purchasing and reselling to your customers.

Repeat steps 1–10 for each Other Charge item you want to add.

CREATING INVENTORY ITEMS

In this section you are setting up your inventory items (the items that you regularly keep on hand to sell to your customers, and that you replenish when necessary).

QuickBooks does an excellent job of tracking the quantities of inventory items on hand and reminding you to reorder if quantities get low. See Chapter 14, "Keeping Track of Your Inventory," for a complete analysis of the ways in which QuickBooks treats inventory.

> QuickBooks tracks inventory using an Average Cost method, which is to say that the value of individual items in your inventory is constantly being revised as you purchase and sell inventory items. This method of inventory valuation does not conform to IRS regulations. See Chapter 14 for information regarding rules and alternative methods for valuing inventory.

Use the following steps to create an inventory item:

1. Choose Yes on the screen provided, and then click <u>N</u>ext. The Inventory Item: Sales Information screen appears.
2. Enter a short name for the item. You are limited to 13 characters and spaces. This name is for your reference, and it is the name that you will use to request this item on a sales form.
3. Enter a description of the item. This is the description that appears on the sales forms that you give to your customers.
4. Enter the price that you normally charge for this item.
5. Indicate if this item is normally subject to sales tax.
6. Click <u>N</u>ext to proceed to the Inventory Item: Income Account screen.
7. Click the down arrow to drop down a list of choices for the income account that relates to this item. Choose the account in which you will record income received for this item, or select Add New if you need to create a new account.
8. The next screen asks you for a purchase description and cost. The purchase description is a specific description of the item that appears on your purchase orders and other documents. If the cost of the item varies each time you make a purchase, leave the cost section blank. Click <u>N</u>ext when you have finished entering this information.
9. You are next asked for information regarding reorder point. Enter the number of items to which your inventory needs to drop in order to trigger a reminder that it is time to reorder. Also, enter the number of items you have on hand as of the start date. QuickBooks calculates the average value of these items based on the cost information that you entered in step 8.

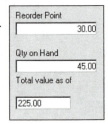

Figure 5.8

Repeat steps 1–9 for each Inventory item you want to add.

ENTERING OPENING BALANCES

In the Opening Balances section of the EasyStep Interview you are asked to enter information, as of the start date, about which customers owe you money (your *accounts receivable*) and which vendors you owe money to (your *accounts payable*). In addition, you enter balances of loan accounts, fixed assets, and other assets and liabilities of your business. If these terms are new to you, don't worry. The process of entering this information is explained in a straightforward way that is easy to understand.

The Opening Balances section of the EasyStep Interview is the place where you enter the balances of all asset and *liability* accounts as of the start date.

Table 5.1 provides you with the information that you need to determine opening balances for many typical balance sheet accounts.

Table 5.1 Determine Opening Balances

Type of Account	Opening Balance
Bank account	Exact amount you had in the bank on the start date.
Current asset (such as deposits, short-term investments, and prepaid items)	Value of the asset as of the start date.
Accounts receivable (amounts owed to you by your customers)	Amount owed by each customer as of the start date.
Fixed asset (such as equipment, vehicles, office furniture, and computers)	Cost of the asset. Also note the amount of *depreciation* recorded against the asset from the date of purchase to the start date..
Other asset (such as securities, long-term deposits, and prepaid expenses)	Value of the asset as of the start date.
Current liability (such as down payments on future delivery of goods, loans expected to be paid off within one year, bank overdrafts, and income taxes)	Amount due as of the start date.
Accounts payable (amounts you owe to vendors, utility companies, and so on)	Amount owed to each supplier asof the start date.
Long-term liability (such as mortgages and long-term notes payable)	Amount due as of the start date.
Credit card	Amount due to the credit card company as of the start date.
Owner's equity	Amount invested by owners of the business as of the start date.

Tip #11 from
Gail Perry

If you don't have all the appropriate balances at your fingertips when you get ready to set up asset and liability accounts, go ahead and set up the accounts anyway, entering 0 as the balance. You can go back later and change the opening balance for any account (as discussed in Chapter 6, "Entering Historical Information").

Entering Customers

Plan on entering each customer who owes you money as of the QuickBooks start date. If you feel ambitious, you can also enter other customers while you are in the EasyStep Interview, even if they don't owe you anything as of the start date. It's not necessary to do this, however, because entering customers later (as you do business with them) is an easy process.

When entering customers, you need the following information:

- Customer name
- List of individual jobs for the customer (if you plan to track jobs separately)
- Amount due from customer either in total or for each individual job

Choose Yes when you are asked to add a customer, and then enter the name of the customer. Be careful when typing the name—if you spell it incorrectly, you can't go back and correct it in the EasyStep Interview; you have to wait until later.

Enter both the name of the first job for which this customer owes you money and the amount owed, or enter the total amount owed by the customer (see Figure 5.9). Continue entering other jobs until you have finished with this customer.

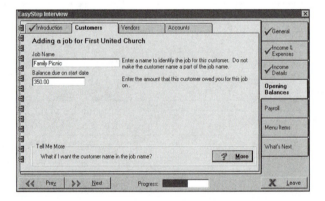

Figure 5.9
Entering jobs helps you separate the work you do for a client.

Follow the same procedure for all the customers that you want to enter at this time.

Note that in the EasyStep Interview you are not given an opportunity to enter addresses and phone numbers of customers, or any other pertinent information such as whether the customer is subject to sales tax or what payment terms are normally applied to amounts due by this customer. This information must be added outside of the interview, in the customer list. See Chapter 8 for information about entering details about your customers.

Entering Vendors

Have ready a list of every person and company to whom you owe money as of your start date, and the amounts you owe.

Choose Yes when you are asked to add a vendor, and then enter the name of the vendor. Be careful when typing the name—if you spell it incorrectly you can't go back and correct it in the EasyStep Interview; you have to wait until later.

Enter the amount that you owe this vendor as of the QuickBooks start date (see Figure 5.10).

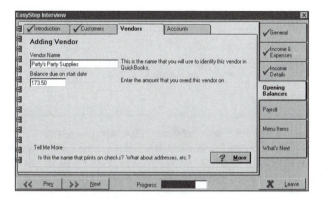

Figure 5.10
Enter the amount owed to this vendor. This amount is combined with all other amounts owed to form your Accounts Payable balance.

Follow the same procedure for all the vendors that you want to enter at this time.

Again, note that you are unable to enter detailed information about the vendor, such as the address and phone and fax numbers. See Chapter 8 for the steps for entering complete vendor information.

CREDIT CARD ACCOUNTS

Does your company have a credit card, or do you use your personal credit card for company business? You can set up a credit card as a separate liability account in QuickBooks; the credit card shows up on your financial statements with the amount due on the account.

When you enter credit card information into QuickBooks, you set up the credit card in a manner similar to setting up a bank account. The opening balance is the balance due to the credit card company, with subsequent purchases and payments entered either as they are made or at the end of each month when you get your statement.

To enter a credit card in QuickBooks, you first enter the name of the credit card (MasterCard or Discover, for example). You are then asked to enter the date of the last credit card statement received prior to your start date (see Figure 5.11) and the amount owed on that statement.

Figure 5.11
Enter the date of your last statement prior to your start date. If you begin doing business on your start date, enter your start date here.

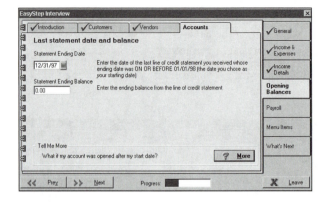

> **Note**
> If you try to enter a credit card statement date that falls after your start date you'll get an error message. The implication is that a balance was due on your start date that is not being properly reflected. If no balance was due on your start date, go ahead and set up the credit card, entering 0 in the Statement Ending Balance text box.

LINES OF CREDIT

A *line of credit* is a type of loan—usually a bank loan—from which you can draw money when needed and pay it back on a predetermined schedule. I used to work for a company that received its revenue seasonally. When it wasn't the season for revenue to come in, bills still had to be paid; so, the company maintained a line of credit with their bank, a short-term loan account on which they were able to draw in the non-revenue season.

To set up a line of credit in QuickBooks, you need the name of the bank or institution issuing the line of credit, the date of the last statement received just prior to your start date, and the amount owed as of the start date. If you don't owe anything on your line of credit as of the start date, enter 0 as the statement ending balance (refer to Figure 5.11).

You are asked if you want to add another line of credit. When you are finished entering lines of credit, answer No to this question. The EasyStep Interview proceeds to the next section, Loans and Notes Payable.

SETTING UP LOANS AND OTHER LIABILITIES

When setting up loans or other liabilities in the EasyStep Interview, you are expected to enter a name for the loan and the unpaid balance as of the start date, and to indicate whether this is a long-term liability (see Figure 5.12).

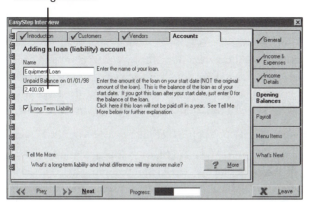

The amount due is the amount of principal—not the total payments including interest.

Figure 5.12
The name of the loan is the name that appears on your financial statements.

Tip #12 from
Gail Perry

Although the loan and liability setup screens seem specifically geared to setting up only loans, you can set up any liability on these screens. Liabilities are obligations to make payments or provide services in the future, and include items such as sales tax payable and prepaid services which you are obligated to perform.

The name of the loan can be tied to what the loan is for (such as Truck Loan or Equipment Loan), or to the name of the lender (Bank of America Loan or First Finance Loan). The name you choose appears on the financial statements and reports for your company.

To determine the unpaid balance of the loan as of the start date, you might need to examine a loan *amortization schedule*, a report that shows the balance of the loan after each payment is made. If your lender didn't provide you with such a schedule, you can contact your lender and ask for the *principal* amount due on the loan as of a specific date. When you contact your lender, ask also for an amortization schedule so that you always know how much of each payment goes toward interest and how much toward principal.

A check box is provided so that you can indicate whether this is a *long-term* liability. A long-term liability is one that is not expected to be paid off within the current year, or, in this case, within the 12-month period starting with the start date. *Short-term*, or *current*, liabilities appear first in the liability section of your company's balance sheet, followed by the long-term debt.

Many large companies split their loans into two pieces on their financial statements; one shows a short-term loan (or current liability) for the amount that will be paid within 12 months of the financial statement date, and the other shows a long-term liability for the amount that will carry over beyond 12 months. Smaller companies often report each loan as a single loan and, in this case, check the Long Term Liability box if any part of the loan will be unpaid after 12 months.

After entering loan and liability information, click Next. You are asked if you want to set up another liability. Choosing Yes returns you to the Adding a Loan (Liability) Account screen. If you choose No you proceed to the section on setting up bank accounts.

Set Up Your Bank Account

Most of your day-to-day transactions ultimately flow through your company bank account. Amounts received from sales get deposited into the bank account. Checks you write result in withdrawals from your account. Until you set up a bank account, the tasks you perform in QuickBooks have nowhere to go. Use the following steps to set up your bank account:

1. Choose Yes when you are asked if you want to set up a bank account; then click Next.
2. Enter the name of the bank account. You can either use the actual name of the bank or a descriptive name for the account (such as Checking Account, Savings Account, or Cash). The name you choose is the name that appears on your company financial statements and other reports. Click Next to proceed.
3. Enter the date of the last bank statement you received prior to your start date. If you are setting up a new bank account where your first bank statement was issued at the end of your first month of business (or sometime thereafter), use the start date as the bank statement date.
4. Enter the ending balance amount from the last bank statement prior to your start date. If you are setting up a new bank account, enter 0 as the balance at the start date.

Repeat the preceding steps for each new bank account you want to set up. You can also follow these steps to set up a petty cash account.

Setting Up Asset Accounts

The setup procedures for all types of asset accounts (current assets, fixed assets, and other assets) are essentially the same from one type of account to the next. Use the following steps to set up an asset account:

1. Indicate that you want to set up an asset by choosing Yes when you are asked; then click Next.
2. Enter the name of the asset. This is the name that will appear on your financial statements and reports.
3. Indicate if the asset is current, fixed, or other.
4. If you chose Fixed Asset in step 3, you are asked if you keep track of *depreciation* for this asset. Answer Yes if you plan to enter depreciation for this asset within QuickBooks.

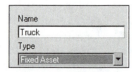

Figure 5.13

Although you can enter depreciation in QuickBooks, the program does not have the capability for calculating depreciation expense. When setting up assets in QuickBooks, you have two options in regard to depreciation:

- Track depreciation in QuickBooks by calculating depreciation yourself (see Chapter 16, "Managing Fixed Assets," for information on how and when to calculate depreciation) and enter the depreciation adjustments into the program in the form of general journal entries.
- Do not track depreciation expense in QuickBooks. Enter your fixed assets at their full value and do not offset that value with depreciation adjustments. This method provides you with statements that accurately reflect the cost of your fixed assets, but do not give you useful information for preparation of your income tax return or for statements to shareholders or lenders. If you choose not to track depreciation in QuickBooks at all, plan on making depreciation adjustments yourself on your tax return and on published financial statements.

One way or another, you must find a way to keep track of depreciation expense so that your tax returns and financial statements provide an accurate reflection of the value of your business. You might want to consult with an accounting professional for help in calculating depreciation or in setting up a system that enables you to make the calculations yourself.

Debits and Credits and Double-Entry Accounting
The accounting terms *debit* and *credit* refer to the left and right, or the plus and minus sides of an account, respectively. An account is increased when an amount makes the account's balance larger and decreased when the balance of the account gets smaller. Some accounts (expense and asset) are increased by a debit, whereas others (income, liability, and equity) are increased by a credit. You don't need to know these terms to use QuickBooks; however, a brief introduction to double-entry accounting might be helpful to you. The theory behind double-entry accounting is that for every debit there is a credit. This is not to say that for every increase in an account there is an offsetting decrease—you can increase an asset account (debit) by making a purchase and at the same time increase a liability account (credit) for the amount of the purchase. Because there is always an offsetting debit or credit, the sum of the balance of all accounts in a company using a double-entry accounting system is always zero. QuickBooks takes care of making your offsetting debits or credits so that you only have to enter one side of the double-entry equation. For example, enter a sale to a customer as income (credit) and QuickBooks makes a corresponding adjustment to your accounts receivable account (debit) for the amount the customer owes you.

Your Equity Accounts

QuickBooks establishes a set of *equity* accounts for you based on the type of business entity you chose when you began setting up your company. An equity account is one that equates to the net worth of the company—the accumulated earnings reduced by accumulated expenses.

An account such as Retained Earnings or Owner's Equity summarizes the net profit of the company, year after year. Corporations have a capital stock account. Partnerships and proprietorships have a draw account for the partner or owner(s).

A strangely named equity account created by QuickBooks is called Opening Balance Equity. It is the nature of double-entry accounting (see preceding sidebar) to offset every entry with an equal amount. QuickBooks creates this Opening Balance Equity account to accommodate offsets for amounts you enter during the EasyStep Interview. So, for example, when you enter a new asset valued at $10,000, the Opening Balance Equity account is offset with $10,000 as is the asset account. You don't need to do anything during the EasyStep Interview with regard to the setup of equity accounts. Later, if you want to add an equity account (say your business takes on a new owner and you want to create a new draw account), or change the name of an equity account, you can do so. The process of adding and changing accounts is described in Chapter 8.

Tip #13 from

Use a journal entry to remove the Opening Balance Equity account before producing financial reports. Journal entries are described in Chapter 16.

SETTING UP PAYROLL

The single most time-consuming part of the EasyStep Interview is the payroll setup. You set up payroll for each of your company's employees, indicating such items as

- Frequency of pay periods
- Regular rate of pay
- Overtime rate of pay
- The state(s) in which your company pays payroll taxes
- Your company's state and federal unemployment tax rates
- The types of deductions withheld from employee paychecks (such as medical insurance, union dues, and local taxes)
- The types of items typically added to employee paychecks (such as mileage and travel reimbursements and reimbursements for other business-related expenditures)
- The name, address, and Social Security number of each employee you plan to enter, as well as the date on which each was hired

When you have a payroll that you plan to set up in QuickBooks and you are asked if you want to set up or skip payroll, consider whether you want to set up payroll through the EasyStep Interview or wait until a later time.

SETTING UP PAYROLL ITEMS

If you choose to wait until later to set up your payroll, I recommend that you at least go through the EasyStep payroll screens and set up the elements of your payroll. Indicate whether your paychecks are issued weekly, biweekly, or semi-monthly; indicate which types of withholding apply to your company's employees and which types of benefits are paid on behalf of the employees. Set up your unemployment tax rates and any local income taxes that might be applicable.

Then, when you are asked if you want to set up the individual employees, you can choose to do this later (see the section on setting up employees in Chapter 18, "Paying Employees and Contractors"), but all your payroll items will be in place and ready to use.

To set up your payroll items, follow these steps:

1. Answer Yes when you are asked if you want to set up payroll.
2. Indicate how frequently paychecks are issued by your company. You can choose more than one frequency. Some companies pay their hourly employees more frequently (weekly or every two weeks) than their salaried employees. Check each box that applies.
3. Check off each state for which you withhold income taxes. Several screens separate this step from step 4. Just click Next at the bottom of each screen to progress to the next screen that asks you for input.
4. Enter the state withholding ID number for each state listed. If you don't know this information, you can enter it later.
5. Enter the state unemployment ID number for each state listed and the rate at which unemployment tax is calculated for each state. Some states require withholding for unemployment taxes (although most states do not). If you pay taxes in such a state, enter a rate in the ER Rate column.
6. Indicate whether your company qualifies for a FUTA credit. The FUTA credit is the result of offsetting federal unemployment compensation taxes by amounts paid to state unemployment agencies.

Figure 5.14

Tip #14 from Gail Perry

State unemployment tax rates change from year to year as states determine your *experience rate*. The experience rate is determined by looking at a profile of your past employees and the claims that they have made for unemployment compensation. In the first years of doing business, an employer pays a high unemployment rate. After you have established that your employees do not make claims for unemployment compensation (usually after three years), this rate decreases.

7. Indicate if your employees are paid hourly, are salaried, or are paid on commission. Check each box that applies.
8. If your company pays different rates for different types of hourly work (such as higher rates for overtime or holiday hours), indicate multiple rates available by checking the various options. You can check as many options as you need. It's wise to check each

item that you think might apply, because the payroll item will be set up for you and ready for use when you need it.

9. Just as your company might pay different rates for hourly workers, there might be different rates for types of salaried work as well. Check all items that apply.

10. Place a check next to each payroll deduction that applies to your company's employees. These items (shown in Figure 5.15) are items that will be paid by employees through payroll withholding. If you want to include a deduction that is not on this list (child care, for example), choose Other Net Deduction.

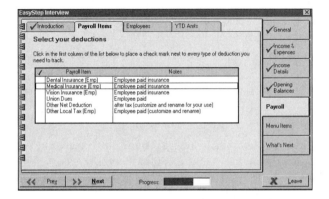

Figure 5.15
Check each item that applies to your employees. Check an item even if it only applies to one employee.

11. Check Mileage Reimbursement if your company has a practice of paying employees for vehicle usage in the form of an addition to their paycheck. If other payments are made to employees in their paychecks (such as moving expense reimbursements), check the Other Taxable Addition(s) item. If you check the Other Taxable Addition(s) item, a series of setup screens appears (see Figure 5.16). On these screens, you are asked for the following information:

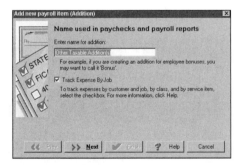

Figure 5.16
Enter the name of the item that you want to add.

- Name of the new item (Moving Expense Reimbursement, for example).
- Indicate an expense account (such as Moving Expenses) for this item.
- As an item that is taxable to the employee, it needs to be included in the employee's compensation, and you are asked to indicate the name of the account you use for compensation (it might be an account called Compensation, or something similar such as Salaries and Wages).
- Indicate which withholding taxes apply to this item.
- Indicate if this item is based on quantity. In other words, if the item is a form of compensation that is based on a number of units sold or a number of phone calls made, check the Based on Quantity box.
- If the compensation is based on quantity, you are asked to enter a rate or an amount. A rate is the value per unit, so if each unit sold is worth $5, enter 5. If the rate is a percent, enter the amount with the percent symbol (2%). If the rate varies from one employee to the next, leave this part blank.
- If there is a maximum annual amount that can be earned for this payroll item ($5 per unit, but no more than $500 total), enter that amount.

12. Check off all company-paid benefits (such as medical insurance). Check Other Comp. Contribution if there is a company-paid benefit that is not listed; you are asked to set up the benefit by answering questions similar to the ones for setting up a compensation item in step 11.
13. Now that all the payroll items are set up you are asked, on a series of screens, to check off the items that apply to all or most employees. By checking off these items, they automatically appear when you are issuing paychecks. You don't have to use the items that appear on a paycheck entry form, but they are there, waiting for you to fill in amounts—and you don't have to search for the items in drop-down lists. For more detailed information about all the questions covered on these screens, see Chapter 18.

After you have checked all items that you want to appear on paychecks, you are ready to either set up actual employees or finish payroll setup. If you plan to set up your actual employees at this point, see Chapter 18.

Entering Starting Balances for Payroll

The final few screens of the payroll setup ask you to enter starting balances for employees and payroll taxes. If you chose to set up employees in the interview and your start date is sometime after the first day of the year, you need to enter the year-to-date payroll and withholding totals for each employee. This causes your payroll tax forms at the end of the year (such as employee W-2 forms) to reflect payroll for the entire year rather than just part of the year.

If your start date is January 1 (or the first day your company begins doing business), that will be the date on which you begin tracking payroll and payroll tax liabilities. If your start date is later in the year, I strongly recommend that you enter January 1 of the current year as the date on which you start tracking payroll and payroll tax liabilities.

You are asked for a date on which your accounts will be affected by payroll transactions. This will also be January 1 of the current year, or the first day on which you began doing business.

Finally, you are asked to enter a date on which you plan to start using QuickBooks to pay your payroll. This is the actual date on which you will begin processing paychecks through QuickBooks.

If you entered employees earlier in the payroll setup, you are now presented with a screen listing all your employees. Select each employee listed, one at a time, and enter any year-to-date payroll information for that employee (see Figure 5.17). If you start using QuickBooks to generate a payroll as of January 1 of the current year, you don't have to enter anything here. This is just to catch up the year-to-date numbers from the first of the year to the time when you start issuing paychecks from QuickBooks.

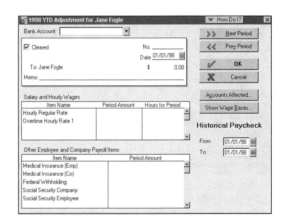

Figure 5.17
Enter all the year-to-date information for the selected employee on this screen. Entering this information is extremely important if you want to use QuickBooks to produce W-2 forms at the end of the year.

If your start date is not January 1 and you had payroll during the year prior to your start date, you need to enter the year-to-date tax payments that you have made. When the Prior Payments of Taxes and Liabilities screen shown in Figure 5.18 appears, click in the area under Item Name. An arrow appears and you can click it to display a drop-down list of all the payroll items you created previously. Choose the items one at a time and enter the related year-to-date amount in the Amount column.

When you have finished entering year-to-date tax and other payroll liability amounts, click Done. A box appears, asking if you want to use these amounts as your liability account balances. If you don't want the payments reflected in your financial statements for the year, answer Do Not Affect Accounts. If you have paid the amounts and you want the payments to come through on your financial statements but don't want to include the payments as reductions of your cash account, choose the second option.

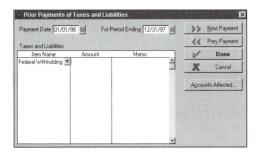

Figure 5.18
Click in the Item Name column to get a drop-down arrow. Then, choose each tax and liability for which you have made payments during the year.

To include the tax payments in your financial statements and to reflect the payments in your cash account as well, choose the third option.

Nearly every company (with exception of companies that are just getting started) have starting balances for payroll tax liabilities. Unless your first payroll checks are issued at the same time that you begin using QuickBooks, you probably owed some payroll taxes as of the end of the prior year. Taxes that were withheld last December aren't due to the government until January, so that withholding is considered a liability as of January 1. If your start date is sometime later in the year, the amount of payroll tax you owe as of the start date is the amount you will enter as your liability.

Finishing the Interview

The last two sections of the EasyStep Interview go by quickly. Answer a few simple questions and the interview is completed. The Menu Items section asks the following questions:

- **Do you expect to use QuickBooks' To Do list often?** Answering Yes to this question places the To Do list in a prominent place on the Lists menu. If you answer No, the To Do list is still available on the Lists menu under Other.

- **Do you want to assess finance charges for customers with overdue invoices?** Answering Yes causes this feature to appear on your Activities main menu. If you answer No, the feature appears on the Activities menu, under the Other category.

- **Do you want to use QuickBooks to help with budgeting?** Again, a Yes answer places this feature prominently on the Activities menu, and a No answer moves the feature to the Other category.

The final section of the interview, the What's Next section, is an information section only. You will read some general pointers about how to get started using QuickBooks, and you will see information about purchasing supplies from Intuit.

Click through these final screens and your interview is finished!

Troubleshooting

Changing Descriptions

I setup an item as a Non-Inventory Part, but it should really be an Inventory Part item. Can this description be changed?

You can't edit the description of an existing item; nor can you merge an item of one type into an item of a different type. The best you can do is create a new item with a similar name, and then make a journal entry to zero out the contents of the item you no longer want and transfer the balance to the new item.

Editing Accounts

During the setup process, I didn't have the opening balances available for all my accounts. Can these amounts be added later?

Edit an asset or liability account and adjust the opening balance by choosing Lists, Chart of Accounts, and then double-clicking the name of the account you want to change. The account register opens. Press Ctrl+Home to see the beginning of the account register, if it isn't already visible; then, make any necessary entries or changes to the opening balance.

Setting Up Payroll

I have a new payroll to set up—several employees with varying pay rates. What's the best way to set up a large payroll?

I recommend going back to the EasyStep Interview to set up your payroll. Even after the interview is completed, the question and answer format takes you step-by-step through the process of entering payroll for new employees, and you'll find that you're less likely to leave anything out.

CHAPTER 6

ENTERING HISTORICAL INFORMATION

In this chapter

Changing Your Start Date   88

Checklist of Items Before You Begin   88

Entering Historical Bills Received   90

Entering Historical Invoices   92

Entering Money Received   94

Entering Bills Paid   99

Entering Deposits Made   99

Entering Payroll Transactions   100

Entering All Other Payments Made   102

Changing Your Start Date

If the start date that you choose for your company is a date from the past, you need to go back to that start date and begin entering the individual transactions that will make your company's QuickBooks file complete. Usually, the first day of the year is chosen as a start date. If it's May and you are beginning to enter information for the year in QuickBooks, you need to enter the transactions from January through May.

> **Note**
> You are not required to keep the start date you designated when you set up your company in the EasyStep Interview. For example, if you chose June 1 as your start date and now you decide you really want to go back to the beginning of the year to enter a full year of transactions, you can change the start date by adjusting the beginning balance and date in your registers, as described in this chapter.

Use the handy checklist in this chapter (see Figure 6.1) to help you gather the documents you need to enter your historical transactions.

Checklist of Items Before You Begin

When you enter historical transactions you must make your entries in a certain order. For example, if you enter the checks you wrote before you enter the bills that you are paying, you can't tie the checks to the bills. Also, if you enter your deposits before entering the customer invoices that were paid, a clear record of what the deposited funds represent will not exist.

Therefore, the transactions that occurred in your bank account are actually the last transactions you enter.

> **Tip #15 from Gail Perry**
> Business doesn't have to come to a standstill while you are entering historical transactions. You can continue entering your current transactions on the schedule that you normally follow. That way, you won't get behind.

The list of documents and information you need for entering historical transactions is presented in the order in which you need to enter those transactions (see the following checklist). By using this convenient checklist, you can gather the appropriate data and perform one task at a time. The detailed instructions for performing these tasks follow the checklist. Check off the task as you do it, and then when you come back to enter more historical transactions you can see where you left off. The checklist is as follows:

> **Tip #16 from**
> *Gail Perry*
>
> Use a special check mark, a rubber stamp, or some noticeable means of marking each document that you enter into QuickBooks to keep you from entering the same document twice.

- **All bills you have received since your start date**—Enter one at a time, in the order in which they were received, just as you might enter a bill that comes in the mail today. Now is a good time to consider getting a date stamp—if you don't already have one—so that you can date bills when you receive them. This is useful if a dispute arises concerning the length of time you were given to pay a bill. Any bills that were outstanding at the time of your start date should already have been entered when you went through the steps of the EasyStep Interview. Any bills that you have paid recently should have already been entered as well. Make sure you don't enter the same bill twice.

- **All invoices from your start date to the present**—Enter these, one at a time, in the order in which they were issued. Enter the invoices in the same way as you might enter an invoice you are issuing today, but make sure that you check the date on the invoice. Note that any invoices that were outstanding at the time of your start date need to already have been entered when you went through the steps of the EasyStep Interview.

- **All money you have received since your start date**—This includes cash, checks, and credit card payments, as well as proceeds from loans, and money from any other sources. Because you have already entered all your invoices, noting the payments made by customers is a matter of checking off which invoices have been paid.

- **All bills you have paid since your start date**—Had you not completed the earlier step of entering the bills you received, you would not be able to perform this step now. Check off the bills that you paid as you normally do, noting any changes in the amounts paid versus the amounts on the bills as you enter the payments. QuickBooks offsets your cash account by the amounts of the bills you paid.

- **All deposits you have made to your bank accounts since the start date**—Because you have already entered the amount of money you have received since the start date, entering the deposits will be a simple matter of checking off the payments to form each deposit. QuickBooks increases the balance in your cash account by the amount of deposits you indicate.

- **Payroll transactions from the start date to the present**—Note that you can't use the QuickBooks payroll feature until all historical payroll information has been entered. By entering historical payroll information, you can produce accurate payroll tax reports and year-to-date payroll statements for the company employees.

- **All other checks written since the start date**—This is aside from the checks written to pay bills.

When all the boxes are checked, you have entered all the historical information necessary to provide you with complete financial statements and tax reports.

After you've collected the documents you use to make entries of historical information, and you've set aside some time to make these entries, you can follow the rest of the instructions in this chapter for getting the historical information into your records in the proper order.

ENTERING HISTORICAL BILLS RECEIVED

The first pieces of historical information you enter are the bills that you received from the start date to the time when you began entering current information in QuickBooks. These are the bills from your vendors, suppliers, and contractors for items and services you purchased.

To make sure you haven't already entered some of these bills in QuickBooks, you can print a list of all bills that you have received—including those that have been recorded as paid—organized by vendor. With this list at your side, you can quickly check to see if a bill has been entered previously. To generate such a report, choose Reports, A/P Reports, Vendor Balance Detail.

> **Tip #17 from Gail Perry**
>
> You can enter historical invoices before bill payments if you do not pass billed amounts through to customers on their invoices. If you pay for items for which you expect reimbursement from your customers, it is necessary that you enter historical bills before invoices, so that all the billed information will be available when you get ready to enter the invoices.

As you enter each bill, QuickBooks adds the amount to your *accounts payable* balance and shows the amount as an expense in the account that you indicate on the bill:

1. Choose Activities, Enter Bills. (If Enter Bills does not appear on your main Activities menu, you can find it under Activities, Other Activities.) The Enter Bills window opens.

> **Note**
>
> Depending on how you answered some of the questions in the EasyStep Interview, some menu choices might be hidden. The Lists menu has a side menu called Other Lists, and the Activities menu has a side menu called Other Activities. You can control which features appear (and don't appear) on these other menus by choosing File, Preferences, and then clicking the Menus icon on the left side of the Preferences window (you might have to scroll down to find the icon). Check items that you want to take away on the Other menus, or uncheck items that you want to move to the main part of the Lists and Activities menus.

2. Choose a vendor from the drop-down list (see Figure 6.1). If the vendor you want to use does not appear in the list, select Add New from the top of the drop-down list and enter new vendor information.

Click Add New to add a new vendor.

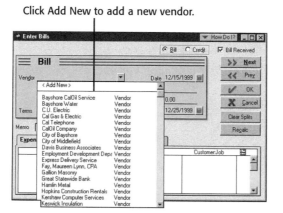

Figure 6.1
Scroll through the drop-down list to find the vendor that you are looking for.

3. Make sure that the correct date appears in the date area, and that the date matches the date on the bill.

4. Enter a memo (optional).

5. If this bill is for the purchase of inventory items, on the tab marked Items (see Figure 6.2), enter the rest of the information right from the bill: item(s) ordered, description, quantity, and rate. If this bill relates to a particular job (if you use the Job Costing feature), enter the job name in the space provided.

Click the Expenses tab to show expenses such as supplies or utilities.

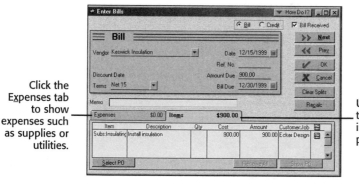

Use the Items tab to reflect inventory items purchased.

Figure 6.2
Enter detailed information right from your bill at the bottom of the Enter Bills window.

6. If this bill is for expenses (such as repairs or supplies), use the Expenses tab and enter the type of expense, an optional memo, and the amount of the bill.

7. Click Next to proceed to the next bill, or click OK if this is the last bill that you intend to enter.

Continue the preceding process until all your bills have been entered.

After you've entered all bills from your start date to the present, the following areas of QuickBooks have been brought up-to-date:

- Records of all inventory purchases since your start date
- Vendor history of all bills received from each vendor since the start date

ENTERING HISTORICAL INVOICES

When you have gathered all the invoices that you issued between the start date and today, you are ready to enter historical invoices into your QuickBooks company file. Stack the invoices in the order in which they were issued, with the earliest on the top.

Before you begin, you might want to see a list of all the invoices you have previously entered into QuickBooks. To generate such a report, choose Reports, A/R Reports, Customer Balance Detail. A detailed list showing all invoices as well as payments received, such as the one shown in Figure 6.3, can be printed by clicking the Print button at the top of the report.

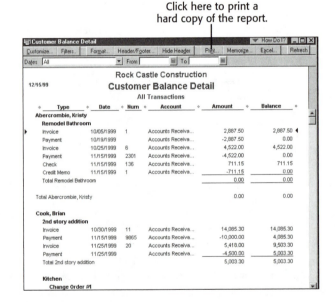

Figure 6.3
Keep this report by your side when entering historical invoices so that you don't enter the same invoice twice.

1. Choose Activities, Create Invoices. The Create Invoices window appears. Note that your invoice window might look different than the one to which I refer in these steps. The type of invoice template you choose (Service, Product, and so on) dictates the fields that appear.

2. Choose a customer from the drop-down list. If the customer name does not appear, select Add New and enter new customer information.

3. Make sure that the date of the invoice is correct.
4. Enter details of the invoice, following right along from the actual invoice you issued: item, quantity, description, and rate (see Figure 6.4).

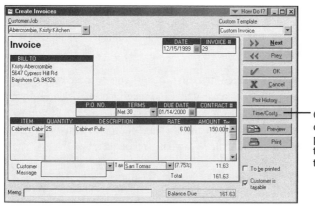

Figure 6.4
In the bottom area of the window, enter the details of each item for which you are billing a customer.

Click here to review costs that have been passed through to this customer from the bills you entered.

5. If an expense was entered from your historical bills that relates to this invoice, click the Time/Costs button in the Create Invoices window to pop up the Choose Billable Time and Costs window. Any items charged to the customer through the bills appear here (see Figure 6.5). Check any item that needs to pass through to this invoice, and then click OK when you are finished.

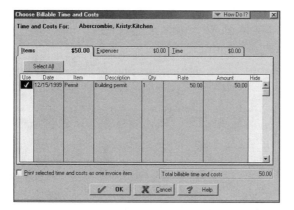

Figure 6.5
Check off each item that you want to include on this invoice by clicking in the Use column next to the item.

6. Click Next to proceed to the next invoice, or click OK if this is the last invoice that you intend to enter.

Continue the preceding process until all your invoices have been entered.

After you've entered all the invoices from your start date to the present, the following areas of QuickBooks have been brought up-to-date:

- Complete record of every item and service you have sold since the start date
- Detailed customer history of all business done with each customer since the start date

Entering Money Received

After all your invoices have been entered, it's time to start recording payments for those invoices. If, in the past, you recorded payments with a receipt book or some form of paper voucher, you can use those receipts or vouchers for entering payments. If you have no such paper trail, you will probably have to refer to whatever documentation accompanies your bank deposits. Collect all the documents for payments received since the start date.

Entering Payments Against Invoices

To enter historical payments, follow these steps:

1. Choose Activities, Receive Payments. The Receive Payments window appears. This window is for recording payments against invoices only. If you want to record payments for sales without linking the sale to an invoice, see the later section, "Entering Cash Payments."
2. Choose a customer name by clicking the drop-down arrow, and then clicking a customer name from the resulting list (or begin entering the letters of the name until the correct name appears). Because the payments are for invoices, and you have already entered all your invoices, the customer names are already in the list.
3. Make sure that the date of the payment is correct.
4. Enter the total amount of payment received in the Amount area on the receive payments form.
5. All invoices that have been created for this customer appear in the Invoices Paid (with this Payment) and Those Still Outstanding list at the bottom of the Receive Payments window (see Figure 6.6). In this area of the window, QuickBooks makes assumptions about how the payment is applied, showing the oldest invoices as being paid first. Check off each invoice to which this payment relates by clicking in the left-most column across from the invoice. QuickBooks applies the payment in the order in which you check off the invoices. You can also override the amounts that QuickBooks enters in the Payment column by deleting the QuickBooks amounts and keying in your own amounts.
6. If the amount of payment was not for the entire invoice, reflect the actual payment by entering the correct amount in the payment column across from the invoice. Any remaining balance due stays with this customer and appears the next time you enter a payment for this customer.

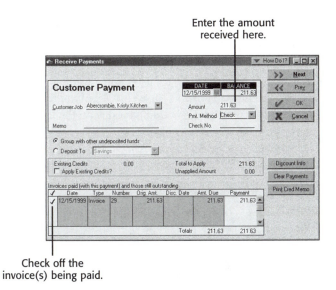

Figure 6.6
This form is used for reporting payments received from customers.

Enter the amount received here.

Check off the invoice(s) being paid.

> Before changing the amount of an invoice to reflect the actual payment due, find out why only part of the payment due was received. If the customer was entitled to a credit or a discount, this is reflected properly instead of merely changing the amount in the Payment column. Otherwise, QuickBooks continues to maintain an amount due from this customer for this invoice. See the section "Reflecting Credits and Discounts" for the proper treatment of these items.

7. Click the Next button to enter another payment, or click OK when you have finished entering payments.

Repeat the preceding steps for each payment that you want to record.

REFLECTING CREDITS AND DISCOUNTS

After entering an invoice in your QuickBooks file, strange things can happen. Between the time that the invoice was issued and the payment was made, there might have been a return of merchandise resulting in a credit. Or the customer might be entitled to a discount for a timely payment. When such events as this occur, the amount of the invoice disagrees with the amount of the payment received.

You can change the amount reflected in the invoice summary at the bottom of the Receive Payments screen, but then you will forever carry an amount due on the invoice that changed.

Instead, you need to accurately record the credit or discount so that the payment for the invoice appears to be correct, the invoice doesn't remain on your books with an amount due (that really isn't due), and your company's income records are correct. To do so, follow these steps:

1. With the Receive Payments window still onscreen, click the Discount Info button.
2. The Discount Information window appears (see Figure 6.7). Select an *account* for the discount (there will already be a discount account in your account list).
3. The discount amount that appears is a result of the terms assigned to the related invoice. You have the option of changing the discount amount. After you're satisfied with the amount, click OK. The discount reduces the amount due on the invoice.

Figure 6.7
Click Discount Info to display this window.

Change the discount amount here if necessary.

Choose the correct account for recording the discount.

To record credits and refunds, use the following steps:

1. Choose Activities, Create Credit Memos/Refunds. The Create Credit Memos/Refunds window appears.
2. Select the customer name at the top of the credit form and enter the correct date.
3. In the Item column, indicate the item(s) for which a credit is being issued (see Figure 6.8). Generally, the item you choose is the same as an item that appeared on an earlier invoice.

Figure 6.8
Enter credits and refunds on this separate form, and then the amounts flow through to the customer invoice.

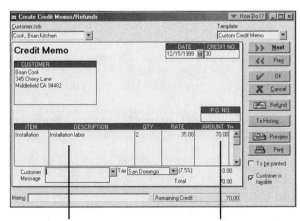

Click here to enter the item for which the credit is being issued.

QuickBooks calculates the amount of the credit based on the quantity and rate you enter.

4. Enter the quantity and rate for the item(s) being credited. Verify whether or not the Customer Is Taxable box needs to be checked.
5. Click OK to issue the credit and record it on your books.
6. Complete steps 1–5 in the earlier section "Entering Payments Against Invoices." When you select Activities, Receive Payments, and choose a customer job, the amount of credit existing for this customer appears in the middle of the screen (see Figure 6.9).

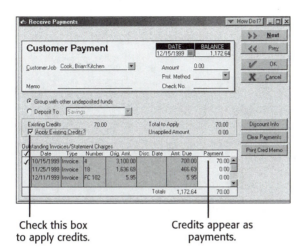

Figure 6.9
Credits appear in the middle of this form, ready for you to apply.

Check this box to apply credits.

Credits appear as payments.

7. To apply credits, check the Apply Existing Credits box. The credits available for this customer appear in the Payment column at the bottom of the form.
8. Complete the Receive Payments form by clicking Next or OK.

ENTERING CASH PAYMENTS

Some circumstances exist in which you have payments to enter, but have no related invoice. For example, your business might conduct cash sales—sales to customers who make purchases on a one-time, walk-in basis, and who are not expected to give you their names. You might have customers who make purchases from you regularly but who do not have an open account with you, so they pay cash at the time of the purchase.

Or you might have decided to streamline your entry of historical information, bypass entering invoices altogether, and just enter cash payments.

Whatever the reason, cash sales might be lurking among the payments received that must be recorded to bring your income and cash records into balance:

1. Choose Activities, Enter Cash Sales. (If the Enter Cash Sales menu choice does not appear, look under Activities, Other Activities.) The Enter Cash Sales window appears.

2. Choose a customer from the drop-down list at the top of the window. If the customer who made the sale is not on the list, you can add a customer by clicking Add New at the top of the list. If you have a lot of cash sales to enter, particularly sales to strangers or one-time only customers, you might want to create a new customer called Cash Sales (or something similar) and use that "customer" name each time you have a cash sale to record.

3. Make sure that the date of the payment is correct.

4. On the bottom section of the Enter Cash Sales form, enter a description of the item for which the payment was received (see Figure 6.10). By choosing an item or items, QuickBooks knows to which income account the cash needs to be directed.

Figure 6.10
Enter a cash payment on this screen.

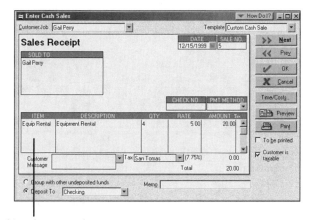

Click in this column to select the item that was sold or the service that was provided.

5. Enter a quantity and rate, if this information is available. Alternatively, you can enter a total amount in the Amount column in the lower section of the form.

6. Click the Next button to enter another payment, or click OK if you have finished entering cash payments.

Repeat the preceding steps for each cash payment that you want to record.

When all payments have been entered into QuickBooks, the following areas of your QuickBooks file have been brought up-to-date:

- Records of all payments received as of your start date
- Complete customer records showing all sales to customers and payments made by customers since the start date
- Complete records of all unpaid invoices as of the current date
- Accurate reflection of income to date in your company accounts

Entering Bills Paid

All the bills that you have paid from the start date to today must now be entered. Otherwise, your records will show that you owe an awful lot of money! Gather all the bills you have paid since your start date. The date and amount paid will be marked on each bill. If you haven't been marking bills paid, now is a good time to start.

1. Choose Activities, Pay Bills. (If you can't find Pay Bills on the Activities main menu, look under Activities, Other Activities.) The Pay Bills window appears.
2. For the first bill you paid, enter the payment date.
3. Click the Show All Bills option in the center of the screen. All outstanding bills appear on the list at the bottom of the screen.
4. Check the bill that corresponds to the payment. If this payment was for only part of a bill, indicate the amount that was paid in the Amt Paid column.
5. Click Next to enter the next payment, or click OK if you are finished entering payments.

Follow the preceding steps until you have entered all your bill payments.

When all bill payments have been entered into QuickBooks, the following areas of your QuickBooks file have been brought up-to-date:

- Records of all bill payments made since your start date
- Complete vendor records showing all acquisitions made by your company and payments made by your company since the start date
- Complete records of all outstanding bills (accounts payable) as of the current date
- Accurate reflection of expenses to date in your company accounts

Entering Deposits Made

You've recorded all the cash you received since the start date and have updated your income and receivables records in the process. But so far, your bank account hasn't been affected by these entries. You need to reflect the actual bank deposits so that your cash balance is accurate.

Gather your deposit slips or other records of the amounts deposited with each bank deposit, and then follow these steps:

1. Choose Activities, Make Deposits. The Payments to Deposit window appears.
2. Click each payment that is part of this deposit. If an amount included in this deposit does not appear on the Payment to Deposit list, don't worry (it's covered in step 5). Click OK, and the Make Deposits window appears.
3. Indicate the bank account to which you are making this deposit.

Part
I

Ch
6

4. Verify the date of the deposit.
5. If this deposit included amounts that were not on the Payment to Deposit list, enter the additional deposit amounts on this screen. This might include money from sources other than customers, such as a bank loan or a cash rebate. In the From Account column, indicate the account to which the amount relates.
6. Click Next to finish recording this deposit and enter a new deposit, or OK to record the deposit and exit this screen.

ENTERING PAYROLL TRANSACTIONS

All payroll transactions must be entered before you begin using the QuickBooks Payroll feature.

If your start date is after January 1 (and after the first day that your company began doing business), you must enter year-to-date payroll amounts for all your company's employees as of the start date. For example, if your company was in business all year and you chose April 1 as your start date, you have to enter January to March payroll amounts for all the company's employees. In addition, you must enter every paycheck written after the start date, with full details of all tax and other withholdings.

If your start date is January 1 (or the first day your company began doing business), you have no year-to-date amounts to enter, but you must enter every paycheck written since the start date.

Gather the details for every paycheck written since the start date as well as information relating to all payroll tax payments made since the start date.

> **Note**
> Payroll setup must be completed before you can begin entering historical payroll. This involves setting up individual payroll items such as types of withholding and benefits paid by the employer. The easiest way to set up payroll is by using the EasyStep Interview. If you need to set up payroll, choose File, EasyStep Interview, and then click the Payroll tab. See Chapter 5, "Setting Up Accounts, Inventory, Fixed Assets, and Payroll," for instructions on setting up payroll.

To enter year-to-date payroll information for your employees, choose Activities, Payroll, Set Up YTD Amounts. The Set Up YTD Amounts window appears.

→ To enter the year-to-date information, **see** "Entering Starting Balances for Payroll" on **p. 83**.

1. Choose Activities, Payroll, Pay Employees. The Select Employees to Pay window appears.
2. Verify the dates for the check and the end of pay period. Also verify that the correct bank account is chosen for this payment.

3. Click to the left of the employee that you want to pay (see Figure 6.11). You can select more than one employee, but the payments you create for all selected employees are recorded on the same date and for the same pay period.

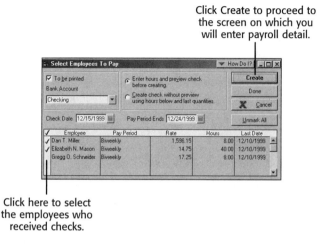

Click Create to proceed to the screen on which you will enter payroll detail.

Figure 6.11
Choose which employees received checks during the stated pay period.

Click here to select the employees who received checks.

4. Click the Create button. The Preview Paycheck window appears (see Figure 6.12).

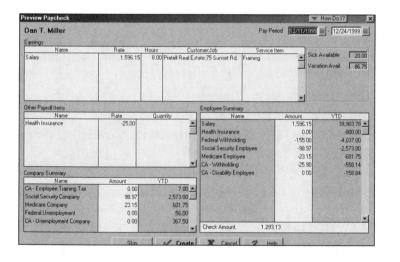

Figure 6.12
Enter all appropriate payroll information for this employee's paycheck.

5. Enter the appropriate information for this employee's paycheck. For a detailed example of paycheck creation, see Chapter 18, "Paying Employees and Contractors."

6. When you have completed this paycheck, click the Create button. If you selected more than one employee in step 3, the next employee screen appears; otherwise, you return to the Select Employees to Pay screen, where you can change the dates and enter additional paychecks, or click Done if you are finished entering paychecks.

When all paychecks and year-to-date payroll information has been entered into QuickBooks, the following areas of your QuickBooks file have been brought up-to-date:

- Year-to-date payroll records for each employee
- Complete payroll tax liabilities for the entire year

Entering All Other Payments Made

The final step in entering historical information involves entering any remaining payments that have been made since the start date. These payments might include rent, loan payments, loans to employees or owners, retirement contributions, and so on.

You need your check register or other record of checks written since the start date. You only enter the checks that have not been entered previously. Use the following steps:

> **Note:** You might inadvertently enter a check that has been entered previously (for example, in the form of a bill payment). See Chapter 15, "Purchase Orders, Accounts Payable, and Paying Bills," for information on how to examine the checks that have been written and how to delete a duplicate check.

1. Choose Activities, Write Checks. The Write Checks window, which looks just like a real check, appears.
2. At the top of the screen, where it says Bank Account, select the bank account from which this check was written.
3. Verify that the correct date is displayed.
4. Enter the name of the payee at the top of the check.
5. Uncheck the To Be Printed box. This enables you to enter the correct check number for this check.
6. Enter the amount paid.
7. At the bottom of the window, enter a description of what you paid or purchased with this check, selecting the account to which the expense needs to be charged (see Figure 6.13). For more information about accounts, see Chapter 7, "Chart of Accounts."
8. Click Next to enter another check, or OK if you are finished entering checks.

Repeat the preceding steps for all the checks that you need to enter.

When all checks have been entered into QuickBooks, the following areas of your QuickBooks file have been brought up-to-date:

- Accurate ending balance in your bank accounts
- Company profit and loss statement for the year to date

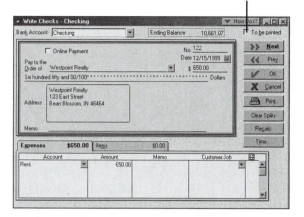

Figure 6.13
Enter all check information, just as it appeared on your original check.

TROUBLESHOOTING

ENTERING BILLS

I want to enter my historical vendor bills, but I seem to have misplaced some of them. What do I do?

Enter the bills you have. For payments that you made but for which you can't find the bill, enter the amount of the payments (from your check register or canceled checks) and make your best estimate of how the amount needs to be categorized. If possible, contact the vendor and ask for information supporting the payment in question. He probably has a record of your payments and can link them to his invoices.

CORRECTING DEPOSITS

While entering my deposits from the past year, I noticed a deposit amount that didn't agree with the invoice. I didn't catch it at the time. How do I enter this in QuickBooks?

You can contact the customer and correct the situation, either by requesting additional payment (if the customer underpaid) or by issuing a credit or refund (if the customer overpaid). If the amount is negligible, you can choose to adjust the invoice to the actual amount paid.

CHAPTER 7

CHART OF ACCOUNTS

In this chapter

Understanding the Importance of Accounting   106

What Is an Account?   106

Types of Accounts   107

Your Company's Liabilities   109

Equity: What Your Company Is Worth   109

Income: Your Company's Bread and Butter   112

Expenses Reduce Business Income   112

QuickBooks Gives You a Standard List of Accounts   112

Numbering Your Chart of Accounts   117

Printing a Chart of Accounts List   119

This chapter is about scary accounting terms such as *chart of accounts, assets, liabilities, equity, debits, credits,* and so on. As a former accounting instructor who taught introductory-level accounting courses to people who were new to these terms, I have a good feel for just how obscure some of this can seem to the uninitiated.

Before you skip ahead to future chapters, give me a few minutes to convince you that there are easy ways to look at these basic accounting concepts and that your experiences using QuickBooks over the years will be better for having learned about them.

Understanding the Importance of Accounting

Accounting is the business of keeping track of all the financial activities of an entity (individual or company). When you use accounting techniques, you provide an opportunity to obtain information about how your company is performing, and you can use that information to make intelligent decisions.

Without accounting, you never know whether your business is profitable or losing money until you either find yourself with too many bills and not enough money to pay them, or find your cash register overflowing with no room to store all the cash. Chances are greater that you will be met with the former scenario if you haven't kept track of your company's performance through basic accounting methods.

With an accounting system such as QuickBooks in place, you can compare results from one year to the next, from one month to the next, or even from one day to the next. You can also do the following:

- Spot trends by comparing performance over time.
- See areas of strength and weakness by identifying the costs of producing different types of income.
- Budget your income and expenses so that you are sure to have enough money to meet your bills when they are due.
- Plan for the future by forecasting anticipated income and expenses based on past performance.
- Report on your performance to lenders and tax authorities.

What Is an Account?

An account is a descriptive title for financial information. On a financial statement that lists all the types of earnings and expenses for a company, or a statement that lists the types of items a company owns and the amounts it owes to others, each individual category is known as an account.

Accounts simplify the way financial information is organized to make the information easy to understand. For example, if you tell your banker that your company earned $100,000 last year and spent $75,000, that probably wouldn't be enough to satisfy his curiosity regarding your ability to pay back a loan.

By separating your financial transactions into accounts, you can provide a more detailed picture of where the company got its money, how the money was spent, what possessions the company has (such as vehicles or office equipment), and what it owes to lenders. Accounts provide the pieces that fit together to make a financial representation of the whole company.

Types of Accounts

Five main types of accounts are used, and all your company's financial activity will fit into these five types. Within each type you can get creative, using descriptions that fit the kinds of financial transactions in which your company engages.

The five types of accounts are

- **Assets**—Your company's possessions are assets. QuickBooks breaks this down into the following categories: Bank (your company bank accounts), Accounts Receivable (amounts due from others), Other Current Asset (assets that will be replaced or used up within one year), Fixed Asset (furniture, buildings, and other fixtures), and Other Asset (assets that don't fall into the preceding categories).
- **Liabilities**—Your company's debts are liabilities. QuickBooks breaks this down into the following categories: Accounts Payable (amounts your company owes to others), Credit Card (balance due on your company charge card), Other Current Liability (debts that will be liquidated within one year), and Long Term Liability (debts that will still be owed after one year).
- **Equity**—The difference between your company's assets and liabilities equals your company's equity.
- **Income**—Your company's earnings are its income. QuickBooks breaks this down into the categories of Income and Other Income. Other Income is income that is not necessarily related to the main reason your business exists (such as interest income).
- **Expenses**—The costs involved in earning income are your company's expenses. QuickBooks breaks this down into the following categories: Cost of Goods Sold (costs of producing your company's inventory), Expense (all other business expenses), and Other Expense (expenses not necessarily related to the main reason your business exists).

Debits and Credits

The concept of debits and credits has confused many beginning accounting students, but it is simple. Applying a strict accounting definition, *debit* means "left" and *credit* means "right."

Traditionally, accounts are viewed like the letter T, with the account name across the top of the T and changes to the account falling on the sides of the T—debits on the left and credits on the right. A *dr* (abbreviation for debit) and *cr* (credit) are placed at the top of the T.

Depending on the type of account it is, amounts on the left either increase or decrease the balance in the account, and amounts on the right do the opposite. For Asset and Expense accounts, an amount on the left side increases, and an amount on the right side decreases. For Liability, Equity, and Income accounts, the opposite is true.

→ For more information about the way accountants look at accounts, see "Debits, Credits, and Double-Entry Accounting," **p. 79**.

In Figure 7.1, the sales account has seen increases of $9,500 and a decrease of $600, for a credit balance of $8,900. Because credits increase an income account, income is increasing.

Figure 7.1
The way accountants see things: Debits on the left, credits on the right. It's the same for every type of account.

```
          Sales Revenue
        dr    |    cr
       600    |   3000
              |   4000
              |   2500
```

ASSETS AND WHY YOU CARE ABOUT THEM

An *asset* is something that belongs to your company, and is part of what gives your company value. Following are examples of assets that your company might own:

- Cash in the bank, petty cash, cash in the cash register, or cash in the safe
- Investments in stocks, bonds, and mutual funds
- Inventory that is ready to sell, inventory that is in the process of being manufactured, and pieces and parts that will eventually become inventory
- Accounts receivable, which are amounts owed to you by your customers
- Prepaid purchases or goods and services
- Amounts on deposit with suppliers
- Furniture, equipment, vehicles, building and building improvements, and land and land improvements
- Loans that your company made to employees or shareholders

Assets get used in the production of your company's income. Sometimes they are used and replenished quickly; for example, you use the cash that is in your bank to pay the expenses of your company, and you replenish the cash each time you sell a product or service. Your inventory (if your company has inventory) turns over quickly as well—you sell products, and purchase or make new products to take their places.

Other assets are used up at a more leisurely pace—office furniture wears out over time, computer equipment becomes obsolete (all right, I admit that doesn't seem to happen at a leisurely pace), and buildings are outgrown or need remodeling.

Over time, your accounting records will show the pace at which assets turn over and need to be replaced, and from this information you can plan for future cash outlays. You can study the impact that time has on your assets and make decisions about how to slow down or speed up the pace at which you use assets.

→ For more information about using QuickBooks to forecast future performance of your company, see p. 471.

YOUR COMPANY'S LIABILITIES

Liabilities are what you owe. When judging the viability of a company, people look the liabilities, and how well the company is able to meet those obligations. Following are examples of liabilities:

- Payables owed to your suppliers, vendors, utility companies, or subcontractors
- Payroll owed to your employees
- Taxes owed to federal, state, and local governments, including income taxes, payroll taxes, and sales taxes
- Retirement contributions owed to your company retirement program
- Amounts your company has received as advance payments, retainers, or deposits from your customers and clients
- Loans owed to banks and other lenders
- Service and product warranties that you have issued to your customers

Just as with assets, some liabilities get turned over quickly—bills get paid and new bills take their places, paychecks get issued regularly, and advances your company has received from customers turn into income as you fulfill your obligations.

Other liabilities stay around for a long time, such as mortgage loans on buildings and lifetime warranties.

By using QuickBooks to keep track of what your company owes and to whom, you can monitor how long it takes your company to meet its obligations and make decisions about what obligations you might be capable of taking on in the future.

EQUITY: WHAT YOUR COMPANY IS WORTH

When describing different types of accounts, the term net worth is often applied to the sum of a company's *equity* accounts. If you add up all the value of the company's assets (items that the company owns), and then subtract the company's liabilities (amounts owed to others), what you are left with is the *net worth* of the company, or its *equity*.

> **Note:** Another common phrase for net worth is Book Value.

Adding assets and subtracting liabilities is the back way into calculating equity. Equity itself is made up of the following types of amounts:

- Amounts contributed to the business by owners and shareholders, including the value of stock issued by the company
- Amounts earned by the company (the amount of income left after the expenses are paid each year) and not distributed to owners

Adding up the preceding amounts gives you the same result as subtracting liabilities from assets.

Understanding Equity Accounts

Following are some special account names that are given to equity accounts (including one account name that is unique to QuickBooks):

- **Capital Stock**—An account that appears only in corporations. It is the name given to the par value of shares of stock issued by the company. *Par value* is the stated value of a share of stock, a value that is determined by the officers of a corporation and printed on the stock certificates. For example, if a company sells 1,000 shares of stock with a par value of $1 per share, the capital stock account shows a balance of $1,000. The amount in this account does not change as the market value of the stock fluctuates.
- **Paid-in Capital**—An account that appears only in corporations. Paid-in capital describes additional amounts contributed to the company that exceed the cost of the stock. For example, the preceding stock, which has a par value of $1 per share, might actually have been sold at $10 per share. In this case, the paid-in capital account reflects the difference between the amount paid for the stock ($10,000) and the par value of the stock ($1,000), or $9,000.
- **Retained Earnings**—Also a corporation account, retained earnings is the name given to the account that represents the net earnings of the company, or the total income minus the total expenses of the company. The amount in this account changes at the end of each year when a company determines its total income and expenses for the year. The difference between total income and total expenses for the year flows into this account and the income and expense accounts start over again with zero balances.
- **Owners' Capital Account**—Also referred to as a Capital Account or a similarly named account, it is the name given to the equity account in a business that is not a corporation.
- **Opening Balance Equity**—An account name that QuickBooks assigns to every type of business organization (see "Understanding the Type of Business" in this chapter). This is an account that is unique to QuickBooks and represents the value of opening balances that are given to accounts during the interview setup process. For example, if you

indicate in your setup that your company has a starting balance of $3,500 cash in the bank, QuickBooks assigns an opening balance of $3,500 to your cash account. An offset to this amount must exist (see "Debits and Credits" earlier in this chapter), and QuickBooks puts the offsetting $3,500 in this Opening Balance Equity account. After your entire setup is complete, a journal entry must be made to clear the opening balance equity account and transfer its balance to the retained earnings account.

→ For more information about making journal entries, **see p. 253**.

Understanding the Type of Business

Your business falls into one of the following types:

- **Corporation**—A form of business entity that is separate and apart from its owners, the business has its own legal existence, files its own tax returns, and can acquire debt in its own name. Owners of a corporation are called shareholders.

- **Personal Service Corporation (PSC)**—A special type of corporation that performs personal services specifically in the areas of medicine, law, accounting, engineering, architecture, actuarial science, performing arts, or consulting. PSCs are subject to special tax rates and can use a cash method of accounting wherein they do not account for accounts receivable or accounts payable. PSCs report income only when it is received and expenses when they are paid, that is to say on a cash basis.

→ For more information on cash basis and accrual basis, **see p. 471**.

- **S Corporation**—Another special type of corporation that, for the most part, pays no income taxes. (However, state laws vary with regard to the tax treatment of S corporations.) An S corporation passes its earnings on to its owners, who report the earnings of the corporation on their personal tax returns. Special limitations exist for S corporations, such as the limitation of no more than 75 shareholders.

- **Sole Proprietorship**—An unincorporated business in which there is only one owner (the *proprietor*). No legal forms are required to establish a proprietorship—you simply begin doing business. Taxable income or loss of the business is reported on Schedule C of the owner's personal tax return, and the assets of the business are not protected if the owner defaults in some other, personal, area of his financial life.

- **Partnership**—A form of business in which a group of people (two or more) decide to form a business organization together. Partners (owners) of the business are personally responsible for the debts of the business (unless the partnership agreement that they all sign assigns a limited partnership role to certain owners, which protects them if the partnership defaults on its liabilities). The partnership files its own tax return but pays no taxes—the income (or loss) of the business is passed through to the partners and is reported on their personal income tax returns.

- **Limited Liability Company**—A relatively new form of business entity in which all owners, called *members*, are protected from creditors of the business. The business operates much like a partnership in that it pays no income taxes but passes income and losses on to its members, who report the activity of the business on their personal tax returns.

Income: Your Company's Bread and Butter

Have you ever filed an income tax return? I know you have, so this is a safe question. Think back to one of your personal tax returns. On the front page of the return you list different types of income, such as wages from your job, interest income, prize winnings, and so on.

If accounts are being discussed, each one of these types of income might be considered an *income account*—just a separate description for the different kinds of income you list on your tax return.

Rather than adding up all your income from all sources and placing one number on your tax return, you use separate lines and descriptions for different types of income, making it easy to see where all your income is derived from.

A business separates its income into accounts as well and uses those accounts as separate descriptions on the business financial statements, tax returns, and other reports that show the financial progress of the business.

The names given to business income accounts vary greatly, based on the type of business. A restaurant and catering business might have income accounts with names relating to catering services and food sales, whereas a manufacturing business might have income accounts with names relating to construction labor and materials.

Expenses Reduce Business Income

On your personal tax return, if you itemize your deductions on Schedule A, you have many types of expenses such as real estate taxes, mortgage interest, and charitable contributions. Each of these can be considered an *expense account*, or a separate description for the different ways that you spend your money.

Businesses have expense accounts too. Expense accounts reflect the costs of generating income and are shown on financial statements as reductions to income. On a business income tax form, for example, income appears first, reduced by business expenses, and the difference, called *net income*, is the amount on which income tax is paid.

Expense accounts, like income accounts, have names that vary depending on the type of business. A restaurant might have expense accounts for the cost of food, laundry (for its linens), printing (for menus), music, and entertainment, whereas a construction company might have expense accounts for subcontractor fees, building permits, and tools.

QuickBooks Gives You a Standard List of Accounts

One of the biggest advantages to using the EasyStep Interview rather than trying to set up your company from the ground up is that QuickBooks assigns a standard list of accounts to your company, based on the company description that you provide.

This standard list of accounts includes accounts of all previously mentioned kinds (asset, liability, equity, income, and expense), geared to your type of company.

You have the option in the interview to not accept this list of accounts and to create your own accounts instead after the interview has finished. I recommend accepting the standard list and then deleting the accounts you don't need and adding new accounts (the process for deleting and adding accounts is explained in the next sections). You save a lot of time by using the standard account list as a starting point.

Adding Accounts

Whether you choose the standard list of accounts for your company or decide to start from scratch, you no doubt have to add some accounts so that all your company's financial transactions can be properly classified. Use the following steps:

> **Note**
> You can add accounts all at once, or add them one at a time at a later date, as your business changes.

1. Choose Lists, Chart of Accounts (or you can press Ctrl+A). The Chart of Accounts window appears, listing all account names currently available to your business.
2. Click the Account button at the bottom of the window, and a drop-down menu appears.

> **Note**
> When viewing the Chart of Accounts List, press Ctrl+N to open the New Account window.

3. Choose New. The New Account window appears (see Figure 7.2).

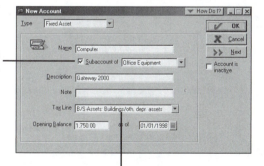

Click here if this is a subaccount.

Choose a tax line (optional) by looking at a tax return for your type of company and determining on which line this account might appear.

Figure 7.2
Enter all the information about your new account here.

4. In the Type field, select the type of account.
5. Enter the name you want to use for this account. This is the name that appears on your company financial statements and other reports.
6. If this account is to appear as a subaccount of another—for example, Room Additions might be a subaccount of New Construction—check the check box and fill in the account of which this is a subaccount (the total of all subaccounts adds up to the total of the main account).
7. Enter an optional description of the account in the designated field. You might also see a field for a note about the account, or a bank number. These fields might or might not appear, depending on the type of account you select.
8. In the Tax Line field, choose the line of your tax return on which this account will be entered, if you plan to use QuickBooks to help you organize your tax information.
9. In the Opening Balance field, enter the balance (if any) in this account as of your start date. (The opening balance and start date fields only appear if the account is an asset, liability, or equity account.)
10. Verify that the start date in the date field is correct.
11. Click Next to add another account, or OK to close the New Account window.

Deleting Accounts

You might find that the standard list of accounts provided by QuickBooks includes some account names that you don't want to use. If you have used an account—entered some transactions into the account—deleting the account is more difficult than it is when the account has never been used.

1. Choose Lists, Chart of Accounts. The Chart of Accounts window appears.
2. Click the name of an account that you are certain you no longer need.
3. Click the Account button at the bottom of the window. A drop-down list appears.
4. Choose Delete. A dialog box appears asking if you are sure you want to delete this account. Click OK, and the account is removed from your Chart of Accounts.

Figure 7.3

> **Note**
> When viewing the Chart of Accounts List, click the name of the account that you want to delete (or scroll down to it), and then press Ctrl+D to delete the account.

Deactivating an Account that Has Seen Some Action

An account that has a balance in it (notice the balances across from the account names in Figure 7.4) cannot be deleted. You can't remove accounts that have balances associated with them—that throws off the total company balances on your financial statements.

This sign means an account is inactive.

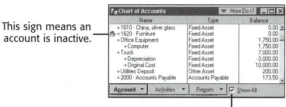

Figure 7.4
Accounts with balances cannot be deleted.

Check this box to display inactive accounts. (This check box might be dim, if no inactive accounts are present.)

If the balance is zero, it seems like you ought to be able to remove the account from your records. Not so. As long as there has been activity in the account, QuickBooks insists that the account stay on your Chart of Accounts list, even if you don't expect to use the account again.

For example, I charged my Rubbish Removal expense account with a $20 purchase of office supplies, and then realized my mistake and reclassified the $20 to the correct account. My rubbish removal account now has a zero balance. I realize I'm not going to need that Rubbish Removal account after all because the property taxes my company pays cover the cost of rubbish removal. It seems I ought to be able to delete the Rubbish Removal account.

But, because there has been some activity in the account, when I try to delete the account I get the message you see in Figure 7.5.

Figure 7.5
Warning from QuickBooks: You can't delete an account that has had transactions in it.

If I really want to get rid of that account, I have two choices. The first choice is to make the account inactive. Making the account inactive doesn't remove it from my Chart of Accounts list. Inactive status does, however, hide the account so that the account no longer appears on my list.

Note
Inactive status applies only to the way accounts are listed in the Chart of Accounts window; inactive accounts can still be used.

1. With the Chart of Accounts window in view, click the name of the account that you want to make inactive.
2. Click the A‍ccount button.
3. From the resulting drop-down list, choose Make Inactive. The unwanted account disappears from the Chart of Accounts list.

You can view inactive accounts on the Chart of Accounts list by checking the S‍how All box at the bottom of the Chart of Accounts window. Inactive accounts appear with a little gray hand to the left of the account name.

To make an inactive account active again, click the account name, click the A‍ccount button in the Chart of Accounts window, and then choose Make Ac‍tive.

DELETING (MERGING) AN ACCOUNT THAT HAS SEEN SOME ACTION

Earlier in this chapter I indicated that QuickBooks doesn't want you to delete any accounts in which there has been activity, even if the balance in the account is zero. Although this is a true statement, you can get around this dilemma if you are bound and determined to delete an account.

The way to delete an account that has had transactions in the past is to *merge* the account into another account. By merging an account into another account, you transfer all the transactions from the original account into the new account. During the merge process, QuickBooks automatically deletes the old account.

Before you begin merging an account, have in mind the exact names of the two accounts you use in this operation: the account you want to remove from the list and the account which will absorb the transactions in the deleted account.

Accounts that are being merged must be at the same level in the Chart of Accounts and must be the same type of account. If one of the accounts being merged is an Other Current Asset, the other account must also be an Other Current Asset. If one account is a subaccount, the other account must be a subaccount too. The two accounts, however, do not need to be subaccounts of the same major account. Use the following steps to merge accounts:

Tip #18 from
Gail Perry

You can easily move the level of an account from subaccount up to major account, from major account to subaccount, from subaccount to sub-subaccount, and so on. With the Chart of Accounts List window onscreen, drag the little diamond that appears to the left of the account name. If you drag to the right or left, the hierarchical level of the account changes accordingly. If you drag up or down, you can move the account to a new location (such as under a different major account) in the list.

1. From the Lists menu, choose Chart of Accounts. The Chart of Accounts list window appears.
2. Click the account that you want to delete.
3. Click the Account button, and then choose Edit (or press Ctrl+E). The Edit Account window appears (see Figure 7.6).

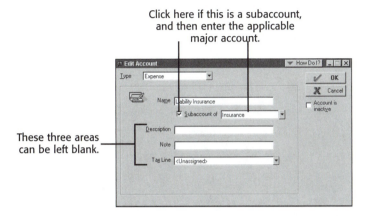

Figure 7.6
The name of the old account appears in the Name section. Replace this with the name of the account into which you want to merge the transactions of the old account.

4. Change the name of the account that you no longer want to the exact name of the account into which its transactions are to be merged. Make sure that you spell the name of the new account correctly, and make sure that you indicate the same subaccount level as that of the new account.
5. Click OK. You see a message that reads, "This name is already being used. Would you like to merge them?" Answer Yes.

All transactions of the original account are now a part of the account into which you merged. The original account has been deleted.

NUMBERING YOUR CHART OF ACCOUNTS

QuickBooks doesn't assign numbers to your accounts when you set them up through the EasyStep Interview. You can assign account numbers yourself in one of two ways:

- Let QuickBooks assign a numbering system for you.
- Choose your own numbering/lettering system.

ASSIGNING ACCOUNT NUMBERS WITH QUICKBOOKS

The easiest way to assign numbers to your Chart of Accounts is to allow QuickBooks to do the work for you. QuickBooks assigns account numbers using the following numbering scheme, and you are welcome to accept these numbers. If you want to change the account numbers to your own numbering scheme, see the following section, "Assigning Account Numbers Yourself."

1. Create all the accounts you think you might want to use.
2. Choose File, Preferences.
3. Click the Accounting icon at the left side of the Preferences window.
4. Click the Company Preferences tab at the top of the window, and then click Use Account Numbers. QuickBooks assigns numbers to each existing account, based on a standard system of numbering as follows:

   1000s: Numbers in the 1000s are assets

   2000s: Liabilities

   3000s: Equity

   4000s: Income

   5000s: Cost of Sales

   6000s: All other expenses

Assigning Account Numbers Yourself

It's harder, but perhaps ultimately more useful to your business, to choose your own numbering/lettering system for account numbers rather than letting QuickBooks choose account numbers for you. In both cases (easy way and hard way), you perform the preceding steps (go to the Preferences window and turn on account numbering). In addition to numbering all your existing accounts automatically, QuickBooks places a new field in your New Account window: the Account Number field. Use the following steps to number your accounts:

1. For all new accounts, enter your own account number in the Number field when setting up the account.
2. For existing accounts, go to the Edit Account window and change the assigned account number to the one that you prefer.

When choosing account numbers, keep in mind that any financial statements or reports that you want organized by account name are now going to be organized by account number. This is because QuickBooks makes your account number part of the account name (almost like the first word in the name). If you want to have your accounts appear alphabetically on your financial statements, assign account numbers to the accounts in alphabetical order.

No provision exists for assigning account numbers during the EasyStep Interview. This is something you must do after the interview has been completed.

Printing a Chart of Accounts List

It is helpful to have a copy of your chart of accounts handy so that you can refer to the chart when assigning accounts to business transactions. Use these steps to print a copy:

> **Tip #19 from Gail Perry**
>
> Do you want to exclude accounts with zero balances on your account list? See the "Troubleshooting" section at the end of this chapter.

1. Open the Chart of Accounts List window by choosing Lists, Chart of Accounts (or by pressing Ctrl+A), and then click the Reports button at the bottom of the Chart of Accounts window.
2. Choose Account Listing from the resulting drop-down menu. A report of your entire list of accounts appears onscreen.
3. Print the report by clicking the Print button that appears at the top-right side of the report (or press Ctrl+P).

Troubleshooting

Printing

I want to print a Chart of Accounts list that only includes accounts containing balances. The filter options don't seem to enable me to produce this type of report.

Although time-consuming, a no-zero-balance-accounts report can be produced. From the Chart of Accounts List window, click each account containing a zero balance. Choose Account, Make Inactive to change the status of the particular account to inactive. After all zero balance accounts have been made inactive, print your account list. To return the accounts to active status, return to the list window, click each inactive account, and choose Account, Make Active.

CHAPTER 8

SETTING UP SERVICES, CUSTOMERS, AND SUPPLIERS

In this chapter

Understanding Items   122

Locating Information with Lists   127

Working With Lists   130

Quick Access to Editing   132

Making Reports Based on Items   142

Creating Reports from the Item List   142

Customers, Vendor, and Employee Lists   149

Customer, Job, and Vendor Type Lists   154

Terms, Customer Messages, and Payment Method Lists   154

Understanding Items

Items are the backbone of QuickBooks, and all items in QuickBooks are organized in lists. If you've gone through the EasyStep Interview, and have therefore entered customers, employees, products, and vendors into their rosters, you've already worked with lists. You'll be back from time to time when you hire new employees, buy from new vendors, and sell to new customers, but unless situations in your company change drastically, you will not again have the chore of building up your lists from scratch.

In QuickBooks, almost everything is an item. An *item* is a description that appears on your purchase and sales forms. An amount is associated with the item, and QuickBooks uses the amount to perform calculations on your forms. Things you buy and sell are items. Discounts you apply and services you perform are also items, as are long-term loans and cash deposits that you make to cover shortages. You'll find all the items listed in the QuickBooks Lists menu.

Customers, vendors, invoices, purchase orders, and accounts are not items. Items are services or products that you sell or buy and the charges related to them.

> **Note** The examples used in this chapter are from the QuickBooks Pro sample company, "Rock Castle Construction." Your company data will appear differently.

Working with Items

Use preparing an invoice as an example of how to work with items. For example, if you finish a job with three components, such as Photography, Layout, and Publishing, enter each of these tasks as items into QuickBooks (using Lists, Items). These are *service items*. Each item represents a type of service that you provide and sell to customers.

In creating your invoice to charge for these services (go to Activities, Create Invoices, or press Ctrl+I), click the area of the invoice below and to the right of the word Item (see Figure 8.1), and then select Photography from the list. Because you've entered Photography as an item, the item is available to you here in the invoice you are creating.

Next, click the line right under Photography and a drop-down menu appears where you clicked. Choose Layout. To add the final task for this job, click the line below Layout and choose Publishing.

As soon as you create an item, that item becomes available for use in all the forms you have yet to create, such as sales receipts, checks, and invoices, as shown here. Each item can be associated with a charge, such as $30 per hour or $500 per job. Figure 8.2 shows a sales receipt generated from the same set of services.

Understanding Items | 123

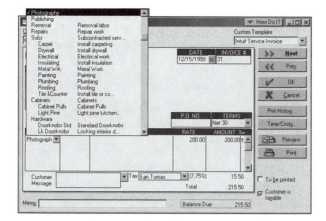

Figure 8.1
Charge for your services by adding an item to an invoice.

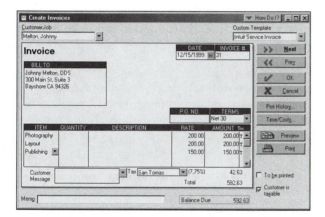

Figure 8.2
A sales receipt created for services provided to a customer.

Other items can be applied to a job that you perform for a client or customer. In these examples, terms of payment and sales tax have been set up as items.

QuickBooks enables you to instantly choose from other items you've created and apply them to various customers and jobs as needed. Perhaps you've established terms of payment with a particular customer, offering them 30 days to pay you in full, with a 2 percent discount applied for early payment. In QuickBooks, you display these terms on an invoice by clicking the drop-down menu near the word Terms, as shown in Figure 8.3, and choosing the applicable item. Click Add New at the top of the terms list to add a new item. Adding terms to an invoice causes QuickBooks to update the customer's information and keep track of how much money is owed to you, by whom, and by what date.

> **Note**
> You might not have to make any changes to the Terms item provided by QuickBooks—the standard terms that come with QuickBooks might be sufficient for your business.

Figure 8.3
Displaying Terms that can be applied to an invoice.

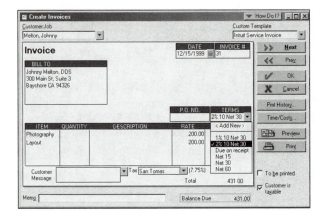

The Tax field at the bottom of the invoice also shows a drop-down arrow, which enables you to choose the sales tax that is applicable to this customer's invoice. In creating a Sales Tax item, you enter the percentages that are applicable to your city and state, and that tax item becomes available to all your sales.

All the items discussed here—job components such as Photography and Layout, and special calculations such as Terms and Taxes—can be applied to any invoice, purchase order, credit slip, and so on, as needed.

Types of Items

There are ten different types of QuickBooks items, and any items you create must fit into one of these ten categories:

- **Service**—Labor charges and professional fees.
- **Payment**—Money received that reduces the amount owed on an invoice.
- **Inventory Part**—Merchandise your company purchases, keeps in stock, and resells.
- **Noninventory Part**—Products you sell but do not normally keep in stock or products you do not purchase (such as livestock that you raised). Following are some examples of special noninventory parts:
  - Livestock that you raise and ultimately sell. You didn't purchase the animals, so there was no inventory purchase cost, but the animals belong to you nonetheless and need to be classified as noninventory parts.
  - A mechanic who occasionally applies custom rims to a car upon request might consider the rims he purchases specifically for a customer to be noninventory parts.
  - Noninventory items also might include prepared food such as fresh-tossed salads (the lettuce might be considered an inventory item, but not the salad).
- **Group**—A group of items can be saved all together as an item. This is helpful if you sell expensive china sets, for example. Most often, you sell the entire set of tableware,

but occasionally, you do sell individual china pieces. Therefore, your regular product set is a group, and occasionally you break this group down into individual pieces. In QuickBooks, both the entire china set and the individual cups and bowls are called items.

- **Discount**—An amount of money subtracted from a total or subtotal cost of an item. Beyond the obvious 10 percent markdowns and such, discounts have multiple uses. Following are two examples:
  - *Tracking a Commission*—If you are paid a commission for each sale of a product, create a discount item for the same percentage as your commission. QuickBooks tracks the discount for all your sales and keeps records of your total commission income.
  - *Forgiving a Charge*—If you provide a service for a client and work 20 billable hours but decide as a courtesy to only charge for 15, you can create a discount item, deducting 5 hours from the final invoice. This way, you can keep track of both the hours that you really did work and the deduction.
- **Sales Tax**—When applicable, you can add a sales tax item to an invoice. QuickBooks automatically calculates the correct amount based on the percentage you set.
- **Sales Tax Group**—Often, the total sales tax you pay is actually a combination of state, county, and city tax. Customers are not accustomed to seeing three tax rates applied to their invoices (for example, 5 percent state tax, 1 percent county, and .6 percent city tax). Therefore, QuickBooks gives you the option to enter a sales tax group as an item.
- **Subtotal**—A subtotal item is important. If you apply shipping charges, discounts, credits, or tax, these items need to be applied after the goods or services themselves are totaled. The total charge before these "extras" are applied is called a subtotal.
- **Other Charges**—Freight, finance charges, late fees, special handling charges, and rush charges can all be applied using an Other Charges item. Other Charge items can also be created to track unusual occurrences. Following are two examples:
  - In the restaurant business, cash drawers often show overages or shortages at the end of the day. Use an Other Charge item to track these discrepancies. This enables you to create reports showing over/short trends in your business.
  - If you are put on retainer, for example if you are a musician who is prepaid to be available to record at a certain time of year, or as a scriptwriter who is prepaid to turn in sitcom episodes before a particular date, the money you are paid is not really income. This money is actually a liability because you owe the related service to the customer. You can create an Other Charge item to keep track of this special sort of situation.

continued

Creating Items to Track Profits

To keep close track of where and how money is being made in your company, you might want to create several accounts that reflect income sources and apply appropriate items to each account. For example, if you have one main office and smaller branches, you might expect supply usage and expenditures to be higher at the main office, but with good tracking, you can still know how profitable each office is without being confused by the differences in expenditures. You can guarantee this by creating unique inventory account items for both the home and satellite office. That way each office can show its own scale of profitability.

Tip #20 from

Gail Perry

As an alternative to tracking different types of profits with items, consider dividing parts of your business into *classes* (*page xx 160*).

CREATING SUBITEMS

Subitems are created as easily as items themselves. You simply create an item, and then check the Subitem of check box, as shown in Figure 8.4. A drop-down menu appears, showing all QuickBooks items. Use this menu to select under which item this subitem is to appear.

Figure 8.4
Creating a subitem.

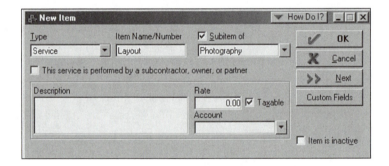

On your QuickBooks Items list, subitems appear indented under the parent item.

Why might you create a hierarchy of items and subitems? Following are two examples:

- Most independent computer stores sell systems cobbled together from individual components, keeping an eye on the falling and rising prices of RAM, hard drives, monitors, and so on. The profitability of the entire system sale is greatly dependent on the total cost of these components. To set a good price on a whole computer, you need accurate and up-to-date tracking of how you are being charged for each component. Use subitems to manage your inventory of parts and pieces; the entire computer package can be presented as an item. Also, tracking RAM and hard drives as subitems enables you to sell these pieces individually and still keep an eye on how many entire computer systems (items) you can package and sell.

- As a service provider, subitems enable you to charge varying rates for different types of work you perform for a client. For example, a lawyer might charge one rate for her own time, and a lower rate for research conducted by a paralegal. Or a medical office might charge one rate for a doctor visit, and another for a follow-up visit by a nurse practitioner.

You can do this in one of two ways: The two rates can be a subitem of the entire charge, as shown in Figure 8.5, or the secondary, lower rate can be a subitem of the primary, higher-paid professional.

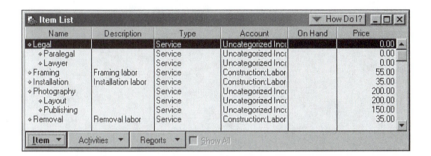

Figure 8.5
An item called Legal shows two subitems beneath it. Each subitem can be charged at a different rate.

LOCATING INFORMATION WITH LISTS

QuickBooks uses lists to organize all the information you use in your company. The items described in the last section are included on one list. Your vendors are on another list, the chart of accounts is a list, and so on. You can add to lists or change entries on lists by opening the list from the Lists menu and working with the entries there. Also, you can add to lists as you use the various QuickBooks forms. These methods are described in this and the following sections.

> **Note**
> In QuickBooks, you seldom need to access a list by clicking a menu at the top of the screen. Instead, use the Navigator to conduct your day-to-day business with QuickBooks. Furthermore, you can open and edit lists from your actual forms.

Figure 8.6 shows the menu options for the lists that are described in detail in this chapter, although the contents of the Other submenu category might not appear this way on your screen. Some lists might be missing, and others might be added or in a different order, depending on the choices you made in the EasyStep Interview.

To add, remove, or move lists as they appear in this Other submenu, select File, Preferences, Menus, and place a check by the items that you want to appear in the Other submenu, rather than in their own respective Lists or Activities menu (see Figure 8.7).

Before looking at specific features of lists, here's a look at how to update lists as you work, merge lists, and view an entire list entry rather than just a name.

Figure 8.6
A look at the lists in QuickBooks.

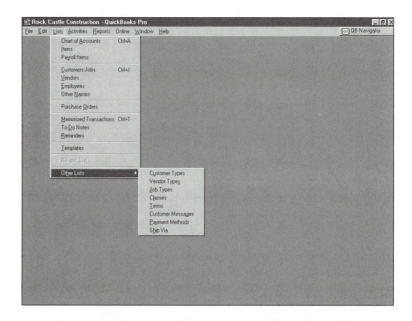

Figure 8.7
Use the Preferences menu option to change list items that appear in the Other submenu.

UPDATING LISTS

While working with any form, if you enter a new entry in an appropriate field, QuickBooks checks to see if your entry is already part of a list. If not, you are prompted to add the entry using one of two methods (see Figure 8.8):

- **Quick Add**—This adds only that particular entry, exactly as you enter it, to the list. For example, if you enter the name of a new customer on an invoice form and choose QuickAdd from the box that appears, only the customer's name is added to the customer list—not the address, phone number, and so on. Later, you can add more supportive detail.

- **Set Up**—QuickBooks opens a window for recording an entire list entry with all the information that is pertinent to the entry.

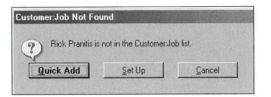

Figure 8.8
In any form, enter an item with which QuickBooks is not familiar, and you see this prompt.

Merging Two List Entries

Merging two list entries can be helpful if, for example, you've been working with a customer at two locations and then find that she's consolidated her business into one location. Merging list entries can also be helpful if you've entered a client into your database twice, using slightly different spellings; merging the two entries keeps pertinent information you might have recorded in both.

Use the following steps to merge list entries:

1. Locate the name that you don't want to use. Do this by selecting the Lists menu, and then choosing the submenu that contains that name.
2. Click once on the name in the list to select it (alternatively, you can double-click the name or press Ctrl+E to edit the name).
3. Select the drop-down menu at the bottom left, and choose Edit.
4. Your goal is to change the name of this entry to match the name that you do want to use. Change the name you don't want by typing the name you do want in its place.
5. Click OK, and then click Yes, indicating that you do indeed want to merge the list entries.

Viewing an Entire List Entry

If you are entering the name of a customer onto a form, for example, and you want to know whether the customer has any amounts due or jobs in progress, click the field on the form in which you enter the customer's name. Press Ctrl+L, and the entire customer list appears in its own window. Locate the customer's name on the list. QuickBooks displays information about that customer, including balances due, notes, status of jobs, and outstanding estimates.

Right-click on the customer name and choose Quick Report for the details of transactions relating to this customer, or choose View Estimate to see the actual estimate for a particular job.

This technique works with any form (Estimates, Invoices, Cash Sales receipts, and so on). Use this method to view whole lists in almost any field of the form, such as Tax, Item, Terms, Customer Message, Payment Method, and Customer.

Working With Lists

In this section, you'll explore different types of items and lists and focus on various ways you can put them to work for you. The QuickBooks manual does a wonderful job of touring each and every field and menu. You'll review some of the less obvious features, and emphasize those that bring you multilevel power for creating reports and getting information that you want quickly. You'll see that you can tailor list items to very specific needs for your business.

Rather than start at the top of the Lists menu, you'll begin with lists that you are more likely to use regularly. First, you'll examine features common to all lists, using the Items list as your example.

Features Common to All Lists

Like the other lists, the Item list (Choose Lists, and then Item) shows a scrollable list of entries with three drop-down menus (Item, Activities, and Reports) at the bottom left (see Figure 8.9).

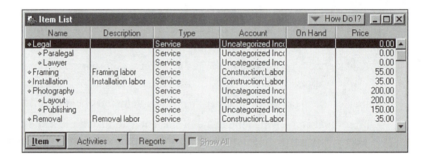

Figure 8.9
The Item list looks similar to other lists.

The items you see here are those you created when you answered questions in the EasyStep Interview as well as any others that you've added along the way. Or, if you are using the QuickBooks sample file (Rock Castle Construction, in QuickBooks Pro) to feel your way around the program, you see the items created for that sample company.

Moving an Item in a List

You can move any list item by clicking and dragging with your mouse over the diamond that appears in front of each item name. When hovering over a diamond, your mouse turns to a four-way arrow (see Figure 8.10). Click and drag the item to a new location, up or down the list. If you click and drag an item with subitems, the subitems move as well. To return the list order to its original state, select Resort from the drop-down menu that is accessible from the left-most button on the bottom of any list.

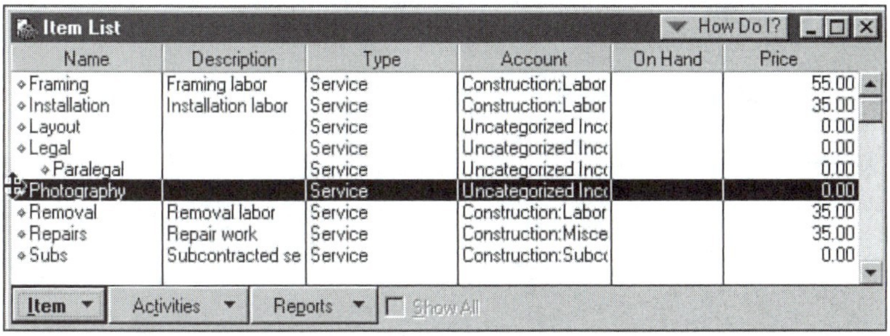

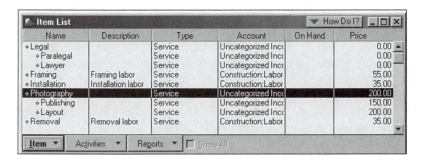

Figure 8.10
When hovering over an entry in a list, the mouse becomes a four-way arrow, enabling you to move the entry to a different location.

Listing Subitems

Subitems are indented, listed under their parent items. As you can tell from the example in Figure 8.11, "Photography" has two subitems beneath it. Under "Photography," you can see the price and availability of two subitems, Publishing and Layout. To the right is the price of each.

Figure 8.11
Subitems listed beneath parent items.

Finding a List Entry

QuickBooks has a powerful Find feature (see Figure 8.12) that enables you to choose Filters to help locate particular transactions, including an individual check, bill, vendor, transaction, memo entry, or even a birthday or email address. Find is always available from the Edit menu (or by pressing Ctrl+F), no matter which window is open.

Use Find by selecting a filter from the Filter list, and then typing text or using the drop-down menu to set criteria for that filter. You'll see your filter choice appear in a list at the upper right of the dialog box, under Current Choices.

After a filter appears there, you can use the Filter menu to choose an additional filter, providing another limit to your search. For example, if you want to find transactions from within a particular range of dates relating to a particular customer, your first filter is the name of the customer, and the second filter is the date range. Your search brings up every document involving that customer that falls within that particular date range.

Figure 8.12
Set up Filters in the Find dialog box to locate transactions that meet particular requirements.

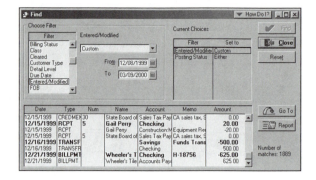

The filters provided by QuickBooks are good at predicting what a businessperson might need to know in a hurry. For example, the filters include Aging, for bills that are fast becoming due; Cleared, for checks that have cleared or not cleared; and Detail Level, which limits the number of duplicate entries you'd have to wade through.

After setting your filters, click Find, and entries that match appear in a list. You can generate a report on that list (click the Report button), or you can double-click any entry to view the original transaction document, such as a check or bill.

Quick Access to Editing

Double-click any item in the list to bring up the Edit Item dialog box. If you ever want to change the rate or price of an item, make the item taxable (or not subject to tax), or specify which account is to receive money when this item is sold, double-click its name in the Item list.

Double-clicking Exterior Door in the Item list, for example, makes the Edit Item dialog box appear, with information about the Exterior Door item. You can see the cost of each door, relative to its price (see Figure 8.13). The cost, as shown in the Cost data field of the Edit Item dialog box, is $105. To the right you can see the sales price of $120.

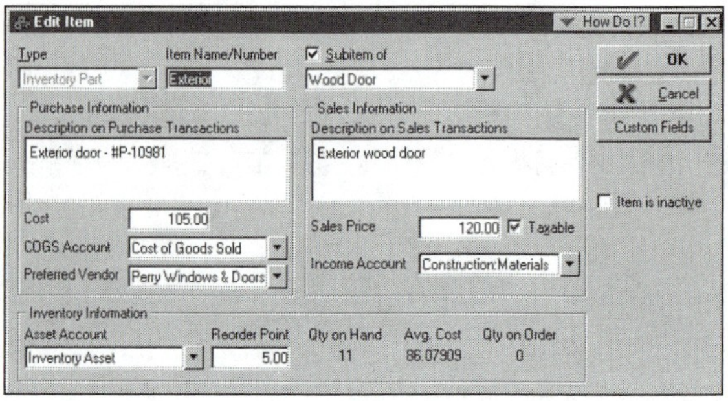

Figure 8.13
Double-click any item in a list to view and edit its settings.

You can execute these steps right from an invoice form on which you are selling the item. Press Ctrl+L from within the Item field of the invoice to bring up the Items list, and then double-click on the item to view its details, and change them if necessary.

CREATING A NEW ITEM

This section continues the use of the Items list as an example, but the procedures explained here apply to all lists. Follow these steps to create a new item:

1. Click the Item button in the Items list window (the left-most button at the bottom of the window), and choose New (or press Ctrl+N). The New Item dialog box appears (see Figure 8.14).

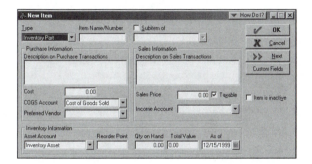

Figure 8.14
The New Item dialog box, shown here with settings for an Inventory Part item.

2. From this dialog box, you can specify item Type, using the drop-down menu, and provide a name and a description.
3. In the Rate field, enter a rate (dollars per hour, for example) or price for this item, and click the Account arrow to pick which account to credit when the item is sold, or when the service is performed.
4. If you click Subitem of, the drop-down list of all the items becomes available. Use this list to select a parent item. Your new subitem appears indented, below the parent item.
5. Click the Taxable option if applicable.

Notice also the Custom fields button, for creating and applying *custom fields* (*page 354*) to forms associated with this item. The custom fields do not appear in the Edit Item dialog box, but are available to forms involving this item.

> **Note**
> The fields available in the New Item dialog box change depending on what type of item you are creating. The options that are available for Inventory Parts, for example, differ from Service Item options.

Using the Items List

After creating an item, the item appears with the others in the items list. The item is now available for use on any form.

> **Note**
> As soon as you open any list from the Lists menu, the QuickBooks Edit menu changes to provide options specific to that list. For example, with the Vendors list open, you can edit or delete a vendor, add a new one, and find a vendor using filters to narrow your search.

Returning again to the Items list (choose Lists, and then Items), notice the Item button (left-most button) at the bottom left, which produces a drop-down menu. Use choices on this menu to print a list, delete an entry, or locate all the transactions in which a particular list entry is found (Find in Transactions). You'll find that every list has a menu offering similar functions, always found at the lower left.

> Pressing the Enter key has the same effect as clicking the OK button—it automatically saves the new item or form you are creating, even if you are not finished making entries. Do not press Enter to move from one field to another; this is done by pressing Tab or clicking in the new field with the mouse. Sometimes, when entering data in a number field, it's tempting to press Enter to see the resulting new calculated value, or to make sure that the decimals line up as expected. New calculations in data fields are adjusted automatically when you move to a new field.

Tip #21 from

> Although the default performance of the Enter key generally closes the current window, you can alter the way in which this key operates so that pressing Enter moves you from one field to the next. Choose File, Preferences, General. On the My Preferences tab, check the Pressing Enter moves between fields box to activate this feature.

Generating Sales, Invoices, and Price Changes

Besides adding and changing entries on a list, there are other activities you can perform from within the List window. Again, the examples here relate to the Items List, but apply to other types of lists as well.

To create a price change, follow these steps:

1. Select any item entry, and click the drop-down Activities menu. Here you can quickly create an invoice for that item, receive items, enter bills, and change prices. Figure 8.15 shows the Change Prices dialog box.

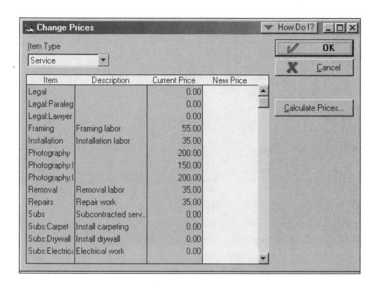

Figure 8.15
To quickly change the price of any type of item, select Change Prices from the Activities menu of the Items list.

2. Select the Item Type that is to be affected by your price change. From the Item Type drop-down menu at the upper left of the screen, choose Inventory, Noninventory, Service Item, or Other Charge. You see a list of all the chargeable items pertaining to the item you clicked.
3. Select an item for a price change, and click across from the item in the New Price column.
4. Change the price of Photography Layout to $170 (see Figure 8.16).

The Activities Menu and Other Lists
All other lists, such as Employees, Customer:Job, and Vendors, have a drop-down Activities menu, similar to the Items list covered here. You'll find that in any list, chores related to paying or receiving money can always be found in the Activities menu. Following are some examples of what you'll find in a list's Activities menu:

Customer:Job list—Create Invoices, Receive Payments, Enter Cash Sales.

Vendors list—Write Checks, Enter Bills, Create Purchase Orders.

Employees list—Pay Employees, Pay Liabilities/Taxes, Process various tax forms.

Chart of Accounts—Write Checks, Make Deposits, Transfer Money.

Figure 8.16
The changed price is displayed in the New Price column.

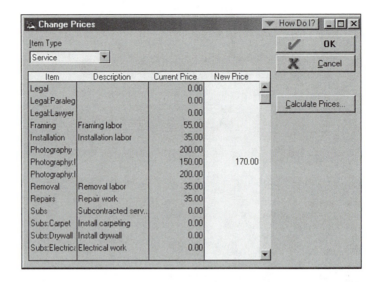

Most often, businesses institute price changes on many items simultaneously. Customers seem to be less taken aback by one blanket price increase, rather than many isolated ones. Also, an "across the board" change makes it easier for you to see the effect of the change on your business. To calculate new prices on a range of items, see the following section.

→ To find more detailed information on using the invoicing feature in QuickBooks, **see p. 183**.

CALCULATING NEW PRICES

If you want to change the price that you charge for an item, follow these steps:

1. With the Items List open onscreen, click the Activities button, and then choose Change Prices. The Change Prices dialog box appears (see Figure 8.17). Choose the Type of item you want to change. You can enter amounts in the column at the right to change prices for individual items.

2. If you want to change prices by a percentage, or change several prices at once by a particular amount, click the Calculate Prices button. On the far left of the dialog box, check the items that are to receive the price change. (The accompanying QCard and instructions seem to indicate that only price increases can be generated here, but that is not the case. You can lower prices as well).

3. In the Mark Up Sales of Checked Items by (amount or %) field, enter a dollar amount or a percentage. The item's price changes by that amount. (For example, enter 10% in the $120 Exterior Door field, and the price rises to $132. Enter -30, and the price falls to $90. Enter -$15, and the door's price is reduced by $15.)

The Price Change window has been discussed as if the changes apply only to prices you charge your customers for the items or services. However, at the bottom of the Change

Prices dialog box shown in Figure 8.17, click Unit Cost to make your changes here apply to what you paid for each item, rather than to the Current Sales Price, which is what your customers pay.

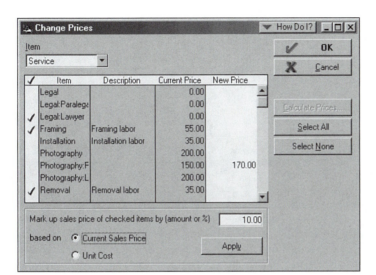

Figure 8.17
In the Change Prices dialog box, check the items that are set to receive price changes.

When you click OK, you are not returned to the Change Prices dialog box. The program assumes that you are finished editing, and you are returned to the List view.

> **Note**
> Notice the Adjust Quantity/Value on Hand menu item in the Activities menu. Here you can view the quantity on hand for each item. After scrolling down the list to see if there are any items you need to reorder soon, you can create a Purchase Order, also found in this same Activities menu.

Receiving Items, Bills, and Credit from a Vendor

In the Activities menu of the Items list, click Receive Items & Enter Bill. Here you can create receipts verifying that merchandise has been received, create a bill for them, and make a record of credit that a vendor has extended to you.

> **Tip #22 from Gail Perry**
> Why create a bill for an item in QuickBooks? After all, hasn't the vendor sent you his own bill? By entering a bill in QuickBooks, you can debit the appropriate accounts for the purchase, generate a check to pay the bill, examine and calculate the terms of payment, and receive a reminder telling you when the bill is due.

The initial screen shows the Enter Bills dialog box (see Figure 8.18), enabling you to select the vendor who has billed you, the terms of the billing cycle, and the dates that the bill was received and due. You can also enter the amount due, reference number, and memo message.

Figure 8.18
The Enter Bills dialog box enables you determine which of your accounts is to shoulder this expense.

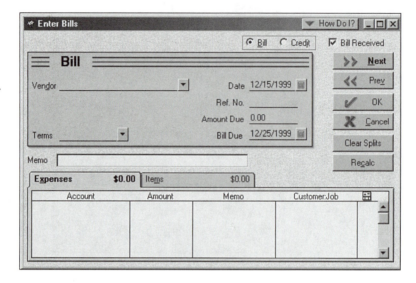

> **Note**
>
> The memo appears in the accounts payable register. This is a good way to write yourself an important note about the item.

In the lower half of the Enter Bills dialog box (QuickBooks calls this the details area), you see two tabs: Items and Expenses. In the Items tab, use the drop-down menu under Items to specify the item for which you are being billed. QuickBooks adjusts the Quantity on Hand to reflect that you've received this merchandise.

Here you can also include other information important for registering bills that have to be paid. Enter the quantity of items you've received. The cost of each item appears in the Cost column, and QuickBooks calculates the total cost of the purchase in the adjacent Amount column. Select a customer with whom to associate this purchase, if applicable.

> **Note**
>
> If you filled out a purchase order for merchandise received, you might not have to enter detailed account crediting and customer information because you probably already did so when you ordered the merchandise.

→ To find more detailed information on receiving, recording, and paying bills, **see p. 239** and **p. 241**.

ACKNOWLEDGING RECEIVED MERCHANDISE

If you received merchandise from a vendor, but no bill, you still need to credit the appropriate accounts and inventory lists with the received merchandise. Use the following steps to do so:

1. From the Lists menu, chose Vendors. The Vendors list appears.
2. Select the Activities drop-down menu, and then Enter Bills, which opens the dialog box shown in Figure 8.19.
3. Remove the check mark next to Bill Received, and the dialog box creates a record of a receipt of items without entering the bill.
4. Specify the vendor, the appropriate date, the items received (you might need to click the Items tab at the bottom of this window), and, if applicable, click the Select PO button (or press Alt+S) to view the purchase order that first generated this transaction.
5. Click Next (or Alt+N) to edit other Bills, or click OK to exit the dialog box.

> **Note**
>
> If a purchase order was created back when this item was ordered, the detail fields of this receipt are automatically filled out from the details of the purchase order. That means you don't have to click the Customer:Jobs list and choose items and accounts manually.
>
> Please note that clicking the Select PO button only applies the data from the appropriate purchase order to this receipt. Clicking this button doesn't bring up the purchase order for you to view it. If you want to view the purchase order, click the Show PO button (see Figure 8.19). This button is not available unless a purchase order was generated at the time of order.

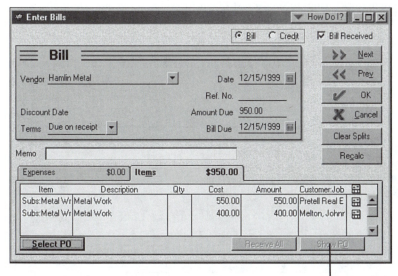

Figure 8.19
The Show PO button is available if there is a PO for you to view.

Show PO button

Changing the Receipt Into a Bill

Later, when the bill arrives, you can change the receipt into a bill using the following steps:

1. Click the Activities menu in the Items list, and choose Enter Bill for Received Items.
2. QuickBooks lists any receipts of unbilled, received merchandise. Click one, and the Enter Bills dialog box appears.
3. Click Bill Received, and the receipt turns into a bill. All the appropriate accounts reflect the fact that money is now due, and you are soon issued a reminder that the bill needs to be paid.

Entering Receipts and Credit from a Vendor

Up until now you've been learning about creating bills from vendors using the Enter Bills dialog box. To enter credits received from a vendor, follow these steps:

1. In the Enter Bills dialog box, check the Credit button, and the title of the form changes to Credit. A Credit Amount line appears.
2. Enter the amount credited to your account by a vendor.

The Checking Credit in the Enter Bills dialog box is for recording amounts that are credited because you returned merchandise to a vendor.

Adjusting Quantity/Value of Inventory on Hand

QuickBooks automatically adjusts your inventory whenever you make a sale or purchase new merchandise. To manually adjust the quantity or value of your inventory, select Adjust Quantity/Value on Hand, at the bottom of the Activities menu of the Items list. This enables you to update information in the Adjust Quantity/Value on Hand dialog box (see Figure 8.20).

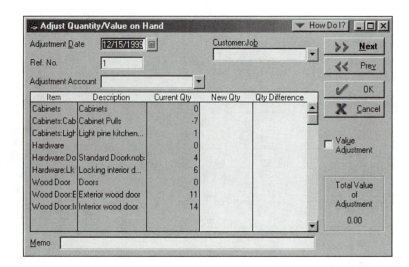

Figure 8.20
To manually adjust your inventory amounts, use the Adjust Quantity/Value on Hand dialog box.

Following are some situations in which you might need to adjust your inventory manually:

- **Theft**—To receive an accurate recount of what was taken
- **Fire or Other Damage**—To accurately report inventory that is still available
- **Counting Discrepancies**—If you recounted and got a total that was different from your records

> **Note**
>
> Because this chapter is discussing lists, it's easy to forget that many QuickBooks features are more easily accessed from the Navigator, including some that are discussed here. For example, to adjust quantity/value on hand, just click the Navigator's Purchases and Vendors Tab. Then click Adjust Qty. on Hand. You find that the Navigator often shortens menu option names, but the features accessed are the same.

Following is a look at other features of the Adjusting Quantity/Value on Hand dialog box.

→ To find more detailed information on counting and valuing your inventory, **see p. 220**.

ADJUSTING NEW QUANTITY

To make an adjustment, locate the item whose numbers you want to change, and enter a new quantity in the New Qty column. The Qty Difference column reflects your change. You can select as many items for adjustment as you like. You can also make an adjustment by typing a number directly in the Qty Difference column. QuickBooks calculates the correct quantity from that figure.

> **Tip #23 from**
>
>
>
> You need to indicate an account for recording the value of changes in inventory. Include this information in the Adjustment Account field. In the example shown in Figure 8.20, an account called "Inventory Loss" was created. Later, you can generate a report that shows inventory losses separately.

ADJUSTING REFERENCE NUMBER

In the Adjust Quantity/Value On Hand dialog box, QuickBooks creates a separate transaction record for each inventory adjustment. By noting the reference number, you can view your adjustments later from this very same Items list, and create reports. Sequential reference numbers are generated automatically. If you want to enter your own, you can do so.

ADJUSTING OTHER IMPORTANT FIELDS

To associate this inventory adjustment with a particular customer's account, click the drop-down arrow in the Customer:Job field. To create a note regarding this adjustment that will appear in a report (explaining its circumstance and purpose), enter text in the Memo field.

Notice that a Total Value of Adjustment panel appears in the lower right of the dialog box, providing a dollar amount based on your inventory changes.

Adjusting Value Rather than Quantity

In the Adjust Quantity/Value on Hand dialog box, you might want to adjust the value of inventory, rather than the quantity on hand (see Figure 8.20). For example, if you sell computer parts, the prices of hard drives and RAM are apt to fluctuate wildly. You might need to periodically adjust the value of your stock on hand, according to the most current prices.

When you click the Value Adjustment check box (on the right side of the Adjust Quantity/Value on Hand dialog box), a New Value column is added. Here you can enter a new dollar value for an item's stock on hand. Please note that you are not changing the value of one item, but rather the entire inventory of that item. This procedure does not alter the number of items on hand, but rather the value of the items in dollars.

> The IRS has specific rules about methods of valuing inventories, and changing the value of your inventory falls under these rules. See the section on "Valuing Your Inventory" in Chapter 14, "Keeping Track of Your Inventory," before you think about making adjustments to any of your inventory accounts.

Making Reports Based on Items

The purpose of items in QuickBooks is not just to make forms more convenient, but to put more meaningful information at your fingertips. QuickBooks enables you to select particular items from lists and generate reports on all (or only) the data you want. *Reports (page 361)* are the key and, as you shall see, are available from a drop-down menu on every list of items.

It's easy to create filters in reports, screening out information that you don't need to see at the moment. After you've created a report, you can memorize the report (retaining the format and scope of the report) even as the data changes over time. Also, you can graph your report. Viewing data pictorially can illuminate seemingly insignificant differences in data.

Even something innocuous such as shipping charges can provide important data in a report. For example, you can learn what percentage of your customers requires out of state shipping, or you can determine if you are getting the best deal from the shipping agency that you are currently using.

Creating Reports from the Item List

In this book, creating reports is thoroughly discussed as each topic arises. For now, this chapter briefly touches on the reports that can be created from lists, and highlights some unique aspects of how each list can create reports that are helpful to your company. You will spend a great deal of time on the Item list reports, using them to create a general picture of what you'll find in other reports.

GENERATING A QUICKREPORT

To generate a QuickReport, follow these steps:

1. Click once on any line in the Items list, and select the drop-down Report menu at the bottom (see Figure 8.21).

2. Click QuickReport. The name QuickReport appears with the name of the item you select, in this case, QuickReport:Drywall.

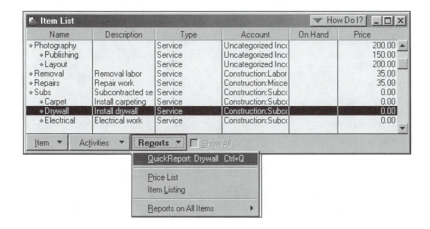

Figure 8.21
Generate a QuickReport on any item you click from the Item List's Reports menu.

QuickBooks creates a report of every activity involving the item you've clicked. Here you see that customers requiring Drywall installation are included on the report (see Figure 8.22). Each line in the report represents a type of document that relates to the item, perhaps an invoice or bill.

> **Note**
> Double-click the magnifying glass on any line to see the document to which the line refers. Click a line that refers to an invoice, and the entire invoice appears. You can then edit the document as you want, although doing so affects other transactions as well. Edits that you make are reflected on the report totals and subtotals, when applicable.

Each line also shows a customer name, the date of the transaction, the amount received, and the quantity that was billed. A transaction number is also included. At the bottom of the report are totals and subtotals of each.

> **Note**
> To change the time scope of the report, click the Dates drop-down menu at the top left corner of the report, or change the From and To indicators at the top of the report to specific dates.

Figure 8.22
Click any line in a QuickReport to view the document to which it refers.

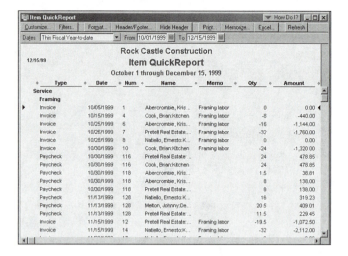

Using Available Item List Reports

From the Reports drop-down menu of the Item list, a number of reports are available. Notice that quite a few reports branch out from the Report on All Items submenu, as shown in Figure 8.23.

Figure 8.23
The Reports on All Items submenu contains submenus to many other reports, which, in turn, contain submenus to additional reports.

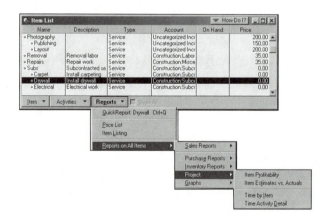

The following is a list of reports that are worth a special glance:

- **Viewing your Inventory Prices**—To create a report that shows how much your inventory items cost (to you and your customers), click Reports on the Item list dialog box, and choose Price List.

- **Viewing Selected Item Details**—To create a report that shows the details that you think are most helpful (use the Customize button to choose fields for viewing), click Reports on the Item list dialog box, and choose Report on all Items. You'll see several cascading submenus. Each submenu reveals a submenu for creating a detailed report or a summarized report.

ITEM SALES REPORTS

From the Item list, Reports menu, there are two types of sales reports available. From the Reports drop-down menu, select Report on All Items, Sales Reports, and choose either By Item Summary or By Item Detail.

- **By Item Summary**—Includes Average Pricing, Gross Profit Margin, and COGS information. Inventory items and complete products that are ready to be sold are summarized together (see Figure 8.24). Click the Collapse button at the top of the report to hide inventory subaccounts. Clicking the Expand button restores subaccounts to the report.

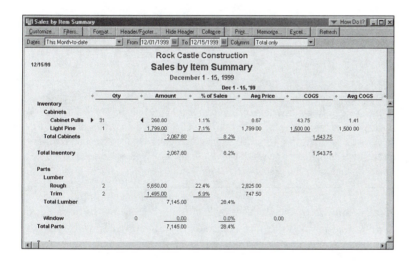

Figure 8.24
This sales report shows inventory information of all items sold.

- **By Item Detail**—Shows the date the item was acquired and the memo (if any), and displays additional price and account balance information.

ITEM PURCHASE REPORTS

From the Items list, Reports menu, six types of Purchase Reports are available. Click Report on All Items from the Reports drop-down menu, and choose Purchase Reports. You'll see the following six options:

- **By Item Summary**—You see a list of items and subitems, displayed with the quantity and amount that you paid for each item, summarized for quick viewing. Click the

Collapse button at the top of the form to further abbreviate the information that is shown.

- **By Item Detail**—You see each inventory item displayed with quantity information, source, purchase and sale price detail, and account balance totals.

- **By Vendor Summary**—Within the Purchase Reports menu, you can use this report to view how much you spent on vendors in any given accounting period (see Figure 8.25).

Figure 8.25
The Purchases by Vendor Summary report summarizes how much you spent on vendors during a given time period.

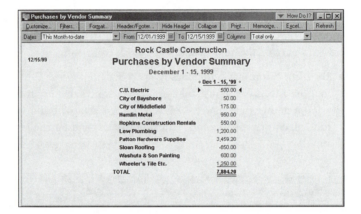

Tip #24 from
Gail Perry

Don't forget that you can change the time scope of any report by using the drop-down Date menu, or by typing new dates in the From and To fields at the top of the report. You can add filters to this vendor report by using the Columns drop-down menu, making this a very powerful reporting tool. For example, you can view the money spent on your vendors according to the Terms on which you pay them, Item Type, Shipping information, and Payment Method.

- **By Vendor Detail**—Similar to the By Vendor Summary, but shows item name, purchase number and date, memo, and more detailed account information for each vendor.

- **Open Purchase Orders**—This report lists all orders for items that you have not yet received. The report includes the purchase order number and the date you expected to receive the merchandise. Display a purchase order by clicking its name in this report.

- **Open Purchase Orders by Job**—Just like the Open Purchase Orders report, this report lists orders for items that you have not yet received. Only purchase orders containing items that have been assigned to specific jobs are included in this report.

Note

If, while viewing a report, you want to learn more about the details of a specific purchase order, double-click on the transaction to view the originating document.

Inventory Reports

Click Reports at the bottom of the Item list, and choose Report on All Items, Inventory Reports. You see several handy reports for showing which items are on backorder, how many of each item you sold during a particular period, delivery schedules, and detailed asset value information. Reports dealing with inventory are covered in Chapter 14. Following are three of the most useful inventory reports:

- **Stock Status by Item**—Under the Inventory Reports submenu is the Stock Status by Item report, which provides detailed quantity, reordering, and item delivery information. Sales information for the week is also available.
- **Valuation Summary**—Generates a report for inventory asset value broken down into item types, percentage of total value, your own inventory costs, retail value, and average cost of each item.
- **Physical Inventory Worksheet**—This form contains a quick list of all your inventory items, featuring the reported inventory quantities. At the far right is a field for you to check off an actual physical count as you walk through the warehouse.

Project

Click Reports at the bottom of the Items list, and choose Report on All Items, Project. Here you can find out how profitable each item in your inventory is, estimated revenue versus actual revenue of inventory items, and how much time was spent on each job item. (This group of reports might not appear in QuickBooks Standard Edition.) Following are a few of the reports listed:

- **Item Profitability**—Under the Project submenu, click Item Profitability to see the actual costs versus actual revenue, and a calculated dollar difference. Click the Collapse button to simplify the report for quicker data.
- **Item Estimates vs. Actuals**—A more complete version of the previous report, featuring how much profit was estimated versus how much was actually realized on each set of transactions (see Figure 8.26).
- **Time By Item**—Click here to find out how much time was spent over a particular period on each type of job item.

Graphs

To see pie and bar graphs of your sales over a given period of time, click Reports at the bottom of the Item list, and choose Report on All Items, Graphs, Sales. These graphs are a very powerful feature of QuickBooks, and the Sales Graph reviewed here is only one of many. QuickBooks graphs have amazing "drill down" capabilities, enabling you to click a pie chart for an entire year and continue clicking down for more detail until a specific invoice appears for a specific transaction. With a single mouse-click, you can print your graph as well.

Figure 8.26
Check profitability of your transactions using the Item Estimates vs. Actuals report.

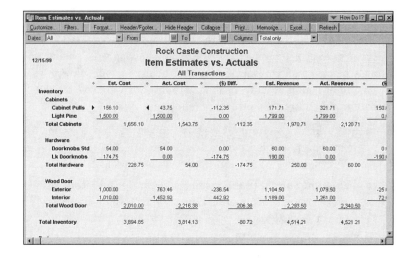

Pictured in Figure 8.27 is a Sales Graph. When the graph first appears, you see a bar graph at the top showing Sales By Month. Each month's total is shown as a bar in thousands of dollars. You can change the date range by clicking the Dates button at the top of the graph and choosing a new range. Enter a custom range in the From and To fields if you want.

Figure 8.27
Graphs enable you to view data over time and by item simultaneously.

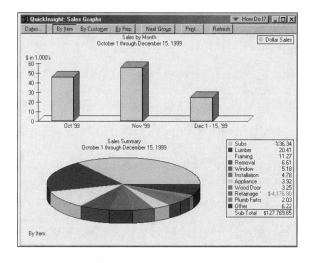

The lower half of the graph shows a pie chart that breaks down all sales for a given period by item. Notice that you can change which data group is represented by clicking any of three buttons at the top of the screen: By Item, By Customer, or By Rep. Clicking these buttons only changes the data shown on the pie chart, and not the bar graph, which measures time.

Going back and forth between these two graphs enables you to narrow your view down to both a specific product or service and a very specific time frame. Double-click any bar in the bar graph or "slice" of the pie to get a close-up view of that specific data group. For example, double-clicking the month of November shows a pie chart that represents sales in that month only. Double-clicking the item Framing in the pie chart shows a new bar graph with the entire date range, but only the data for sales of Framing services is shown.

If you've drilled down far enough (by double-clicking) to show a single month and data group, double-clicking again opens a list of invoices for that month. Double-click any invoice in the list to view the originating document full-screen. After it's open, you can edit the document or view more details.

> **Note**
>
> Although only a Sales Graph is available from the Items list, QuickBooks includes dozens of graphs that are highly customizable. Graphs are covered in more detail in Chapter 21, "QuickBooks Reports and Graphs."

Customer, Vendor, and Employee Lists

From the Lists menu, you can view and edit Customer, Vendor, and Employee information. Here, you can also see all your currently open Purchase Orders, Memorized Transactions, and Reminders.

Customer:Job List

The Customer:Job list (see Figure 8.28) is where you store information about a particular customer, such as name, address, credit limit, and internal account information. Information about jobs that you do for this customer is also stored here. This includes the type of job, its pending status, the completion date estimate, and so on.

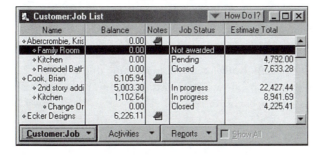

Figure 8.28
The Customer:Job list. Leave yourself a note as a reminder of important details regarding a particular customer or job.

After creating an entry in the Customer:Job list, you can access that entry from any form using the drop-down Customer menu. These include purchase orders, invoices, and cash sales forms. All the information you save with your Customer:Job list is available to these forms, as are checks, bills, classes, and ledgers.

Tip #25 from

Even your minor business transactions relate to a particular customer or job. Someone must benefit from the fact that you are running to the hardware store for the third time today! In an effort to keep track of where your moneys and energies are being spent, whenever possible, associate each task with a particular customer and job, even if that task or expense is not going to be billed to that customer.

You probably made some entries into the Customer:Jobs list when you used the EasyStep Interview to set up QuickBooks. It is those entries that you see when you click List, Customer:Jobs. However, at some point you'll probably need to add new customers. To do so, from the List menu, click Customer:Jobs, and select New from the Customer:Job submenu. You see the three tabs of the New Customer dialog box (see Figure 8.29).

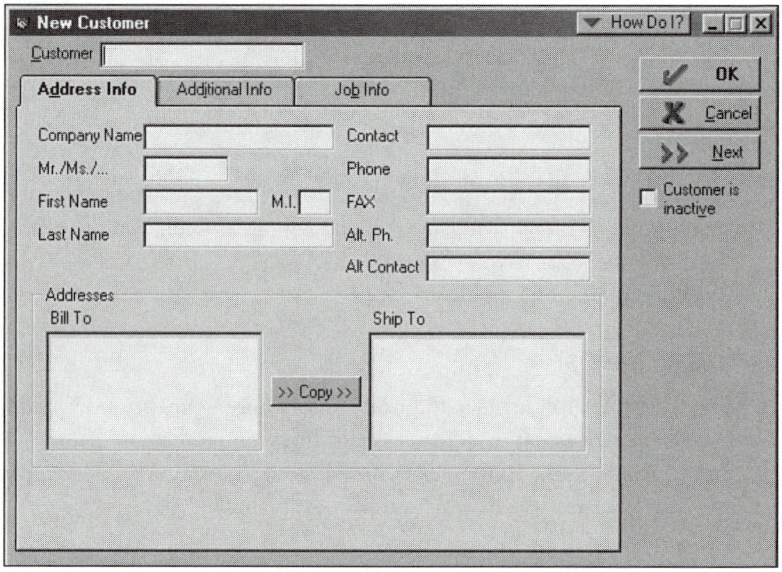

Figure 8.29
The New Customer dialog box contains three tabs for storing customer information.

CUSTOMER FIELD

Above the tabs is the Customer field. Enter the customer's name in this field. The name that you enter here gets added to the Customer:Job list, and is always the first field used any time you apply this entry to a form, check, or ledger.

ADDRESS INFO

In the first tab, Address Info, you include company name, customer name and address, and contact information. If this customer's shipping address differs from his billing address, this tab is the place where you include both.

Additional Info

The second tab, Additional Info, is where you enter a customer number (one you create as your own internal reference), and choose Job Type, Terms, and Sales Rep, if applicable. Custom fields that you design appear here as well.

Job Info

On the third tab, Job Info, type an estimated job completion date, start date, job status (awarded, pending, closed, for example), and job description. This job description appears on many forms.

> **Note** In the Customer:Jobs list, you can have more than one job associated with a customer. You have to fill out a new item for each job, however. In the Customer:Jobs list, each job appears indented below the customer with whom it is associated.

Making a Note about a Customer

If you want to enter descriptive information about a particular job, you can click the Customer:Job button in the Customer:Job List window and choose Edit (or press Ctrl+E). In the Edit Customer dialog box that appears, at the far right, is the Notes button. Click this button to enter a note to yourself that is pertinent to this job. After you've done so, a small Notes icon appears next to that particular job in the Customer:Jobs list. Double-click the icon to view the note. Notes are helpful to remind yourself of an agreed-upon time to make a delivery, call a business associate, or any small detail that defies categorization.

Notes and To Do lists are explored more thoroughly later in this chapter.

Vendors List

Besides creating new vendors and editing existing ones, the Vendors list is where you can print 1099 forms, write checks, pay bills, enter credit card balances, print QuickReports on vendors, and create reports and graphs. In addition, you can perform standard list activities such as making vendors inactive, deleting vendors, and finding specific vendors in any transaction.

When you set up QuickBooks, you entered vendors as part of the process. Vendors are businesses that regularly sell you goods. Most often with vendors, you've established a routine, a relationship of purchasing, billing, and paying. A vendor trusts you to pay within an agreed period of time. It's desirable to deal with vendors, rather than having to run to the store and pay cash for things.

Vendors and taxes

Dealing with vendors presents a special tax issue: the 1099 form. The IRS likes to make sure that it gets its share of all transactions conducted by even small informal business relationships. Therefore, if you pay more than $600 per year for services performed by an unincorporated vendor, you are required to create a 1099 form for that vendor, to report the income. QuickBooks keeps track of how much you've paid each vendor. You can use QuickBooks to produce 1099 forms at year-end.

If you think you will purchase at least $600 in services from an unincorporated vendor during the year, click the Vendor Eligible for 1099 check box on the Additional Info tab of the New Vendor dialog box.

ADDING A NEW VENDOR

To add a new vendor to the Vendor list, select New from the Vendor drop-down menu (see Figure 8.30), and type all pertinent contact information.

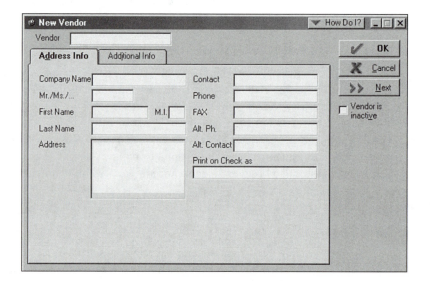

Figure 8.30
Create a new vendor using the by-now-familiar tabs to include all the necessary information.

The Address Info tab of the New Vendor dialog box prompts you for name, address, and phone information, as well as what you want printed on the checks that you make out to the vendor. The Additional Info tab enables you to include an account number and sales tax information, and it enables you to chose which Vendor type and credit terms are to be associated with this vendor. Credit Limit and Tax ID fields are also available. If this customer's purchases begin to approach the figure you set in the Credit Limit field, QuickBooks issues a warning.

All the information you enter in these fields is used by QuickBooks in creating reports.

Tip #26 from Please note that you only add an opening balance figure if you are just now beginning your QuickBooks company. Otherwise, leave this number at zero and begin entering transactions, such as purchases and payments.

EDITING A VENDOR

To edit a vendor, click on the vendor name on the list, click the Vendor button, and chose Edit from the resulting drop-down menu (or double-click on a vendor name). Make any changes you want in any of the fields. You can also add and customize fields using the Define Fields features on the Additional Info tab.

EMPLOYEE LIST

You might have entered employees when you first set up your QuickBooks company. As your company grows, you'll probably hire more; if you've never had an employee, the time might indeed come when you'll need to get some help. Here's a look at how to add new employees to your company and edit the information on those that you have. Setting up an employee can be a rather complex process because of the various agencies involved. State and federal withholding, health insurance, disability, and social security are some of the liabilities you are responsible for when you truly and officially hire someone.

When you add an employee to your company, choose Employees from the Lists menu, and click New from the drop-down Employee menu (or press Ctrl+N). The first two tabs, Address Info and Additional Info, prompt you for name and address, date hired, account number, and other information. The third tab, Payroll Info, is where income and deduction information for the employee is entered. The complete job of setting up a new employee is explained in Chapter 18, "Paying Employees and Contractors," but for now, you'll take a quick look at what's required.

On the Payroll tab of the New Employee window, use the drop-down menu in the Name field to select a payroll item, such as Salary or Overtime Pay. To the right, in the Hour/Annual Rate field, enter the actual rate of each payroll item.

Use the drop-down menu to the right to specify Pay Period.

Use the bottom half of the Payroll Info tab to enter additions and deductions just as they appear on the employee's paycheck. These include health insurance, mileage reimbursements, flexible spending account contributions, FSLA adjustments and such. You can enter a percentage amount and a cap (limit) that a particular deduction or contribution cannot exceed. To add a new type of deduction or contribution, click the drop-down menu arrow in the Name field and choose Add New. The Add new payroll item Wizard appears. Here you can specify a Type and Name for your contribution or deduction, set a percentage or amount limit, and associate this payroll adjustment with a particular account.

Customer, Job, and Vendor Type Lists

In a submenu of the Lists menu, you find Other Lists. Of particular interest here are the Type lists. Types enable you to further break down your lists into subgroups that make sense for your business. Following are three examples:

- If you sell merchandise, you might have different terms for wholesale, commercial, and retail customers. QuickBooks can account for these as Customer types.
- As a wedding photographer, you might have a standard picture package you offer and a deluxe package. Each service can be identified in QuickBooks as a Job type, under the main item Job Photography.
- As a restaurateur, perhaps you purchase consultation and marketing services to come up with plans to bring in more customers. You do not group these transactions in the same expense category with ordering paper cups and food inventory. In this case, you'd set up two Vendor types.

As with other lists, click the drop-down menu at the bottom left to create new list entries, to delete and deactivate old ones, and to print the list contents. Use Find in Transaction to locate all active transactions using the item list you've specified.

When you create a new Customer, Job, or Vendor type, the name appears in the list and is available to all relevant forms from the drop-down list on the form. After a new customer, job, or vendor is created, you can associate charges with these new entries, create estimates for services, prepare invoices, receive payments, and otherwise include these new types in the daily business routines that you record in QuickBooks.

Next, briefly look at Terms, Customer Messages, Payment, and Method lists. These are also found in the Other Lists submenu. You'll take a fast look at the Ship Via list as well.

Terms, Customer Messages, and Payment Method Lists

From the Lists menu, click Other Lists, and then choose Terms, and you see the Terms List dialog box. You do not need to come here to apply terms to a transaction. To do that, open any form (Sales Receipt, Customer Payment, or Invoice, for example) and click the Terms drop-down menu. However, to create a new set of terms, edit existing ones, or view a list of all transactions to which certain terms have been applied, use this list.

Editing and Creating Payment Terms

Figure 8.31 shows the Terms list. Double-click any existing term to edit it (or click on a term and press Ctrl+E). In this example, the Term 1%10Net30 was double-clicked. The following steps look at the dialog box to show you how to edit an existing term, as well as how to create new ones.

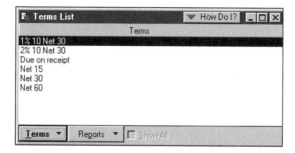

Figure 8.31
Double-click on a term description to edit it, or press Ctrl+N to add a new term.

1. In the Terms field, enter any change you want to make to the name of this term:
   - This example, 1%10Net30, means that if the customer pays the amount due within 10 days, the total is discounted by 1 percent. In any event, the total payment is due within 30 days.
   - If the terms were 1%10Net15, payment within 10 days brings a 1 percent discount, and the entire payment is due within 15 days. Whatever you enter in the Term field, however, is simply a title. The term is set by filling out the fields that follow.
2. For creating standard terms, use the fields below the Standard radio button. In the Net due in ( ) Days field, enter the number of days until the entire payment is due.
3. In the Discount percentage is field, enter the percentage discount offered if payment comes early.
4. In the Discount if paid within ( ) days field, enter the number of days for which this discount is effective.

Click Date Driven if you want to set up your terms to apply to dates of the month rather than days from the current date. Clicking Date Driven causes a new set of options to appear.

To create a terms discount based on dates in the month, complete the following steps:

1. First, enter the day of the month on which the entire payment is due.
2. Next, use the Due the next month if issued within ( ) days of due date field to create a condition that enables the customer to slide until next month. For example, say that you are accustomed to getting paid by all your customers on the 15th of the month, but this sale was made on the 14th. Rather than force this customer to pay by tomorrow, QuickBooks enables you specify that if a sale was made ten or 15 days before the normal due date, you'll let the due date slide until the following month. This way you don't have to alter your payment routine just for one customer.
3. In the next field, enter a discount percentage for early payment. Enter zero if no discount is offered.

4. Below that field, enter the day of the month on which this bill must be paid by to receive the discount.

You can create a new set of terms using this same dialog box. The dialog box can be accessed by choosing New from the Terms drop-down menu of the Terms list. After you've created new terms, they are available on any applicable QuickBooks form, by clicking that form's drop-down Terms menu.

Printing, Deactivating, and Locating Terms in Use

Click the Terms drop-down menu from the Terms list, and options appear, enabling you to print the terms currently in use on your QuickBooks forms. You can also make terms inactive and use Find in Transactions to locate any current transaction that uses a set of terms that you specify.

> **Note** There has been an emphasis on creating terms in QuickBooks that you apply to your customers, relating to the payments that they make to you. You also need to make QuickBooks aware of terms that your vendors apply to you. To make your purchase orders and payments fully accurate, use the Term list to create a term item used by each of your vendors.

Use the following steps to create a report of the terms:

1. Click the Term item for which you want to run a report, and choose Quick Report from the Reports drop-down menu. You see a list of all relevant bills, invoices, and payments.
2. From this report, double-click any document in the list.
3. The document opens, ready for you to edit. Make any changes you want, or just view the contents.

Customer Messages List

On most QuickBooks forms, you can enter a message to your customers ("Thank you for your business," "Happy Holidays"), or you can use the provided drop-down menu to apply messages that you've already created and saved. Customer messages can actually be created on-the-fly by clicking Add New from the Customer Message drop-down menu on any form and typing a new message. Your message is saved. To view and print all the customer messages you've created and saved, click Other Lists from the List menu, and choose Customer Message. From this list, you can also create new messages, delete old ones, make a message inactive, and print a list of all the messages you use.

Payment Method List

This list enables you to create new payment methods, delete and deactivate existing payment methods, and locate any transactions that use a payment method that you specify. You can also view and print reports. To access the Payment Method list, click Other Lists from the Lists menu, and choose Payment Methods. Typical payment methods are check, cash, and various types of credit cards. One of the principal conveniences of the Payment Method list is to create separate lists for each credit card you own, enabling you to keep track of which card got charged for what merchandise. However, when you are setting up a payment method, you are not creating an account or terms for handling those methods—you are merely typing a name that appears in appropriate forms and on reports.

To view all the transactions conducted using a particular payment method, select from the list the Payment Method that you want to track, and click the Report drop-down menu. Then choose Quick Report. To edit a payment method, double-click its name in the list.

When you create a Payment Method by clicking New from the Payment Method drop-down menu, you are providing a name that will appear in the Payment Method drop-down menu found in many forms, such as Sales Receipts, Customer Payments, and Bills.

TROUBLESHOOTING

DISPLAYING INACTIVE CUSTOMERS

I've lost some customers that I know I created, but they're no longer on the list.

At some point you might have chosen to make the customers inactive. Display inactive customers on your Customer:Job list by clicking the Show All button.

PRINTING A CUSTOMER LIST

How do I print a customer list?

From the Customer:Job List window, choose Reports, Phone List, to display an alphabetical list of all customers and their phone numbers. Choose Reports, Contact List, to display an alphabetical list of all customers, the phone and fax numbers, current balance, and contact name. Print these lists by clicking the Print button at the top of the report screen.

SETTING UP SEPARATE ITEMS

I charge two different prices for the same item. I've chosen one price as the standard price for the item, and half of the time I have to override that price on my invoices. Is there a way to have two prices in the system for the same item?

You must set up two separate items if you want to have two separate prices available without having to override the price on your invoice. You might consider setting up the main item with two subitems, one at each price.

CHAPTER 9

SEPARATING YOUR COMPANY INTO LOGICAL DIVISIONS

In this chapter

What's a Class? 160

Setting Up Classes 160

Reporting on Classes 164

Does your company have locations, divisions, departments, funds, or other areas that it needs to track separately? Perhaps you want to track income by the person who brings the income to your company (such as lawyers, accountants, salespeople) for purposes of paying commissions and bonuses, or to judge performance.

Or your company might engage in several types of business, for example a construction company that performs residential and commercial construction, and it is beneficial to track the performance of each type of work.

If these or other scenarios apply to your company, you can use the QuickBooks class feature and report on each area of your business separately.

What's a Class?

A *class* is a label that you attach to your income, expense, and payroll transactions to identify the transaction as belonging to a particular group. Only one class can be applied to a single transaction.

You have the option of setting up subclasses of classes, so as to further classify and separate income and expenses.

For example, a law firm that practices in the areas of criminal law, family law, and personal injury might want to have a class for each of these types of law, and then a subclass for each attorney. That way the firm can create reports that show how the family law practice as a whole is doing, and then a report showing how each lawyer within the family law practice is doing, and so on.

Setting Up Classes

Before you can use classes, you must activate the QuickBooks preference for class tracking. (During the EasyStep Interview, you were asked whether you wanted to use classes.)

→ To find information on setting up classes during the EasyStep Interview, **see p. 59**.

If you answered Yes to the interview question about classes, the class preference has already been activated. If you didn't request classes during the interview, follow these steps to turn on the feature:

1. Choose File, Preferences. The Preferences window appears.
2. Click the Accounting icon at the left (you might need to scroll to find this icon). Make sure that the Company Preferences tab is selected (see Figure 9.1).
3. Check the Use class tracking box to turn on the class tracking feature.
4. Click OK to close this window and save your settings.

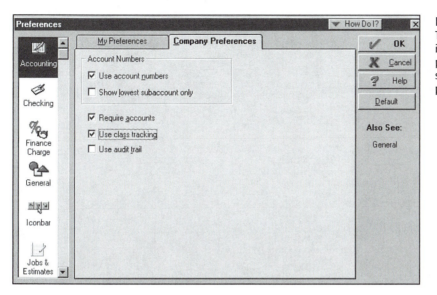

Figure 9.1
Turning on class tracking enables you to prepare reports that show how each class performs.

If class tracking is turned off, either inadvertently or intentionally, your class designations are still stored with your transactions and you can still prepare reports based on class designations—you just can't assign future income and expense transactions to classes until you turn the feature on again.

If you turn on class tracking after transactions have been entered in QuickBooks, you can go back to past transactions and enter the class.

Creating a List of Classes

When you are ready to set up your classes, you can open the Class List window and enter each class as follows:

1. Choose Lists, Classes (Or Lists, Other Lists, Classes, depending on your setup). The Class List window appears.
2. Click the Class button, and then choose New from the drop-down list (or press Ctrl+N). The New Class window appears.
3. Enter the name of the class that you want to create in the Class Name field.
4. If this class is to be a subclass of another class, check the check box and choose the name of the class from the drop-down list; or choose Add New to enter a new class name (see Figure 9.2).
5. To continue entering classes, click the Next button; another New Class window appears. If you are finished entering classes, click OK to close the window.

Figure 9.2
Create new classes in this window.

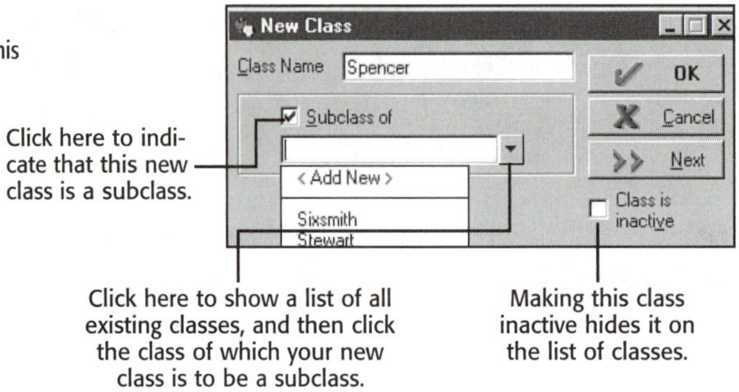

Click here to indicate that this new class is a subclass.

Click here to show a list of all existing classes, and then click the class of which your new class is to be a subclass.

Making this class inactive hides it on the list of classes.

Other Features of the Class List Window

Several other operations are available to you in the Class List window.

From the Class drop-down menu, you can perform the following tasks:

- **Edit (Ctrl+E)**—Click a class name on the list, and then choose Edit to change the spelling of a name.
- **Delete (Ctrl+D)**—Click the name of a class that you no longer need, and then choose Delete to remove the name. You cannot delete a class name if transactions have occurred in that class.
- **Make Inactive**—Click the name of a class that you no longer want to see on the class list, and then choose Make Inactive to remove the name from the list. The name is still available for use on transactions, and it still appears on reports.
- **Find in Transactions**—Click a class name, and then choose Find in Transactions to search for all transactions for this class.
- **Print List**—Print a complete list of all your classes.

From the Reports drop-down menu, you can prepare the following reports:

- **Quick Report (Ctrl+Q)**—Click a class name, and then choose Quick Report to display a report of all the transactions that refer to the selected class.
- **Profit and Loss by Class**—This is one of the most useful class reports you will find. Prepare the P&L by choosing Reports, Reports on all Classes. A side menu appears, from which you can choose Profit and Loss by Class. This report shows you all income and expenses for the year to date, with a separate column for each class. You can change the date at the top of the screen to select the time period that the report covers (see Figure 9.3).

SETTING UP CLASSES | 163

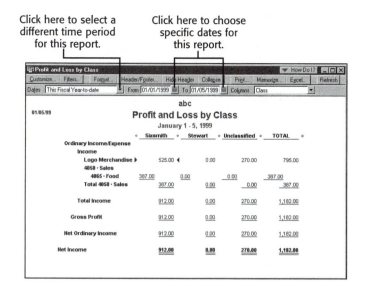

Figure 9.3
This useful report shows you all income and expense transactions, with a separate column for each class.

- **Balance Sheet Itemized**—Choose Reports, Reports on All Classes, and then pick Balance Sheet Itemized to display a balance sheet with class listings. Most balance sheet accounts aren't affected by classes, but the detail of your accounts receivable and accounts payable includes class information, which might be useful to you.

- **Graphs**—Choose Reports, Reports on All Classes, Graphs to select either graphs depicting Income and Expense Items by Class, or Budget versus Actual by Class.

→ To find information on the reports and graphs that are available in QuickBooks, **see p. 361**.
→ To find more information about other tasks that you can perform within List windows, **see p. 121**.

CREATING CLASSES ON-THE-FLY

If you want to, you can just wait until you need a new class designation, and create it on-the-fly.

On an invoice, purchase order, bill, or any form on which you are entering a transaction that ultimately affects an income or expense account, a class field appears (see Figure 9.4).

Click the drop-down arrow in the class field, and then choose Add New; the New Class window appears. Enter the name and (optionally) the subclass information for the class that you want to create, click OK, and presto! A new class is born!

Figure 9.4
Create a new class on-the-fly on any screen where you see a class field.

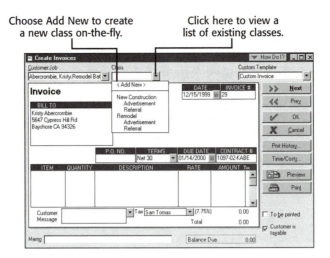

REPORTING ON CLASSES

Many reports support reporting by classes, but following are some reports with which breakdowns by class might be especially useful:

- **Profit and loss statements**—From the Reports menu on your main QuickBooks screen (as opposed to the Reports button in your Class List window), choose Profit and Loss, and then choose from the reports that are listed. When a report is onscreen, it can be filtered to show only the results of a particular class or group of classes. QuickBooks has done part of this job for you already with one of its standard reports. If you choose Reports, Profit and Loss, By Class, your company profit and loss statement appears with a separate column for each class.

→ To find guidance on filtering reports by classes, and to find information about other filtering techniques, **see p. 372**.

- **Sales reports**—From the Reports menu, choose Sales Reports, and then choose from the list that appears. You can request that any sales report be filtered by class, thus showing sales for only one class or for a selected group of classes.

- **Purchase reports**—From the Reports menu, choose Purchase Reports, and then choose from the list that appears. If you are interested in displaying purchase information by class, choose a purchase report and filter the report for a particular class or group of classes.

A much more detailed discussion of reports can be found in Chapter 21, "QuickBooks Reports and Graphs."

TROUBLESHOOTING

INDICATING CLASSES

The box for indicating classes isn't appearing on my forms.

Choose File, Preferences. When the Preferences window appears, click the Accounting icon on the left. Click the Company Preferences tab, and then check the Use class tracking box. Click OK to close the Preferences window.

CHANGING CLASSES

I assigned the wrong class to a transaction. Is there a way to change the class after the transaction is finished?

You can always go back to a transaction and change the class designation. Open the transaction (such as an invoice or bill), make the change, and then save the transaction again. You might want to reissue any reports that you have produced that will be affected by this change.

PART II

TAKING CARE OF BUSINESS

10 Job-cost Estimating and Tracking 169

11 Invoicing, Monthly Statements, and Accounts Receivable 183

12 Recording Income 197

13 Reporting Sales Tax 205

14 Keeping Track of Your Inventory 217

15 Purchase Orders, Accounts Payable, and Paying Bills 233

16 Managing Fixed Assets 253

17 Entering Cash Transactions 263

CHAPTER 10

Job-cost Estimating and Tracking

In this chapter

Setting Up Jobs   170

Optional Job Information   171

Creating an Estimate   174

Invoicing Against an Estimate   176

Revising Estimates   179

Reporting on Work in Progress   180

Depending on the type of business you have, you might find that you have a need for keeping track of your costs on a per-job basis. Many businesses do this: construction companies, specialty manufacturing companies, architectural companies, caterers, law firms, accounting firms, and so on.

Any type of business that needs to keep track of separate jobs for the same customer can benefit from job-tracking. If you never do repeat business for a customer, you probably have no reason to track jobs. Or if you want to reflect each job as if it were a separate customer, you can do that as well, without the QuickBooks Pro job-costing feature.

With job-costing you can have the luxury of producing reports for a single customer, summarizing all the jobs performed for that customer, or producing reports for the individual jobs.

Note that you must own QuickBooks Pro to do job-costing. The regular version of QuickBooks does not support this feature. If you use the regular version of QuickBooks, you can skip this entire chapter.

Setting Up Jobs

There is no limit to the number of jobs you can set up for a customer.

You learned how to set up your customer list in Chapter 8, "Setting Up Services, Customers, Suppliers," and you might have taken the opportunity to set up some jobs during the EasyStep Interview (see "Entering Customers" in Chapter 5). This section presents the complete steps for setting up jobs.

You must have a customer already set up before you can set up a job for that customer. To review, you set up a new customer by opening the Lists menu and choosing Customer:Job. Then click the Customer:Job button in the window that appears, choose New, and enter the appropriate information for your new customer.

Use the following steps to set up a job:

1. Open the Lists menu and choose Customer:Job. The Customer:Job List window appears.
2. Click a customer for whom you want to create a new job (the customer must be on the list before you can add a job).
3. Click the Customer:Job button at the bottom of the window. A drop-down menu appears.
4. Choose Add Job from the menu. The New Job window appears (see Figure 10.1). The customer name appears in the Customer field of the Address Info tab. Verify that this is the correct customer.

Optional Job Information

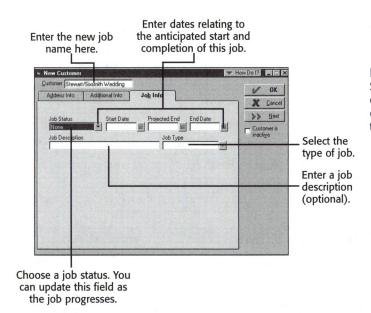

Figure 10.1
Set up a new job for an existing customer by choosing Add Job from the Customer:Job menu.

5. Enter a name for this job in the Job Name field at the top of the window. You are limited to 41 characters, including letters, numbers, and spaces. You can use a combination of upper- and lowercase letters.

6. You can add optional job information (discussed in the next section) by moving to the Job Info tab. When you have finished entering information about this job, click OK. The job is added to the Customer:Job list, alphabetized, and indented under the name of the customer you have chosen.

Optional Job Information

You can add several pieces of information about a job when you are setting up the job. These include the job status, the dates of the job, a job description, and the job type.

Enter or update these options by clicking a job from the Customer:Job list, clicking the Customer:Job button, and choosing Edit.

The following sections contain descriptions of the various descriptive job options.

Job Status

Job status is a distinction that you can assign to a job to indicate where in the completion process this job falls. QuickBooks provides you with a standard list of job status options from which you can choose. You can also modify this list if your company uses different terms to identify job status.

The standard job status options offered by QuickBooks include the following:

- **Pending**—Use this option to describe a job when you have provided an estimate but have not yet heard if your company has been awarded the contract.
- **Awarded**—Use this option to describe a job that has been awarded to your company but on which you have not yet begun work.
- **In Progress**—Use this option to describe a job on which you are currently working.
- **Closed**—Use this option to describe a completed job.
- **Not Awarded**—Use this option to describe a job on which you provided an estimate but for which you did not receive a contract.
- **None**—Leave None as the status if you do not use the job status option for your jobs.

> **Tip #27 from Gail Perry**
> Double-click a job name in the Customer:Job list to edit information about that job.

Only five status options (plus None) are available for your use. If, however, the options you see are not appropriate for your business (perhaps, for example, your business is a law practice and you prefer to use terms such as Meeting, Discovery, Pre-Trial, Trial, and Appeal to describe the status of a legal case), you can change any or all the five options to suit your business needs.

Use the following steps to change a job status option:

1. Open the File menu and choose Preferences. The Preferences window appears.
2. Click the Jobs & Estimates icon at the left of the window. You might have to scroll to find this icon.
3. Click the Company Preferences tab at the top of the screen to see the five job status options (see Figure 10.2).

Figure 10.2
Enter your own job status descriptions in the Jobs & Estimates Preferences.

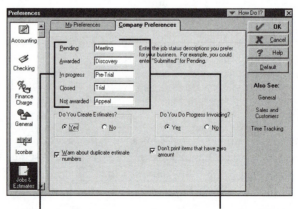

These standard descriptions for the fields don't appear anywhere in your lists and reports.

Create any status descriptions that will be useful to your business.

4. Change the name of any job status by deleting the name you see and entering your own choice for a job status. You are limited to 12 characters, including spaces. You can use upper- and lowercase letters or numbers.

5. When you have entered all the job status options you plan to use, click the OK button to save your changes.

Any jobs for which you have already assigned a job status are updated to reflect the changes that you make to these options.

If you use the Job Status field to describe the progress of your jobs, remember to edit your jobs regularly, updating the status. Select a job in the Customer:Job list by clicking it, click the Customer:Job button, choose Edit, and update the status on the Job Info tab.

Whenever you display the Customer:Job list, you can quickly see the status of all jobs in the Job Status column.

Job Dates

If you want to use QuickBooks to help keep track of the dates on which you begin and end a job, you can enter information in the three date fields on the Job Info tab.

Enter a start date for the job. This is the date on which you actually begin, or expect to begin, working on the particular job.

Indicate an anticipated job completion date by entering a date in the Projected End field. This date is an estimate.

When the job is completed, enter the actual date by filling in the End Date field.

When you have entered dates in any or all these fields, you can produce reports based on these dates. See the "Reporting on Work in Progress" section later in this chapter for more information about the different types of job-related reports that you can create.

Job Description

You can enter an optional narrative description of the job. No standard entries are provided for this field, so you can be creative; or perhaps your company wants to set up standard job descriptions of its own and make a printed list available to anyone entering job information in QuickBooks Pro (there is no provision for a drop-down list in this field).

For example, if you are a tax practitioner, some standard descriptions for the type of tax work you perform might include the following:

- Quarterly Estimates
- Annual Tax Planning
- Individual Income Tax Returns
- Corporate Income Tax Returns
- Payroll Tax Forms

Job Type

You have the option to define the Job Type field. Unlike the Job Status field, no standard entries are available in the Job Type field; therefore, you can customize job types to go with your business. For example, a construction company's job types might include New Construction, Repairs, and Renovation. Job types can be subtypes of other job types; for example, the New Construction job type might include the subtypes Commercial and Residential.

You can create a job type on-the-fly while you are setting up a new job by clicking the arrow in the Job Type field, clicking Add New, and entering a new job type in the window that appears.

An advantage of using job types is that QuickBooks considers job types to be an *item (page 55)*. A drop-down list in the Job Type field provides an easy way to choose from existing job types. Also, if you open the Lists menu and choose Other Lists, and then choose Job Type from the submenu, you can create quick reports, easily edit job types, and search for job types in your transactions.

Creating an Estimate

When you use job-cost tracking, you have the option of preparing and working with estimates. An estimate is very similar in appearance to an invoice, but serves an entirely different purpose.

An invoice is a final statement of the work performed and materials purchased for which the customer owes your company; an *estimate* is a preliminary listing of the costs and time you anticipate will be associated with a particular job.

An estimate is prepared in advance of getting a job, as a summary of what the job is expected to cost. Typically, a businessperson or company presents a prospective customer with an estimate, hoping to get the job. The customer considers the estimate, often comparing it to estimates received from competitors, and decides whether to award the job.

A company might agree that the cost of the job will not exceed the amount on the estimate, or there might be agreement that the estimate can be exceeded with the customer's approval. These terms must be decided before the job is accepted.

An advantage of creating an estimate in QuickBooks Pro rather than just writing the estimate down on a piece of paper is that you can create invoices right from the estimate. With the QuickBooks Pro Progress Billing feature, you can indicate which individual items on an estimate are to be invoiced, or you can request to invoice a percentage of an estimate (for example, if 40 percent of the job is completed, you can invoice 40 percent of the total amount on the estimate).

Another advantage of using estimates in QuickBooks Pro is that you can create reports showing the amount of work in progress based on the unbilled portions of your estimates.

QuickBooks Pro provides a way to revise an estimate at any time if the job situation changes.

To create an estimate, follow these steps:

1. Open the Activities menu and choose Create Estimates. Or, from an open Customer:Job List window, right-click the customer job and choose Create Estimates from the pop-up menu. You can also click the Estimate button on the iconbar to open the Create Estimates window (see Figure 10.3).

→ For more information about displaying and using the Iconbar, **see p. 390**.

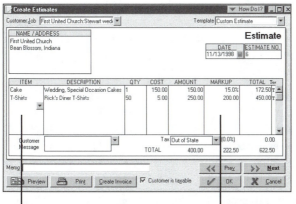

Figure 10.3
Enter all anticipated costs for this job in the Create Estimates window.

Click in this column to display a drop-down list showing all your company's items.

Enter a markup amount or percentage in this column. This figure won't print on the customer copy of the estimate.

2. Enter the job name in the Customer Job field at the top of the window (or verify the job name if one is already present).

3. If you use classes, choose a class in the Class field (or choose Add New to create a new class). If you want to activate the Classes feature, open the File menu and choose Preferences. Click the Accounting icon in the Preferences window and check the Use class tracking box.

4. In the Template field, choose the form of estimate that you want to use. You'll find only one form to choose (Custom Estimate) unless you have created additional estimate forms yourself.

→ For more information on creating your own custom forms, **see p. 338**.

5. Verify the date of the estimate.

6. Click in the Item field and choose from the drop-down list of available items (or create a New Item).

7. The Description field fills in automatically, as do the Cost and Amount fields if information for these fields is available. You can override any information in these fields by deleting the information that appears and entering what you want.

> If you press the Enter key while entering information on an Estimate form, QuickBooks thinks that you have finished and takes you to the next form. If you press Enter inadvertently, click the Prev button to return to the form that you were working on.

8. Enter an amount in the quantity field.//
9. The Estimate form includes a Markup column. In this column you can enter either an amount or a percentage by which you want to increase the calculated cost of an item. The original cost and the markup amount do not appear on the printed estimate—this is for your information only. Only the amount in the Total column appears on the printed estimate.
10. If you want to, enter a customer message that will print on the estimate. QuickBooks offers several friendly messages from which you can choose, or you can click Add New on the drop-down message list to create your own message.
11. You can also enter an optional Memo at the bottom of the Estimate form. This field is for your information only and does not print on the estimate.
12. Click the Preview button if you want to see the estimate before printing it. Click the Print button to send the estimate to the printer. Click the Create Invoice button only if you are ready to invoice the customer for this estimate. Usually you won't create an invoice until some portion of the job has been completed.
13. Click Next (or press Enter) to proceed to the next Estimate form, or click OK to save this Estimate and close the window.

You can use the Print button on the Estimate form if you want to print the estimate right after you complete the form. Estimates don't queue for printing in QuickBooks the way other forms do (invoices, checks, and so on). If you want to print the estimate at a later time, first display the estimate on the screen by opening the Customer:Job List, clicking the job, opening the Activities menu, and choosing View Estimate. Then click the Print button on the estimate form.

INVOICING AGAINST AN ESTIMATE

If you have created an estimate for a customer, you don't have to start over when you are ready to send an invoice to the customer. You can create an invoice right from the estimate—for the entire estimated amount, for a percentage of the amount, or for specific items on the estimate form.

If you plan to invoice the customer for the full value of the estimate, follow these steps:

1. From the Lists menu, choose Customer:Job. The Customer:Job List window appears.
2. Click the job for which you want to prepare an invoice. Click the Activities button and choose View Estimate. The estimate you prepared appears in its Create Estimates window (as shown in Figure 10.3). If you need to make any changes to the estimate, you can do so at this time.

3. Click the Create Invoice button at the bottom of the Create Estimates window. (Note: If the Progress Billing window appears, you have turned on the Progress Billing feature in QuickBooks Pro. Choose Create invoice for the entire estimate—100%—and click OK.) If you make any changes in the estimate, you are asked to confirm that you want to record your changes. Click Yes. A notice now appears, indicating that the entire estimate has been copied to an invoice and reminding you that you can make changes in the invoice if necessary. Click OK when you see this notice (you don't have any other choice).

4. An invoice appears onscreen, listing all items from the estimate with prices that agree with the amounts in the Total column of the estimate. You can make changes if you need to; then click OK. The invoice is stored until you are ready to print it, or you can click the Print button and then click OK to print immediately.

At times you might want to create an invoice from an estimate before the job is completed. In such situations, you want to invoice only part of the estimate. You have two choices: You can either request an invoice for a percentage of the estimate (such as 40 percent or 75 percent) or you can request an invoice for particular items from the estimate (for example, the drywall and electrical work but not the flooring and ductwork).

Before QuickBooks creates an invoice for a portion of an estimate, you must turn on the Progress Billing feature. To turn on this feature, or to check to see if it has been turned on (you might have indicated that you plan to do progress billing when you answered the EasyStep Interview questions), follow these steps:

1. From the File menu, choose Preferences. The Preferences window appears.
2. Click the Jobs & Estimates icon on the left side of the window (you might need to scroll to find this icon).
3. Click the Company Preferences tab if it is not already selected.
4. Choose Yes in answer to the question, "Do You Do Progress Billing?"
5. Click OK to close this window and save your changes.

Now that you have turned on the Progress Billing feature, you can create an invoice from an estimate and use only part of the estimate.

To create an invoice for a portion of an estimate, follow these steps:

1. Display the estimate from which you want to create an invoice (open the Customer:Job list, select a job, click the Activities button, and choose View Estimate).
2. Click the Create Invoice button at the bottom of the estimate form. The Create Progress Invoice Based On Estimate window appears.

> **Note**
> If you start a new invoice (either by clicking the Invoice button on the iconbar or opening the Activities menu and choosing Create Invoice) and indicate a customer for whom an estimate is pending, QuickBooks Pro displays a message about that estimate and asks if you want to create the invoice from the estimate. If you answer Yes, the estimate appears and you can follow the steps in this section.

3. Select from the following three choices:

    - **Create invoice for the entire estimate (100%)**—This option creates an invoice based on all the items on your estimate (as shown in Figure 10.4). If you have already created an invoice for a certain percentage, this option reads, *Create an invoice for the remaining amounts of the estimate.*

Figure 10.4
Indicate how much of this estimate you intend to invoice the customer for at this time.

    - **Create invoice for a percentage of the entire estimate**—If you choose this option, you must enter a percentage (less than 100%) in the % of estimate field.
    - **Create invoice for selected items or for different percentages of each item**—Choose this option if you want to indicate which items on the estimate will be included in the invoice and at what percentage these items will be invoiced.

4. Click OK when you have made your choice. If you choose the third option, the Specify Invoice Amounts for Items on Estimate screen appears, listing each item on the estimate. Click the two check boxes on this screen so that you can display a full view of the cost, quantity, and percentages for these items (see Figure 10.5). In the white columns (you can't make entries in the gray columns), enter the quantity or percentage of each item that you want to invoice at this time. Any previously invoiced amounts appear in the Prior columns in the center of the screen. Click OK when you have finished.

5. Click OK and the invoice appears, showing the items and amounts as you requested. Click OK to store this invoice for printing (or click Print and then OK to print the invoice immediately).

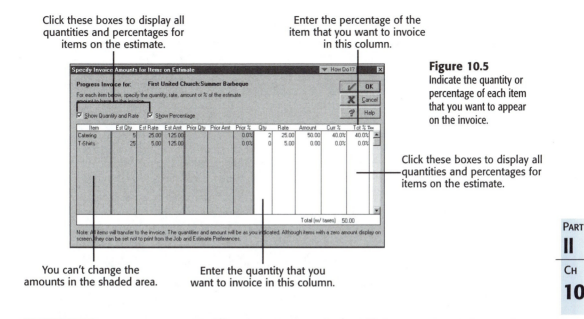

Figure 10.5
Indicate the quantity or percentage of each item that you want to appear on the invoice.

Note

You might notice that when you create an invoice based on selected items from an estimate, all the items from the estimate appear on your invoice—even items that you didn't want to include on this invoice. Never fear! Although it's true that the onscreen version of the invoice shows every item from the estimate, the printed version of the invoice only displays the items that you indicated you wanted to include. You can verify what actually appears on the invoice by clicking the Preview button in the invoice window.

Revising Estimates

In the normal course of business when you are working on a job, you might find that you need to revise your original estimate. Perhaps the nature of the job has changed, the customer has asked you to perform more or less work, the price of parts you expected to purchase has increased, or you found that the work is going to take longer (or not as long) as you originally anticipated.

Instead of waiting until you complete the job to prepare the final invoice, you can make adjustments to your estimate as you go along. This way, you can always bill from the estimate, eventually billing 100 percent of the job as estimated.

Tip #28 from

> You must be cautious about making decisions to change your estimate. Your company's reputation and future work for a customer might be affected by your decision to increase the cost of a job from your original estimate. If you think circumstances might warrant changing your estimate, put a disclaimer on the original estimate, noting that the prices are not guaranteed. Also, of course, notify the customer of changes and receive approval before continuing the job.

To change an existing estimate, view the estimate onscreen (open the Customer:Job list, select the job, click the Activities button, and choose View Estimate). Make any changes that are required, and then click OK to save those changes.

REPORTING ON WORK IN PROGRESS

One of the main reasons you want to enter estimates into QuickBooks Pro instead of scribbling them on pieces of paper is so that you can view reports showing the status of your work as it is in the process of being performed.

Several interesting and useful reports are available to you when you use estimates:

- **QuickReports**—Display the Customer:Job list and click any job. Then click the Reports button and choose QuickReport, the first option on the list. A summary appears, showing all estimates and invoices issued on this job, as well as all payments received to date (see Figure 10.6).

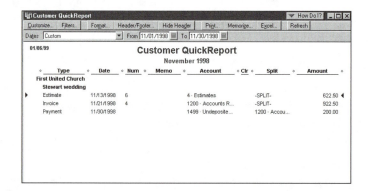

Figure 10.6
The Customer QuickReport gives you a detailed history of all estimates, invoices, and payments on the selected job.

- **Open Balance Report**—How much does this customer owe you? The Customer Open Balance report is the second report on the Reports drop-down menu in the Customer:Job list box. Choose this report to view exactly how much has been billed to this customer and how much is outstanding.

- **Profit & Loss Statement by Job**—Take advantage of the fact that you have taken the time to set up separate jobs for each of your customers. The Profit & Loss Statement by Job report gives you a complete breakdown of every job you have worked on in a designated time period, how much the job has cost you, and how much you have billed for the job. View this report from the Customer:Job window by clicking Reports (you don't need to select a job first) and then choosing Reports on All Customer:Job, Profit & Loss, By Job.

- **Job Profitability Summary**—Are you making any money on your jobs? The Job Profitability Summary provides a job-by-job report of how much you have earned on each job versus how much it cost you to get the job done. Prepare this report by opening the Reports menu, choosing Project Reports, and then choosing Job Profitability Summary.

- **Job Progress Invoices vs. Estimates**—Prepare a report showing all jobs in progress, their current status, the total of the estimate prepared for the job, the amount of the estimate that has been billed, and the percentage of the progress on the job (this calculation is based on the percentage of the amount of the estimate that has been billed). Open the Reports menu, choose Project Reports, and then choose Job Progress Invoices vs. Estimates.

- **Unbilled Costs by Job**—You might have assigned costs to a particular job (for example, you might have paid a subcontractor and indicated on the bill that the costs relate to a particular job), but perhaps those costs have not yet been billed. Your company is out the money and will eventually recoup it, but for now the costs are unbilled. To view a summary of all costs you have assigned to jobs but have not yet billed, open the Reports menu, choose A/R Reports, and then choose Unbilled Costs by Job. Each job is listed individually on the report, showing the source of the unbilled costs and the amount not yet billed to the job.

Troubleshooting

Overriding the Estimate

The job costs were higher than expected and the amounts that appear on the customer's invoice are different from the original estimate.

The estimate can be used as a guide for creating your invoice, but you always have the right to override the estimate, assuming that you have advised your customer that the estimate is just an estimate, and that the actual costs might differ.

Removing an Estimate

I created an estimate but didn't get the job. The estimate continues to appear on my Estimate vs. Actual Report. How do I remove the estimate from the system?

You can delete the estimate by opening the estimate form and choosing Edit, Delete Estimate, or by pressing Ctrl+D with the estimate form active. Unfortunately, there is not a report filter that enables you to filter out estimates with a Not Awarded or Closed status.

CHAPTER 11

INVOICING, MONTHLY STATEMENTS, AND ACCOUNTS RECEIVABLE

In this chapter

Creating an Invoice   184

Creating a Monthly Statement   188

Tracking Accounts Receivable   191

Your company might be immensely successful when it comes to earning money, but that success is diminished if you don't possess the tools for collecting the money in a timely manner.

The process of collecting money includes preparing and sending invoices to your customers, following up on late payments with monthly statements, assessing finance charges to encourage timely payment of invoices, and learning to use an accounts receivable aging schedule to help you budget and plan for overdue payments.

CREATING AN INVOICE

Unless your customers pay you in cash at the time of sale or at the time that you perform a service for them, you need to send invoices so that there is a paper record of the amount due.

The invoice provides your customer with a receipt for the purchase of merchandise or services and sets out exactly how much is owed.

When you create an invoice, your income account is increased by the amount of the invoice, and your accounts receivable account is increased as well.

You might find it convenient to create an invoice every time you complete a sale or a project, or you might wait to create invoices on a schedule, for example on one particular day each week. Whether you create one invoice at a time or prepare many invoices at once, the process is the same.

→ If you use the Estimating feature in QuickBooks Pro, and want to prepare invoices directly from your estimates, **see p. 176**.

Note Some of the fields to which I refer in the following steps might not appear on your invoice form. The style of form that you choose controls which fields are present.

If you used the EasyStep Interview to set up your company, you were asked if you wanted to use one of four types of invoice forms: professional, service, product, or custom. Choosing an invoice style in the interview doesn't prevent you from using one of the other styles. The style you choose is the one that appears by default when you begin creating an invoice.

The following types of invoices are available in QuickBooks:

- **Professional invoice**—Includes the following fields: Terms, Item, Description, Quantity, Rate, and Amount.
- **Service invoice**—Includes the following fields: P.O. Number, Terms, Item, Quantity, Description, Rate, and Amount.
- **Product invoice**—Includes the following fields: Ship To, P.O. Number, Terms, Rep, Ship, Via, FOB, Quantity, Item Code, Description, Price Each, and Amount.

- **Custom invoice**—Can be *customized* (*page 338*) to include any of the fields from other invoice styles and any other fields that are useful to you.

Follow these steps to create an invoice:

1. Choose Activities, Create Invoices (Ctrl+I), or click the Invoice button on your iconbar. The Create Invoices window appears (see Figure 11.1).

Choose an invoice style by clicking here.

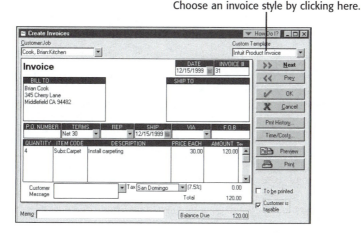

Figure 11.1
The fields that you see on your invoice depend on the type of template style you choose.

2. In the Customer:Job area of the invoice form, click the arrow to display a list of all customers (and jobs, if you use the job feature in QuickBooks). Choose a customer (and related job) from the list, or click Add New at the top of the list to set up a new customer name.

3. Verify that the correct template is in use by examining the list of available forms in the template area of the invoice form. To choose a different form, click the down arrow in the template area and choose from the drop-down list.

4. Verify that the date shown is the date that you want to appear on the invoice. Change to the correct date if necessary.

Tip #29 from
Gail Perry

Do you date your invoice as of the date that you completed the job, as of the date on which you prepare the invoice, or as of the date on which you plan to put the invoice in the mail? The date you use on your invoice is especially significant if you assess finance charges for late invoices, and if those finance charges are based on how many days past the invoice date a payment is received. Choose whether you want finance charges assessed based on the invoice date or the due date by setting a preference for one or the other. See "Sales and Customer Preferences" in Chapter 22 for more information.

5. QuickBooks automatically assigns an invoice number and increments the numbers by one each time you create a new invoice. Verify that the number that appears is the correct number.

→ QuickBooks has a warning system to keep you from issuing duplicate invoice numbers. To learn more about this feature, **see p. 402**.

6. The Bill To address appears automatically when you choose a customer for this invoice. Verify that the information is correct, and make any necessary changes. If changes need to be made to the customer address information, choose Lists, Customers, and then double-click on the customer name. Make your changes, and then close the customer windows; you are returned to your invoice form.

7. Depending on the type of invoice template you choose, there might be a Ship To address field (the product invoice form includes a Ship To address field, and your custom invoice form can include this area as well). If the Ship To address field appears, the address fills in automatically. Verify that the information is correct, and make any necessary changes.

8. Enter a P.O. number, if applicable. This number appears on the purchase order that is issued by your customer.

9. In the Terms area of the invoice, click the down arrow to view a list of available payment terms, and then click the terms that you want to use. This information might appear automatically, if you have already *associated payment terms* with this customer.

10. In the Rep field, click the down arrow to see the initials of your sales representatives and select the appropriate initials.

11. The Ship field contains the date that the product shipped. Verify that this date is correct and change it if necessary.

12. Choose the appropriate shipment carrier by clicking the down arrow in the Via field. Enter the appropriate FOB status in the FOB field. You can instruct QuickBooks to fill in both the shipment carrier and the FOB status on your invoices by choosing File, Preferences, and then clicking the Sales & Customers icon. Choose the Company Preferences tab and enter the standard shipment information that you want to automatically appear on your invoices.

Tip #30 from

Gail Perry

FOB is an abbreviation for the phrase, *Free on Board*, which is a term used to describe when ownership of a product is transferred. Typically, if the FOB is your business location, the ownership transfers to the new owner as soon as the shipment leaves your location. If the FOB is the customer's location, the shipment is owned by you until it reaches the customer. The significance of FOB comes into play when determining who must pay the shipping costs for the item—typically the shipping costs are paid by the company that owns the product during transit. Additional concerns are liability and insurance. If the shipment is damaged, which company is responsible, and which company insures the product during shipment? These are factors to consider and discuss with your customers before a sale is consummated.

13. Click in the Item column of the invoice and a down arrow appears. Click the arrow to display a list of all the items that your company sells. Click an item on the list to place the item on your invoice. Click Add New at the top of the list if the item you want is not on this list. The item name and description fills in automatically. The price can fill in as well. Verify that all information relating to the item is correct, and make any necessary changes. Enter a quantity for this item, if the quantity field is available on this invoice form. QuickBooks calculates the amount due.
14. Click again in the Item column to add additional items to this invoice.

> **Note** To delete an item from an invoice (or from any form), click the line containing the item. Right-click to display a pop-up menu. Choose Delete Line. The item is removed from the invoice.

15. If you have charged time to this customer through the QuickBooks Timer feature or through your payroll, or if you have charged expenses to this customer and are expecting reimbursement, you can automatically transfer these items to the invoice by clicking the Time/Costs button. Any amounts charged to this customer appear on a Choose Billable Time and Costs window where you can check off any items that you want to transfer to this invoice.
16. Click in the Tax column across from the item if you expect to collect sales tax on this item. A *T* appears in the field, indicating that the item is taxable. The *T* can appear automatically, depending on how the item was set up.
17. If you are charging sales tax, verify that the correct taxing authority has been selected in the Tax field under the item area of the invoice. To change the tax, click the down arrow in the Tax field and choose the correct taxing authority. Click Add New at the top of the drop-down list to add a new tax item.
18. Click the arrow in the Customer Message area to choose an optional customer message. Click Add New to add a new message.
19. The Memo area at the bottom of the invoice form is optional, and you can enter any information you want in this area. The memo does not appear on the printed copy of the invoice; however, this information appears on statements issued to this customer (see "Creating a Monthly Statement" later in this chapter), and on reports that include this invoice. There is no limit to the number of characters you can enter in this field.
20. Click the Preview button to see how this invoice will look before you print.
21. Click the Print button to print this invoice immediately. Alternatively, click To be printed to place a check mark in this box if you want to hold this invoice for future printing. The invoice is held by QuickBooks until you are ready to print invoices. To print all invoices, choose File, Print Forms, Print Invoices. The Select Invoices to Print window appears, and you can check off all the invoices that you want to print.
22. Click the Next button if you are finished entering information on this invoice and want to proceed to the next invoice. Click the OK button if you are finished entering all

invoices; the invoice window closes. Clicking the Cancel button closes this invoice window without saving the invoice.

The invoice process might seem like a lot of steps, but when you use the form regularly, you will find that the process becomes automatic.

CREATING A MONTHLY STATEMENT

Although it would be nice if everyone paid on time, chances are that you will have customers who are slow with their payments. One way to remind customers that they have payments due is to send monthly statements.

You can create statements in QuickBooks that summarize all outstanding amounts for a customer. You can also instruct QuickBooks to assess finance charges to late invoices and list these charges on your statements.

Use the following steps to create a monthly statement:

1. Choose Activities, Create Statements. The Select Statements to Print window appears.
2. By default, QuickBooks uses a standard statement form (see Figure 11.2). If you have created a *custom statement (see page 358)*, or if you want to create a custom statement at this time, click the down arrow in the Print format field and choose the statement style that you prefer.

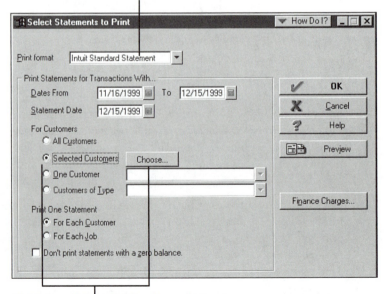

Figure 11.2
Choose which customers will receive statements.

3. Click the Finance Charges button to pop up the Assess Finance Charges window, which shows all the customers with overdue balances (see Figure 11.3). Uncheck any customer who won't be assessed a finance charge.

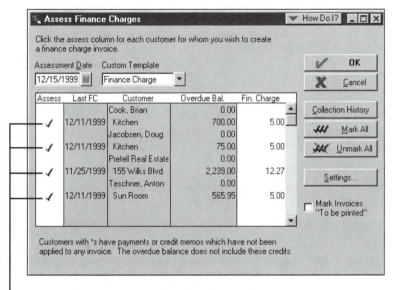

Figure 11.3
You can include or exclude specific customers when assessing finance charges.

Each customer who needs to be assessed has a check mark.

4. Choose the range of dates for which you want to prepare statements. All customers for whom charges were assessed (finance charges or regular invoice charges) during the specified date range are considered for statements.

5. Verify the date that appears on the statements in the Statement Date field.

Frustrated that you can't display your statements onscreen? **See** "Troubleshooting" at the end of this chapter for some pointers.

6. Select the type of customer for whom you want to prepare statements, and then click OK to return to the Select Statements to Print screen:

    - **All Customers**—Statements are issued for all customers with outstanding invoices and finance charges issued during the period that you indicated in step 3.

    - **Selected Customers**—Click the Choose button (see Figure 11.2) to view a list of all customers. Click each customer or job for which you want to print a statement. This list is a little misleading because it lists all customers and jobs—even if there are no amounts due from the customers—and you can't see if any amounts are due. If you check a customer from whom no amount is due, a statement with a zero balance is prepared. You can click on a customer, and then click the Collection History button to see a detailed list of outstanding transactions with this customer.

- **One Customer**—Choose this option if you want to prepare a statement for one particular customer, and then indicate the name of the customer or job for which you want to prepare the statement.
- **Customers of Type**—If you designate *types* for your customers (*see page 154*), you can request that statements be prepared for customers of a particular type.

7. Indicate if you want to print statements for each customer, or separate statements for each job.
8. Check the box at the bottom of the window to prevent QuickBooks from printing statements with zero balances.
9. Click the Preview button to examine statements before printing.
10. Click the OK button when you have finished selecting statement options. The Print Statements window appears (see Figure 11.4). There is no option for saving statements to print at a later date—they must be printed at the time that they are created.
11. In the Print Statements window, indicate if the statements are to be printed on Preprinted forms, Blank pages, or Letterhead.
12. Click the Print button to print the statements.

Figure 11.4
You must print statements at the time that they are created.

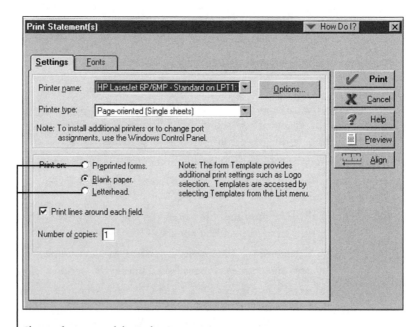

Choose from one of these three paper types.

Tip #31 from Gail Perry
If one statement does not print properly and you have to reprint it, be sure to mark *VOID* across the incorrect statement so that you do not send it to the customer by mistake.

Many companies find that if they follow a practice of sending monthly statements and assessing finance charges for late payments, their customers are more likely to pay on time.

Tracking Accounts Receivable

The balance in the accounts receivable account is the total of all amounts due to your company. Every time you record an invoice or a finance charge, this balance increases. Each time you record a payment against an invoice, the balance in accounts receivable is reduced.

Tip #32 from Gail Perry
From time to time you need to monitor the level at which your accounts receivable increase or decrease. Unless you have made a change to your company's credit policy, receivables need to increase or decrease at a rate comparable to your level of income. If your income increased 15 percent this year over last year, expect an increase in your receivables of roughly 15 percent as well.

→ To learn more about recording payments received, **see p. 198**.

You can view all the transactions that have passed through your accounts receivable account by examining the accounts receivable register. In addition, there are several reports that you can view or print that give you information about amounts that are currently due.

Viewing the Accounts Receivable Register

The accounts receivable register contains every transaction that has occurred in the accounts receivable account since you started recording information for your company. This means that the register information can go back several years.

You can easily obtain a customer's history from the accounts receivable register. You can also view and edit the form from which an accounts receivable transaction was created.

To open the accounts receivable register, choose Lists, Chart of Accounts; or press Ctrl+A. Click the Accounts Receivable account, and then click the Activities button in the Chart of Accounts window. Choose Use Register; the accounts receivable register appears onscreen (see Figure 11.5). Alternatively, double-click on Accounts Receivable in the Chart of Accounts list.

Scroll through the register to view past transactions. Click a customer name, and then click the Q-Report button at the bottom of the register window to view a report showing all transactions for that customer.

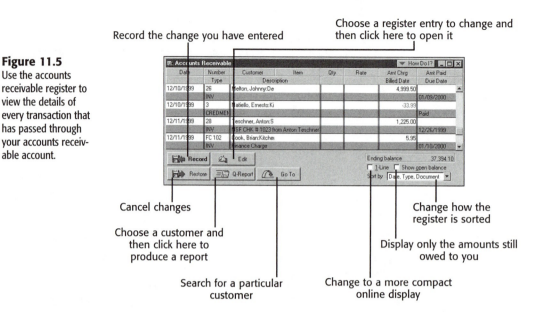

Figure 11.5
Use the accounts receivable register to view the details of every transaction that has passed through your accounts receivable account.

To find a particular customer, click the Go To button. In the Go To window that appears, choose Payee/Name as the field to search, and then enter the customer name (and job name, if applicable) in the Search for field. Click the Next button to proceed through the register, stopping on each occurrence of that customer or job. Or click the Prev button to progress backward through the register.

Double-click any entry in the accounts receivable register to view the form that created the entry. If there is an error on the form, you can edit the invoice, credit memo, or customer payment form and click OK in the form to save your changes.

Either click the x in the upper-right corner of the accounts receivable window or press the Esc key to close the window.

Accounts Receivable Reports

Several QuickBooks standard reports help you examine the contents of your accounts receivable register. Choose Reports from the overhead menu, and then choose A/R Reports to view accounts receivable reports. Depending on the information that you want to find, choose from the following reports:

- **Aging Summary**—The Accounts Receivable Aging Summary report shows the total amount due for each customer and job, with a breakdown of how much has been due for under 30 days, 31–60 days, 61–90 days, and more than 90 days. Use this report to determine which customers might be candidates for formal collection proceedings. Print this report monthly and examine the reports over a period of time to determine whether your collection processes are giving you the results that you desire. Determine when payments are normally received (more than 30 days but within 60 days, for example) to aid in budgeting and projecting cash flow.

- **Aging Detail**—The Accounts Receivable Aging Detail report gives you a breakdown of every amount due from every customer and job, with information on exactly how many days an amount is overdue. The report information is grouped by how many days the amounts are overdue (current receivables are listed first, and then amounts up to 30 days overdue, and so on). Use this report in conjunction with the Aging Summary report to determine exactly which parts of a customer's billing are overdue and need collection attention. If a customer is late in paying every bill, you might want to rethink the credit that you extend to the customer. If the customer is late on only one bill, consider that the bill might have gotten misplaced.

> **Tip #33 from**
>
> Don't sit idly by and allow your customers to determine when it's most convenient for them to pay you. If it seems that the amounts in your accounts receivable account are getting a little moldy, you can encourage your customers to keep up with their bills by offering discounts for early payment, or by charging penalties for late payment.

- **Open Invoices**—Much like the Aging Detail report, the Open Invoices report shows the detail of all amounts due for each customer and job. The items on this report are grouped by customer and job, whereas the items on the Aging Detail report are grouped by when the invoices are due.

- **Collections**—To be used when preparing to make contact with customers who have overdue balances, the Collections report includes the details of all overdue amounts, grouped by customer and job, and includes the contact name and phone number of the customer.

- **Customer Balance Summary**—This report lists each customer with an accounts receivable balance, and the total amount due.

- **Customer Balance Detail**—This report lists each customer and all the transactions that have occurred with each customer. View every invoice, credit memo, and payment made by each customer, and a current balance due from each customer.

- **Unbilled Costs by Job**—View a detailed report of all amounts that have been incurred but not yet billed for your jobs. This includes time charged by employees and subcontractors that is billed through to customers and expenses that are billed to customers.

You can view a graph of accounts receivable aging by choosing Reports, Graphs, Accounts Receivable (see Figure 11.6). Right-click any bar or pie piece of the graph to see the dollar amount that it represents.

Double-click any bar on the main graph screen to see a pie graph of which customers make up the total. Double-click a pie piece to see a detailed report of the transactions for that customer.

Double-click any piece of the pie on the main graph screen to see a bar graph depicting the aging for that particular customer. Double-click any bar of the resulting graph to see a detailed report of all transactions for that customer.

Figure 11.6
The bar graph shows how much of your receivables fall into each of the aging categories. The pie graph shows a section for each customer.

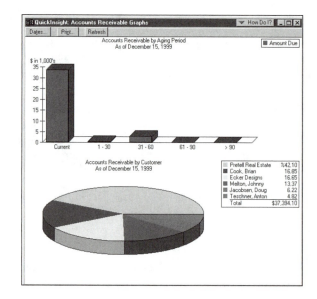

TROUBLESHOOTING

VIEWING OUTSTANDING CUSTOMER TRANSACTIONS

QuickBooks doesn't display my monthly statements before they print. Is there a way to see the detail of the customer's transactions before applying the finance charge?

Although you can't display the actual statement, you can click on a customer name in the Assess Finance Charges window, and then click the Collection History button to see a list of all outstanding transactions with this customer. For more details, open the Customer:Job list—you can do this while the Assess Finance Charges window is still open—and click on a customer name. Then choose Reports, Reports on All Customers:Jobs, A/R Reports, Aging Summary. This report provides you with the details necessary to determine how the finance charges are being computed.

Keeping Track of Customer Payments

I need to keep track of long-term information regarding some customers. If a customer is perpetually late on making payments, how can I record this information to remind myself the next time I do business with him?

You can use the QuickBooks Notes feature to keep track of important information about your customers. Open the Customer:Job List and click in the Notes column next to any customer name. A Notepad window appears in which you can enter any pertinent information about this customer. Each time you open the Customer:Job list in the future, you will see a little notepad icon next to the customers for whom you have entered notes. Double-click on the icon to view the notes for any customers. Also, from any transaction window, you can press Ctrl+L in the Customer:Job field to quickly view the Customer:Job list and see if there are notes about this customer.

CHAPTER 12

Recording Income

In this chapter

Receiving Payments for Your Invoices   198

Receiving Cash   199

Making Deposits   201

Receiving Advances and Down Payments   203

Recording the fruits of your labors is one of the main reasons you invested in QuickBooks. In the last chapter you learned how to create invoices so that you can tell your customers how much they owe you.

In this chapter you learn what to do when your company receives money. You learn how to record full and partial payments, down payments, and retainers. You read about making bank deposits and recording the receipt of cash that isn't associated with an invoice.

Receiving Payments for Your Invoices

When you record an invoice, an account receivable is formed, showing the amount owed from a customer. When you receive money from your customers and associate the receipt of that money with the appropriate invoice, the accounts receivable records are updated, and the amount you received no longer shows as being owed to you.

To record the payment of an invoice, follow these steps:

1. Open the <u>A</u>ctivities menu and choose Receive Payments (or choose Receive Payments from the Sales and Customers tab on the Navigator). The Receive Payments window appears (see Figure 12.1).

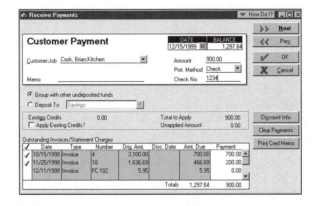

Figure 12.1
Use the Receive Payments window to enter all information about the money you receive and the invoice that generated this income.

2. Click the arrow in the Customer:Job area and choose the name of the customer from whom you received payment. Because you have previously entered an invoice for this customer, the customer name is on the list; you do not have to enter a new customer. Any outstanding invoices for this customer automatically appear in the Outstanding Invoices/Statement Charges area at the bottom of the window.

3. In the Date field, verify the date of this transaction, and change the date if necessary.

4. Enter the amount received from this customer in the Amount field. The amount that you enter should not exceed the amount shown in the Balance field at the top of the form. You can enter an amount that is less than the entire balance due. QuickBooks automatically applies the amount that you enter to outstanding invoices, and to the earliest invoice first. To override this automatic application of payment, see steps 10 and 11.

If you find that the automatic application of your payment to the earliest invoice is regularly a problem, see "Troubleshooting" at the end of this chapter.

5. In the Pmt. Method field, choose the method of payment (Check, Cash, or any of a variety of credit cards), or choose Add New to create a method of payment that is not on this list.

6. In the Check No. field, enter the number from the customer's check, if applicable.

7. Optionally, you can type a memo in the Memo field.

8. If this payment is to be deposited in a group with other payments, choose the Group with other undeposited funds option. If you plan to deposit this payment immediately, click Deposit to and choose the name of the bank account to which it is to be deposited.

→ To learn more about depositing money that you receive, **see p. 201**.

9. If any credits have been issued to this customer, an amount appears in the Existing Credits area of the form. Check the Apply existing credits? box to apply credits to outstanding invoices at this time.

10. If QuickBooks has not applied the payment to the correct invoice, click in the column to the left of any invoice against which this payment is to be applied. A checkmark appears next to each invoice that you click.

11. Verify that the payment amount in the Payment column is correct and is applied to the correct invoice. Make any necessary changes, indicating the amount actually received for each invoice listed.

12. Click Next to save this receipt and proceed to the next one, or click OK to save the receipt and close the Receive Payments window.

Repeat these steps until all the payments have been recorded.

Receiving Cash

Companies that do business in cash, such as retail stores and other types of companies that support walk-in business without prior invoicing, need to enter cash receipts so that income is properly recorded.

The example shown here assumes that you are using the standard QuickBooks Cash Sales form. If you have customized the cash sales form to include fields that are different from the standard form, some of these instructions might not apply.

To enter cash received when there is no invoice relating to the cash, follow these steps:

1. Open the Activities menu and choose Enter Cash Sales. The Enter Cash Sales form appears (see Figure 12.2).

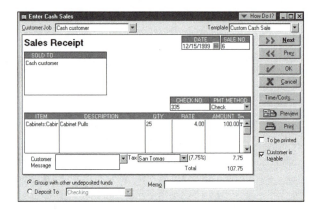

Figure 12.2
Use the Enter Cash Sales form to enter information about money that you receive when there was no previous invoice.

2. Click the arrow in the Customer:Job field and click a customer name (or, if applicable, a job name) from the resulting drop-down list. If the customer name is not on the list, you can choose Add New to add a new customer to the list. If this is a cash sale for which you don't need a customer name, you can leave the customer field blank.

> **Tip #34 from**
> *Gail Perry*
>
> You might want to create a separate customer name for customers whose names you don't know. For example, if yours is a retail store where customers purchase items without disclosing their names, you might want to create a customer name such as *Cash Sale* or *In-store Purchase* to classify these customers. If all similar sales are grouped under one customer name, you can produce reports under that customer name to see how much you earned from cash sales.

3. Verify that the date is correct. If necessary, change the date by clicking the little calendar icon to the right of the DATE field and then clicking the correct date.

4. The SALE NO. automatically increments each time you record a cash sale. You can override this number if you want to use a different number; however, if you override the automatic number with one of your own, QuickBooks ignores your number on the next cash sales form and continues incrementing from the number at which QuickBooks left off. For example, if QuickBooks says this is cash sale number 12 and you change that number to 1012, the next cash sales form displays the number 13—not 1013.

5. In the CHECK NO. field, enter the check number that corresponds to the number on the check you receive from your customer. Entering anything into this field is optional.

6. Choose a method of payment (such as Check, Cash, or any of a variety of credit cards) in the PMT METHOD field if you choose to track the type of payment received.

7. Click in the ITEM column; an arrow appears. Click the arrow and choose an item from the drop-down list. If the item you sold or the service you provided does not appear on the list, click Add New at the top of the list and add the new item.

8. Verify that the description is correct, and make any changes that are necessary.
9. Enter the quantity of the item sold in the QTY column.
10. If the rate is not already filled in correctly, enter the correct amount in the RATE column. QuickBooks calculates the amount based on the entries in the QTY and RATE columns.
11. Optionally, you can enter a customer message. Some choices appear when you click the down arrow next to the Customer Message field—you can use one of these or add a new message to the list.
12. Check the Customer is taxable box at the right of the form if this customer pays sales tax.
13. Choose the taxing authority if any items on this form are subject to sales tax. Verify the sales tax rate. QuickBooks calculates the amount of sales tax.

→ To learn more about grouping items for the purpose of applying different sales tax rates, **see p. 210**.

14. If this payment is to be combined with other funds for deposit at a later time, click the Group with other undeposited funds button at the bottom of the form. Otherwise, click the Deposit to button and indicate the account to which this amount is to be deposited.
15. Optionally, you can enter a memo at the bottom of the form. This Memo area is for your onscreen benefit only and does not print with the form.
16. Click the Next button to save this form and proceed to the next Enter Cash Sales form. Or, if you have finished entering cash sales, click the OK button to save and close this form.

Repeat the preceding steps until all cash sales have been recorded. In a retail setting, you might leave this form onscreen for the entire day while the store is open, recording all the sales of the day.

Making Deposits

After you enter the payments that you receive (both payments against invoices and cash payments without invoices), you need to record a deposit to your bank account. Until you record the deposit in QuickBooks, the undeposited amount is listed on your balance sheet as an Other Current Asset called Undeposited Funds. The balance in your cash account is not affected by the deposit until the deposit is actually recorded.

When you are ready to make a deposit, follow these steps:

1. Open the Activities menu and choose Make Deposits, and the Payments to Deposit window appears (see Figure 12.3). All undeposited funds are listed in this window.

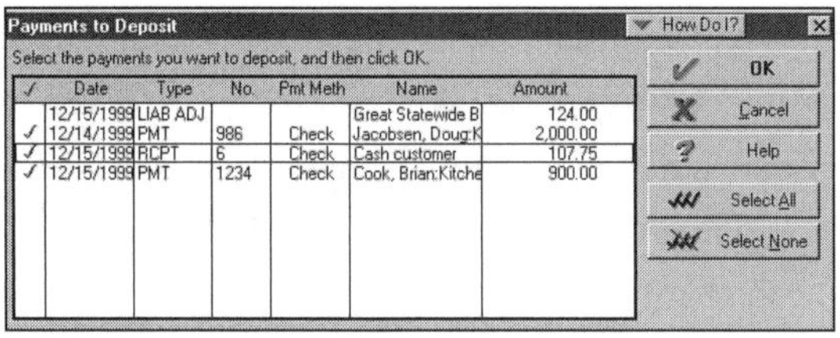

Figure 12.3
You can check any or all items on the Payments to Deposit screen to add them to your deposit.

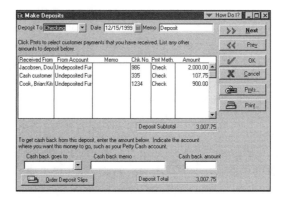

2. Click to the left of all the items that you want to deposit to place a checkmark next to each item; then click OK. The Make Deposits window appears (see Figure 12.4).

Figure 12.4
The amounts listed in the Make Deposits window agree exactly with the amount that you deposit in your bank account.

3. In the Deposit To field, select the account to which this deposit is to be made. Deposits can only be made to one account at a time. If you plan to deposit to more than one account, you need to repeat these steps for the other accounts. For example, you might have received $5,000 from one customer and plan to deposit $3,000 to checking and $2,000 to savings. Make one deposit to your checking account, showing only $3,000 as the deposit (see step 5). Make a different deposit to your savings account, showing the remaining $2,000 as the deposit.

4. Verify that the date in the Date field matches the date of the actual deposit.

5. Verify that the amounts in the Amount column agree with the amounts that you plan to deposit. If there is a discrepancy (as in step 3, for example), you can change the amounts in the amount column.

6. Did you forget to check something off on the Payments to Deposit window, or did you check something by mistake? Click the P<u>m</u>ts button in the Make Deposits window if you need to return to the Payments to Deposit window.

7. If you plan to withdraw cash from this deposit, fill in the bottom part of the window: Enter the account that is affected by the cash withdrawal (such as Petty Cash), enter an optional memo regarding the cash withdrawal, and enter the amount that you intend to withdraw.

8. Click the Print button if you want to print a deposit slip and a deposit summary. You also have the option of printing a deposit summary only. You can order pre-printed deposit slips from Intuit (click the Order Deposit Slips button in the Make Deposits window for more information) for use with QuickBooks. Otherwise, you can choose to print the deposit summary and fill out your own deposit slip.
9. Click Next to record your deposit information and proceed to another Make Deposits window, or click OK to record your deposit information and close the window.

I recommend printing deposit summaries (see step 7 in the previous exercise) and saving them in a notebook or file so that they are easy to find. Deposit summaries provide useful information at the end of the month when you *reconcile your bank account* (*page 248*).

Receiving Advances and Down Payments

Sometimes you might receive money in the form of an advance from a customer for whom you have agreed to perform some work, as a retainer from a client who plans to use your services in the future, or as a down payment on a future purchase.

If you created an invoice for a prepayment from a customer or client, treat the receipt of cash just as you treat any money received against an invoice (see the section "Receiving Payments for Your Invoices").

If, however, the customer gives you a down payment and you have not created any paperwork for this amount, you can still deposit the money to your bank.

Use the following steps to record deposits:

1. Open the Activities menu and choose Make Deposits. The Payments to Deposit window appears, with all undeposited funds listed. Because the advance payment is not related to an invoice, it is not listed with any other undeposited funds.
2. From the list of undeposited funds, you can check any items that you want to deposit at this time. The list might be blank if all other money has been deposited. Click the OK button, and the Make Deposits window appears.
3. Choose the account in which you plan to deposit the money.
4. Verify that the Date field reflects the actual date of the deposit.
5. Click in the Received From column of the Make Deposits window. If items are already listed in this column, click in the white area beneath the list. An arrow appears.
6. Click the arrow in the Received From column and choose the name of the customer or client from whom you received this money. If the customer is not on the list, click Add New to add a new customer.
7. In the Amount column, enter the amount that you plan to deposit.

8. Click in the From Account column; an arrow appears. Click the arrow to see a drop-down list showing all your accounts.

9. Click the account in which you want to record this advance payment. The account is probably a current liability account and might have a name such as Advances, Downpayments, Prepayments, or Retainers. If this is the first time you have entered a prepayment, you might need to click Add New to add the account to your account list.

10. In the appropriate columns, enter any optional memo, check number, and payment method information that you want to record with this transaction.

11. Click OK when you finish entering information.

When you perform the work for which you received a prepayment, create an invoice for the work just as you do under normal circumstances. The process of creating the invoice increases your income account by the amount of the job.

Creating an invoice also increases your accounts receivable account. Because you have already received the cash from your customer (so there is no accounts receivable), you need to create a general journal entry to remove the amount from your accounts receivable account (credit) and also to remove the amount from the down-payment liability account (debit).

Troubleshooting

The Automatic Payment Application Feature

QuickBooks automatically applies customer payments to the oldest outstanding invoice. The problem is that sometimes I forget to change this and the payment gets applied incorrectly. Is there a way to tell QuickBooks not to apply the payment so that I am forced to look at the invoices and associate the payment with the correct charge?

You can turn off this automatic payment application feature by choosing File, Preferences, and then clicking on the Sales & Customers icon. Choose the Company Preferences tab, and uncheck the Automatically apply payments box. Click OK to save your change.

Payment Details

I received a payment from a customer and want to quickly find out what invoices that payment covered.

Open the Chart of Accounts list (Ctrl+A), and then double-click on the Accounts Receivable account. The Accounts Receivable register appears. You can double-click on any Amount Paid transaction in the Accounts Receivable register to see the details of the payment.

CHAPTER 13

REPORTING SALES TAX

In this chapter

Understanding How Sales Tax Works   206

Getting Ready to Collect Sales Tax   206

Creating a Sales Tax Item   207

Charging Sales Tax to Customers   210

Taxable Versus Non-Taxable Sales   212

Tax-Exempt Sales   212

Monthly Sales Tax Reports   213

Paying Sales Tax   214

If you sell items at retail and the items you sell qualify for sales tax, you are expected to collect sales tax from your customers at the time of the sale.

In QuickBooks, you can set up a sales tax item with a fixed percent so that QuickBooks can calculate the sales tax for you and make the assessment on your invoice. You have the capability to set up more than one sales tax item, so if you sell in different locations—each with its own sales tax rate and taxing authority—QuickBooks tracks the amount of sales tax you owe to each government agency. If you are required to charge different rates of sales tax for different types of sales, you can set up a separate item for each rate, and then choose the applicable rate on your invoice form.

Understanding How Sales Tax Works

When you issue an invoice or record a cash sale for a taxable item, QuickBooks adds the sales tax to the total sale and records an increase to your sales tax payable account.

At regular intervals, you will create sales tax reports and pay the amount due to each appropriate government agency. These payment intervals are determined by the government to which you pay the sales tax and are based on how much sales tax you charge over a certain period of time. Companies that don't have many taxable sales do not have to remit sales tax as frequently as companies that sell taxable items every day.

QuickBooks establishes a sales tax payable account when you set up your company. The government agency to which you pay the sales tax is set up as a sales tax item. Sales tax reports are created based on each government agency or each sales tax item.

Contact your state revenue department for specific rules on collecting and paying sales tax in your state. If you do business in more than one state, you might be responsible for paying sales tax in other states as well. Addresses and telephone numbers for all state revenue departments are listed in Appendix D, "State Revenue Agencies."

Getting Ready to Collect Sales Tax

If you indicated in the EasyStep Interview that you plan to collect sales tax, QuickBooks set up a sales tax payable account for you. This liability account tracks the sales tax that you bill to your customers and is relieved each time you make a remittance of sales tax to the taxing authority. If you already have a sales tax liability account, you can skip this section.

If you didn't initially set up sales tax but you want to set it up now, follow these steps to create your sales tax payable account:

1. Choose Lists, Chart of Accounts (Ctrl+A). The Chart of Accounts window appears.
2. Click the Account button at the bottom of the window and choose New (Ctrl+N). The New Account window appears (see Figure 13.1).

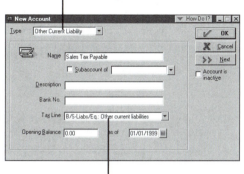

Classify Sales Tax Payable as an Other Current Liability.

Figure 13.1
Set up your Sales Tax Payable liability account so that QuickBooks can track how much sales tax you owe to the government.

Fill in the tax line information if you plan to use QuickBooks to help prepare your income tax return.

3. Click the down arrow in the Type field and choose Other Current Liability.
4. In the Name field, enter *Sales Tax Payable* as the name of the new account.
5. If you use tax lines and your business entity type is something other than a sole proprietorship (such as a corporation or a partnership), choose B/S-Liabs/Eq.: Other current liabilities for your Tax Line.
6. If you have already been collecting sales tax and a balance exists in your liability account, enter that amount as the Opening Balance. Choose the date that you want to use to start tracking sales tax liability.
7. Click OK to close this window and save your entries.

Use the next step to set up your sales tax items. The items are the actual rates that you charge your customers.

CREATING A SALES TAX ITEM

A sales tax item is created for each type of sales tax that you pay. Depending on where you do business, you might pay sales tax to many different states—or one state might require different sales tax rates for different types of taxable items. Each rate and each government require a separate sales tax item.

Tip #35 from Gail Perry

> Some companies have to charge different rates of sales tax for the various types of items they sell. Food sold in a food store might be taxed at one rate, for example, but food prepared and sold for consumption in a restaurant might be taxed at a different rate. If you own a restaurant that is combined with a specialty food store, you might be required to charge sales tax at two different rates. Each rate is set up as a separate item in QuickBooks.

By creating separate sales tax items for each rate and government you pay, charging sales tax to your customers is a simple matter of selecting the appropriate sales tax item from a drop-down list on the invoice or cash sale form. QuickBooks takes it from there, calculating the sales tax due and adding it to the balance due from the customer. At the same time, your sales tax payable account is increased, keeping track of the amount that you owe to the government for tax on items sold.

SETTING UP A SALES TAX ITEM

The EasyStep Interview enables you to set up only one sales tax item. If you need more than one sales tax item, you must set up the additional item(s) yourself. Following is the procedure that you perform after the interview to set up your sales tax items.

Use the following step to set up a sales tax item:

1. Choose Lists, Items. The Item List window appears.
2. Click the Item button and choose New. The New Item window appears.
3. From the Type list, choose Sales Tax Item (see Figure 13.2).
4. Enter a name for the type of tax. You are limited to 13 characters, including spaces. This is the name that you refer to when choosing which tax to apply. If I am charging Indiana Sales tax of 5 percent, for example, my name might be *Ind Tax 5%*.

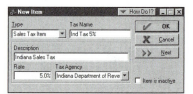

Figure 13.2

5. Enter a description for the tax. The description appears on your customer invoices.
6. Enter the rate at which this tax is to be calculated. QuickBooks assumes that you are entering a percentage, so you don't need to type the percent symbol. Five percent is entered as 5, five and one-half percent is entered as 5.5, and so on.
7. Enter the name of the tax agency to which you make payments of this tax. This tax agency is set up as one of your vendors.
8. Click OK. If the tax agency has not yet been set up as a vendor, you are asked to set it up at this time (see Figure 13.3). Choosing Quick Add enables you to set up only the name of the vendor, but no additional information (such as the agency address). Choosing Set up provides you with a setup screen for entering all pertinent information about the tax agency.

Figure 13.3

→ To learn more about setting up vendors, including sales tax agencies, **see p. 152**.

Telling QuickBooks to Charge Sales Tax

Before you can begin using the sales tax feature in QuickBooks, you must indicate to QuickBooks that you plan to charge sales tax. Otherwise, no option is available for charging tax on your invoice forms.

Note that you must set up your sales tax items before completing these steps.

> **Tip #36 from**
> *Gail Perry*
>
> If you need to charge your customers more than one type of sales tax, you might want to consider setting up a sales tax group. With a group, you include multiple tax assessments under one title. If you need to collect both county and state sales tax, for example, your group might be called simply *Sales Tax*, and that is the name that appears on invoices. The assessment, however, combines rates from both taxing authorities. To create a sales tax group, set up a new item by choosing Sales Tax Group as the item type. A checklist appears in which you check off each of the sales tax items that you want to include in the group. All your sales tax items must be set up before you can create a group.

Use the following steps to set up sales tax:

1. Choose File, Preferences. The Preferences window appears.
2. Click the Sales Tax icon on the left. You might need to scroll through the list to find this icon. Choose the Company Preferences tab.
3. Choose Yes in answer to the question, "Do You Charge Sales Tax?"
4. Indicate whether you expect to pay sales tax monthly, quarterly, or annually. If you are new to collecting and paying sales tax, your state government provides you with this information.
5. Indicate that your company is a cash basis or accrual basis company by choosing whether you owe sales tax As of invoice date (accrual basis) or Upon receipt of payment (cash basis).
6. Choose the sales tax item that you charge most frequently as the Most common sales tax. If you don't charge one type of sales tax any more frequently than any other type, you must still select one sales tax item. This item appears automatically on your invoice forms, but you can always choose a different tax item if necessary.
7. If you want QuickBooks to print a *T* on customer invoices next to taxable items, check the box at the bottom of the window.
8. Click OK to save your changes. The Updating Sales Tax window might appear (see Figure 13.4).
9. In the Updating Sales Tax window, indicate whether all current customers need to be designated as subject to sales tax, and whether all existing inventory and non-inventory part items that you sell need to be designated as taxable. Click OK to close this window.

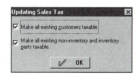

Figure 13.4

In the future, when you set up new customers you will notice an option in the customer setup screen for designating the customer as subject to sales tax (see Figure 13.5). Check the box to enable QuickBooks to charge sales tax to this customer.

Figure 13.5
The customer setup screen includes an option to designate whether a customer is subject to sales tax.

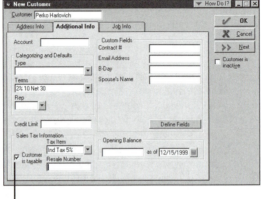

Click here to turn on sales tax for this customer.

When you set up new inventory or non-inventory part items, you have the opportunity to indicate whether the item is subject to sales tax (see Figure 13.6).

Figure 13.6
The item setup screen includes an option to designate whether an inventory item is taxable.

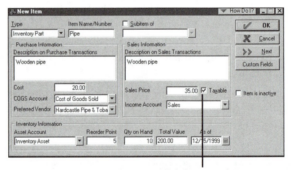

Click here so that QuickBooks charges tax when you sell this item.

Charging Sales Tax to Customers

Tip #37 from
Gail Perry

If you have customers who purchase various items that are subject to different sales tax rates, you can't use the sales tax rate at the bottom of the invoice because this rate applies to the entire invoice. To apply separate rates to different items on the invoice, use a sales tax rate of 0 percent at the bottom of the invoice, and then enter tax items as needed in the item list of the invoice (see Figure 13.8). You might need to subtotal the items that are subject to tax, and then apply the tax rate to the subtotal.

When a customer purchases a taxable item from you, indicate the correct tax amount on the invoice or cash sale form.

Use the following steps to apply sales tax to a purchase:

1. Prepare the invoice as you normally do, including the customer name, job name (if applicable), terms, and items sold.
2. In the Tax area at the bottom of the invoice form (see Figure 13.7), the tax you set up as the common sales tax is already chosen. To accept this tax, do nothing. To switch to a different sales tax, click the drop-down arrow and choose from existing tax items, or click Add New to add a new sales tax item.

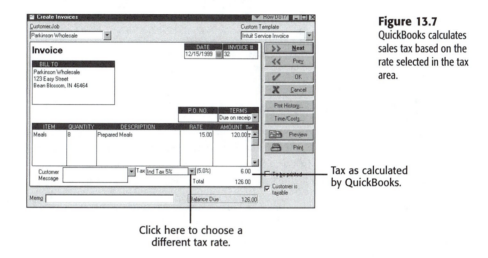

Figure 13.7
QuickBooks calculates sales tax based on the rate selected in the tax area.

3. All items that are subject to sales tax are marked with a *T* in the item area of the invoice. If some items are to be excluded from tax, click the *T* to remove it. If some items need to be taxed but are not marked, click in the Tax column to place a *T* next to the item.

→ To learn more about creating subtotals to be used as items on a form, **see p. 121**.

Figure 13.8
You can calculate sales tax at different rates on one invoice.

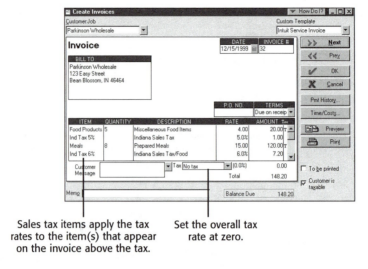

Sales tax items apply the tax rates to the item(s) that appear on the invoice above the tax.

Set the overall tax rate at zero.

TAXABLE VERSUS NON-TAXABLE SALES

If an item you are selling is not subject to sales tax (services such as consulting, legal, or accounting services often are not subject to sales tax), set up this item as nontaxable when it is created (refer to Figure 13.6). In addition, you can double-check your customer invoice to make sure that there is no *T*, which generates a sales tax charge, next to the item.

To determine which items are subject to sales tax, contact your taxing authority. Usually this is the department of revenue for the state in which you live. Each state has different rules regarding which items are subject to sales tax, and sometimes different rates apply to different types of items.

TAX-EXEMPT SALES

Sometimes you sell items that are subject to tax, but you sell them to customers who are exempt from paying sales tax. It is important that you check with your state taxing authority regarding the rules for dealing with tax-exempt customers.

In general, before you can permit a tax-exempt sale, you must request a tax resale number from the customer and keep that number on file. The customer will probably be happy to supply you with this number.

To enter the customer's tax-exempt number, follow these steps:

1. Choose Lists, Customers:Jobs (Ctrl+J). The Customer:Job list window appears.
2. Click the customer name, and then click the Customer:Job button and choose Edit. The Edit Customer window appears.

3. Click the Additional Info tab. At the bottom of the window (as shown in Figure 13.5), uncheck the box indicating that the Customer is taxable and enter the customer's resale number in the space provided.
4. Click OK to save your changes.

The next time you issue an invoice to this customer, no sales tax is calculated.

Monthly Sales Tax Reports

You need to prepare sales tax reports and submit them to your government taxing agency. Generally, these reports are prepared monthly; however, you might report sales tax less frequently, depending on the rules of your state.

→ To find a complete listing of taxing agencies for all states, **see p. 513**.

Although QuickBooks prepares your sales tax payment for you (see "Paying Sales Tax" later in this chapter), it is up to you to prepare the tax form required by your government.

Because each state requires a different tax form, QuickBooks is not equipped to produce the actual forms for you. However, you can produce reports in QuickBooks that provide you with all the information that you need to prepare your monthly sales tax reports.

Follow these steps to produce the Sales Tax Liability report:

1. Choose Reports, A/P Reports. A side menu appears.
2. Choose Sales Tax Liability Report. The report that appears includes total sales, nontaxable sales, taxable sales, tax rate, the total tax due for the current period, and the total tax due for all your taxing jurisdictions (see Figure 13.9).

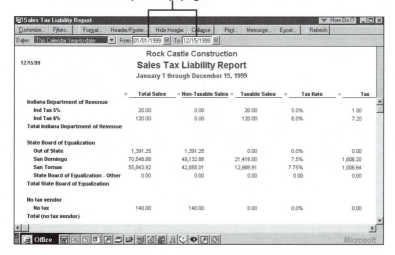

Figure 13.9
Prepare this report so that you can see exactly how much sales tax you owe.

3. At the top of the report window, verify that the dates agree with the period for which you are paying tax. If you pay monthly, you want to produce a report for the prior month. However, if you want to view the amount of tax you owe so far for the current month, change the dates to reflect the current date.

4. Print a copy of the report by clicking the Print button at the top of the report.

In addition to the Monthly Sales Tax Report, you can produce a quick report showing the detailed transactions that make up your tax liability. Choose Lists, choose Items, click the name of the taxing authority, click the Reports button, and choose QuickReport. Adjust the dates on the report so that the detail you view is for the correct time period. Double-click any item on this report to see the invoice or cash sale form that generated the tax.

Paying Sales Tax

QuickBooks is ready to help you make your sales tax payments. Choose Activities, Pay Sales Tax; the Pay Sales Tax window appears (see Figure 13.10). Verify that the date shown in the Show sales tax due through area coincides with the end of the period for which you are paying sales tax (usually, this is the last day of the previous month).

Figure 13.10
Check off the sales tax amounts that you want to pay at this time.

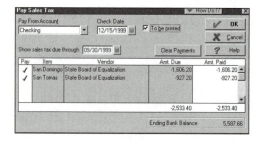

If you pay tax to more than one agency, each agency is listed. Check off all items that you intend to pay at this time. Adjust the amount if you do not intend to pay the full amount due.

Tip #38 from
Gail Perry

The frequency with which you must make sales tax payments is determined by the laws of the taxing agency. Many state and local taxing agencies require monthly payments of sales tax, but check with your government tax agency to be sure. Late sales tax payments are subject to costly fines, so it is imperative that you learn the laws governing your situation.

> **Tip #39 from Gail Perry**
>
> Taxing agencies take a pretty hard line when it comes to collecting tax on time. With sales tax in particular, the government accepts few excuses for late payments because you have already collected the tax from your customers. The penalties are harsh, and the government has the right to seize your company's assets when taxes are not paid. If your company is having cash flow problems, look for other ways to make ends meet rather than holding back taxes owed to the government. While you're at it, take a look at Chapter 26, "Budgeting," where you can find some advice for getting a handle on your finances.

Verify that the account shown at the top of the window is the account from which you want the payment to be drawn. Check the To be printed box if you want QuickBooks to print this check. Leave the box blank if you plan to prepare the check by hand. Click OK and QuickBooks issues the payment for your sales tax.

→ To learn about writing checks in QuickBooks, **see p. 233**.

TROUBLESHOOTING

COLLECTING SALES TAX

I've not collected sales tax before. How do I get started?

Names, addresses, and phone numbers of all state revenue agencies are listed in the back of this book, in Appendix D. Contact the revenue agency for each state in which you do business and ask for a packet of information for a new company collecting sales tax.

NONTAXABLE CUSTOMERS

Some of my customers are tax-exempt; however, most are not, so I've set up my items as taxable items. Do I have to manually remove the sales tax on each invoice to a tax-exempt customer?

Even though your items are taxable, you can indicate right on an invoice form that the customer is not taxable (uncheck the Customer is Taxable checkbox), and no sales tax is applied.

SALES TAX LIABILITY REPORT

I pay sales tax to more than one jurisdiction. When I request the Sales Tax Liability Report I get sales tax owed to all jurisdictions. Is it possible to produce a report for just one jurisdiction at a time?

Produce the Sales Tax Liability Report as you normally do, and then click the Filters button. From the Filter List, choose Item; then, in the Item box, choose the name of the jurisdiction that you want to appear on the report. You can perform this step again to include multiple jurisdictions in the report, or you can remove the filter to include all jurisdictions in the report.

CHAPTER 14

KEEPING TRACK OF YOUR INVENTORY

In this chapter

What is Inventory?   218

Raw Materials, Work in Progress, and Finished Goods   218

Determining the Average Cost of Inventory Items   219

Using the QuickBooks Inventory Features   220

Setting Up Inventory Items On-the-Fly   221

Setting Up Inventory Items in General   223

Editing Items   224

Adding to Your Inventory   224

Reports About Inventory   226

Taking a Physical Inventory Count   227

Adjusting Quantity and Value of Inventory Account   228

Alternatives to the QuickBooks Inventory Feature   229

QuickBooks provides a full, interactive inventory feature that constantly tracks and updates your company's inventory totals. Each time you receive new items in stock, your inventory quantity increases; each time you sell an item, your inventory quantity decreases. A reorder feature reminds you when supplies are getting low, and tells you that you need to order more.

QuickBooks also has a serious shortcoming in the area of valuing inventory: The only way that QuickBooks provides to value inventory is the *weighted average* method. Many Companies need to use other methods to value their inventory items. The weighted average method of valuation is described in this chapter, as are other common methods. This chapter also discusses alternatives to using QuickBooks to account for the value of your inventory.

What is Inventory?

Merchandise that you own and expect to sell to others is *inventory*. Inventory includes finished goods or partly finished goods that you have produced. Raw materials and supplies that will eventually become part of goods available for sale are also considered to be inventory.

Items that you own but have placed on consignment with someone else or on display in a showroom or booth away from your place of business are part of your inventory.

Inventory includes items that you have contracted to sell, but to which you have not yet relinquished ownership.

If a container is sold as part of the inventory item, the container itself is also considered inventory. A container for which a deposit has been received from the customer to guarantee the return of the container is not considered part of inventory.

Inventory is considered a current asset; its value is presented on your balance sheet. The value of your inventory increases the value of your business.

Raw Materials, Work in Progress, and Finished Goods

If your company is a manufacturing company producing products from raw materials or parts and supplies, you will find that QuickBooks falls short of being capable of providing you with the inventory accounting that you need. You can keep track of individual raw material items with the QuickBooks inventory feature, but no provision is made for transferring these items to a Work in Progress or Finished Goods status.

The only way to properly account for manufactured goods in QuickBooks is to record raw materials or parts as inventory items at acquisition. Then, when the end product has been manufactured, create a sale to yourself of all the individual parts, and create a purchase of the finished product item into a new inventory account.

This process of selling yourself parts and purchasing a finished product as a way to record items in inventory is cumbersome, subject to error, and not the way a manufacturing process is envisioned to work. No sale actually occurs—just a change in the status of the inventory items.

QuickBooks doesn't pretend to offer this scenario as a solution to accounting for manufactured inventory. Instead, the makers of the program (in their printed material) recommend against using QuickBooks for tracking manufactured inventory: "If you do manufacturing, do not use the QuickBooks inventory feature."

Determining the Average Cost of Inventory Items

The cost of your inventory is determined by the cost of the merchandise that you purchase for resale. If you are a manufacturer, the cost of your inventory is represented by the cost of materials and supplies that will ultimately become part of your finished goods.

As business unfolds on a day-to-day basis, QuickBooks constantly updates the value of your inventory asset account by using a weighted average method of valuing the inventory that you have on hand.

As each item is added to the total inventory, the cost of the new item is added to the cost of all the pieces of the same item that you have on hand to provide a total. When an item is sold, the total cost of all inventory items is divided by the number of pieces on hand to determine an average cost. This cost is reflected at the time of sale as the cost of sales for the item sold.

This method is contrary to more traditional methods of inventory costing on two levels:

- Although the averaging method of determining the cost of items sold is not uncommon in very small businesses or in businesses where sales of inventory are not a major part of the operation, many companies prefer to use methods of inventory costing that perhaps more accurately reflect the way the company or the industry performs, such as FIFO, LIFO, and Specific Identification (see the following sidebar for descriptions of these methods).

- The more traditional method of accounting for inventory is to charge all purchases of inventory items during the year to a purchases expense account. Then determine the value of your inventory at the end of the year by taking a physical inventory count and using one of the valuation methods to calculate the value of the inventory on hand. The difference between the value of the inventory on hand and the value of the inventory at the last time that you counted gets added to—or deducted from, if the value of inventory has decreased—the purchases expense account in order to determine the cost of sales for the year.

Because QuickBooks does not address these issues of alternative costing and year-end adjustments, you might find the accounting method used for inventory in QuickBooks to be unacceptable. If that is the case, see the "Alternatives to the QuickBooks Inventory Feature" section later in this chapter.

If the average-costing method of valuing inventory is acceptable to you and you appreciate the opportunity to have your inventory updated instantly each time a sale is made, continue with this chapter for more detailed information about how this inventory feature works.

FIFO, LIFO, and Specific Identification: Methods for Valuing Inventory
The three most popular methods of inventory valuation are not supported by QuickBooks:

- **FIFO (First In, First Out)**—Users of this method make the assumption that the first items that you purchase are the first items you sell. You'll notice a grocery store prefers to sell items on this basis, always moving the items with the earliest date to the front of the shelf so that there is never any old stock on hand. The value of inventory at the end of the year (or reporting period) is determined by taking a physical inventory count and then matching the costs of the most recently purchased items to the quantity of items on hand. The cost of the earliest items purchased is then added to the cost of sales. By using this method, your inventory is always valued at its most current cost.

- **LIFO (Last In, First Out)**—Users of this method make the assumption that the last items (the most recent items) that you purchase are the first items you sell. Imagine a clothing store, where the latest fashions are the ones that sell, whereas the older articles of clothing stay on the racks. Items remaining in your inventory are assumed to be the oldest items, and are therefore valued at the cost of the oldest items purchased.

- **Specific Identification Method**—Users of this method have an inventory that lends itself to tracking of individual items. As each item is sold, the value of the inventory on hand is reduced by the actual cost of the specific item. For example, all automobiles have a VIN (Vehicle Identification Number), so it is easy to track automobiles that go in and out of inventory.

Using the QuickBooks Inventory Features

If you choose to use QuickBooks to keep track of your inventory, you will find it is a luxury to know that every single item of your inventory is accounted for on an individual basis. At any time, you can request a report of all inventory items in stock or a complete listing of all items on order.

With the QuickBooks reorder feature, you can indicate a point at which new stock needs to be ordered for each inventory item. Then, when sales of your inventory indicate that quantities are running low, you receive a reminder from the program that it is time to reorder.

Although you can create invoices in QuickBooks for inventory that you do not have in stock, the program gives you a message indicating that present quantities are too low to fill the order for which you are invoicing.

→ To set up inventory and reorder points, **see p. 71**.

SETTING UP INVENTORY ITEMS ON-THE-FLY

When you set up your company with the EasyStep Interview, you might have set up several inventory items. As your business grows, you probably need to set up additional inventory items. You can do this on-the-fly by waiting until you are ready to use the item on a form (such as a purchase order or invoice) and then entering the name of the new item in the Items area of the form. You'll see an Item Not Found window onscreen (see Figure 14.1). To add the item to your inventory list, click the Set Up button. Items must be set up before you can use them; if you click the Cancel button, QuickBooks does not allow you to use the item on your form.

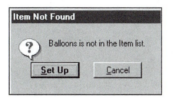

Figure 14.1
Click Set Up if you want QuickBooks to enable you to use your new item.

When you click the Set Up button in the Item Not Found box, the New Item window appears. In this window you set up all the information you have about this new inventory item.

To move from one field to the next in the New Item window, press the Tab key (or press Shift+Tab to move backward through the fields). You can also click in each field. Do not press the Enter key until you are finished entering all the information about this item.

To set up a new inventory item, follow these steps:

1. Verify the description (Inventory Part) that appears in the Type area of the New Item window. If something else appears here, click the drop-down arrow and choose Inventory Part (see Figure 14.2).

2. The item name that you entered on your transaction form appears in the Item Name/Number area. You can revise this if necessary. If this item is to be a *subitem* of another item (*page 126*), check the Subitem of box and choose the item that is the parent of this item.

3. Enter a Description for Purchase Transactions. This description appears on your purchase orders when you order the item, and on your bills when you enter bills that you receive for the item. This description also appears on inventory and purchase reports.

4. Enter the cost that you typically pay for this item. You can override this amount when it appears on a purchase form, and you can also change the amount by editing the item in your Items list (explained later in this chapter). If the cost of the item changes frequently, you might want to leave this area blank; however, QuickBooks uses this amount to estimate the value of any of these items that you currently have on hand (see step 12).

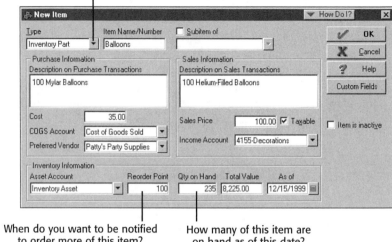

Figure 14.2
Enter all the information about your inventory item in the New Item window.

5. Verify that the Cost of Goods Sold (COGS) account that is shown is the account in which you want to record the cost of purchases of this item. You might have designated subaccounts to identify the costs of specific items sold, or perhaps you set up an account called Purchases instead of Cost of Goods Sold. If the account needs to be changed, click the arrow at the end of the COGS Account field and choose the appropriate account.

6. From the drop-down list in the Preferred Vendor field, choose the name of the vendor that you use most frequently for purchases of this item. If you use this optional field, QuickBooks displays the name of the vendor on your stock status report and your physical inventory worksheet (these reports are discussed later in this chapter).

7. Enter the description that you want to see on sales transaction forms. This description also appears on the invoices that you present to your customers. You can use the same description that you use on your purchase transaction forms.

8. Enter the Sales Price that you generally charge for this item. The amount that you enter appears automatically on invoices for this item. If necessary, you can override this amount on the invoice form. If the sales price changes frequently, you can leave this area blank and fill in the sales price each time you invoice for the item.

9. Choose an Income Account for this item. This is the account in which income from sales of this item is reported.

10. Indicate the Asset Account in which to record the value of this asset. QuickBooks has already chosen an inventory asset account for you, but you might have a specific subaccount where you want to track information about this particular inventory item.

11. Enter a Reorder Point. If the number of pieces of this item drops below this reorder point, you receive a reminder that it is time to reorder.

12. In the Qty on Hand area, enter the number of pieces of this item that you currently own, if any. QuickBooks uses the cost that you entered earlier when calculating the total value of the items that you have on hand.

13. QuickBooks assumes that the information you are entering is current as of today's date. If another date is more appropriate, change the date in the As of field at the bottom of the New Item window.

14. If you want to enter more information about this item but no field is available, you can click the Custom Fields button, and then the Define Fields button to designate up to five custom fields. Enter a description for the field that you want to create (see Figure 14.3), check the Use box to indicate that you want to use this custom field, and then click OK. The custom field(s) you define won't appear on the New Item screen, but they are now available if you click the Custom Fields button. Any custom fields that you create also appear as a choice if you customize a form such as an invoice, so you can choose to have the custom field actually appear on the form.

> **Note**
> Custom fields that you create on one inventory item are made available to every inventory item. Therefore, you only need to create a custom field once to have access to it on all your inventory items.

15. When you finish entering all the information for this new item, click the OK button. The information is saved, the inventory item is added to your Items list, and you are returned to the form on which you were working.

→ To add customized fields to forms, **see p. 354**.

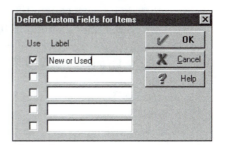

Figure 14.3

Setting Up Inventory Items in General

If you prefer to set up your inventory items all at once rather than on-the-fly, you can open the Items list (from the Lists menu, choose Items, or click the Item button). Click the Item button in the Items List window that appears, and choose New (or press Ctrl+N). The New Item window appears.

Select Inventory Part from the Type drop-down list. Enter all the information for a new item. The fields will differ on this screen depending on the type of item that you choose. Click Next when you're ready to proceed to the next new item. When you have finished entering all items, click OK to close the New Item window.

Editing Items

You can change the specifications of any of your inventory items by displaying the Items List window, clicking the item that you want to change, opening the Item menu, and choosing Edit to open the Edit Item window. Alternatively, click on the item that you want to change and press Ctrl+E, or just double-click on the item to open the Edit item window. Make your changes to any of the fields in this window and then click OK to save your changes.

Adding to Your Inventory

Whether you receive a bill when you receive inventory items or separately from the receipt of the items determines how the receipt of inventory is recorded.

Receiving Items Without a Bill

If you receive the inventory items that you order without an accompanying bill from your supplier, follow these steps to record the receipt of items:

1. Open the Activities menu and choose Inventory; then choose Receive Items from the submenu. (Or, with the Items List open, click the Activities button and choose Receive Items). The Create Item Receipts window appears.

2. Select from the Vendor drop-down list (see Figure 14.4). If a purchase order has been issued for this vendor and items ordered on the purchase order have not yet been received, you see a message onscreen asking if you want to receive against the outstanding order (see Figure 14.5). Click Yes to verify the purchase order(s) to which the received items relate. If no outstanding purchase orders exist for this vendor, skip to step 5.

3. If you have open purchase orders against which you are receiving items, the Open Purchase Orders screen appears, listing the date and purchase order number of each outstanding purchase order for this vendor. Click in the check mark column next to the purchase order that you want to associate with this order (see Figure 14.6). Click OK to return to the Create Item Receipts screen.

4. If you indicated a purchase order in step 3, the items listed on that purchase order appear in the Items area at the bottom of your Create Item Receipts screen. You can change any information in this area so that the items noted on this form correspond to the items actually received. If you want to view the purchase order from which these items were generated, click the Show PO button to display the original purchase order form. Click OK to close the purchase order form.

5. If you did not indicate a purchase order in step 3, click the Items tab in the center of the Create Item Receipts screen. Click in the Item column and then click the arrow to open a list of all items. Choose an item by clicking it, or set up a new item by clicking New Item. Enter the quantity and, if necessary, the cost of the item in the appropriate columns. Repeat this step for as many different items as were received in this shipment.

ADDING TO YOUR INVENTORY | 225

Enter receipts of items in the Create Item Receipts window.

You can check this box if the bill arrives while you are filling out this form.

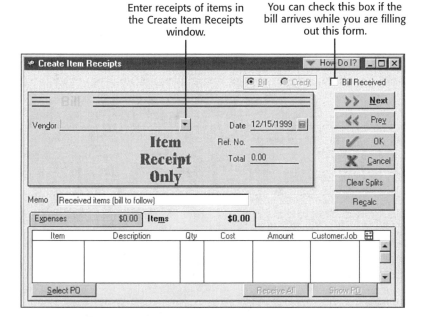

Figure 14.4
Enter receipts of items in the Create Item Receipts window.

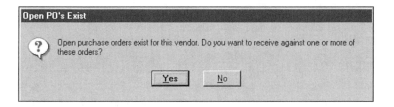

Figure 14.5
The Open PO's Exist message appears if a purchase order exists for items that have not yet been received.

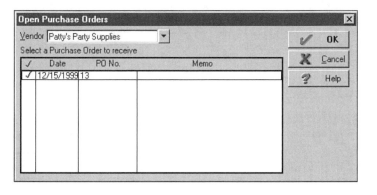

Figure 14.6
Click in the check mark column to associate a purchase order with the receipt of the item(s).

6. When all items have been entered, click Next to proceed to the next Create Item Receipts screen, or click OK if you have finished entering receipts.

After you have completed all the preceding steps, your inventory records are increased by the quantity of items that you indicated that your company received.

Receiving Items with a Bill

If you receive a bill at the same time that you receive your inventory items, you want to enter both the items and the bill in the system. Open the Activities menu and choose Inventory. Then choose Receive Items and Enter Bill. The Enter Bills window appears.

Follow steps 2–6 from the preceding section to enter all information from the bill and to record the receipt of inventory items, but use the Enter Bills window rather than the Create Item Receipts window.

Reports About Inventory

QuickBooks provides several standard inventory reports with which you can obtain information about your inventory. Find out how many items you have on hand and what your inventory is worth by choosing from the following inventory reports:

> **Note**
>
> The inventory reports are not visible on your Reports menu if you have not activated the Inventory feature for your company. To activate Inventory, open the File menu and choose Preferences. Click the Purchases & Vendors icon at the left of the window. On the Company Preferences tab, click the Inventory and purchase orders are active box.

- **Inventory Stock Status by Item**—This report lists each item in your inventory and tells you how many are currently in stock, how many are on order, and when you can expect to receive the orders. The report also calculates the average sales of each item on a per-week basis. Open the Reports menu, choose Inventory, and then choose Stock Status by Item to display this report.

- **Inventory Stock Status by Vendor**—This report displays the same information as the Stock Status by Item report, but the items are grouped by vendor so that you can quickly find out how many items are on order from a particular vendor, and which inventory items get ordered from each vendor. Open the Reports menu, choose Inventory, and then choose Stock Status by Vendor to display this report.

- **Inventory Valuation Summary**—This report shows the worth of each item in your inventory, based on the average cost method. The report also shows what percentage of the total inventory each item accounts for, what the items retail for, and what percentage of the total retail value each item accounts for. Open the Reports menu, choose Inventory, and then choose Valuation Summary to display this report.

- **Inventory Valuation Detail**—This report takes the Inventory Valuation Summary one step further and shows you the complete details of every inventory transaction (each purchase and each sale) for the requested period of time. Open the Reports menu, choose Inventory, and then choose Valuation Detail to display this report.

- **Item Price List**—Prepare a report that shows the price of each item in your inventory as well as all your company's other items. Open the Reports menu and choose List Reports, Item, Price List to display the report. To display a price list of only inventory items, click the Filters button, choose Item in the Filter box at the left, and then select All Inventory Items as the Item filter.

Taking a Physical Inventory Count

Typically, the value of the inventory is determined by taking a count of physical inventory items on hand at a specific time. Quantities of inventory items are confirmed, and cost is determined by using one of the several costing methods described earlier in this chapter.

The more frequently you count inventory, the more likely you are to be aware of any loss or damage to your inventory. Most companies count inventory once a year—at the end of the year when they are preparing their year-end financial statements.

QuickBooks makes taking a physical inventory easy by providing you with a physical inventory worksheet as one of its standard reports. The worksheet, shown in Figure 14.7, lists all the inventory items that you have set up for your company. From the Reports menu, choose Inventory Reports, and then choose Physical Inventory Worksheet to produce this report; then print a copy so that you can use it while you count your inventory.

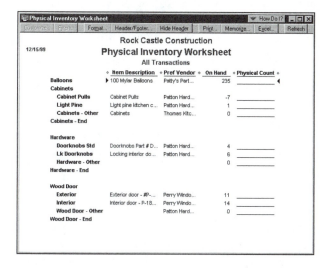

Figure 14.7
A sample worksheet for use in counting the inventory that you have on hand.

The Physical Inventory Worksheet includes any descriptive information that has been set up for these items, the preferred supplier of each item, and the quantity QuickBooks thinks is on hand as of the date that you request the report.

In the far right column, next to the amounts expected to be on hand, is a series of blank lines where you can fill in the actual amounts on hand as you make your count.

As you make your physical inventory count, you might find a disagreement between the inventory in QuickBooks and the inventory that you actually have in your warehouse or other business premises.

Large discrepancies must be explained, and it is up to you and the other members of your company to determine what constitutes a large discrepancy to your business. If your inventory is made up of many small parts, such as nuts and bolts and screws, you might not feel a discrepancy of 20 bolts is worth investigating. If your inventory is made up of computers and printers and other high-tech equipment, you'll probably consider 20 missing computers an unacceptable loss.

Adjusting Quantity and Value of Inventory Account

When you take your physical inventory count, you might find that your actual inventory totals don't agree with the quantity of items that QuickBooks thinks you have. Perhaps some items were damaged or lost, perhaps there was a theft, or there might be other reasons—which you will want to determine—for the discrepancies in your inventory totals.

QuickBooks adjusts its count of your inventory quantities whenever a sale takes place. When changes in quantity occur that aren't attributable to a sale, you have to adjust your QuickBooks records yourself so that they show the exact quantity on hand.

To make an adjustment in the quantity of inventory items on hand, follow these steps:

1. Open the Activities menu and choose Inventory; then choose Adjust Qty/Value on Hand (the Inventory feature must be activated for this menu option to be available). The Adjust Quantity/Value on Hand window appears (see Figure 14.8). All inventory items owned by your company are listed in the Item column at the left. The quantity on hand, according to QuickBooks, is shown in the Current Qty column.

2. If your physical count shows the quantity on hand to be different from the quantity on hand according to QuickBooks, enter the correct quantity in the New Qty column. QuickBooks makes the necessary changes to your records to reflect this change.

3. In the Adjustment Account field, enter the name of the account that you want QuickBooks to use when making an adjustment in the value of your inventory. QuickBooks adjusts your inventory by the average cost of the items that you enter. You might want to set up a new account called Inventory Shrinkage (or something similar) so that you can easily spot the changes you make to your inventory. The account you create to track inventory shrinkage is typically an expense account.

4. Click OK.

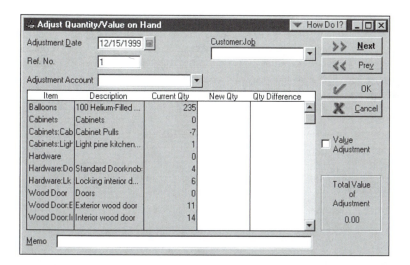

Figure 14.8
Adjust your inventory quantities based on the difference between your physical count and the amount that QuickBooks shows in the Adjust Quantity/Value on Hand window.

Note that there is also a Value Adjustment check box on this screen. If you check this box, two more columns appear: Current Value and New Value. The Current Value column shows the total cost of all inventory items. You can use this column to adjust the value of your inventory.

If you use an outside program to value your inventory, as discussed in the "Alternatives to the QuickBooks Inventory Feature" section, you might find that you can make your year-end adjustments right on the Adjust Quantity/Value on Hand screen, rather than making an adjustment in the general journal (also discussed in the next section).

→ To find more information on passwords and limiting access to the file, **see p. 485**.

ALTERNATIVES TO THE QUICKBOOKS INVENTORY FEATURE

As mentioned earlier in this chapter, some inventory matters can't be accomplished with QuickBooks. Manufacturers are encouraged to seek other methods of accounting for inventory. Furthermore, if you use a valuation method such as LIFO, FIFO, or Specific Identification, it is very difficult to account for inventory with QuickBooks.

Tip #40 from

Gail Perry

Although it is difficult, it is not impossible to track inventory in QuickBooks using a LIFO or FIFO method. You can choose to set up each differently priced set of inventory items as separate items, thus establishing what is known as tiers of inventory. For example, suppose you are in the business of silk-screening T-Shirts and you purchase solid-colored T-Shirts from a supplier. Your purchases include 1,000 T-Shirts acquired at $3.29, 1,000 T-Shirts at

> $3.33, and 1,000 T-Shirts at $3.37. QuickBooks indicates that you own 3,000 T-Shirts valued at $3.33 (the average cost). If you set up each block of T-Shirts as a separate item with its own price, you can track each group of shirts individually and the cost is not averaged. Having to identify from which lot a shirt is chosen results in a lot more work on your part, but at least the accounting will be accurate.

So how does your company proceed if you want to use QuickBooks for other accounting but find the inventory feature unacceptable?

Several alternatives to QuickBooks are available, all of which require you to account for inventory outside of QuickBooks, and then make a year-end general *journal entry (see page 258)* to adjust inventory and cost of sales amounts.

For example, if the value of inventory at the end of the year is $5,000 more than the value of inventory at the beginning of the year, you need to make a general journal entry to adjust the amount in your inventory account on your balance sheet. The journal entry debits inventory by $5,000 (increasing the account because debits increase assets) and credits cost of sales (decreasing the account because all purchases were charged, or debited, to the cost of sales account during the year, but $5,000 of these purchases presumably are still in inventory and need to be reclassified to the inventory asset account).

→ To find more information about debits and credits, **see p. 107**.

THE SPREADSHEET ALTERNATIVE

You can use a spreadsheet program, such as Microsoft Excel, Lotus 1-2-3, or Corel's Quattro Pro, to track your inventory. If you use a spreadsheet program, you might want to set up a separate sheet for each inventory item, or a separate column on one large sheet for each item.

All purchases of inventory items are recorded on these spreadsheets, which carry over from year to year as long as the inventory items are carried in your stock.

If you change your inventory items frequently, selling out of older items and not replacing them but acquiring newer models instead, it makes sense to use a separate spreadsheet for each item rather than one sheet with a column for each item. By using separate sheets, you can stop using a particular sheet altogether when an item is retired.

In a FIFO environment, the oldest items on the spreadsheet are retired after the physical inventory count at the end of the year. Some notation shows that these are the items that were sold during the year. The rest of the inventory carries forward to make up the beginning inventory for the next year.

Companies using LIFO calculations show a retirement on their spreadsheets of recent acquisitions, while maintaining a value for their year-end inventory made up of the cost of the earliest purchases.

Companies who use the Specific Identification method of costing inventory note on their spreadsheet each individual item sold, adding up the cost of each remaining item to arrive at a total for valuing their inventory at year-end.

Creating a spreadsheet system for tracking and costing your inventory might require the time and expense of an outside programmer.

If you have a large inventory with thousands of different pieces, large quantities of each piece, and frequent turnover of the pieces, you will find that a spreadsheet is a time-consuming method of evaluating inventory costs. Also, spreadsheets have size limitations: a maximum of 65,536 rows (some have only 8,192 rows) and 256 columns. When you consider that you intend to track your company's inventory for many years, you might find that these limitations are a problem.

The Database Alternative

Database programs such as Microsoft Access, Corel's Paradox, Oracle, and so on can accommodate millions (and even billions) of records, thus lending themselves much more easily to tracking large inventories.

You can create a database that retires inventory items as they are sold. Ending inventory quantities can be compared to the quantities determined in the physical inventory count, adjusted as necessary, and the value calculated instantaneously based on the valuation method that your company uses.

Many retail stores use point-of-sale database programs that keep track of each item of inventory, providing cost and availability information right at the cash register. Although QuickBooks can provide this point-of-sale information, a sophisticated database program can go farther by tracking raw materials and transferring the materials into finished goods as inventory is produced.

Creating a database program for tracking and costing your inventory might require the time and expense of an outside programmer.

Other Software Alternatives

Several programs on the market are designed specifically to track inventory. A little time searching through software stores or poring over computer catalogs might result in a program that fits the needs of your company.

I have found, through searching the Internet, several inventory programs, including some specifically designed for users of QuickBooks. An easy search for *Inventory AND Software* yielded about a dozen links to companies that provide software programs designed to combat the shortcomings of accounting programs such as QuickBooks.

Some programs are specifically designed to track manufacturing inventories, with easy transitions for raw materials becoming finished goods.

Many of the programs that I found on the Internet offer demos and limited-time samples of the programs so that you can try out the programs and see if they will do the job for you.

TROUBLESHOOTING

ADDING INVENTORY ITEMS

When entering a cash payment for a purchase, I entered the amount on the Expense tab of my Writing Checks screen, rather than on the Items tab. What kinds of problems can this cause?

The problem caused by entering the purchase of an inventory item as an expense is that the item won't be added to your inventory. QuickBooks has no way of tracking the quantity of the item or of advising you when it is time to reorder. Also, the expense goes right to your income statement as a current expense, instead of being added to your inventory as a company asset.

ACCOUNTING FOR THEFT

I lost some inventory due to an employee theft. How do I account for this?

Adjust the quantity of your inventory items to record shrinkage due to theft. You don't need to wait until the end of the year to make this adjustment. If you know how much you lost, you can make the adjustment at any time.

CHAPTER 15

PURCHASE ORDERS, ACCOUNTS PAYABLE, AND PAYING BILLS

In this chapter

Using Purchase Orders   234

What's on Order?   238

Tax-Exempt Purchases   238

Receiving Goods   239

Paying Bills   241

Writing Checks in QuickBooks   243

Printing Checks   245

The QuickBooks Check Register   247

Voiding Checks   248

The Monthly Ritual of Bank Account Reconciliation   248

There's an old saying: "It takes money to make money." It costs money to develop, build, or purchase the things that you sell. In addition, the overhead cost of operating a business includes rent, utilities, office salaries, equipment, supplies, repairs, cleaning, and so on.

When you record your company's income, you know how much money is coming into the business, but you can't get a sense of how much money the business is actually making without recording the expenses as well. All the costs of operating a business must become a part of your QuickBooks recordkeeping.

Using Purchase Orders

Purchase orders are an optional part of QuickBooks. The idea behind a purchase order is that you issue a document that lists the items you are ordering, and that you send that document to your supplier. The purchase order acts as a written record of your order, providing more accuracy than a verbal order might offer.

If you have not yet advised QuickBooks that you plan to use the purchase orders feature, do so now.

To turn on the preference for purchase orders—or to check to see whether this feature has been activated—follow these steps:

1. Choose File, Preferences. The Preferences window appears.
2. Click the Purchases & Vendors button at the left side of the window. You might need to scroll to locate this button.
3. Click the Company Preferences tab at the top of the window.
4. Check the first box, Inventory; purchase orders are now active.
5. Click OK to save your changes and close the window.

After the purchase order feature has been activated, you can create purchase orders in QuickBooks. Use the following steps to create a purchase order:

1. Choose Activities, Create Purchase Orders. The Create Purchase Orders window appears (see Figure 15.1).
2. Select the vendor by clicking the arrow at the right of the vendor field. If the vendor from whom you are purchasing is not on the list, click the Add New button and enter information for a new vendor.

> **Note**
>
> As you're entering information in QuickBooks, you might notice occasions when QuickBooks seems to know just what you're thinking because it fills in the rest of the name or item. This feature is known as QuickFill. If you type a P in the Vendor area, for example, QuickBooks searches the vendor list for the first name beginning with a P and fills in the rest of the name, which might be Partington Supply. If the vendor you are really trying to

type is Pranitis Heating and Cooling, continue typing. By the time you have typed Pr, QuickBooks has filled in the rest of the name; you don't have to type anything more. Just click the next field or press Tab to proceed.

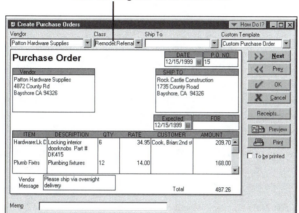

Figure 15.1
Create a purchase order with this form.

3. Choose a class if you use the QuickBooks class-tracking feature (described in Chapter 9, "Separating Your Company into Logical Divisions"). The class field is not visible if this feature has not been activated.

4. If you plan to use something other than the standard purchase order template, click the arrow in the template field to choose another template.

→ To find more information about creating custom templates, **see p. 337**.

5. Verify the address information in the Vendor Address area. This information fills in automatically when you select a vendor; it is based on the information you entered when you set up this vendor. If you change the information in this field, a message appears onscreen when you attempt to save this purchase order, asking if you want to see the changed information next time (see Figure 15.2). If you answer Yes, the permanent address information for this vendor is updated to reflect your changes.

6. The date field contains today's date, which QuickBooks fills in automatically. Change the date of the purchase order, if necessary.

7. If a Ship To field appears on your purchase order, verify that the information in this area is correct. This is the address to which you want the ordered items shipped. QuickBooks automatically fills in your company name and address, but your company might have additional locations, or you might want the items shipped directly to a customer. You can change any information in this area.

Figure 15.2
Click Yes to update the permanent information for this vendor. Click No to leave the vendor file intact. Click Cancel to return to the purchase order form.

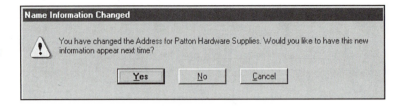

→ Remember that you can add fields, such as the Ship To field, to your purchase order. **See p. 337**.

8. If the Expected area appears on your purchase order, enter the date that you expect the order to arrive. QuickBooks automatically fills in today's date, but you can change this information. If you expect the ordered items to arrive on different dates, decide whether you want to enter the first date of arrival or the last date of arrival. QuickBooks uses this date on inventory stock status reports to show the date on which ordered items are expected to arrive.

9. If an FOB field appears in your purchase order, enter the *FOB status* (*page 186*) for this order, if you know it. Sometimes the vendor determines this status, so you might not have this information when you place the order.

10. Click in the Item area. An arrow appears. Click the arrow to display a drop-down list of all the items you have entered in your QuickBooks file. Choose an item from this list by clicking it. If the item that you want to order is not on this list, click Add New at the top of the list and enter information for a new item.

→ To find more information about setting up new items, **see p. 122**.

11. The item description fills in automatically. You can alter this description, if necessary.

12. In the Quantity area, enter the number of pieces of this item that you want to order.

13. Verify that the rate is correct. QuickBooks fills in the rate automatically if this information was entered when you set up the item. If no amount appears in the Rate column, enter the appropriate amount at this time. If you do not know the cost of the items you are ordering, you can leave this column blank.

14. Enter a Customer:Job if you plan to charge the cost of the items being ordered to a specific customer.

15. The amount calculates automatically based on the rate that you fill in. You can override the amount, if necessary.

16. Repeat steps 10–14 until all the items you want to order from this vendor are listed.

17. Optionally, you can enter a message in the Vendor Message area. For example, you might want to provide special shipping instructions ("Our warehouse will be closed the week of July 17. No deliveries will be accepted that week," or "Please ship via overnight delivery."), or you might want to enter other information here. Your message appears at the bottom of the printed purchase order.

18. Optionally, you can enter a memo in the Memo area at the bottom of the purchase order form. This memo is for internal use only and does not print on the purchase order form.

19. Check the To be printed box (see Figure 15.3) unless you plan to print this purchase order immediately. Checking this box places the purchase order in a holding area, and QuickBooks reminds you that the form is waiting to be printed. To print a purchase order after you have closed the Create Purchase Order form, choose File, Print Forms, Print Purchase Orders. Click each purchase order on the list to select that document for printing. Then click the Print button to print the selected forms.

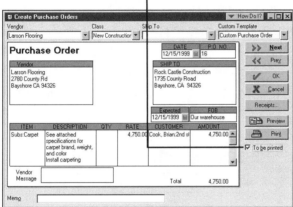

Click here to request that the form be printed later.

Figure 15.3
Enter all information about the items that you want to purchase on this form.

20. After you have entered all pertinent information on this purchase order, choose from the buttons at the side of the purchase order form:

   - **Next**—Click Next to save your changes on this purchase order and display the next available purchase order form.
   - **Prev**—Click Prev to save your changes on this purchase order and display the order that was created just before this one.
   - **OK**—Click OK to save your changes on this purchase order and close the Create Purchase Order window.
   - **Cancel**—Click Cancel to close the Create Purchase Order window without saving this purchase order.
   - **Receipts**—After you have received items from this purchase order and have noted those receipts in QuickBooks (discussed later in this chapter), you can check to see which items have been received by viewing this purchase order and clicking the Receipts button.

- **Preview**—Click Preview to see how the purchase order will look before you print it.
- **Print**—Click Print to print the purchase order immediately. If you do not plan to print the purchase order at this time, be sure to check the To be printed box.

After you have created purchase orders in QuickBooks, you can take advantage of their existence and quickly see what items have been ordered.

What's on Order?

When you issue a purchase order for inventory items, QuickBooks keeps track of the quantity of items on order. At any time, you can get an update of the number of items in stock and the number on order by following these three steps:

1. Choose Lists, Items. The Items list window appears.
2. Click an item for which you want to check the quantities on hand and on order.
3. Click the Reports button at the bottom of the window and choose QuickReport at the top of the drop-down menu. A quick report for the particular item appears (see Figure 15.4), listing all activity relating to the in-stock quantities and outstanding orders for the item.

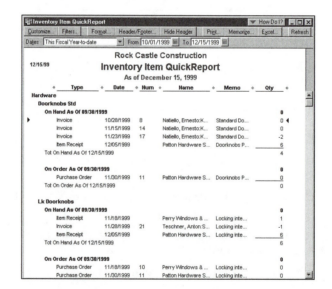

Figure 15.4
QuickReports for inventory items show how many items are in stock and how many are on order.

Tax-Exempt Purchases

Some organizations are entitled to make purchases that are exempt from sales tax. For example, if your company purchases items that will ultimately be sold to your customers you are considered a reseller, and your purchases are not subject to sales tax; this is because you presumably collect sales tax from your customers when you sell the items, and sales tax needs to be collected only once on the sale of an item.

State Resale Numbers
The state in which your company does business will provide you with a resale number when you register to collect sales tax from your customers. See Appendix D, "State Revenue Agencies," for a complete list of state revenue agencies that can provide you with more information about registering a business in your state.

Your organization might be tax exempt under IRS rules that protect schools, churches, and other charitable organizations from paying tax.

If you are exempt from sales tax, you need a tax-exempt number from your state revenue department. This number needs to be provided to each of your vendors whenever you make a purchase.

The Vendor Message area near the bottom of the purchase order form is an excellent place to display your tax-exempt number.

Receiving Goods

When you receive inventory items, your QuickBooks records need to be updated so that your listings of available inventory items is up-to-date. When you make a sale, QuickBooks checks against the quantity of items you have in stock and determines if you have enough items to sell.

You can record the receipt of goods in two ways: goods received before you are billed and goods received with a bill. The processes for entering both types of goods are almost identical.

When you enter goods before receiving a bill, QuickBooks increases the value in your inventory account and increases your accounts payable account. The quantity of items on hand in your inventory records is increased so that your inventory records are accurate.

Goods Received Without a Bill

To enter goods received without an accompanying bill, follow these steps:

1. Choose Activities, Inventory, Receive Items. The Create Item Receipts window appears (see Figure 15.5).
2. In the Vendor area, enter the name of the vendor from whom the items were received. If you have entered purchase orders for this vendor, a message such as the one displayed in Figure 15.6 appears.
3. If you received the message described in step 2 and chose Yes, the Open Purchase Orders window appears (see Figure 15.7). In the Open Purchase Orders window, check off each purchase order against which you are receiving items. Then click OK. These items appear on the Item Receipt form, where you can adjust the quantity to reflect the amount actually received.

Figure 15.5
Enter items received in this window so that QuickBooks can update your inventory records.

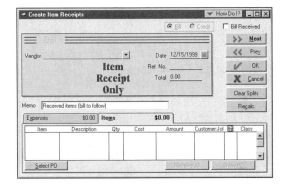

Figure 15.6
Click Yes when this message appears to display a list of open purchase orders. Click No if you are receiving items for which a purchase order was not prepared.

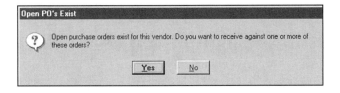

Figure 15.7
Click to the left of any purchase order against which you received items. The items from this purchase order appear on your Item Receipt form.

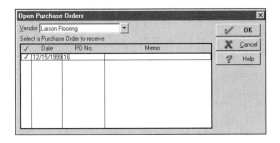

4. If you choose not to record items received against a purchase order and click No in step 3, but later realize that you are receiving against a purchase order—or if you just want to view a list of all outstanding purchase orders for this vendor—click the Select PO button at the bottom of this screen. The Open Purchase Orders window appears.

5. To add items to your Item Receipt form, click in the Item area. An arrow appears. Click the arrow to display a drop-down list of all the items you have entered in your QuickBooks file. Choose an item from this list by clicking it. If the item you have received is not on this list, click Add New at the top of the list and enter information for a new item.

6. Enter the quantity of any items received in the Qty column. Adjust the cost to reflect the cost per item. QuickBooks automatically calculates the total amount.

7. If, as you're entering information on this form, you realize that you have received a bill for this shipment, check the Bill Received box at the top of the form. Two extra fields

appear on the form if you check this box—the date on which the bill is due and the terms of payment.

8. Click Next to save this receipt form and advance to the next form; click Prev to save this receipt form and view a prior form; or click OK to save and close this window.

GOODS RECEIVED WITH A BILL

To enter goods at the same time that the bill is received, follow these steps:

1. Choose Activities, Inventory, Receive Items and Enter Bill. The Enter Bills window appears.
2. Enter the vendor in the Vendor field. If an open purchase order exists for this vendor, the message shown in Figure 15.6 appears. Click Yes or No to indicate whether you want to receive items against the open purchase orders.
3. Verify and change, if necessary, the Amount Due, the date on which the bill is due, and the Terms of payment. If any items appear on the Items tab in the lower portion of the screen, verify the description, quantity, and cost of all items received in this shipment. To remove an item from the bill, click the item to be removed, and then choose Edit, Delete Line (or press Ctrl+D). Alternatively, you might want to leave an unreceived item on the bill but change the quantity to zero.
4. To charge this amount to a Customer:Job, click in the Customer:Job column and choose a job from the drop-down list. When you charge items to a job, a little invoice icon appears in the column to the right of the job name. This icon indicates that the amount will be automatically billed to the customer. To override that decision and tell QuickBooks not to automatically invoice the customer, click the invoice icon; an *x* appears over the icon.
5. Click Next to save this bill and advance to the next bill; click Prev to save this bill and view a prior bill; or click OK to save and close this bill window.

PAYING BILLS

Receiving merchandise and bills is only half the fun! Now that you have a pile of bills, you need to figure out how to pay for all this fun.

Paying bills is more than simply writing checks when the mood strikes. Well-run businesses plan for their expenses by *budgeting* (*page 464*) and predicting cash flow.

Many businesses pay bills on certain days of the month, for example the 15th and the last day of the month. Paying bills on a regular, predictable timetable can help you plan for the times that you need to have cash on hand; furthermore, your vendors can depend on the knowledge that their bills will be paid on a particular day.

When you pay a bill in QuickBooks, your cash account is reduced by the amount of the payment, and your accounts payable account is reduced to reflect the bill that is no longer due.

Use the following steps to pay bills in QuickBooks:

1. Choose Activities, Pay Bills. The Pay Bills window appears (see Figure 15.8), listing all the bills that are currently due. This list is not comprehensive because bills that have been received but have not reached their due date are not included in the list.

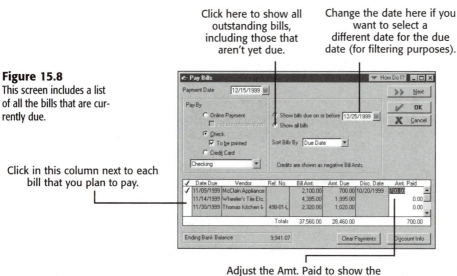

Figure 15.8
This screen includes a list of all the bills that are currently due.

Click here to show all outstanding bills, including those that aren't yet due.

Change the date here if you want to select a different date for the due date (for filtering purposes).

Click in this column next to each bill that you plan to pay.

Adjust the Amt. Paid to show the actual amount that you plan to pay.

2. In the Pay By area, indicate your preferred method of payment: online (this only appears if you are set up for online bill services—see chapter 23, "Going Online with QuickBooks," for more information about making online payments), check, or credit card. Also indicate which bank account you plan to draw from, or which credit card you plan to use. If you plan to print this check in QuickBooks, check the To be printed box.

3. Select the due date for which you want to display bills. All bills due up to the selected date appear in the bills list at the bottom of the screen. Alternatively, you can choose to display all bills (Show all bills), whether or not they are currently due.

Caution

If you choose a due date other than the one QuickBooks has chosen for you, the screen does not automatically refresh to show the bills that fit the new date you have chosen. To be sure that you see all the correct bills, change the due date, choose Show all bills, and then click the top option to show bills on or before the selected date.

4. Check off each bill that you intend to pay, and change the amount in the Amt. Paid column if you don't intend to pay the full amount. If you choose to pay less than the full amount, the bill remains in this list. If an error exists in the amount shown as due for this bill, reopen the bill and correct the amount.

5. If you plan to take a discount on a bill, click the bill, and then click the Discount Info button at the bottom of the window. The Discount Information window appears (see Figure 15.9), displaying the available discount for this bill. In this window you can choose to accept or override the calculated discount amount. Choose a discount account for recording the discount. You might have to set up an account if this is the first time you are recording a discount. Click OK to save the information in this window.

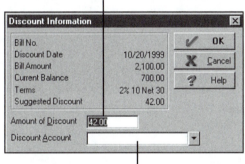

Figure 15.9
The discount terms that appear here were derived from the bill.

QuickBooks has calculated the discount amount. You can revise this amount, if necessary.

Choose the account in which the discount is to be recorded.

6. Click Next to save your payment choices and refresh the window, removing all the bills that you have indicated you want to pay in full. Or click OK to save your payment choices and close the window. Cancel closes the window without recording any of your payments.

WRITING CHECKS IN QUICKBOOKS

Not all your company checks are written in response to bills. You write some checks regularly, without ever receiving a bill—rent, for example. Or perhaps you have to run out to make a quick purchase and you don't plan to bother with a purchase order or entering a bill—you just want to write the check for the purchase.

Use the following steps to enter a check without creating an associated bill:

1. Choose Activities, Write Checks (or click the Check icon). The Write Checks window appears (see Figure 15.10).

Figure 15.10
Write checks on this form, which looks like a real check.

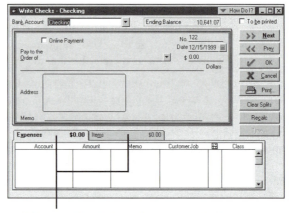

Click on a tab to indicate if you are paying for expenses (such as repairs or utilities) or items (such as inventory).

2. In the Bank Account field, choose the account from which the money for this check is to be drawn.

3. Verify the check number and the date of the check. Change this information, if necessary.

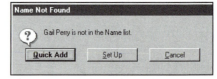

Figure 15.11

4. Enter the name of the payee in the Pay to the Order of field. A drop-down list of all your vendors is available in this field, or you can choose to enter a name not on the vendor list. If you enter a new name, QuickBooks displays the message shown in Figure 15.11. The Select Name Type window then appears (see Figure 15.12), asking you to indicate if this is a vendor, a customer, an employee, or something else.

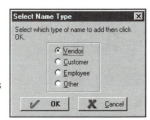

Figure 15.12

> **Note**
> When entering a new payee, you are prompted to either Quick Add or Set Up this payee in the QuickBooks file. You must choose, or QuickBooks won't allow you to use this payee name. Choose Quick Add if this payee is someone to whom you will not write additional checks, or if this is someone for whom you don't need to save any additional information. Choose Set Up if additional information about this payee—such as address, phone number, personal contact, and so on—is useful to you.

5. Enter an amount for this check.

6. Verify that the information in the Address area is correct and that you want this information to print on the check. You have the option of deleting information in the

Address area and leaving this area blank. If you plan to use the QuickBooks *online payment feature (see page 422)*, the payee's name and address must be filled in.

7. In the lower part of the Write Checks dialog box (as shown in Figure 15.10), choose whether you are paying for E<u>x</u>penses (such as rent and repairs) or Ite<u>m</u>s (such as inventory, shipping, or subcontract work) by clicking the appropriate tab.

8. Enter the items or expenses for which you are paying by filling in the appropriate information at the bottom of the check form.

9. Click the Print button if you plan to print this check immediately (the next section discusses printing checks). If you want to print this check later, check the To <u>b</u>e printed box at the top of the form. If you write this check by hand, don't click either print option.

10. Click Next to save your information and proceed to the next check; click Prev to save your information and view the prior check; click OK to save your information and close this window; click Cancel to close the window without saving your check.

PRINTING CHECKS

When you write checks in QuickBooks, you indicate whether you want to print the check immediately (by clicking the Print button), print it at some future date (by checking the To <u>b</u>e printed box), or not print it at all (by not choosing either print option).

If you have indicated that you want checks to be printed, QuickBooks provides you with a list in your Reminder window of the outstanding checks that are waiting to be printed. Don't overlook this task! Creditors won't look too favorably on someone who says he entered the information for the check in QuickBooks weeks ago but forgot to print the check.

To print checks that have been entered into QuickBooks, follow these steps:

1. Choose <u>F</u>ile, Prin<u>t</u> Forms, Print <u>C</u>hecks. The Select Checks to Print window appears (see Figure 15.13).

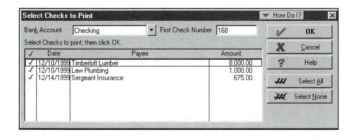

Figure 15.13
Click OK to print the selected checks.

2. Verify that the account listed in the Ban<u>k</u> Account area is the one from which you want to print checks.

3. If you use pre-printed check forms that are already numbered, verify that the first check number shown in this window corresponds with the check number on the first available pre-printed check form.

4. All the checks that are awaiting printing have been check marked. If you don't want to print some checks at this time, click the checks, and the check mark disappears. Only check-marked checks are printed.

5. Click OK when you are ready to print the checks. The Print Checks window appears. Alternatively, click Cancel if you've changed your mind and don't want to print checks at this time.

6. On the Settings tab (see Figure 15.14), choose the printer, the type of sheets you use, and the style of checks you use. Indicate how many checks are on the first page of checks. Also indicate whether you want QuickBooks to print your company name or a logo on your checks. If you choose to print a logo on your checks, you are asked to direct QuickBooks to a bitmap (.BMP) file that contains the logo.

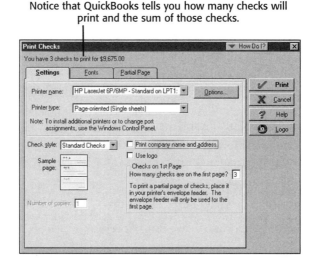

Figure 15.14
Use this window to tell QuickBooks what kind of checks you use and where to print them.

Notice that QuickBooks tells you how many checks will print and the sum of those checks.

7. If you want to choose the typeface that will print on the checks, click the Fonts tab, and then click the Font and Address font buttons to change the fonts on the main part of the check and the company name and address section, respectively.

8. You can print less than a full page of checks without confusing QuickBooks by clicking on the Partial Page tab and choosing the type of check form that you plan to use.

9. Click Print when you are ready to print your checks. Or click Cancel to close the window without printing.

The QuickBooks Check Register

In the good old days of writing checks by hand, there was always a check register where each check was recorded, along with the number, the date, the payee, the amount, and maybe a little memo about what the check was for. Also, every deposit that was made was recorded, along with the date, the amount, and the source of the deposit.

QuickBooks still keeps that check register for you, and you can view it at any time. Follow these steps to open the register for your checking account (or for any account):

1. Choose Lists, Chart of Accounts (or press Ctrl+A). The Chart of Accounts list window appears.
2. Click the name of the account for which you want to view the register.
3. Click the Activities button at the bottom of this window, and choose Use Register from the drop-down menu (or double-click on the account name). The QuickBooks register for the chosen account appears (see Figure 15.15).

Deposits to the account appear in this column.

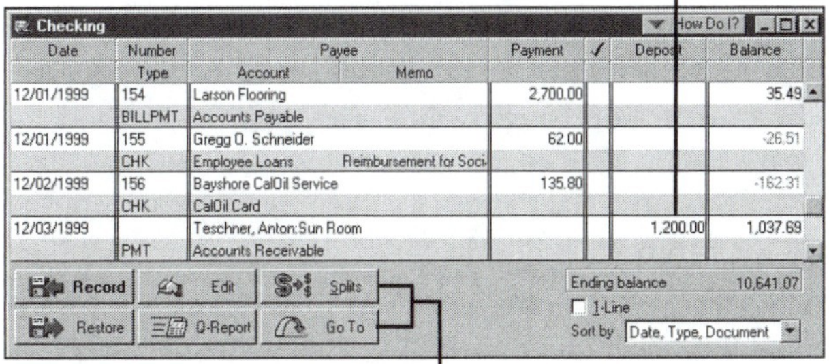

Figure 15.15
Just like a hand-written check register, the QuickBooks register records all the transactions in and out of the account.

See Figure 11.5 (in Chapter 11, "Invoicing, Monthly Statements, and Accounts Receivable") for information on how the register commands work.

4. After you have finished examining the transactions, click the *x* button in the upper-right corner of the window to close it.

If you are looking for a particular transaction, you can search for items in your check register. Click the Go To button at the bottom of the screen. The Go To window appears (see Figure 15.16).

Figure 15.16
Enter the search criteria for finding an elusive transaction in your register, and then click Prev to search the register backward or Next to search forward.

Choose a field in which to search. You might want to search for transactions of a particular amount, in which case you choose the Amount field. To search for checks payable to a particular party, search the Payee/Name field. In the Search For area, enter the amount or name for which you are searching. Then click Prev to search backward or Next to search forward for the missing transaction.

Although you can make entries directly in the register, such as recording checks that you wrote by hand or deposits that you made to your account, you ensure a more complete accounting of transactions if you use the standard QuickBooks forms, such as the bill paying form, the invoice form, the cash receipt form, and so on.

VOIDING CHECKS

At times, you might write a check and discover later that you must void the check. Perhaps you paid for an order, only to find that the order is defective and the supplier told you he is tearing up your check. Or maybe you wrote a check for the wrong amount and want to destroy the check.

The process for voiding a check involves finding the check in QuickBooks, and then requesting that QuickBooks void the check. It is possible to delete a check in QuickBooks, but deleting is irreversible and leaves a trail that is more difficult to follow. Because voiding a check leaves a record of the existence of the check, it is the preferred method.

Follow these steps to void a check:

1. Find the check that you want to void. Probably the easiest way to do this is to open the register (see "The QuickBooks Check Register"), scroll through or search the transactions until you find the check that you want to void, and double-click the check. The check appears onscreen.

2. Choose Edit, Void. The amount of the check changes to zero, and the Amt. Paid area at the bottom of the check also changes to zero. All other information on the check remains intact.

3. Close the check window. A message appears, asking you to confirm your actions. Click Yes. You are returned to the register, where you can see that this check appears with a zero amount.

4. Click the *x* at the top of the register window to close the register.

THE MONTHLY RITUAL OF BANK ACCOUNT RECONCILIATION

Reconciling your bank account has never been so much fun. Fun? QuickBooks makes it seem like fun because it is quick and easy. After you get your bank statement and are ready to begin the reconciliation process, follow these steps:

The Monthly Ritual of Bank Account Reconciliation

1. Choose Activities, Reconcile. The Reconcile window appears (see Figure 15.17).

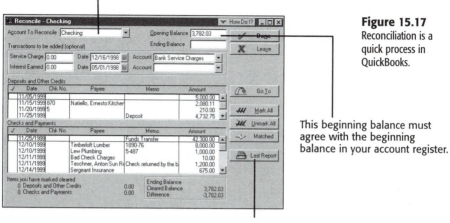

Choose the bank account that you want to reconcile.

Figure 15.17
Reconciliation is a quick process in QuickBooks.

This beginning balance must agree with the beginning balance in your account register.

View the prior reconciliation report by clicking this button.

2. In the Account to Reconcile area, choose the account for which you received a bank statement.
3. Verify that the opening balance agrees with your bank statement. If you find a discrepancy, you must make a change in your register so that the amounts agree. The only time you should see a discrepancy is the first time that you reconcile this account. Transactions that were outstanding with the bank might not have been entered in your register. Make sure that all transactions have been entered and that the opening balances agree.
4. Enter the Ending Balance from your bank statement.
5. In the Service Charge area, enter any service charge applied by the bank and the date that it was applied. This information appears on your bank statement.
6. In the Interest area, enter any interest income that your bank account earned and the date that it was received. This information appears on your bank statement.
7. The amounts you see in the Deposits and Other Credits area represent the amounts from your register. Check off all items that appear on your bank statement. Click an item to check it off.

Tip #41 from Gail Perry

When reconciling, you might find discrepancies between your bank statement and the amounts you recorded in QuickBooks. When this happens, first verify who is right. Banks can make mistakes—don't take their word for it that they are correct. However, if you find that the bank is right and your transaction was entered incorrectly, open the register

continues

continued

> (leave the reconciliation window open as well), find the transaction in question, double-click it to get to the original entry form, and make a correction. The correction flows through to your register and, ultimately, to your reconciliation. If you find that you are missing an entry, open the appropriate window and enter the transaction in QuickBooks, making sure that the transaction is dated properly. The transaction then appears in your reconciliation when you return to it.

8. The amounts that you see in the Checks and Payments area represent the amounts from your register. Check off all the items that appear on your bank statement. Click an item to check it off.

9. At the bottom of the screen you see a running balance of all the deposits and checks that you have checked off. You also see an Ending Balance (the amount from the bank statement), a Cleared Balance (the amount of items that you checked off), and a Difference amount. When all items from the bank statement have been checked off, the Difference amount is zero. If it is not zero, go back through every transaction on the bank statement, comparing it carefully to the items that you checked off. Correct any discrepancies.

10. After the reconciliation is finished (and the Difference amount at the bottom of the window is zero), click the Do*n*e button to save your work and close the reconciliation window. If you need to close the reconciliation window before you have finished, click the Leave button. Your work is saved, and when you return you can start right where you left off.

11. When you have finished, you are given the option to print a reconciliation report (see Figure 15.18). The Full reconciliation report gives you a detailed list of all the transactions that cleared your account during this time period as well as all outstanding transactions (amounts that have not yet cleared the bank). The Summary reconciliation report gives you the totals of all the amounts deposited to and deducted from your account during the specified time period. Printing either report is optional.

Figure 15.18
Choose from a Full report which shows all transactions, a Summary report which gives only totals, and no report at all.

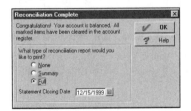

You will find that when you get into the habit of reconciling your bank account with the QuickBooks reconciliation feature, you actually look forward to this process because it is such an easy task.

Troubleshooting

Using the Reconcile Window

I'm in the middle of reconciling my bank account and it's time to quit for the day. How do I stop and pick up again tomorrow?

When you're ready to close the Reconcile window, and you haven't yet finished reconciling, click the Leave button. Everything you checked off is saved, and the next time you open the Reconcile window, you can pick up right where you left off.

Voiding a Check

Can I void a check right on a check form?

As an alternative to voiding checks in the checking account register, you can right-click on a check form and choose Void from the pop-up menu that appears.

Check Forms

If I'm going to print checks from QuickBooks, do I have to purchase check forms from Intuit?

Standard check forms are available at many office supply stores. It makes sense to shop around and do some price comparison before settling on a supplier for your forms.

CHAPTER 16

MANAGING FIXED ASSETS

In this chapter

Why Do We Have to Use Depreciation?   254

Accounting for Fixed Assets   254

Calculating Depreciation   255

Recording Depreciation   258

Following the Audit Trail   260

Selling Depreciable Assets   260

Alternatives to QuickBooks for Fixed Asset Tracking   261

Fixed assets are assets of a durable nature that are acquired for use in the business rather than for resale, and that are expected to last for a number of years. Rather than taking a deduction for the cost of a fixed asset in the year in which it is acquired, as you might for the cost of office supplies or small tools, the investment for these assets is assigned to future periods and deducted through periodic charges to a depreciation expense account.

Examples of fixed assets include furniture, equipment, buildings, large tools, vehicles, computers, machinery, and animals.

A company's balance sheet lists the cost of the asset in total, with the accumulation of depreciation charges summarized beneath the cost. A *net asset value*, commonly referred to as *book value*, is shown as the difference between the original cost and the depreciation charges to date. Even after a fixed asset has been fully depreciated, the asset and its accumulated depreciation remain on the company balance sheet as long as the asset is still in use, with a net value of zero.

Why Do We Have to Use Depreciation?

The purpose of using depreciation accounts to report the expense of the cost of assets is to match the cost of the asset with the income it produces.

If an asset is expected to function and produce income for several years before it becomes outdated or no longer works properly, spreading the cost of the asset over a similar period of time seems reasonable. Deducting the cost of the asset all in one year distorts the process of matching income with expenses.

Accounting for Fixed Assets

When you use QuickBooks to account for fixed assets, you group similar assets in a single account. For example, you might have one account for office furniture, another for computer equipment, and so on. As you purchase new assets, the cost of each new asset gets added to the appropriate account. If you purchase five office desks, each costing $400, your office furniture account increases in value by $2,000 (5×$400).

Depreciation expense for all assets is added to a single depreciation expense account. At the time that the depreciation expense account is increased, an *accumulated depreciation* account is increased by the same amount. The accumulated depreciation account is a type of asset account, but because its purpose is to offset the value of the assets by the amount of the accumulating depreciation, it is referred to as a *contra asset* account.

On the balance sheet, the accumulated depreciation account is listed with the assets, reducing the value of the related fixed asset account. The following is an example of how fixed assets might appear on your balance sheet:

Fixed assets

Office furniture	4,000	
Accumulated depreciation	3,000	
Total office furniture		1,000
Computer equipment	12,000	
Accumulated depreciation	12,000	
Total computer equipment		0
Total fixed assets		1,000

Calculating Depreciation

The accounting profession, in conjunction with the IRS, has established many complicated rules for calculating depreciation expense—rules certain to confuse even the most savvy businessperson. Following are some of the basics.

Even though the process of calculating depreciation is designed to spread the cost of a fixed asset over the useful life of the asset, you don't need to guess about the useful life of your assets. The IRS has already decided what the useful life is for most assets, and you are expected to use these standard lives when determining your depreciation expense. The following is a list of several common asset types and the standard lives assigned to those types, courtesy of the IRS:

Depreciable Asset	Depreciable life
Automobiles	5 years
General-purpose trucks	5 years
Computer equipment	5 years
Office equipment	5 years
Office furniture	7 years
Residential rental property	27.5 years
Office buildings/factories	39 years

Tip #42 from Gail Perry

The standard lives are the lives currently recognized by the IRS. The rules for determining standard lives and calculating depreciation are always subject to change; consult with an accountant to determine the rules that are in place when you purchase assets.

Depreciation was originally established as a means of spreading the cost of an asset evenly over the expected useful life of the asset. Over the years, Congress has enacted laws that enable you to accelerate the rate at which assets are depreciated—taking larger deductions in the earlier years of asset ownership.

Businesses often use accelerated methods of depreciation for calculating the depreciation expense they take on their business income tax returns, but use a more even, conservative depreciation expense for the amount they show on the company's financial statements. Deciding which method of depreciation to use and when to use it is a decision that you need to make with the help of an accountant.

Because of the complications in this area of accounting and tax law, the discussion in this chapter is limited to the two most common methods of calculating depreciation: straight-line and Modified Accelerated Cost Recovery System (MACRS).

STRAIGHT-LINE DEPRECIATION

A *straight-line* method of calculating depreciation expense results in spreading the cost of an asset evenly over the anticipated useful life of the asset.

The cost of the asset is divided by the number of years of estimated useful life (following the IRS guidelines). For the first and last year of depreciation expense, only half a year of expense is taken. For an asset that cost $5,000 and has a useful life of five years, the depreciation expense calculation using the straight-line method actually results in six years of depreciation deductions, calculated as follows:

Year 1	$500
Year 2	$1,000
Year 3	$1,000
Year 4	$1,000
Year 5	$1,000
Year 6	$500

MACRS DEPRECIATION

Depreciation expense calculated by using the *MACRS* method of accelerated depreciation results in greater deductions in the earlier years of asset use. Some negative side effects of using MACRS include a greater taxable gain if the asset is sold before its useful life is over and some potential additional adjustments for tax purposes.

The company choosing to use MACRS depreciation calculations is well advised to obtain a copy of IRS Publication 946, *How to Depreciate Property*. This publication can be obtained by calling the IRS at 1-800-TAX-FORM, or it can be downloaded from the IRS Web site on the Internet at www.irs.ustreas.gov. You might also find it useful to seek advice about depreciation from an accountant.

If you choose to use the MACRS method for calculating depreciation, you can use tables published by the IRS to perform the calculations. Some of these tables are reproduced here; others are available in the IRS publication mentioned earlier.

MACRS Depreciation Tables

The MACRS depreciation tables reproduced in this book are the tables most commonly used for 5- and 7-year assets (see Tables 16.1 and 16.2, respectively). However, additional tables are available for use in situations in which the majority of assets are purchased in a particular quarter of the year. The best approach is to consult an accountant when determining which method of depreciation fits your situation.

TABLE 16.1   MACRS Depreciation Deduction for 5-Year Property

Year	Percentage*
1	20.00%
2	32.00%
3	19.20%
4	11.52%
5	11.52%
6	5.76%

*Multiply the percentage by the cost of the property to determine the depreciation deduction for the year.

TABLE 16.2   MACRS Depreciation Deduction for 7-Year Property

Year	Percentage*
1	14.29%
2	24.49%
3	17.49%
4	12.49%
5	8.93%
6	8.92%
7	8.93%
8	4.46%

*Multiply the percentage by the cost of the property to determine the depreciation deduction for the year.

Recording Depreciation

After you figure out how much depreciation expense to deduct for each of your assets, you must record this depreciation.

You might choose to record an entire year's worth of depreciation at the end of the year, or you might make monthly or quarterly adjustments for depreciation so that the financial statements you produce during the year reflect an accurate amount for depreciation.

There is no provision in QuickBooks for calculating or recording depreciation expense. You must perform the calculations on your own, and then record the amount of depreciation yourself.

In QuickBooks, you make a *general journal entry* to reflect the depreciation expense and the adjustment to your accumulated depreciation account. General journal entries are adjustments made to the balances in your accounts without the use of forms such as invoices, bills, and checks. A general journal entry must always have two sides—a debit and a credit.

→ To find more information on debits and credits, **see page 107**.

If an amount was misclassified, for example, a general journal entry can be made to correct the classification of the amount. If $100 was recorded as a repair expense when it was supposed to be an expense for office supplies, you can make a general journal entry to reduce the repairs expense account by $100 and increase the office supplies account for $100 without having to open any forms.

A general journal entry is necessary to record depreciation because depreciation isn't generated by any of the traditional forms. When you record depreciation expense, an offsetting amount is recorded as accumulated depreciation.

For example, if your depreciation expense for the period is $500, of which $300 is for computer equipment and $200 is for office furniture, a general journal entry looks like the one in Figure 16.1.

Figure 16.1
This general journal entry records depreciation expense and accumulated depreciation.

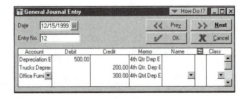

Creating a General Journal Entry

Take the following steps to create a general journal entry:

1. From the Activities menu, choose Make Journal Entry. The General Journal Entry window appears.
2. Verify that the date of the entry is correct. The entry date doesn't always coincide with today's date. For example, you might have some end-of-the-year journal entries to make, which are dated 12/31, but not actually have the information to make these entries until sometime in January (see the following section, "Following the Audit Trail").
3. Enter a number for this journal entry in the Entry No. area. Typically, general journal entries are numbered consecutively.

> **Caution**
>
> Using journal entry numbers is a process that is completely at your discretion. QuickBooks does not number journal entries, nor does it care if you duplicate journal entry numbers. You must enter the number of your choice on each journal entry, being careful not to reuse numbers.
>
> When you begin creating a journal entry, it is recommended that you click the Prev button to view the previous journal entry so that you can see what the most recently used number is. Then click Next to return to the new journal entry where you can enter the next consecutive number.

4. Click in the Account column; an arrow appears. Click this arrow to display the drop-down list, and then click the name of the account to be debited (Depreciation Expense is being debited in Figure 16.1).
5. Click in the Debit column and enter the amount of the debit.
6. Optionally, you can enter a memo in the Memo column across from the debit amount. In the example shown in Figure 16.1, the memo description is *4th Qtr Dep Expense*.
7. Use the Name column if this journal entry is to be charged to a specific customer or job. Depreciation expense is probably not charged to a job unless a piece of equipment is purchased for a specific job and is only used for that job.
8. Repeat steps 4–7 if more than one account is to be debited.
9. Click in the Account column again and choose the name of the account to be credited.
10. Click in the Credit column and enter the amount of the credit.
11. Optionally, you can enter a memo in the Memo column across from the credit amount.
12. Use the Name column to choose a customer or job if this amount is to be reflected on the records for a specific customer.

13. Repeat steps 9–12 if more than one account is to be credited. In the example shown in Figure 16.1, two different accumulated depreciation accounts are being credited.
14. When you have completed your journal entry, click the OK button to record your entry and close the General Journal Entry window, or click Next if you need to make additional journal entries.

Following the Audit Trail

QuickBooks comes with a feature called the Audit Trail, which is a summary of all the transactions and changes to transactions made in your QuickBooks file. If you have a tendency to change transactions (to go back to previous forms and make changes), you might find the Audit Trail useful in identifying when these changes occurred. If more than one person has access to your company's QuickBooks file, the Audit Trail provides a certain amount of security in that no changes can be made to any forms or amounts in your file without a record of the changes appearing in the Audit Trail.

> **Note:** The Audit Trail works completely in the background and doesn't interrupt your day-to-day QuickBooks activities.

If you use an outside accountant to examine your records and help with year-end adjustments, your accountant will probably request that you use the Audit Trail.

To turn on the Audit Trail, open the File menu and choose Preferences. When the Preferences window appears, click the Accounting icon at the left side of the window. On the Company Preferences tab, check the box next to Use audit trail.

Only transactions that occur while the Audit Trail is turned on are stored in this list. To view the listed transactions, open the Reports menu and choose Other Reports. Then select Audit Trail from the submenu.

Selling Depreciable Assets

When you sell an asset that you have been depreciating, the sale of the asset must be recorded in such a way as to relieve both the asset account and the accumulated depreciation account of the value of the sold item.

Consider the following example: You purchased a piece of equipment for $3,500, and over the years you took deductions for $1,250 in depreciation expense relating to this piece of equipment. The book value of the asset is therefore $2,250 ($3,500–$1,250), and you sell the asset for $1,700. The following accounts are affected by the sale:

Cash	$1,700	(debit)
Fixed asset: Equipment	$3,500	(credit)
Acc. depreciation: Equipment	$1,250	(debit)
Sale of assets	$550	(debit)

The cash account is increased (debited) as cash is received in the company. The fixed asset account is decreased (credited) to remove the asset from the company balance sheet. The accumulated depreciation account is decreased (debited) to remove accumulated depreciation relating to this asset from the company balance sheet. The sale of assets account is decreased (debited) to reflect a loss (amount by which the book value exceeds the sale price) on the sale of the asset.

If the preceding asset is sold for $3,000 instead of $1,700, the cash account shows an increase of $3,000 instead of $1,700, and the sale of assets account shows an increase (credit) of $750 to reflect the gain (amount by which the sales price exceeds book value) on the sale.

Uncle Sam Is Watching

In the previous example, an asset and its related accumulated depreciation are both reduced to zero to remove them from the company's balance sheet, cash is increased to reflect the cash received, and a gain or loss is recorded for the difference.

Be aware that sales of assets are often recorded differently on a company's tax return than they are on a company's balance sheet. This is especially common when a company uses an accelerated method of depreciation. When selling assets, consult a tax professional to determine the proper treatment of the sale for tax purposes.

The sales of your business assets are reflected on tax form 4797, *Sales of Business Property*, which is prepared and filed with your company income tax return. For more information about reporting sales of assets for tax purposes, you can request Publication 544, *Sales and Other Dispositions of Assets*, by calling 1-800-TAX-FORM. You can also download this publication at the IRS's Web site,
http://www.irs.ustreas.gov/prod/forms_pubs/forms.html

Alternatives to QuickBooks for Fixed Asset Tracking

Notice that there is no provision within QuickBooks for calculating depreciation on assets. The information provided in this chapter relating to calculating depreciation might be enough to get you started, or you might feel the need to consult with an accountant who can advise you in this area.

If you know the calculations that you need to make, you can use a spreadsheet program to create a spreadsheet that calculates and keeps track of depreciation for you. An accountant or a computer professional can help you set this up.

An alternative method to help you with your depreciation calculations—especially if you have many assets for which you need some method of tracking depreciation—is to seek out another software program to help with depreciation.

An Internet search for depreciation yields several programs designed to perform depreciation calculations. Many of these programs offer demonstration disks or trial periods so that you can test the software and see if it will be helpful to you. Intuit's TurboTax program also provides depreciation calculations.

TROUBLESHOOTING

ENTERING DEPRECIATION

I forgot to record my monthly depreciation expense last month. Do I record double the expense this month?

Consider, instead, going back to last month and making the depreciation journal entry, and then reprinting financial statements for last month. If this is not possible, you can record a double expense this month, but first check your company policy for such matters.

ENTERING YEAR-END ADJUSTMENTS

My accountant gave me some year-end adjustments to my accounts. How do I enter these changes?

Use the General Journal Entry feature to enter your accountant's changes. See "Creating a General Journal Entry" in this chapter for more information.

ENTERING ADDITIONAL FIRST YEAR DEPRECIATION

I want to enter additional first year depreciation (Section 179 depreciation) for new assets I purchased. How does this get treated?

Under the rules of Internal Revenue Code Section 179, business are entitled to take a deduction for up to $19,000 (the allowable amount changes each year—this is the 1999 amount) of the cost of certain assets in the year of acquisition. Use a General Journal Entry to enter your Section 179 deduction.

CHAPTER 17

ENTERING CASH TRANSACTIONS

In this chapter

Forms of Cash   264

Quick Cash Entry   264

Daily Cash Summaries   265

Cash Over or Short   266

Depositing Cash   268

Credit Card Payments from Customers   268

Many businesses deal in cash—retail stores, filling stations, lawn care services, and so on. When these businesses receive cash, they must have a method of recording the cash and reporting the amount received.

Forms of Cash

Cash is more than just a handful of bills and coins. You can receive cash in any of several guises:

- Currency, including bills and coins
- Checks
- Traveler's checks
- Credit card transactions

When you receive cash, your immediate reaction might be to run for the bank to make a deposit. Before you make that trip, however, perform some QuickBooks tasks that will help you keep track of all this cash, where it came from, and what you plan to do with it.

Quick Cash Entry

One way to enter cash in your QuickBooks company file is to use the Cash Sales form. This form is similar in appearance to the invoice form, but the following major differences exist between an invoiced sale and a cash sale:

- When you enter a sale on an invoice, it is for the purpose of billing the customer, so it is important that you know the name and other pertinent information about the customer. In fact, QuickBooks does not accept an invoice that does not have a customer name filled in. In the case of a cash sale, you can record the sale without filling in the customer area of the form. Cash sales often occur without the vendor (you) knowing who the customer is. The Enter Cash Sales form has a field for Customer:Job entry, but the form can be prepared even if this field is left blank.
- The accounting for cash sales is different from the accounting for invoices. When you record an invoice, QuickBooks increases an income account by the amount of the sale and increases accounts receivable for the same amount. With a cash sale, income is increased, but accounts receivable is not affected. Instead, cash received but not yet deposited goes into an asset account called Undeposited Funds (or you might have set up a cash holding account with a different name).

For a comprehensive example of entering a cash sale in QuickBooks using the Enter Cash Sales form, see the section "Receiving Cash" in Chapter 12, "Recording Income."

Daily Cash Summaries

During the day, you can collect money in your business establishment by placing cash in a cash register (or your pocket!). At the end of the day, you need to get all that cash information into QuickBooks.

One way to enter your day's cash activities into QuickBooks is to prepare a daily cash summary. The summary is like creating one giant sales form that adds up all the sales for the day. This might be sufficient in terms of tracking sales, unless you need to track each individual sale. Create a summary of daily cash sales with the following steps.

> **Tip #43 from Gail Perry**
>
> Some companies don't need a specific record of each sale; they find that a daily summary gives them all the information they need. Others find the information about individual sales necessary and useful. If the time that each sale occurs is important to you—so that you can see which times of the day your store is busy, for example—you will want an individual record of each sale. Alternatively, if your business flows evenly throughout the day, or if you already know your peak periods, you might not need to know at what time sales occurred. If you have employees who are paid on a commission, tracking individual sales is important to that calculation. But if your employees are all paid at the same rate and are all considered to be adding to the value of the sale, the individual sales by employee are not useful to you.

Follow these steps to create a summary of daily cash sales:

1. Choose <u>A</u>ctivities, Enter Cash <u>S</u>ales. The Enter Cash Sales window appears, just as it does when you plan to enter only one sale at a time.

2. In the area labeled Customer:Job, enter a name that describes this cash sale summary (see Figure 17.1); for example, you might want to enter *Daily Sales Summary* or *Summary of Cash Sales*. If this is the first time you have used this description, you are notified that no customer exists with that name. Choose <u>Q</u>uick Add to add the name to your customer list so that it is accessible to you in the future.

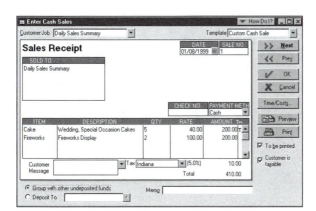

Figure 17.1
Use a cash sales form to create a daily cash summary.

3. If you use classes, enter the correct class in the space provided. You can be entering the daily cash sales from your downtown division, for example, which falls into a class that you have named *Downtown*.

4. Verify that the date is correct. The date that appears on this form is the date on which the sales were made, which is not necessarily today's date.

5. If you use a cash sales template that you have designed especially for recording the cash sales summary, choose the template that you want by clicking on the arrow in the template area. If you choose a template that you have customized, the steps that follow might differ, depending on which fields appear on your customized cash sales form.

→ To find more information on customizing forms such as cash sales entry forms, **see p. 337**.

6. You can leave the Check No. and the Pmt Method areas blank.

7. In the Item area at the bottom of the form, list each item that was sold during the day and the quantity that was sold. This way, QuickBooks can update your inventory records to reflect items that are sold and no longer in stock. If you don't use QuickBooks's inventory tracking feature, the information in the Item area can still be useful because it tells you which services or non-inventory items you sold during the day.

8. Enter a Qty (optional) if you plan to record quantities of items sold, and enter a Rate if you want QuickBooks to calculate the total amount based on a unit rate. Alternatively, you can enter the total amount yourself in the Amount column.

9. If the amount you received is to be deposited immediately to your bank account, you can choose the name of the account at the bottom of the window in the Deposit To area. If you plan to hold the deposit so that it can be combined with other deposits, click the Group with other undeposited funds button.

10. To enter another daily summary (from a store at a different location, for example), click the Next button; otherwise, click OK. Your entries have been saved, and you're ready to read the "Making Deposits" section in Chapter 12.

When you create the daily cash summary, QuickBooks enters the total amount as income and offsets that amount with an entry to your undeposited funds account.

Cash Over or Short

What happens if the actual cash that you count up doesn't agree with the amount reported on your cash sales forms for the day, or on your daily cash summary form? This is a frequent occurrence, especially in retail stores where a large quantity of cash is handled each day.

You need to create an account that gives you a place to report these overages and shortages. You can then note a discrepancy in cash when you fill out your daily cash summary form. Create a new account to track cash overages and shortages by following these steps:

1. Choose Lists, Chart of Accounts. The Chart of Accounts list window appears.
2. Click the Accounts button at the bottom of the window and choose New. The New Account window appears (see Figure 17.2).

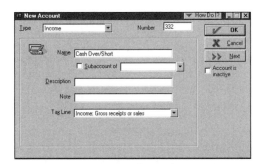

Figure 17.2
Create a new account for recording cash discrepancies.

3. Decide whether you want this account to reside with your income accounts or your expense accounts. Consider past performance, and if your company seems to experience more cash overages than cash shortages, choose Income for the type of account. If the opposite is true, choose Expense for the type of account.
4. Enter a name for this account—such as *Cash Over/Short*—so that its purpose is easy to understand.
5. Enter a tax line if you plan to use QuickBooks to help you with your income tax return.
6. Click OK to save your new account information, and close the window.

Before you can use your new cash over/short account, create an item so that you can apply the cash overage or shortage right on a cash sale or daily cash summary form. Create a new item for cash overages and shortages by following these steps:

1. Choose Lists, Items. The Item list window appears.
2. Click the Item button at the bottom of the window and choose New. The New Item window appears (see Figure 17.3).

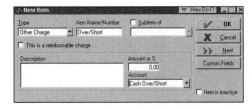

Figure 17.3
Creating an item for cash discrepancies enables you to enter the item on a cash sale form.

3. Choose Other Charge for the type of item.
4. In the Item Name/Number area, enter a name for this item. Cash Over/Short won't fit because the item name can have a maximum of 13 characters, including spaces. Instead, think of some other appropriate name, such as *Over/Short*, *Adjustment*, or *Reconcile*.
5. In the Account area, choose the Cash Over/Short account that you just created.
6. Click OK to save your new item and close the window.

Now that you've created both a new account for recording your cash overage and shortage amounts and a new item so that you can enter these amounts right on your cash sales form, you're ready to record a cash discrepancy.

Imagine it's the end of the day and you have created a daily cash summary report such as the one described in the last section. You arrive at a total for the cash that you expect to deposit for the day. But when you count your cash, you find you are $2.00 short of the expected total.

After you enter all the items that you sold today, click again in the item area of your cash summary form, and then choose your new Over/Short item. In the Amount column, enter the amount of an overage as a positive number. Enter a shortage as a negative number by entering a minus sign before you enter the number.

Depositing Cash

After you've entered your individual cash sales or your daily cash summary in QuickBooks, you need to deposit the money you've received.

For detailed steps to make and record a deposit in QuickBooks, see the section "Making Deposits" in Chapter 12.

Credit Card Payments from Customers

When a customer uses a credit card such as MasterCard or Visa to pay you, the credit card receipt gets deposited just like cash.

Later—usually monthly—you will receive a statement from the institution to which your credit card payments are deposited. The statement includes a fee. If you pay this fee by writing a check, follow the procedure for paying bills that is described in Chapter 15, "Purchase Orders, Accounts Payable, and Paying Bills."

On the other hand, if the bank withdraws the fee from your deposited money, you must make a general journal entry to record the increase in your expense account for the bank fee (a debit) and the reduction in your cash account (a credit).

Examples of general journal entries and a discussion of this type of accounting procedure appear in Chapter 16, "Managing Fixed Assets."

Troubleshooting

Using an Over/Short Account

My deposit for the day doesn't agree with the sales on the cash register. Now what?

Use an over/short account to reflect minor discrepancies in daily cash sales. Major and frequent discrepancies require investigation into the cash counting methods and controls in place in your business.

PART III

PAYING EMPLOYEES AND CONTRACTORS

18 Paying Employees and Contractors 273

19 QuickBooks and Payroll Taxes 307

CHAPTER 18

PAYING EMPLOYEES AND CONTRACTORS

In this chapter

Determining Employees and Independent Contractors   274

Gathering Payroll Information   275

Paying Employees Versus Paying Independent Contractors   277

QuickBooks Payroll and Employee Setup   278

Setting Up Employees   279

Updating Year-to-Date Amounts   284

Updating Payroll Tax Tables   288

Payday   291

When you first set up your QuickBooks company with the EasyStep Interview, part of that process is choosing how to pay the people who work for you. Not everyone that works for you is an employee. QuickBooks defines employees as people that you pay for services, and from whom you deduct taxes, sending that money in the employee's name to state and federal tax agencies. Independent contractors—people you hire to do a particular job—are not your employees, and you don't withhold taxes from their paychecks. Additionally, do not consider yourself an employee of your own company unless you pay yourself via payroll accounts as you do all your other employees. A business partner is also not an employee, unless she or he is actually on the payroll.

Determining Employees and Independent Contractors

Sometimes it's difficult to determine whether someone who works for you is an employee or an independent contractor. The IRS has published a list of 20 questions to help answer this one question. The more positive answers you get to these questions, the more likely the person is an employee rather than an independent contractor. Following are the questions that you can ask to determine the status of someone who does work for you:

1. Do you (as the person paying the worker) give the worker instructions that he is expected to obey?
2. Does your company provide the worker with training?
3. Are the worker's services integrated into the regular business operation of your company?
4. Is it a requirement that the worker, personally, provide the services?
5. Is the worker prohibited from subcontracting the work?
6. Is the business relationship between your company and the worker an ongoing one?
7. Do you set the hours for the worker?
8. Is the worker expected to work full time for your organization?
9. Is the work performed on your company's premises?
10. Do you instruct the worker regarding the order in which to perform his tasks?
11. Is the worker expected to submit reports (oral or written) that summarize his work progress?
12. Does the worker receive payments at regular intervals, such as weekly or monthly?
13. Does the worker get reimbursed for business and travel expenses?
14. Does your company supply the tools and supplies for this worker?
15. Does the worker have little or no significant investment in the tools used to perform the job?
16. Is the company responsible for absorbing any loss resulting from the work performed?

17. Is the worker prohibited from working for more than one company or person at a time?
18. Is the worker prohibited from making his services available to the general public?
19. Is it the company's responsibility if the worker does not perform to the specifications of the project?
20. Is the company responsible if the worker causes any damage?

Gathering Payroll Information

When you first began setting up your QuickBooks company, you began reading about payroll, tax, and insurance withholding; perhaps you didn't have all the information handy for setting up your payroll during the EasyStep Interview. It's easy to add or change payroll information after the interview is completed. It might appear that if you answered QuickBooks's questions the wrong way, undoing what you've done is a major chore. Not so!

If you chose to learn more about payroll—or to take the time to gather more information—before responding to some of the payroll questions, rest assured that your EasyStep Interview remembered everything you answered, and that all the information you provided will still be there when you come back. Clicking the Leave button in the EasyStep Interview does not mean that you have to start from scratch. When you return to the interview (by choosing File, EasyStep Interview), you can continue entering payroll information where you left off.

> **Note**
> If you did not do an EasyStep Interview for your company and are entering company information as you go, special tasks that you need to go back and do are addressed throughout this chapter.

Your Personal Experience With Payroll

If you've never set up a payroll before, you'll read through this chapter and realize that the onerous task of deducting money from people's paychecks and making sure it gets sent to the right agencies is now part of your job. Payroll is serious business; you are dealing with other people's money. You might never appreciate having QuickBooks so much as when an employee comes to you about discrepancies in a paycheck. QuickBooks makes such record-keeping virtually painless. It is easy to draw up reports and show exactly how much sick time an employee has coming, how much overtime was worked, and exactly when it is time to send the government its quarterly tax payment for each employee.

If you have worked with payroll before—perhaps using another program—or with a couple of bank accounts and a calculator, you've already had a taste of having to keep track of health insurance premiums, state disability payments, worker's compensation, accrued vacation time, and so on. You'll enjoy how easy QuickBooks makes it to create separate payroll items for all those deductions, printing out paychecks that accurately break down what each person is really owed month after month. QuickBooks makes it easy to provide mileage reimbursements, set up voluntary contribution accounts that are specific for each employee (such as Flexible Spending accounts), and determine AEIC eligibility. You can even automate bonuses and create different commission rates for each employee. You'll be happy to learn that QuickBooks knows which payroll adjustments are computed on gross pay and which are computed on net. After you do the initial work of setting up employees and their payroll deductions and contributions, you'll find that regular payroll tasks can become completely automated.

Planning Payroll

Regardless of whether you use the EasyStep Interview, there are several steps for setting up and paying employees. The following are tasks that you must accomplish before using QuickBooks payroll. These are necessary to keep accurate records of how much you've paid each employee, and to keep accurate totals for taxes, contributions, and accrual of benefits such as sick time and vacation. After listing these tasks, they are explored step-by-step in the following sections:

- Determine who is an employee and who isn't. Understand the distinction between paying an employee and a contractor (see previous section in this chapter).
- Make sure Payroll is turned on in the Preferences menu.
- Make final decisions about how often you'll pay your employees, and think about which employees are salaried and which are paid by the hour.
- Determine if you want to have special types of payroll accounts (one for supervisors, and another for labor, for example), rather than the standard payroll related accounts that QuickBooks automatically creates.
- Review the payroll items that QuickBooks sets up. These are the items that QuickBooks uses to make deductions from employee paychecks, to generate reports, and to make payments to tax agencies, insurance firms, and so on.
- Determine whether you need to create other payroll items. When QuickBooks sets up payroll, it includes familiar payroll items such as Federal Income Tax and Medicare contributions, state tax deductions, and so on. However, QuickBooks needs to know about all deductions and contributions such as 401Ks, mileage reimbursement, and anything that has a positive or negative effect on your payroll and liability accounts.
- Create new items, if necessary. Examples include company-paid insurance and union dues.

Tip #44 from

Gail Perry

If you pay your employees variable commissions or bonuses, or if you reimburse mileage at different rates for each employee, you don't need to create new payroll items to account for each variable. You can set a distinct rate for each employee in the employee information section, using the same payroll item.

- You can then enter data for all your employees and make individual changes in their deductions and contributions, as you deem necessary. Use the Employees List to add new employees or to edit existing ones.
- Decide on a company *start date (page 40)*, if you haven't already done so.
- Enter all payroll history from the beginning of the year up to the start date of your QuickBooks company. This includes all wages paid to employees, taxes, deductions, and contributions. This needs to be done before you use QuickBooks payroll, so that QuickBooks knows when to stop deducting certain taxes and withholdings for that year. This payroll history includes money paid to any employees who have worked for you during the current year, *even if you no longer employ them*. You need not create adjustments for new employees whom you have not yet paid.
- Determine how you want to use timesheets. Do you want to print them for each hourly employee? Do you want to use the QuickBooks Timer to have employees enter their hours from the Timer? Do you want employees to enter their own hours into QuickBooks, or are you the one doing it?
- Finally, QuickBooks generates regular paychecks using the Timer or the hours that you manually enter, or by salary or project. All you need to do is select Pay Employees from the Employees Items list. All accounts are appropriately debited and credited, and checks are printed.
- QuickBooks also generates checks to tax agencies and other payroll liabilities such as insurance and retirement plans. This occurs at the intervals that you set, or when you click Pay Liabilities/Taxes from the Employee Item List.

The following sections look closely at these steps.

→ If you haven't done so already, this is a good time to think about keeping your payroll information secure. To learn more about setting up passwords and limiting access to parts of your QuickBooks company file, **see p. 480**.

Paying Employees Versus Paying Independent Contractors

If someone is your employee, you pay his taxes as well as his wages. The complexity of setting up payroll encourages lots of businesses to work with independent contractors whenever possible. However, there are some tax issues at stake when you employ a contractor. Independent contractors are required to report their income to the IRS and pay tax on that income. You play a part in this process by providing your contractors with a record of the amounts that they receive from you. The IRS requires you to report independent contractor amounts of $600 or more per year on form 1099.

QuickBooks enables you to track all independent contractor payments and prepare the 1099 forms. This process is explored in detail at the end of this chapter.

Tip #45 from

The best way to work with independent contractors in QuickBooks is to set them up as vendors. You can pay your contractors just as if you were paying a bill to a vendor. This enables you to keep track of the yearly totals, seeing how much money you pay out to contractors and how much is paid as wages and salary to employees. Payments to independent contractors are discussed later in this chapter.

QuickBooks Payroll and Employee Setup

Before getting into the nuts and bolts of actually setting up employees, here is an examination of the two accounts that QuickBooks sets up when you turn on payroll. You'll see that QuickBooks can do so much more than simply set up a roster of the people who work for you. QuickBooks creates vitally important accounts that help you keep track of all employee deductions, in addition to making it easy for you to make sure all that money gets sent to the correct agency.

Payroll Expense and Liability Accounts

When you first turn on the QuickBooks payroll feature, QuickBooks creates two new accounts: Payroll Expense and Payroll Liability accounts. (Figure 18.1 shows the Payroll Liability account in the Chart of Accounts. The Payroll Expense account is much farther down the list, appearing with other expense accounts.) Also upon turning on Payroll, QuickBooks automatically assigns the most obvious payroll expenses (wages, company-paid payroll taxes, employee deductions) to one of these two accounts.

Figure 18.1
The Payroll Liabilities account as it appears in the Chart of Accounts.

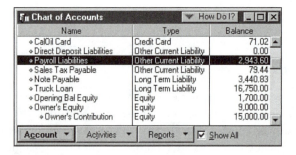

Understanding Payroll Expenses and Payroll Liabilities

When you issue paychecks, each of these payroll accounts has its balance decreased or increased as is appropriate. If you create additional payroll items (union dues, voluntary employee deductions such as United Way, or 401K plans, for example), QuickBooks assists you in choosing the right account. Here's why, and here's what's at stake:

- **QuickBooks sets up the Payroll Expense account to handle pure company expenses**—These are wages that you owe to employees, company bonuses, and so on. The wages and any employee benefits you pay are recorded as expenses. The company-paid portions of taxes, such as social security and Medicare, are also expenses that are paid when they are due (usually quarterly).

- **QuickBooks sets up a Payroll Liability account to handle amounts you owe, but have not yet paid**—These include each employee's share of state and federal taxes. The Payroll Liability account helps you keep track of money that is not your own and that is just waiting to be sent to the appropriate tax agencies. QuickBooks calculates and deducts the correct amount from each employee for taxes based on your choices in Employee Setup (see next section), and it records the totals in your Payroll Liability account. When you issue paychecks, you see your Payroll Liability account increase because you are now holding on to even more of your employee's money than you were before—so it's considered an increased liability.

Setting Up Employees

Setting up employees includes making QuickBooks aware of all the paychecks you've written since the beginning of the year, up to the date you that you designate as your QuickBooks *start date*. You can't record new paychecks for employees unless QuickBooks knows the history of the employees, so you'll learn how to set up employees and enter all payment data since the beginning of the year. The purpose of this long way around is to ensure that at the end of this process, you can issue paychecks to your company's employees, with all deductions accurately accounted for and credited, and that you can produce year-to-date reports summarizing your employees' earnings.

For the purposes of bringing QuickBooks up to speed with where your business is in the real world, this employee list has to include all employees that have worked for you during the current year—including those who no longer do.

From the QuickBooks Navigator, select the Payroll and Time tab, and click the Employees Icon. The Employee List appears (see Figure 18.2).

Figure 18.2
Set up employee data from the Employee List.

Select New from the Employees drop-down menu at the lower left, and you see the New Employee dialog box. It has the following three tabs:

- **Address Info**—Fill in basic statistics such as Name, Address, and Phone Number. Also include Social Security Number and Hire date. If the employee ever leaves, you'll record that information here as well.

- **Additional Info**—This tab has extras such as Birthday, Date of Last Raise, and Spouse's Name. If there is other incidental information that you want to keep track of for each employee, for example department, team, or travel preferences, this is where you create it. The Define Fields button enables you to create new fields to appear on the Additional Info tab for each employee. Note that you can create fields for Customer and Vendor forms from this same dialog box. Employee Account Numbers or birth dates can be recorded here, if your company uses them.

> **Note**
>
> If you create a new field for one employee, it is available for you to use with every employee. When filling in data for the Additional Info tab, consider whether there is any sort of useful information you might want to track. For example, if your company has to relocate, you might want to speak with each employee about the chances of them relocating with you. Create a field here to keep track of the results of those conversations.

- **Payroll Info**—The Payroll Info tab is where you record how much you pay this employee, how often, and what deductions you remove from his regular paychecks. You also manage employee sick time and vacation time pay rates from this tab, specifying the rate at which these items accrue for this employee and whether you want unused sick time and vacation to *zero out* (start over) at the year's end. Tax withholdings and preferences are also managed from the Payroll Info tab. Specify how often this employee is to be paid by choosing a Pay Period from the drop-down menu.

→ To find more information on creating custom reports, **see p. 361**.

SPECIFYING EARNINGS

To specify how much you are going to pay this employee, click the top line in the Name field of the Earnings panel. A drop-down menu appears, containing the following items:

- To pay this employee a particular hourly wage, select Regular Pay from the drop-down menu. Specify an hourly rate by typing a number into the Hour/Annual Rate field. The number you type there is how much this employee makes per hour.

- To pay this employee a yearly salary, select Salary from the drop-down menu. After determining how much per year you want to pay, type that number into the Hour/Annual Rate field.

Use this same Earnings panel to specify an overtime, a sick time, and a vacation time pay rate for this employee (see Figure 18.3). Type an hourly rate even if the pay rate for sick and vacation time is the same as the regular hourly rate.

SETTING UP EMPLOYEES | 281

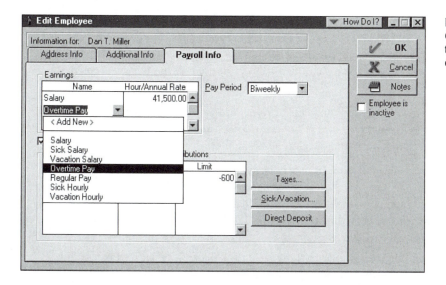

Figure 18.3
Creating a new overtime item for an employee.

Remember that in the Earnings field, the title Name does not refer to the name of the employee, but to the name of the payroll item that you are applying to this employee.

If you are using QuickBooks Pro, you'll see a Use Time Data to Create Paychecks check box. Click this if you want to calculate paychecks from QuickBooks *time tracking (page 443)*.

APPLYING NEW PAYROLL ITEMS

If you've created other payroll items that apply to earnings, such as a special rate for working weekends, holidays, and night shift, use the drop-down menu to include those rates as well. To include more than one type of payroll item in the Earnings field, just click the line below the item you just added, and you see a new drop-down menu (as shown in the preceding figure). The same choices are available from this menu, but they now apply to this new line. Don't forget to type an hourly rate for each new item you add. If the number of items you use exceeds the number of visible lines, just use the scrolling button to view the lower ones.

Each payroll item and rate that you add to this employee's record is available for you to apply to his paycheck. To learn how to create a new Payroll Item, see the following section.

CREATING A NEW PAYROLL ITEM

The Payroll Info tab of the New Employee dialog box enables you to create new Payroll Items on-the-fly by clicking Add New at the top of each drop-down menu.

From the Names field of the Earnings panel, you can create a new Hourly or Yearly Salary Payroll Item. This adds a new category of payment that you can apply to any employee's paycheck. You can make a new salary or hourly wage item if you are creating a new job and job description in your company—one that is easier to manage if you can track it separately from other employees. When you create the new item, you are asked to specify either hourly wage or salary, and to choose the account from which this new payroll item is to be paid. As you choose an account type, explanations as to the purpose of each account appear beneath your choice.

If you want to create a new Additions, Deductions, and Company Contributions item, click in an empty line below the Earnings panel, and choose Add New. A dialog box appears. Each of the items has features that need to be pointed out:

- **Commission**—When creating a new commission item, the rate that you enter here can be overridden on a paycheck-to-paycheck basis. You can create a new commission rate on-the-fly for each employee. The rate that you type here only applies if no other rate is chosen on the paycheck itself. Again, click Track Expense by Job if you want more powerful reports that associate this payroll expense with an employee's job.

- **Addition**—Fill in fields similar to those used for a deduction, but in this case, the Calculation Type feature becomes more important. For example, if you are creating a new mileage reimbursement item, click As a Dollar Rate Times a Quantity; you are prompted to enter the number of miles this employee drove, and, therefore, to pay her for every mile she drove rather than just for one. Also, if you are planning to pay an employee for piecework, for example five dollars for each blouse sewn, click Based on Quantity; you can specify in each paycheck the number of blouses sewn. Click Track Expense by Job if you want to create reports that link this addition to the job accounts that this employee has been working on.

- **Deduction**—When you create a new deduction, specify its name, to whom the deduction is to be paid, and whether the deduction is to be applied to net or gross pay. Also include an amount or percentage for this deduction and an annual limit dollar amount if it's the same for each employee.

- **Company Contribution**—The Company Contribution dialog box requires the same type of input as the preceding payroll items. Create a new company contribution item if your company is contributing to a particular fund or company on behalf of its employees.

Tip #46 from

Gail Perry

When creating a new payroll item, specify only dollar or percentage amounts for an item (at the time that you are creating it) if the sum is the same for each employee. If you anticipate applying different amounts to each employee, don't specify an amount at this time. Later, when you apply the item, type an exact amount on each employee's paycheck.

CREATING ITEMS FOR WEEKEND PAY AND SHIFT DIFFERENTIALS

Many employers pay more per hour for working weekends and night shifts, and sometimes employees who work holidays get extra compensation as well. Often, these amounts are calculated as an additional amount per hour. For example, an employee whose *base pay rate is*

$16 per hour might make an additional $8 per hour for working overtime. With QuickBooks, it's best to create an item called *overtime* that pays out at the full $24 per hour rate, rather than creating an item for $8 per hour that you can tack on as extra when applicable.

ADDITIONS, DEDUCTIONS, AND COMPANY CONTRIBUTIONS

Use the Additions, Deductions, and Company Contributions portion of the Payroll Info tab of the New Employee dialog box to specify all types of regular adjustments to an employee's paycheck, except for taxes. Apply payroll items such as union dues, 401K deductions, health insurance, mileage reimbursement, and employee bonuses.

To apply an addition, deduction, or company contribution to an employee, click the first available blank line in the Names field, as shown in Figure 18.4. A drop-down menu appears. From this list, select any item to make it appear on that line. In the fields to the right of the Name field, type an amount and yearly limit for this item. When you type an amount for a deduction, the number automatically turns to negative. Rather than a simple dollar amount, you can also specify a percentage.

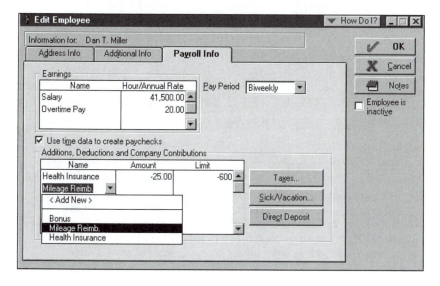

Figure 18.4
Adding a deduction or addition item to the employee's paycheck.

To learn how to create this type of payroll item, see the previous section, "Creating a New Payroll Item."

SETTING UP PAYROLL TAXES

Chapter 19, "QuickBooks and Payroll Taxes," is dedicated entirely to payroll taxes. For now, know that you need to click the Taxes button—found on the Payroll Info tab—to set withholdings, allowances, and filing status. You see three separate tabs for setting up taxes: Federal, State, and Other.

Establishing Sick and Vacation Time

Click the Sick/Vacation button to open the dialog box shown in Figure 18.5.

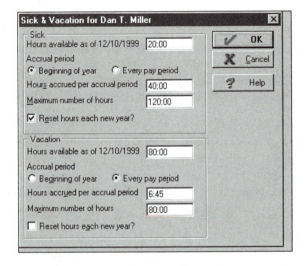

Figure 18.5
Setting up sick and vacation time for an employee.

In this dialog box, you determine the accrual rate for sick and vacation time and type the number of hours available as of the current date. Click the Every Pay Period button to allow the employee to accrue a certain amount of hours per pay period toward this benefit, or click Beginning of Year to front load the employee with a certain number of hours for the entire year. You can also specify if sick and vacation time is to zero out at the beginning of the year.

Tip #47 from	Some companies institute a *sick bonus* for employees who seldom call in sick. After resetting sick hours at the beginning of the year, a bonus is awarded to the employee. This bonus can be set up as a payroll item or simply applied spontaneously to the final paycheck of the year. If you were to set such an item up as a company contribution, for example a certain dollar amount per hour, make sure you've clicked the Based on Quantity button, which applies this set dollar amount to every hour of remaining sick time.

Updating Year-to-Date Amounts

After completing the previous sections, an employee is set up for regular payroll activity. (You might want to review payroll taxes in Chapter 19 before actually printing out checks.)

Because we are moving through the process of initially setting up payroll, we'll explore how to enter information about all employees so that your withholding, contribution, and deduction totals are all up-to-date.

Entering Year-to-Date Paycheck Amounts

At this time, you need to locate records for any paychecks that you've written to any employee from January of the current year to your QuickBooks start date. You need the total amounts that you've paid to each employee, as well as all deductions and contributions during that period.

To update year-to-date paycheck amounts, follow these steps:

1. Click the Payroll and Time tab of the QuickBooks Navigator and choose the YTD amounts icon. You see the dialog box shown in Figure 18.6.

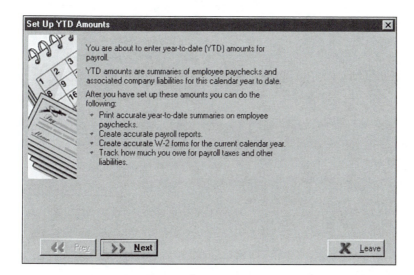

Figure 18.6
Bringing all your payroll accounts up-to-date.

2. Read the instructions and click Next. The next two dialog boxes prompt you for the following three dates:
    - Your QuickBooks start date
    - The date you want to show QuickBooks Year-to-Date summaries as truly affecting your bank accounts
    - The day you'll start paying employees with QuickBooks paychecks

    After answering questions about these dates, you see a dialog box for entering data about each employee (see Figure 18.7)

3. Double-click an employee's name to enter new data. Just like the Payroll Info tab of the New Employees dialog box, use the drop-down menus that appear to enter wage data in the upper fields, and use the lower fields to enter deductions and contributions (see Figure 18.8).

Figure 18.7
Select an employee for whom data needs to be updated. Click Enter Summary after clicking on the employee's name.

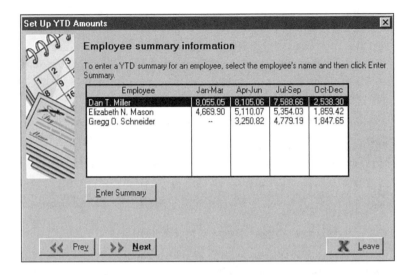

Figure 18.8
Adding employee payment data from the beginning of the year up to the QuickBooks start date.

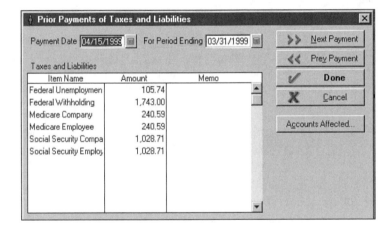

4. Use the Pay Period Summary panel at the lower right to specify the time frame that is covered by each adjustment. This is your *adjustment period*. In the following sidebar, learn the advantages and disadvantages of choosing monthly, quarterly, or a single adjustment period starting at the beginning of the year.

Choosing an Adjustment Period
Before you begin entering YTD amount data, you have to choose an *adjustment period*. You can enter a sweeping sum for each employee from the beginning of the current year until now, or you can break down the data into quarterly (or even monthly) chunks and enter it that way. The amount of detail that is available for QuickBooks reports depends on this choice. The smaller your adjustment period is, the more accurate QuickBooks can be with its projections and period summaries. Breaking down your adjustment period into shorter periods is more work, and you might not have detailed enough paper documents to warrant it; but if you do, your QuickBooks reports will be of more help to you.

Keep in mind that tax agencies such as the IRS often expect you to pay employee taxes quarterly, so you might want to set up QuickBooks employee records to create quarterly reports for tax deductions. When those taxes are due, your quarterly tax calculation is easy to find.

Keep in mind that choosing an adjustment period is a different concept from choosing a QuickBooks start date. You can choose to start your QuickBooks company mid-year or at the previous quarter, but in this Year-to-Date Amount dialog box, employee data needs to be entered for the entire year up to the QuickBooks start date.

After you choose an adjustment period and have entered employee data, you cannot change it unless you delete all YTD adjustments for every employee.

5. After you choose the adjustment period, use the Next Period button to move from one time period to the next. For example, if you've used the pay period summary dates to indicate that you want to enter data for the entire year up to now in one summary, you won't need to use the Next button because you've chosen to type all yearly figures in one summary. However, if you've chosen a monthly or quarterly adjustment period, make sure you have your figures from your older documents divided into these periods. Enter data for only that one period. Then, use the Next Period button to move forward to the next quarter, month, or pay period.

6. Add all relevant data for an employee. Then click OK, and move on to another employee.

When you've updated payroll for your entire work force, you'll be back at the Set Up YTD Amounts dialog box (pictured previously in Figure 18.8).

ENTERING PRIOR PAYMENTS OF TAXES AND LIABILITIES

Use the following steps to enter prior payments of taxes and liabilities:

1. Click the Next button in the Set Up YTD Amounts dialog box. You see a dialog box prompting you to enter data for all special the payments that you've made toward health insurance for your employees, pensions, or any company contributions.

2. Click the Create button and you see the Prior Payments of Taxes and Liabilities dialog box (see Figure 18.9).

3. Select any blank line to choose a contribution type from the drop-down menu. Again, use the date boxes to choose an adjustment period. Here, enter any checks you've mailed this year to tax agencies, insurance groups, or any payment that might help QuickBooks create a correct up-to-date picture of where your payroll accounts stand as of the start date. You can write a memo to yourself regarding this adjustment. To add more adjustments, click the line under the adjustment you just created, and a new drop-down menu appears.

4. If applicable, you might see a dialog box that prompts you to enter any unpaid carry-over liabilities from the previous year. You need to enter this as well to make QuickBooks aware of any payments from last year's payroll liabilities that you have yet

to make. Again, choose an item to add and adjust by clicking the top line in the Item Name field. A drop-down menu appears, as usual.

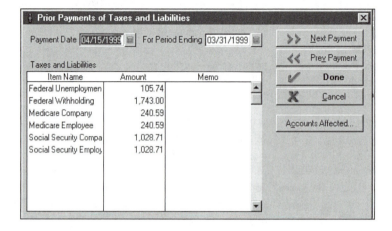

Figure 18.9
Use this dialog box to enter all the company contributions that you've made since the beginning of the year.

Tip #48 from

Some of the payroll dialog boxes, such as those shown in Figures 18.8 and 18.9, have an Accounts Affected button. Click it if you want the payments that you've made to affect an account other than the Payroll Expense and Payroll Liabilities accounts. If you do not want the adjustments that you are making here to affect the Payroll Expense and Payroll Liabilities accounts, click this button and choose another account from the list. The adjustments that you make here still affect the amounts on your Year-to-Date Payroll Reports.

UPDATING PAYROLL TAX TABLES

When you use the Employee List to add a new employee or to edit an existing one, click the Taxes button on the Payroll Info tab to specify withholding and deduction information for each employee (see Figure 18.10). Based on your choices, QuickBooks accurately calculates the amount of taxes owed, deducts the correct amount from each check, and places the sums in the correct accounts. It does this for state taxes as well as for federal; you simply have to select a state from a drop-down menu. You might be wondering how QuickBooks does this. After all, aren't tax withholding calculations time-sensitive, subject to new congressional laws and changes in the tax code?

It is true that tax withholding calculations are time-sensitive. QuickBooks maintains a Tax Table (select Payroll and Time from the Navigator, and click the Tax Table Icon; see Figure 18.11), and uses it to calculate all federal and state taxes. When you first purchase QuickBooks, you need to make sure that your version comes with the latest tax table. Just because you are using QuickBooks 6 does not mean you have the latest version of the table. Intuit updates QuickBooks from time to time by issuing *maintenance releases* that you can download from their Web site (www.intuit.com). In between full new versions of its products, Intuit might offer several maintenance releases to fix small problems and offer the latest information to its customers.

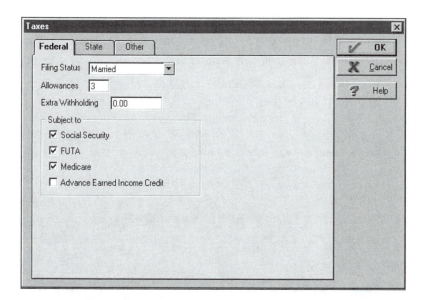

Figure 18.10
Enter Employee Tax Deductions in the Taxes dialog box.

> **Note**
> You can verify if the tax tables you are using are up-to-date by calling Intuit at 800-771-7748. To subscribe to the update service—if you don't have Internet access—call 800-644-8371.

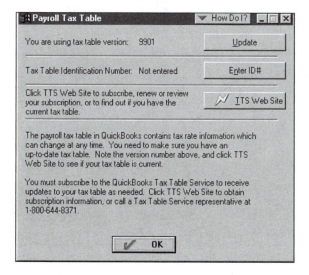

Figure 18.11
The QuickBooks Tax Table, which is used to keep your tax deduction rates up-to-date.

As a QuickBooks owner, you can download one Tax Table update from its Web site for free. You must do this within 60 days of your purchase. After downloading one new Tax Table, you must subscribe to Intuit's Update Service, which currently costs $59.95 for 12 months, to obtain later versions.

You might want to wait until that 60 day period has nearly arrived so you'll stand the greatest chance of obtaining the newest Tax Table before the offer expires.

How do you know if you are using the most recent Tax Table? Click the Tax Table Icon from the Payroll and Time tab, and you see a panel indicating which version you are using. Then, log on to Intuit's Web page. You are prompted to search for a product or a service. Click Tax Table Service, and locate the page on which you are prompted to type your current Tax Table number (see Figure 18.12). If your number matches its most recent release, you do not need to download the new one. If you do need to replace your Tax Table, download the newest one and follow the directions for installation.

Figure 18.12
Intuit's Tax Table Service Web page, where you can make sure your QuickBooks Tax Table is up-to-date.

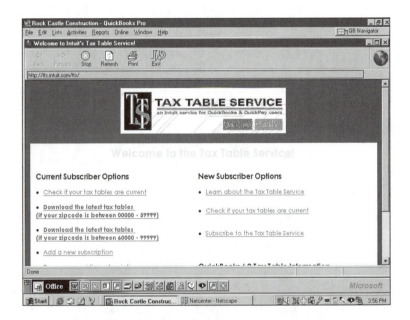

> **Note**
>
> No matter which version of QuickBooks you are using, it's helpful to know which maintenance release you are using. Before downloading a new version from Intuit, find out which version you have running. To do this with QuickBooks running, press Ctrl+1. The information you want appears at the top of the panel. Then log on to Intuit's Web site, locate their Service and Update page (currently, the URL is http://www.intuit.com/support/updates), and see which version Intuit is offering as the latest.

Payday

If you fully set up Payroll, entering each employee's past and current data and creating any additional payroll items you need in addition to the ones generated by QuickBooks, you are pretty much ready to print checks and pay your employees.

> **Note**
> Please take a look at Chapter 25, "QuickBooks Pro and Time Tracking," to learn how to set up timesheets, use the QuickBooks Pro Timer, and associate payroll time with a single job and customer. After reviewing that chapter, you'll know how to automate payroll hours.

Preparing Paychecks

QuickBooks knows that paychecks are due to your employees when hours have been entered into weekly timesheets, or when they've performed billable activities (this topic is also covered in Chapter 25). So after having set pay rates and salaries for each employee, as well as setting up vacation and sick time accrual rates, payday is simply a matter of preparing the paychecks and printing them. Use the following steps to prepare paychecks:

1. Click the Payroll and Time tab on the QuickBooks Navigator and select the Create Paychecks Icon. You see the Select Employees to Pay dialog box (shown in Figure 18.13).

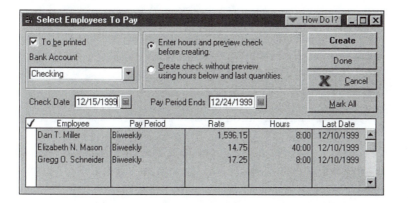

Figure 18.13
Review a list of all the employees to whom paychecks are due, and the amounts that are due.

2. Select the Bank Account from which these checks are to be paid. In the example shown here, Checking is selected. Of course, you need to make sure that you've got enough money in this account to cover the checks.

3. Verify the Check Date and the pay period dates covered by this paycheck. QuickBooks tracks pay periods by indicating the final day of that pay period (Pay Period End). You'll be drawing up checks for the pay period shown.

4. Specify whether you want to preview the paychecks before they fly out to your printer, or just view the information here in this dialog box and be done with it.

5. Place a check to the far left of each employee to whom a paycheck is due. If every employee visible in this dialog box is going to be getting a check today, click the Mark All button.

6. View and verify the employee information that is available here: name, pay rate, pay period covered by this paycheck, and pay period type (in this case it is biweekly). If you see something amiss, you can fix it later in this process.

7. Click Create, and you see the Preview Paycheck dialog box.

Previewing Your Checks

In the Preview Paycheck dialog box (see Figure 18.14), each check is presented in sequence and with the employee's name at the top. When you are done previewing and adjusting, click Create (at the bottom of the dialog box) to go to the next employee.

Figure 18.14
Review all employee deductions and totals before printing the check.

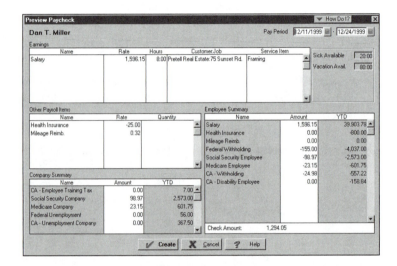

This is basically your last chance to gracefully edit paycheck components and totals. Here you can change hours and regular deductions, and add new payroll items. Payroll items such as health insurance, mileage reimbursement, and even sums you'd think of as being written in stone—such as Social Security and Medicare deductions—all can be edited here.

To review and edit paycheck amounts, follow these steps:

1. Review the amounts in the Earnings panel of the Review Paycheck dialog box. Type a new amount if you want. Also, use the Customer: Jobs area and Service Item to assign this paycheck to a particular job account. Use the drop-down menu to select a customer account and item, if necessary.

2. Review the Other Payroll Items and Company Summary panels, and use the drop-down menus to make changes. (Menus appear when you click a line.) Manual

adjustments can be helpful if you realize that it's someone's bonus day and you just want to tack it on quickly, or if someone came in on a weekend and forgot to tell you about it formally, but you still want to pay them.

3. Quickly compare the Company Summary, Employee Summary, and Check Amount, just to make sure nothing is amiss.

4. When you are happy with how a check looks, click Create. If you have a sound card in your computer, you'll hear the reassuring clangs of a cash register, telling you that a check has been processed and is awaiting printing.

5. When you've finished this process for all the checks, all that remains is viewing the actual facsimile of each check (if you so desire) and printing them out.

Notice that you can also associate each payroll item in the Earnings section with a particular job and customer. Use this option when applicable because the reports that you generate later will better indicate which jobs are more profitable.

> **Caution**
>
> As you click in fields and make changes to any of these totals, don't press Enter until you are entirely finished with this paycheck. Pressing Enter confirms your edits and moves you on to the next employee. To see the result of your tinkering, just make an edit, click in another field or press Tab to move to another field, and then watch the check amount at the lower right adjust itself.

VIEWING THE CHECKS

To retrieve and view the paychecks, follow these steps:

1. With Intuit's checks loaded into your printer, select Reminders from the List menu.

→ To find information about using the QuickBooks Reminders feature, **see p. 16**.

2. Click Paychecks to Print, as shown in Figure 18.15.

3. Double-click Paychecks, and you see a list of each paycheck that you processed earlier, as well as any other paychecks that had not previously made it this far.

4. Double-click the check at the top of the list, and you see a check facsimile, as shown in Figure 18.16.

5. If you want to make any changes, click the Check Detail button at the bottom of this dialog box. You'll notice that it returns you to the Preview Paycheck area that you were just working with.

6. By default, the To Be Printed check box at the upper right of each check is selected. However, if this is a direct deposit check that you are making a record of, or if you are recording a paycheck that got paid in some other way, you can uncheck the To Be Printed check box.

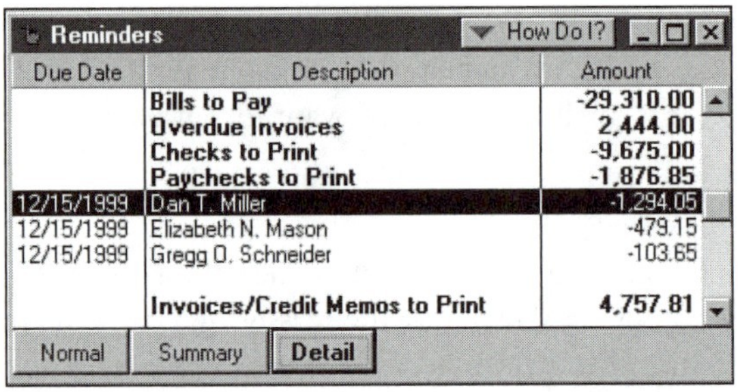

Figure 18.15
The Reminder List is the fastest way to retrieve the paychecks that are ready to print.

Figure 18.16
Previewing a check facsimile before you actually print it.

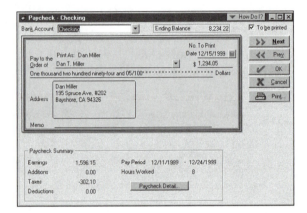

7. At some time you might have to void a paycheck. Perhaps it didn't print correctly, or maybe an error was discovered. To void a paycheck while it is displayed on your screen, click the Edit menu (at the top left, as shown in Figure 18.17), and then choose Void Paycheck. The paycheck still shows up in your chart of accounts—but it appears voided.

8. From the same menu, you can also delete the paycheck. This entirely removes the transaction. To void and delete paychecks at some other time, select the Chart of Accounts from the List menu, and click the account responsible for this check. Scroll down and locate the check that you want to void or delete. Select either command from the Edit menu, as previously described.

Note

You can purchase checks from Intuit that work with most commercial printers. They come in a variety of formats and styles, and can be ordered from www.intuitmarket.com.

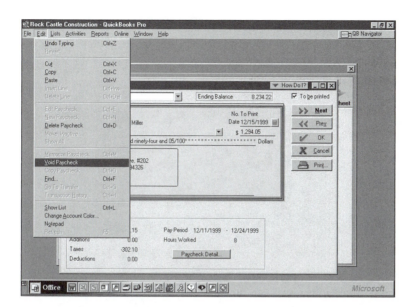

Figure 18.17
Use the Edit menu to void a paycheck.

Printing Paychecks

To print your paychecks, click the Print button next to the check facsimile and make any adjustments to Check Style (See Figure 18.18). Check the Print Company Address button if you want this information on the paycheck.

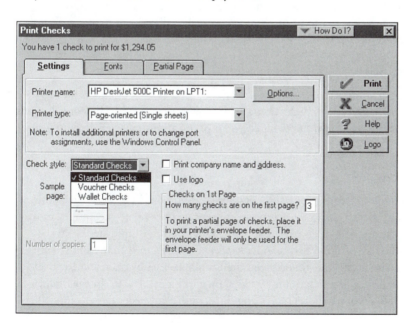

Figure 18.18
By adjusting the Check Style, you can accommodate several different check sizes and shapes.

Printing a Logo

If you are interested in using a logo on your check, click the Logo button on the right side of the Print Checks dialog box; choose a .BMP file for your logo by clicking the File button (Figure 18.19) and locating an applicable file.

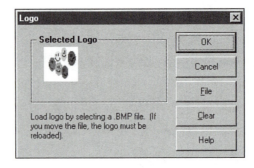

Figure 18.19
Click File to search your hard drive for a .BMP logo for your check.

You do not need to move the bitmap image to the same folder as QuickBooks; if you do move the file, however, you'll have to pinpoint its location again, using this same dialog box.

Printing a Partial Page of Checks

Checks are not cheap, and if you only want to print one or two right now (or if you printed a partial page of checks previously, and don't want to waste the rest of the page), click the Partial Page tab of the Print Checks dialog box. Using the Print Envelope feature of your printer, you can get QuickBooks to print a single check. The dialog box makes it clear how to position your check in the printer.

Special Payroll Reports

You can generate lots of reports associated with Payroll, such as QuickReports on each employee, reports that summarize deductions, types of pay, various company contributions, and YTD liabilities that summarize how much you owe to various tax agencies and health insurance firms.

Controlling Overtime

Reports are helpful for controlling overtime. Rather than find out long after the fact that a job has not been profitable because of overtime, use reports to regularly keep track of overtime. You can display a report of all payroll items, summarized by employee. From the Reports menu of the Payroll Item List, choose Reports on All Payroll Items and select Summary. You can also access this report from the Employee List by choosing Reports, Reports on All Employees, Payroll, Summary, as shown in Figure 18.20. (In the Standard Edition of QuickBooks, your Reports might appear in a different order.)

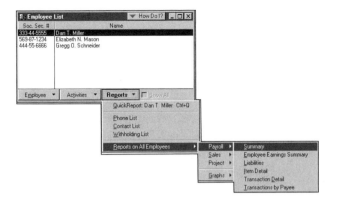

Figure 18.20
Use this report to view payroll items as totals, by employee, or with many details.

The third report item from the top shows overtime use for each employee (Figure 18.21). You have to scroll to the right to see each employee.

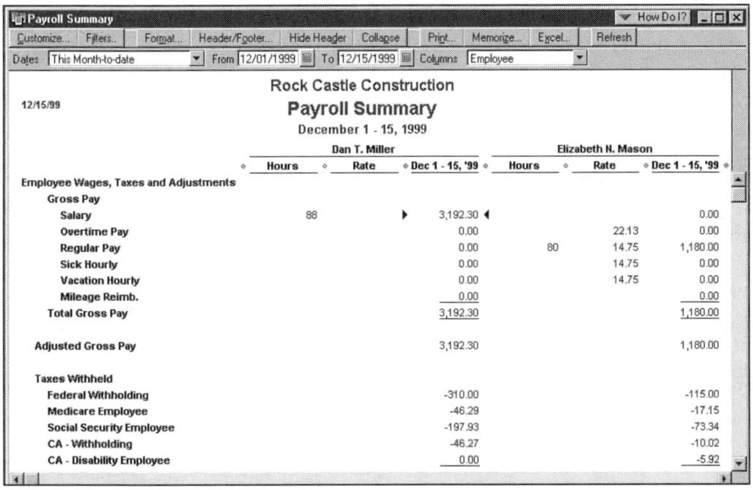

Figure 18.21
The Payroll Summary by Item Report shows how much overtime each employee uses.

It's possible to create a specific report detailing only overtime usage.

Use the following steps to create an overtime report:

1. Click Filters from the report that is shown in Figure 18.21. The Report Filters dialog box appears (Figure 18.22).
2. Scroll down the Filter list, and click Payroll Item.
3. In the field to the right, scroll down and select Overtime.
4. Click OK; a report appears that shows only overtime use for each employee.

Figure 18.22
Use the Filters dialog box to limit what is shown on a report.

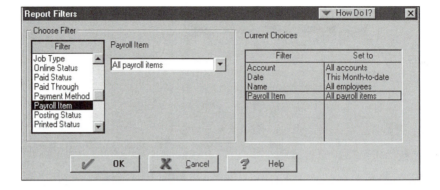

Viewing Year-to-Date Payroll Liabilities

QuickBooks can generate a helpful report showing your company's year-to-date payroll liabilities as a summarized dollar amount (see Figure 18.23). Select Reports on all Items from the Reports drop-down menu of the Payroll list, and then choose YTD Liabilities, as shown. You can click any item in the list—click any individual sum, not its item name—to see more specific information about any particular deduction or owed amount. (The Standard Edition refers to the report as Liabilities, not YTD Liabilities.)

Figure 18.23
Quickly view all your payroll liabilities in a single report.

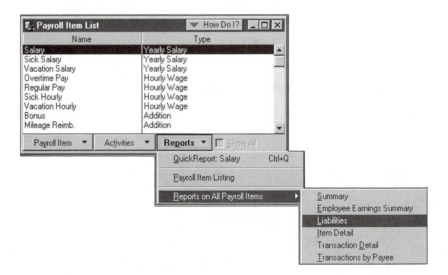

Working with W-2s

At the end of the year, an employer must complete a record of all wages paid to and taxes deducted from each employee. This yearly information is summarized on a federal W-2 form. One copy of the W-2 form goes to each of the following: the federal, state, and local tax agencies. One copy goes to the employee, and one copy is saved for your records.

Additionally, an employer must submit a W-3 form, which summarizes all W-2 information, to the tax agencies.

W-2 forms—and their accompanying W-3 summary forms—must be mailed by January 31st of each year to each employee; they must be mailed by February 28th to the appropriate government agencies.

QuickBooks makes dealing with W-2 and W-3 forms very easy. If you made all your year-to-date adjustments to your payroll accounts, as specified earlier in this chapter, all the W-2 data generated by QuickBooks is accurate. Here's how QuickBooks handles W-2s:

- Gathers all tax and wage information on each employee and generates a W-2.
- Displays each employee's W-2 on the screen, enabling you to make adjustments to any field.
- Prints W-2s onto forms that you can order from Intuit. These forms work on any standard laser or inkjet printer.
- Assists you in reviewing and printing a W-3 form (a summary of all W-2s), which the government also expects to receive from you.

Ordering and Printing onto Blank W-2 Forms
Although QuickBooks prepares and prints W-2 data for each employee, you cannot print W-2s on standard paper. Also, the blank W-2 forms that you can order from the IRS are set up for multifeed printers (tractor printers) and typewriters. These forms are designed to make triplicate copies all at once, and you can't use them on laser or inkjet printers. You can order blank *computer-friendly* W-2 forms from Intuit by calling 1-800-433-8810, or you can buy them from most office supply stores.

Because you need to print out several copies of each form, the following question arises: "Do I collate?" The answer is no. QuickBooks prints out all the Copy A forms, and then all the Copy B forms, and so on. Therefore, when loading blank W-2 forms into your printer, load as many copies of each form as you have employees, and then load the next form.

REVIEWING AND EDITING YOUR W-2S

Start reviewing W-2s by selecting the Payroll and Time tab on the Navigator and clicking the Process W-2 icon. (You can also click Process W-2s from the Activities menu of the Employee List.) You see the dialog box shown in Figure 18.24.

You have the following options:

- To review all W-2s for the current year, click the Mark All and then the Review W-2 buttons.
- To review select W-2s rather than all of them, place a check at the left of each name whose form you want to look at, and then click the Review W-2 button.

Figure 18.24
Click the Process W-2 icon in the Navigator to see a list of W-2s for all your employees.

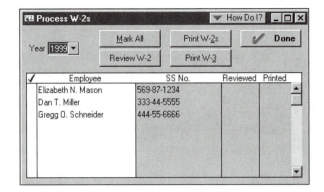

In either case, you see the Employee W-2 screen; here you can simply review the data, or you can make changes by hovering your mouse over any field until it turns into a magnifying glass, and then double-clicking. When you use this zoom feature to see a close up of one field (as shown in Figure 18.25), you can type an adjustment in the Amount field. Any number you include here is added to the amount previously shown.

Figure 18.25
Click any W-2 field to make an adjustment.

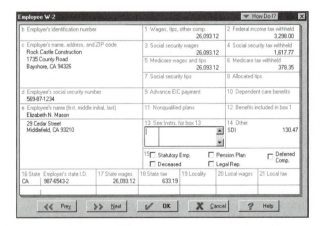

> **Note**
> If you are not sure of the significance of any W-2 field, press F1 while the W-2 is onscreen and QuickBooks's help system displays a clickable representation of the W-2 form. Click any field for a helpful description and instructions on how to change or add data to that field.

> **Tip #49 from Gail Perry**
>
> If you want to see W-2 data from previous years, select Process W-2s from the Payroll and Time tab of the Navigator, and use the Year drop-down menu to select the year that you want to review. You can also print out forms from previous years.

Please note that this is your last chance to gracefully make changes in an employee's W-2. There are some instances in which you might really need to. For example, if you've provided a day-care service for your employees and want to obtain the dependent care tax credit for it, this is your last chance to put the fair market value of this service on an employee's W-2. Or, if you've provided scholarships or relocation assistance to employees and want to take tax credit for its fair market value, you can make the change here.

After finishing with one employee's W-2, click Next to move on. When you are finished reviewing each, click OK. The Process W-2s dialog box reappears. If you've reviewed an employee's W-2, a Reviewed check appears near their name.

Printing W-2 Forms

In QuickBooks, you cannot print W-2s until you've reviewed all of them. After you've done so, click the Print button. QuickBooks prepares to print any employee W-2 that has a check to the left of their name in the Process W-2s dialog box. Because government regulations require W-2s to have a certain appearance, there are very few alternative options available when printing out these forms. Make sure that the correct printer and printer type are selected, and take the time to run a test print before loading up all your blank W-2s, clicking Print, and running to get coffee. You might want to read the preceding sidebar, "Ordering and Printing onto Blank W-2 Forms," before continuing.

Printing Form W-3

The W-3 form is a single summary of all the data from your W-2s, and QuickBooks only enables you to print them out after you've properly reviewed (and, ideally, printed) all your W-2s. To print one or more copies of your W-3 (all tax agencies want to see a copy), open the Process W-2s dialog box and click the Print W-3 button.

Paying Independent Contractors

Contractors are people that you pay to work for you, but who are not your employees. In QuickBooks, contractors are tracked as vendors, and they are not paid from your payroll accounts. Independent contractors have special tax issues that need to be examined. Each contractor to whom you pay more than a certain dollar amount (currently $600 per year) needs to receive an annual 1099 form from you (the $600 threshold does not apply to attorneys who are to receive a 1099 form reporting all payments for legal services made during the year). You'll also send a copy to the IRS. Because you might not know at the year's outset which contractors will reach this $600 threshold, QuickBooks helps you keep track of how much contractors are paid and manage the compiling and printing of 1099 forms at the end of the year.

You must supply each Form 1099 recipient with a copy of the 1099 form by January 31 of the following year. State government agencies and the IRS require that copies of the forms be filed by February 28 of the following year.

> **Tip #50 from**
> *Gail Perry*
>
> It might seem like a lot of trouble to prepare and file 1099 forms, and you probably even have some people who work for your company who might prefer that you just don't bother with the form.
>
> Be aware, however, that there are penalties that the taxing authorities gladly charge if you don't comply with the law in this area. There is a $50 per form penalty for not providing 1099 forms to payees. Other penalties can apply for not filing the required copies of these forms with federal and state government agencies.
>
> It is definitely in the interest of your company to file all required forms in a timely manner.

To pay independent contractors, follow these steps:

1. Turn on tracking for 1099 forms in the Preferences menu and specify a 1099 category.
2. Create or choose an account to be used for paying 1099-elegible vendors. Having this special account makes it easier at the end of the year to track all contractors who've reached that payment threshold and need to receive the 1099 form.
3. As you add vendors that you want to track as independent contractors, make sure that you select Eligible for 1099 when setting up their information.
4. If you create a Service Item performed by a subcontractor, (For Example *Brickwork* or *Proofreading*,) check This Service is Performed by a Subcontractor in the New Item dialog box.
5. Finally, at the end of the year, you can run 1099 reports, check and verify totals, and print out your 1099 forms.

Following is a look at how to collect and print out all the 1099 data you need (first, turn on 1099 Tracking):

1. Select Preferences from the File menu, and click the Tax 1099 button on the left (See Figure 18.26). Make sure the Company Preferences Tab is showing. Answer Yes to the question "Do you file 1099-MISC forms?"
2. Although many category options are available, Box 7 is the one used to track non-employees who are being paid for services. Move your mouse down to the Box 7 line.
3. In the Account field, choose an account to follow payments made to independent contractors. By default, QuickBooks sets up a subaccount called Subcontractors (under Job Expenses) for this purpose. You can choose this account, or you can create a new one.
4. In the Amount field, type a threshold amount. This amount is currently $600. To find out if it has changed, call Intuit at 1-800-771-7248.

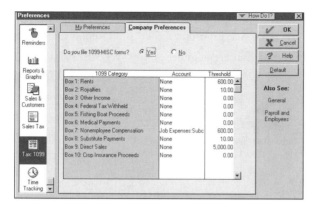

Figure 18.26
Set up tracking for 1099 forms in the Preferences menu.

The following steps go over how to set up an Independent Contractor and retrieve 1099 information at the year's end:

1. Create a Vendor Item as usual, selecting New from the Vendor menu of the Vendor List.

2. Click the Additional Info tab (see Figure 18.27). Enter any additional information that your company requires for this contractor. You can define custom fields if necessary. Be sure to fill in the Tax ID number for the contractor (Social Security number for an individual, or federal identification number for a business). The IRS requires that you obtain this information. Failure to obtain this number can result in your company being held responsible for the tax due on the fees paid to your contractors.

3. Check the Vendor Eligible for 1099 box. After doing this, QuickBooks tracks how much money you pay this vendor throughout the year, and makes such information available for reports—and for creating 1099 forms.

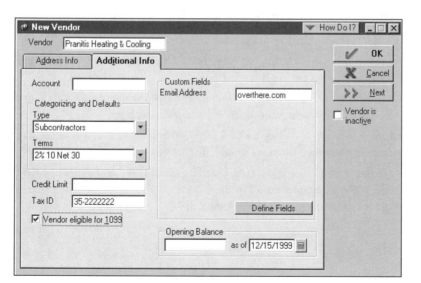

Figure 18.27
Setting up a Vendor for 1099 eligibility tracking.

4. At the end of the year, open the Vendors List and select the Reports drop-down menu.
5. Choose Reports on all Vendors, A/P report, and then 1099 Report (see Figure 18.28).
6. You see a list of all the vendors that are eligible for 1099 reports. Printing the actual 1099 forms is covered in the very last section of this chapter, titled "Printing 1099 Forms."

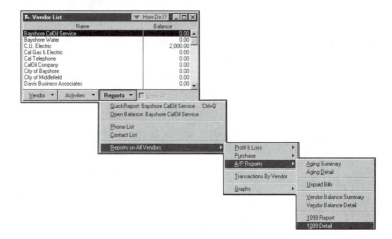

Figure 18.28
Choosing a report that prepares you for mailing 1099 forms to vendors.

→ For information about obtaining tax forms from the IRS and state governments, see Chapter 23, "Going Online with QuickBooks."

CHECKING YOUR 1099 LIST FOR MISSING VENDORS

Sometimes a Vendor can be missing from the list. Following are some steps for making sure every eligible vendor is on your list.

Use the following steps to Check for missing vendors:

1. Open the 1099 report, as outlined in the preceding section.
2. Use the three drop-down menus at the top (see Figure 18.29) to view all vendors, and then view all the vendors that are eligible for 1099.
3. If you notice someone who should have been set up for 1099 forms but wasn't, double-click that vendor's name; this brings up the Edit Vendor dialog box.
4. Click the Additional Info tab and place a check by Eligible for 1099. You now see that vendor's name among the others who are eligible for 1099s.
5. If you think someone is still missing, use the Use Threshold drop-down menu at the upper right of the 1099 report to view all qualifying vendors regardless of their threshold amount. Perhaps someone just squeaked under the qualifying amount.

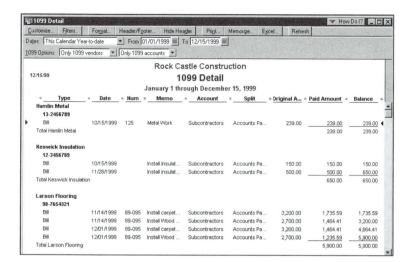

Figure 18.29
The drop-down menus to the right help track down the vendors that are missing from 1099 reports.

Printing 1099 Forms

After verifying that every vendor that needs to be on the 1099 report is there, open the Vendor List (From the List menu, select Vendor). Select the Vendor drop-down menu on the bottom left of the list, and choose Print 1099. You must use standard government 1099 forms. These forms are available from Intuit and can be ordered on the QuickBooks Web site; they are also available at many office supply stores.

Troubleshooting

Employee or Contractor?

One of my workers wants to be paid as a contractor, but I'm concerned that the IRS expects me to withhold taxes. How do I find out how to treat this worker?

There's no hard and fast rule for determining if someone is an employee or an independent contractor. The IRS expects you to consider the list of 20 questions presented earlier in this chapter. The more questions that you answer positively about your worker, the more likely the worker is an employee.

Adding an Item to Payroll

I'm in the middle of entering my payroll information, and realize that I need to set up an item for Overtime Meal Reimbursements. Can I leave the payroll set up, set up the item, and return to the place where I left off?

An even better solution is to set up the item on-the-fly. In the Other Payroll Item area of your Preview Paycheck screen, click the arrow in the Name field and choose Add New from the drop-down list. Set up your new item without leaving the Preview Paycheck screen, and you can continue with your payroll without missing a beat.

CHAPTER 19

QUICKBOOKS AND PAYROLL TAXES

In this chapter

Creating Checks To Pay Your Taxes   309

Reports That Help With Tax Corrections   326

Common Problems With Tax Figures   329

Setting Up Advanced Earned Income Credit   332

As an employer and business owner, your basic responsibilities regarding taxes are as follows:

- Making sure that you've set up each employee to have taxes deducted from his paycheck. QuickBooks does not create state disability or state unemployment tax items, so you have to create those yourself. See the previous chapter for instructions on how to create payroll tax items.
- Send Federal taxes that you deducted to Federal tax agencies such as the IRS and the Social Security Administration.
- Send state and local taxes that you deducted to state tax agencies. To do this, you might have to calculate a *wage base* (*page 315*), which QuickBooks does for you. A wage base actually helps ensure that you do not pay too much. This is explored in detail in this chapter.
- Create and send state unemployment tax forms reporting your share of state unemployment liability to your state taxing agency.
- Create and send quarterly 941 forms to the IRS, stating your tax liabilities.
- Create and send a yearly 940 form to the IRS, which reports your federal unemployment tax (FUTA) liability.

 Wondering where to find tax forms and addresses? **See** "Troubleshooting" at the end of this chapter.

Note

> For QuickBooks to have an accurate picture of all your tax liabilities, make the necessary adjustments using the YTD Amounts feature (see Chapter 18, "Paying Employees and Contractors").

The following are your tools for managing the aforementioned tasks:

- Use the Employee List to set up tax status, withholding, and allowances for each employee.
- Create checks for payment of your taxes by clicking the Pay Liabilities icon on the Payroll and Time tab of the Navigator (see Figure 19.1).
- Double-check the amounts you owe by looking over the three main Payroll reports— Summary by Employee, Employee Journal, and Liabilities by Item. (The names of these reports might vary slightly for QuickBooks standard version users.)
- Create 941 forms by clicking the Process 941 icon on the Payroll and Time tab of the Navigator. (Figure 19.2 shows a 941 form.)

There are some things QuickBooks cannot do, and preparing Schedule B of your Form 941 is one of them. To find information relating to this topic, **see** "Troubleshooting" at the end of this chapter.

- Create 940 forms by clicking the Process 940 icon on the same tab.

Figure 19.1
Pay taxes by clicking the Pay Liabilities icon.

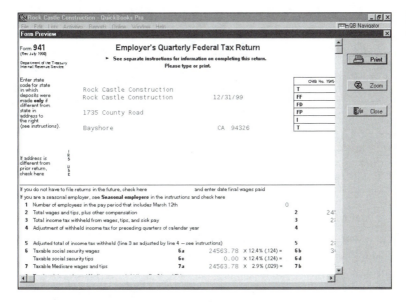

Figure 19.2
A completed form 941.

Creating Checks To Pay Your Taxes

Regarding Federal taxes, when you obtain your Employer ID number, you also receive a booklet of coupons that will accompany your tax payments. If you do not receive such a coupon book, contact your nearest IRS office and they will be happy to supply you with what you need. The taxes that you pay are the amounts you've collected from employees' paychecks for various Federal taxes, and these amounts need to be turned over to the taxing authorities regularly. The frequency with which you submit your payments is determined by the amount of taxes you withhold. Contact the IRS if you have questions about your company's role in collecting and paying employment taxes. Including the tax coupons with your payment assures that you will receive credit for your payment.

To pay all tax-related liabilities that have been set up as payroll items (see Chapter 18, "Paying Employees and Contractors"), click the Payroll and Time tab on the Navigator, and then select the Pay Liabilities icon. You see the Pay Liabilities dialog box. (See Figure 19.3. The tab might be called Payroll and Employees, depending on the version of QuickBooks you are using.)

Figure 19.3
In the Pay Liabilities dialog box you can choose what taxes to pay at the moment, or you can pay them all with one click.

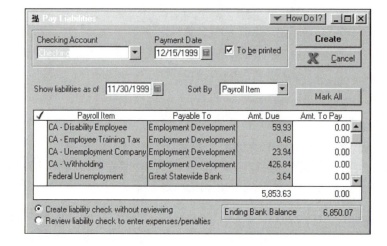

Among other things, the choices you make here determine how much you pay on each payroll item, and which account to use in payment.

To Make a payroll tax liability payment, follow these steps:

1. When you're ready to pay taxes, click the Pay Liabilities icon on the Payroll and Time tab of the Navigator, which opens the Pay Liabilities dialog box.

2. By default, payment is made from your checking account. You can choose a different account if you want.

3. The Show liabilities as of field shows all taxes not yet paid, up to the end of the previous month. If you pay more often than once a month, choose a more recent date.

4. To create a check that will be issued at a later date, change the Payment Date field. QuickBooks reminds you of this date when the time to issue the check draws near.

5. To use QuickBooks's checks for these payments, click to place a check mark in the To be printed box. If you're writing the check by hand, remove the check mark.

6. Click to check off the far left area of the liabilities that you intend to pay now, or click the Mark All button.

Note

When setting up each liability payroll item, you also named a tax agency or a bank as a vendor to receive the check. If, however, one of the payroll items you've set up is not associated with a vendor (if, for example, you weren't certain where the payments were to be

> made when you set up the liability), you receive a warning; that item's edit dialog box opens, prompting you to select a vendor. The vendor you choose needs to be a bank empowered to handle your tax disbursements or the tax agency itself.

7. Review the payroll items and the amount due, making sure that the amounts seem right to you. (Later in this chapter, you learn how to find errors in the Amount Due, and to make adjustments.)
8. By default, QuickBooks creates checks for the entire amount due. If you want to pay a different amount, click any line in the Amount to Pay field and type a new amount. The Amount Due total at the bottom of the dialog box decreases by the amount you choose to pay.

Caution
> After typing in a new amount in the Amt to Pay window, view your change by clicking any other line. Pressing Enter has the same effect as clicking the OK button. The Pay Liabilities box disappears, and QuickBooks records your transaction as complete.

9. Using the options at the bottom left, indicate whether you want QuickBooks to create the checks without your review, or whether you need an opportunity to make adjustments.
10. Click OK, and your accounts are appropriately updated. If you've indicated that you want to review the check before finalizing it, a check appears on the screen. Make adjustments as necessary. Click OK to add the check to the printing queue.

Although you can make manual adjustments in the checks that you write to tax agencies, it's best to try tracking down the actual mistakes in your Liability accounts. Making liability adjustments and reports that help you find the errors is discussed later in this chapter.

Writing Two Tax Liability Checks to the Same Vendor

Most employers establish a relationship with a single bank, empowering it to actually distribute the payment to the various tax agencies. When QuickBooks sees a single vendor name listed to receive tax liability payments (see Figure 19.4), it simply issues one check to that vendor. If you are paying two separate tax liabilities, you might want to issue separate checks.

Use the following steps to send two liability checks to a single vendor:

1. Create a new vendor item using a dummy name.
2. Assign one of the amounts to that new vendor. Two checks are printed.
3. When you are finally reviewing the checks before you print them, change the vendor name of the dummy vendor back to the real vendor.
4. Two checks are still printed, both to the same vendor.

Figure 19.4
Although this check is payment for many taxes, there is only one payee.

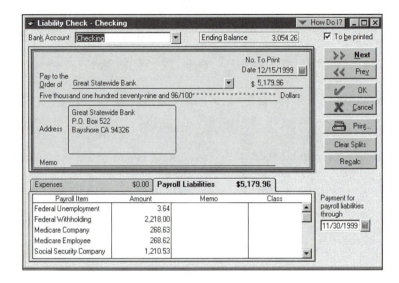

Setting Up Employee Tax Status, Withholding, and Allowances

When you create an employee item, you will notice three tabs (see Figure 19.5). One of them is Payroll Info. Chapter 18 described using Payroll Info to set up earnings and specific tax items for each employee, but you have not yet learned how to make QuickBooks aware of the standard tax information that every new employee provides when hired.

Use the following steps to set up an employee's tax status:

1. Select Employees from the Lists menu, and click New from the Employee drop-down menu.
2. Select the Payroll Info tab (see Figure 19.5).
3. Click the Taxes button, and you see the Taxes dialog box (see Figure 19.6).

The Taxes dialog box is divided into three tabs: Federal, State and Other.

Federal Taxes

Select the Federal taxes tab to enter employee federal tax options.

Follow these steps to set up federal tax options for an employee:

1. Click the drop-down arrow to select a Filing Status for this employee. Choose from Single, Married, Head of Household, or Don't Withhold.
2. In the indicated boxes, type the number of Allowances and any applicable dollar amount for Extra Withholding.
3. In the Subject To panel, indicate whether there are any taxes to which this employee is not subject. By default, every check box is selected, except for Advance Earned Income Credit. (see "Setting up Advance Earned Income Credit" later in this chapter.)

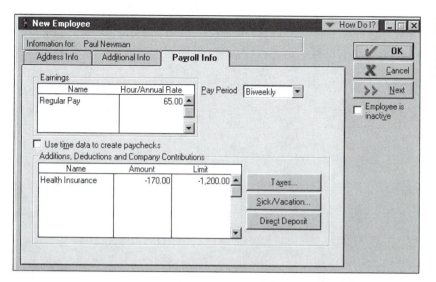

Figure 19.5
The Payroll Info tab, for storing payroll information on an employee.

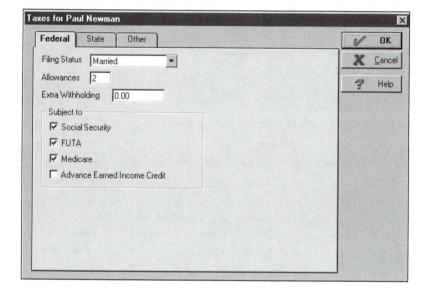

Figure 19.6
Use the Taxes dialog box to keep a record of the tax status of an employee.

4. Click the State tab to set up state tax information for this employee.

STATE TAXES

Select the State taxes tab (see Figure 19.7) to choose options for this employee's state tax status.

Figure 19.7
Click the State tab to enter state tax information for an employee.

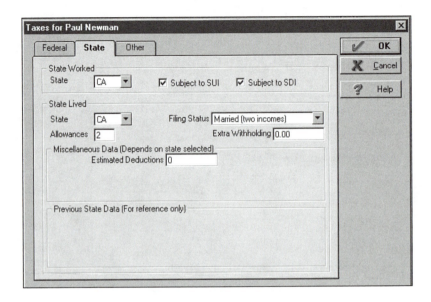

Set up state tax deductions by following these steps:

1. Click the drop-down arrows to choose the state in which this employee works, and—if it is different—the state in which he lives.

2. Indicate with the check boxes whether this employee is subject to State Unemployment Insurance (SUI) and State Disability Insurance (SDI). Check with your accountant or your state tax board for more information about this choice.

> **Note**
> If you do not see an SDI option, don't worry. Your state might not deduct for state disability insurance.

3. Most states require that an employee specify filing status (single, married, head of household), allowances, and extra withholding amounts. If your state is among those that want this information, fill in the various windows in the State Lived panel.

4. QuickBooks includes a Miscellaneous Data area for some states. For example, California requires employees to include estimated deductions, if applicable. Enter the appropriate information in this area.

5. Click OK when you are finished, or if a special tax needs to be applied (perhaps a local or unique state tax) select the Other tab.

OTHER TAX

If a tax was created that does not fall into the categories of state or federal, click the Other Tax tab (see Figure 19.8) to apply it to this employee.

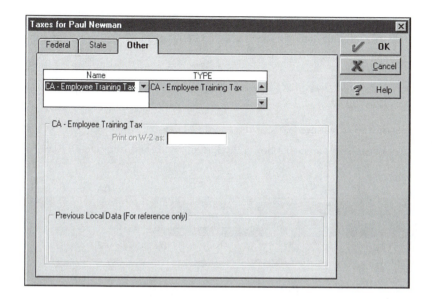

Figure 19.8
For city or county taxes, click the Other Tab. QuickBooks has predefined taxes for a number of U.S. municipalities (note: this tab is only visible if you have set up an Other Tax payroll item).

Use the following steps to apply an Other Tax to an employee:

1. Click the drop-down arrow in the Name field to choose an Other Tax to apply to this employee. If you need to create this new tax item, just click Add New at the top of the drop-down list.
2. If you choose Add New, you see the New Payroll Item dialog box (discussed in the later section "Creating a New Tax Payroll Item").
3. An option or two might appear below the Name field. If so, enter the appropriate information.
4. Click OK, and you're finished setting up tax information for this employee.

SUPPLYING WAGE BASE INFORMATION FOR STATE TAXES

QuickBooks does not print state payroll tax forms, but the program can help you prepare the information you need, making it much easier to fill them out.

Some states calculate state taxes on a wage base. A wage base is an employee's taxable salary, and can be defined as follows:

- If an employee has pretax deductions such as 401K and flexible spending accounts, these sums are subtracted from the total wages, and the remainder is the wage base.
- In some instances, a wage base excludes employee overtime hours and shift differential payment.
- The wage base also refers to annual limits on certain taxes. For example, only the first $7,000 of an employee's annual salary is subject to federal unemployment tax. Likewise,

employees and employers do not pay Social Security tax on earnings of more than $72,600 annually (this amount changes each year; $72,600 is the 1999 amount for maximum wages subject to Social Security tax).

You can locate every employee's wage base by opening the Payroll Item Detail report as follows:

1. Click the Reports drop-down menu, from the Employee List.
2. Choose Reports On All Employees, followed by Payroll, and then Item Detail (see Figure 19.9).

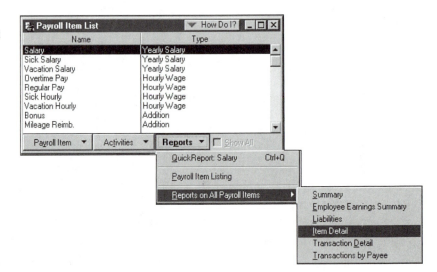

Figure 19.9
The Item Detail report lists wage base information.

3. Every employee is represented in this report, and it shows the following details:
   - Each row represents a salary type paid to an employee.
   - Near the bottom of the report, other payroll items such as deductions and contributions are reported, row by row.
   - If you have not customized the report, the sixth column from the right lists the wage base for each employee's salary.
4. Note every employee's wage base, and include those numbers as needed in your state tax forms.

SETTING UP PAYROLL ITEMS TO COLLECT STATE TAXES

In Chapter 18, you learned how to set up new payroll items. You can create payroll items to collect taxes at a certain rate or dollar amount, and they can be applied to each employee's paycheck. (If you have employees that work in other states, see the Out of State Employees sidebar.) However, you might not have to create new payroll items for state taxes because when you conduct the EasyStep Interview, you make QuickBooks aware of your company's location. As part of the setup process, QuickBooks uses the current tax table data to set up state-related payroll items for your state. Therefore, you might not need to set up any additional payroll items in order to collect adequate state taxes from each employee. (You still have to set up each employee's state tax status, withholdings, and so on, as outlined in the previous section.)

→ To find more information on keeping your payroll tax tables current, **see p. 288**.

Following is a list of state tax items that are likely to appear in your Payroll Items List:

- Withholding
- Disability
- Unemployment
- Employee training

CREATING A NEW TAX PAYROLL ITEM

To create a new payroll item for deducting taxes from employee's paychecks, select New Item from the Payroll Item List's drop-down Payroll menu. You see the Add New Payroll Item dialog box (see Figure 19.10). Check the type of item that you want to create. You can only choose from selections that you have not already used. If you do need to set up an additional state or local tax, follow these steps:

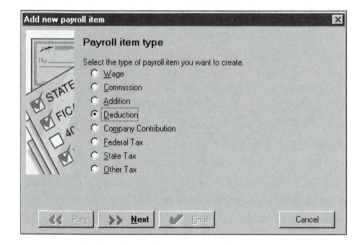

Figure 19.10
Create a new Tax Payroll item just as you do any other payroll item.

1. Open the Payroll Item List and click the Payroll button to produce a drop-down menu. Choose New Item (or press Ctrl+I).

2. The Add new payroll item dialog box appears. Select a payroll item type and click Next.

3. If you selected Other Payroll Item, indicate whether this tax is to be paid by your company or by the employee. Click the Other Tax drop-down list (see Figure 19.11) to see whether QuickBooks has created a predefined tax that suits your needs. If you select a State Tax Item, your options depend greatly on which state you previously chose.

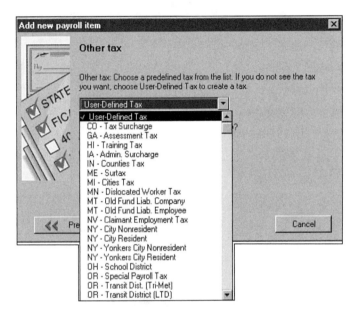

Figure 19.11
Review one of QuickBooks's Other Tax options to see whether a predefined tax suits your needs.

4. Whether you select Other Tax or State Tax, you're prompted by a series of dialog boxes to do the following:
    - Enter the name of the tax item that you are creating.
    - Assign an account to the item.
    - Indicate the agency that is to be paid.
    - Provide the employer number by which your company is identified with the agency.
    - Select an option that describes how this tax item is tracked on tax forms.

5. You might be asked to indicate if this item is to be calculated based on a quantity that you specify.

6. You are asked to fill in a default tax rate (a percentage that applies equally to all employees) and a ceiling amount for this tax (see Figure 19.12).

7. Finally, in the Taxable Compensation dialog box, verify all wage types that have an effect on this tax (see Figure 19.13), and uncheck any that don't apply. Removing a

check from a wage type means that money earned via that particular wage type is not taxed. Click the Finish button.

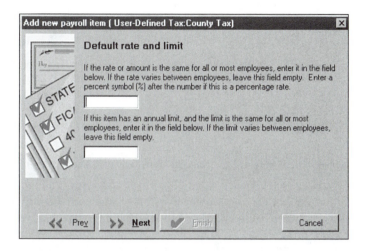

Figure 19.12
QuickBooks asks how your new payroll item is to be calculated.

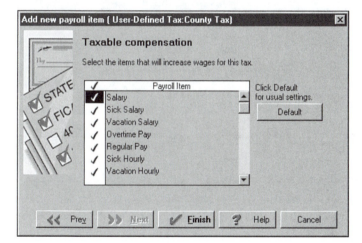

Figure 19.13
If you want certain income types to not be affected by this new tax, remove the check by its name.

8. Your new tax item appears on the Payroll Item List with all the others, and can be applied to the paycheck of any employee who lives in the state or city in question.

Tip #51 from

Gail Perry

If you have an employee who lives out of your state, check the reciprocity laws for the two states to find out for which state you are to be withholding and paying taxes. You can contact the state government for this information (see Appendix D, "State Revenue Agencies," for addresses, telephone numbers, and email addresses of all state taxing agencies).

CREATING A REPORT OF STATE PAYROLL TAXES

Sometimes it's helpful to see various breakdowns of the state taxes you deducted, either by Payroll Item or by Employee. The difference is as follows:

- Viewing a state tax report By Employee enables you to see in a simple list how much state tax was deducted from each employee.
- Viewing a report By Item enables you to see each state tax deduction, paycheck by paycheck.

For this example, look at By Employee.

Use the following steps to create a state tax report for each employee:

1. Open the Employee List, and then click the Reports button to produce a drop-down menu.
2. Click Reports on All Employees, Payroll, Employee Earnings Summary (Figure 19.14 shows a sample report). Standard Edition users might find that the report has a slightly different title.

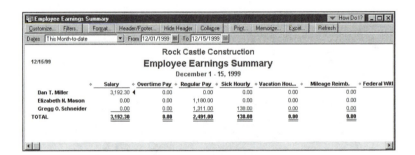

Figure 19.14
The Employee Earnings Summary report can generate a report of state taxes.

3. If necessary, adjust the time frame (From and To date range) of the report to suit your needs.
4. To refine the report to include or exclude particular items, click the Filters button in the upper left of the Report.
5. This example produces a report that displays state withholding for each employee. In the Filters window, scroll down and click Payroll Item (see Figure 19.15). Notice the drop-down menu next to the Filter list changes to read Payroll Item.

CREATING CHECKS TO PAY YOUR TAXES | 321

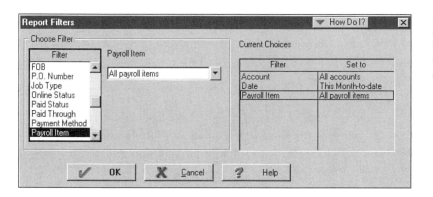

Figure 19.15
Creating a filter to include or exclude a certain payroll item in a report.

6. Click the drop-down menu, and then click Selected Payroll Items, near the top of the menu. A new window called Select Payroll Items appears.

7. Scroll down and locate the State Withholding item created for your state. In this example, CA-Withholding is selected (see Figure 19.16).

8. Notice that the Current Choices window on the Filters dialog box now includes an entry: Selected Payroll Items. (It might be simply titled Payroll Items.) Click OK to view the Report.

9. The report now shows a list of employees and the amounts deducted for state tax withholding.

10. To view paycheck by paycheck detail, double-click a deduction amount next to any employee's name (shown in Figure 19.17).

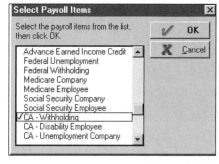

Figure 19.16

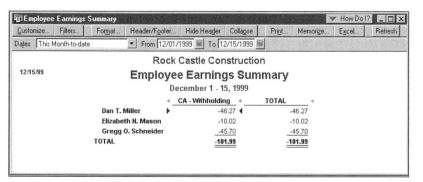

Figure 19.17
In a report, you can select a specific transaction by double-clicking it.

Preparing, Reviewing, and Printing Form 941

Form 941 is a quarterly payroll tax form on which you report federal income tax withheld, as well as social security and Medicare tax. Because these taxes are based on the total wages you paid your employees, QuickBooks makes creating this form very easy.

Create and mail Form 941 at the end of every quarter; creating one is as easy as clicking the Process Form 941 icon on the Payroll and Time tab of the QuickBooks navigator (this feature is also found on the Activities menu, on the Payroll menu). After you click the icon, QuickBooks steps you through a Wizard that creates form 941 information line by line, just as if you were filling out the paper version. You're asked to provide the following information:

- Number of employees paid
- Wages paid and income withheld from wages
- Social Security and Medicare tax withholding
- Withholding adjustments that you need to make carried over from last quarter

The good news is that as you click Next and move through each set of questions, QuickBooks has already filled in the answers. Most often, you just salute the numbers as they sail by. In the final screens, you see the following:

- You're asked whether you want to apply an overpayment (if there is one) to the following quarter or be mailed a refund.
- In creating Form 941, QuickBooks asks you how to apply an overpayment.
- You receive a chance to make final adjustments to each month in the quarter.
- Finally, you can print or preview the form as it will appear when it's printed. (Form 941 can be printed on a blank, 8 1/2×11-inch piece of paper.)

The bad news is that QuickBooks does not produce the Schedule B portion of the 941. If you are required to submit Schedule B, you must prepare this part of the form manually.

Making Adjustments

You can make adjustments if you need to, typing in new numbers as you go along. Figure 19.18 shows a typical dialog box from the Form 941 Wizard.

Notice that numbers are provided; you can adjust the numbers simply by clicking the Yes button. The question arises, though: Where do I get the information to make these adjustments? How do I know whether the numbers are right or wrong? This is discussed momentarily.

Beyond simply stepping through the Form 941 Wizard and double-checking the salary and deduction dollar amounts that QuickBooks uses to create the final form, there is not much here that can throw you. You are, however, asked the following three questions while completing the form, and you might want to have the information handy:

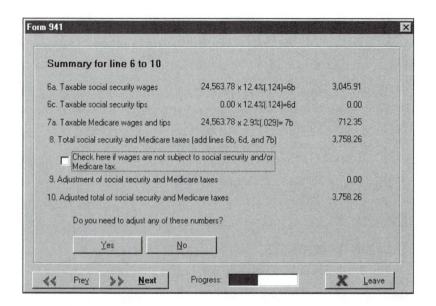

Figure 19.18
In this typical 941 Wizard dialog box, you can approve the numbers by clicking No, or click Yes to edit them.

- Are you obligated to file 941 forms in the future? If not, on what date will you be issuing your final paychecks? (This only applies if your company will no longer have a payroll.)
- Are you a seasonal employer? (Special rules apply.)
- If your monthly tax liability is particularly high, isn't it better to pay biweekly instead? The IRS might think so, too. Even if you don't voluntarily start paying biweekly, you might be required to do so.

CREATING FORM 940

Form 940 is an annual payroll tax form on which you report your federal unemployment tax (FUTA) liability (see Figure 19.19). The form is due each year by January 31 (for the prior year). Deposits of federal unemployment tax are due quarterly whenever the amount due exceeds $100. (You can skip your payment for a quarter if the current amount due is less than $100, and just pay the amount with the next quarter. Be sure to check each quarter to see if you need to make a payment.) All payments for the year are due by January 31 of the following year.

Follow these steps to organize your FUTA information and create Form 940:

1. Click the Payroll and Time tab of the Navigator and select the Process 940 icon (or choose Activities, Payroll, Process Form 940). The Form 940 Wizard appears.
2. Fill out Form 940 by stepping through a series of dialog boxes, acknowledging the information that QuickBooks has already provided in each of the windows (see Figure 19.20).

Figure 19.19
A QuickBooks-generated Federal Form 940, which is filed yearly.

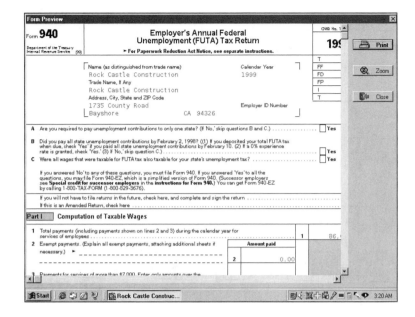

Figure 19.20
Step through the form 940 dialog boxes to fill out the form.

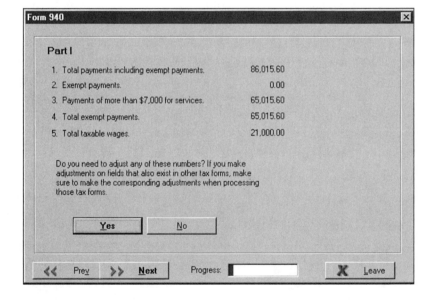

3. As with Form 941, you can edit the information at any time simply by clicking the Yes button, as shown in the preceding figure; or, later, you can reopen the Form 940 Wizard and choose to edit the form, rather than create a new one.

4. The following are some of the questions that you have to be prepared to answer, and numbers that need your approval.

- Indicate whether you are required to pay unemployment contributions in only one state.
- Indicate whether you paid all the previous year's unemployment contributions by January of this year.
- Specify whether all wages that were taxable for federal unemployment tax were also taxable by your state unemployment tax.
- Verify total wages paid, and verify any prior FUTA payments during the current year. As QuickBooks fills out form 940, notice that the income taxable by FUTA equals $7000 times the number of employees you have. Notice that in the preceding example (Figure 19.20), the QuickBooks sample company has three employees; therefore, the total FUTA taxable income is $21,000.
- Verify any carryover unpaid FUTA tax from the previous year.

5. If you are to receive a refund, you're asked whether you want to apply it to the following tax year or be issued a refund check.

6. Finally, you're given an opportunity to make any adjustments to unemployment liability for each quarter of the year (see Figure 19.21), and you are asked whether you want to print or preview your Form 940.

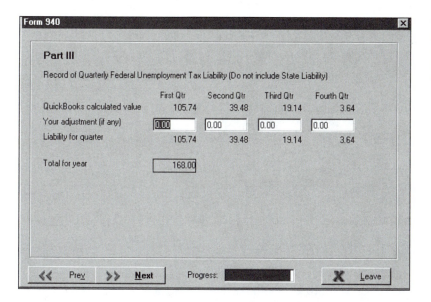

Figure 19.21
Before final approval and printing of your Form 940, you can make adjustments to any quarter of the year.

Tip #52 from Gail Perry

You pay federal unemployment taxes only on the first $7,000 of an employee's income. Therefore, your FUTA taxable income will be no more than the number of employees you have, times $7,000, times the FUTA tax rate (usually .8 percent). You might, however, owe more than that if there were payments not made in the previous year, and you might owe less than that if you made contributions to a state unemployment tax.

Reports That Help with Tax Corrections

As was mentioned earlier, when paying taxes with QuickBooks, the process is mostly a matter of stepping through dialog boxes, clicking Next, and verifying the numbers used to generate the payments. The same goes for creating tax forms. You answer a few questions about special circumstances, previous payments and such, and examine the figures that QuickBooks presents. The trouble is, what if you sense that something is amiss? How do you track down the error? Do you have reports that break down the figures for you, perhaps paycheck by paycheck? Yes, you do.

You have essentially three reports that break down the amounts that you've deducted from each employee's paycheck, contributions, and prior payments, as well as reports that specify your company's total tax liability for any given period of time. They are listed as follows (the reports might have slightly different names depending on the version of QuickBooks that you are using):

- Employee Earnings Summary
- Payroll Summary by Item
- Quick Reports

> **Tip #53 from Gail Perry**
>
> When viewing a report that includes standard federal and state taxes, it's helpful to understand how they are named. Some taxes, such as Social Security, are contributed to by both the employer and employee. Some contributions are made only by the employer, and others are made by the employee. In any tax generated by QuickBooks, look at the final word of its name to see who the contributor is. For example, The payroll item Medicare *Company* refers to the company's share of the Medicare tax. Social Security *Employee* refers to the employee's share of social security.
>
> Some taxes, as you can see, are comprised of two items: one item collects the employee's share and the other collects the employer's share. Keep this in mind as you scroll through reports, interpreting the items to which they refer.

Employee Earnings Summary

The Employee Earnings Summary report shows each employee's gross pay (which includes salary, hourly wages, commissions, and any other additions), as well as sick and vacation pay. Employees are divided into rows, and each Payroll Item has its own column (shown in Figure 19.22). Access this report by clicking the Reports button in the Payroll Item List window, and then choosing Reports on All Payroll Items, Employee Earnings Summary.

The following information from this report is of particular interest during tax time:

- Deductions from gross pay
- Gross pay after deductions
- Taxes withheld

- Deductions from net pay
- Net pay after deductions
- Employer-paid taxes and contributions

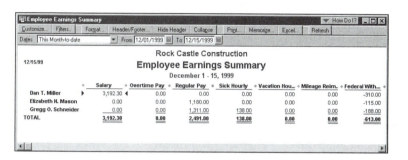

Figure 19.22
The Employee Earnings Summary Report.

Please note that The Employee Earnings Summary Report is wider than your computer screen, so you might have to scroll to the right to see additional columns (see accompanying tip).

Tip #54 from

You can view more of a report by reducing the width of the columns on the report. Place your mouse on the dot that separates the column titles. Your mouse pointer changes to a four-sided arrow. Drag the mouse to resize the column. You are given an opportunity to apply this new size to each column.

Payroll Summary by Item

The Payroll Summary report is similar to the Employee Earnings Summary, except that each employee has his own set of columns, and Payroll Items are broken into rows. To access the report, click the Reports button on the Payroll Item List, choose Reports on all Payroll Items, and then choose Summary.

Searching For More Specific Information

View a Quick Report on any payroll item by clicking on the item in the Payroll Item List, and then clicking the Reports button and choosing the top item in the drop down list. The Quick Report that appears displays every transaction that has affected the selected item for the entire year (you can also change the time period of this report to reflect a span of time other than the entire year).

Using the Quick Reports, you have three ways to quickly *drill down* to find the information that you might be looking for.

Change the Date Range

At the top of every report are Date fields. Use the drop-down button in the Dates field to select a new time scope for your report. When searching for the source of an error, it helps to be able to quickly include or exclude more dates from your report. To choose a very specific date range, use the From and To fields at the top of the report, specifying only the dates you have in mind.

Use Filters To Isolate Specific Payroll Items

Suppose that you have a strong suspicion that an error is occurring because somebody is being taxed twice for sick hours. You can check to see whether sick hours were double-reported (stranger things have happened). The following steps show how a report can help:

1. Open the report that you want to filter.
2. Click the Filters button at the upper left of the report. The Report Filters dialog box opens (this box was displayed previously, in Figure 19.15).
3. In the Filters window, scroll down and click Payroll Items.
4. The drop-down menu to the right of the Filters window is now labeled Payroll Items (see Figure 19.16, earlier in this chapter). Click that drop-down menu.
5. Click Selected Payroll Items. The Selected Payroll Items dialog box appears.
6. This dialog box shows all payroll Items. Scroll down and click the item that you specifically want to see.
7. On the Report Filters dialog box, the Current Choices Window now includes the filter that you selected.
8. You can go back to the Filters drop-down menu and add more filters if you want—for example, you can narrow your search to a specific Job Type.
9. When you are satisfied with your choices, click OK; a new report is generated, showing only the items that you want to see.

You might drill down further, clicking a specific line to see the check in question, as outlined in the following section.

Double-Click a Specific Transaction

When you find a line in a report that refers to some transaction that might be the source of your problem, double-click it, and drill down even further to see the source document from which a particular line is taken.

Use the following steps to locate a paycheck deduction that might be in error:

1. Open the Payroll Summary or Employee Earnings Summary report, and locate a line that shows a figure that is perhaps too high or too low.
2. Double-click the line containing the questionable figure. Figure 19.23 shows the user clicking the Medicare Employee line for a particular employee.

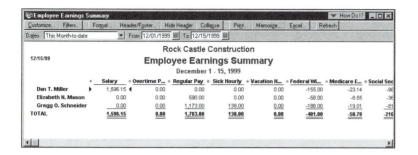

Figure 19.23
Looking closely at Medicare deductions, paycheck by paycheck.

3. You see a brief report that breaks down that employee's check-by-check contribution to Medicare.

4. Double-click a specific line in that new report. That line refers to a specific check paid out on a specific date.

5. An actual check appears on the screen. View the numbers here to see whether something is amiss.

6. Return to the first report that you opened by clicking the X in the upper-right corner of the reports that you want to close (or press Esc to close a report). Repeat steps 2–5 to examine the details of any other check that seems questionable.

Common Problems With Tax Figures

Following is a look at a few typical situations that cause your liability account to report inaccurate numbers.

Federal Unemployment Tax Seems High

If the amount that you owe for Federal Unemployment tax seems higher than you expected (you see how much your FUTA tax is when creating a Form 40), you probably forgot to apply the state contributions tax credit.

To get QuickBooks to acknowledge FUTA tax credit, follow these steps:

1. First, check with your accountant to make sure you can take this credit. If you pay state unemployment on a timely basis, you probably qualify for the credit.

2. Locate the payroll item called Federal Unemployment in the Payroll Item List.

3. Double-click it to edit it.

4. Click the Next button twice, and you see the Federal Unemployment Tax Rate dialog box (shown in Figure 19.24).

5. Select 0.8 percent, rather than 6.2 percent (see Figure 19.24).

Figure 19.24
Make sure that you are getting credited for your state unemployment payments by editing the Federal Unemployment tax Payroll Item.

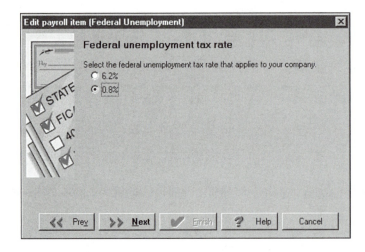

6. Continue to click Next until you arrive at the final screen, and then click Finish.
7. Click the Process 940 icon on the Payroll and Time tab. One of the final screens shows how much you owe for federal unemployment tax. The amount is much lower now.

LIABILITY AMOUNTS SEEM INCORRECT

Following are a few things to check when you select Pay Liabilities from the Payroll and Time tab of the Navigator, and the amount that QuickBooks says that you owe seems wrong:

1. Verify the Show liabilities as of date.

   By default, the Pay Liabilities window shows amounts due as of the last day of the previous month. If you made a payment during the current calendar month, the Pay Liabilities dialog boxes do not show correct amounts. To be credited for this most recent payment, move the Show Liabilities As Of date forward to include the date of your recent payment.

2. If you used the Write Checks window to make payments on any tax liability, the Pay Liabilities window does not credit these payments. To receive credit, you have to make a manual adjustment using the Adjust Liabilities window (see next section). For proper accounting, you have to use the Pay Liabilities feature to make tax payments of any type.

3. Pay attention to Tax Tracking. Perhaps the payroll item itself was applied on an employee's paycheck incorrectly. When you add a new deduction or contribution to an employee's paycheck, you use the Payroll info tab of the New Employee dialog box to specify how deductions and additions affect salary and taxable income.

4. The Tax Tracking window of the Add New Payroll Item dialog box enables you to determine exactly how this item affects the employee's taxes. When you select a Tax

Tracking option from the drop-down list, QuickBooks shows a paragraph or two explaining how that particular item affects taxable income.

Tip #55 from	Payroll additions and deductions all affect tax liability, but you often need to specify whether this payroll item taxes gross pay or net pay. Also, the sequence of payroll items as they appear on an employee's Paycheck Detail can make a difference. For example, if you set up a payroll item that pays an employee extra for working weekends, that item needs to appear above any company contribution that is a percentage of gross pay.

Correcting Liability Amount Errors

Following are two examples of potential errors in your QuickBooks liability account records:

- You once paid an employee from an account not associated with QuickBooks.
- You used the Write Check Window to pay last month's liabilities, and QuickBooks did not credit your payment.

Now that you've figured out why your numbers were off, what do you do about it? How do you make QuickBooks aware of the additional income or deductions that you need to apply?

Here's how to fix tax liability errors:

1. Note the amount of the adjustment you need to make, and the type of payroll items you want to adjust. (For example, if you made a company-contributed health insurance payment last week from your paper checkbook, you need to update the Health Insurance Company payroll item.)
2. Select the Payroll and Time tab from the QuickBooks Navigator, and click the Adjust Liabilities icon. The Liability Adjustment dialog box opens (shown in Figure 19.25)
3. The current Date appears in the Date field at the upper left. Make sure the Effective Date field shows the pay period that is affected by this adjustment.
4. Specify whether this adjustment affects a particular employee or a company payment or contribution.
5. In the Item Name field, use the drop-down menu to choose a Payroll Item to adjust.
6. Type a dollar amount in the Amount field.
7. Include a memo to later jog your memory regarding this adjustment.
8. In the Item Name field, click additional lines to make adjustments to other items, if necessary.
9. If you really did use a QuickBooks account to make this payment, but just used the Write Checks window to write the liability check, click Affected Accounts and check Do not Affect Accounts.

Figure 19.25
The Liability Adjustment dialog box.

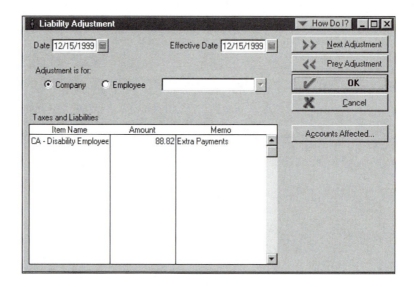

10. If you are making QuickBooks aware of a payment made from a source that had nothing to do with QuickBooks (for example, a paper checking account you don't normally use for this purpose), click Affected Accounts, and check Affect Liability and Expense Accounts.

11. If your adjustment requires you to calculate from a Base Wage, click the Show Wage Base button to view it momentarily.

12. If you are making adjustments for several pay periods, Click Next Adjustment to move on.

13. After making your final adjustment, click OK.

Setting Up Advance Earned Income Credit

If an employee meets the requirements to qualify for the Earned Income Credit, you can help him receive the tax credit through his current paycheck with the Advance Earned Income Credit. Following are some facts about how this process works:

- The Earned Income Credit is a way to qualify individuals who expect to pay little or no federal income tax to avoid having to wait until the end of the year to file for a tax refund.

- To establish eligibility for Advance Earned Income Credit payments, your employee must fill out and return to you a W-5 form, also known as an Earned Income Credit Advance Payment Certificate. Call 1-800-829-3676 to obtain a form.

- QuickBooks has created a payroll item called Advance Earned Income Credit, which you can quickly apply to any qualifying employee's paycheck; the payments can be generated automatically.

- You, the employer, actually make this payment to the employee as part of the regular paycheck process and, in turn, deduct what you paid the employee from the amount of tax you have to deposit.
- At the end of the year, when you create a Form 941, notice that a provision exists on line 12 for listing your Advance Earned Income Credit payments.
- Finally, in order to feed the right Advance Earned Income Credit figures to your Form 941, you need to generate a report showing how much you paid out. Simply use the Payroll Summary by Item report, creating a filter as previously outlined. QuickBooks includes an Advance Earned Income Credit payroll item for which you can easily create a report.

Troubleshooting

State Taxes

I need to get set up to withhold and pay state taxes. How do I find out how much to withhold and where to make my payments?

The address, phone number, and email address of every state taxing agency are listed in Appendix D. Contact the agency for the state in which you think you need to pay taxes and get the forms and information you need. Many forms can be downloaded from the state Internet sites.

Federal Form 941

I need to fill out Schedule B of my federal Form 941. QuickBooks doesn't provide this schedule. How can I get the information I need in order to prepare this form?

Prepare a payroll Item Detail report to extract the information you need for Form 941, Schedule B. Notice also that Line 17 of Form 941 is supposed to be left blank for Schedule B filers, but QuickBooks fills in this part of the form. I don't think that this is very significant, but you might want to delete the information on Line 17 of Form 941 if you are preparing a Schedule B.

County Taxes

My employees are subject to county taxes at more than one rate. QuickBooks only provides an opportunity to add a payroll item for one county rate in my state. How can I get around this problem?

Set up additional county or local tax rates within your state by choosing Other Tax as your new payroll item, and then choosing User-Defined Tax. You can enter as many user-defined tax types as you need.

PART IV

Making QuickBooks Work for You

20 Customizing QuickBooks Forms 337

21 QuickBooks Reports and Graphs 361

22 Setting Preferences 383

CHAPTER 20

CUSTOMIZING QUICKBOOKS FORMS

In this chapter

Customizing a Form 338

Moving and Resizing Fields 348

Customizing Tips 357

There are many reasons why you might want to customize a form. You can

- Add your name, address, or company logo at the top of the form.
- Create unique invoices for various types of customers you have.
- Add fields for customer-specific information, such as shipping and handling charges.
- Specify that certain information is to be seen on the onscreen version of your form, but is not to be printed.
- Create custom sales slips, adding fields for new information to one version while removing them from another.
- Use the Layout Designer to move and resize fields and columns. This is helpful, for example, if you create a large logo that you want to appear prominently on your form.
- Create a special Packing Slip for checking the total of ordered goods versus the number that actually arrives in a particular shipment.
- Add fields that enable you to keep track of specific aspects of your client base, such as a special distinction for those who have placed especially large orders in the last year, or those who are more than three months behind in their payments.
- Create a field that tracks clients by industry. You can have one form available for customers from the entertainment business and another for publishers and journalists, for example. After you have this industry-specific information on hand, you can create a direct mailing tailored for each type of client, and, most importantly, note which type of industry is most highly represented among your newer clients.

Note

QuickBooks enables you to quickly specify which fields of a form you want to see onscreen and which are to be printed. For example, the customer's birthday might be handy to know, but you probably don't want it printed on an invoice or purchase order.

CUSTOMIZING A FORM

In QuickBooks, you can quickly customize a form by adding and removing fields. For more substantive changes, you can alter the form's layout, moving fields around the form and resizing them.

Tip #56 from
Gail Perry

If you find yourself scribbling important numbers or memos in the margins of your purchase orders, invoices, or credit slips, consider creating a new field specifically for that data. Also, check out QuickBooks and Your Industry (choose QuickBooks and Your Industry from the Help menu) to see how others in your field have customized QuickBooks forms to suit their needs.

Most of the examples in this chapter are invoices, although the methods used for customizing any sales form or statement are identical. These include Credit memos, Cash Sales slips, and even purchase orders. Because you're using an invoice as your example, I'll point out that you might customize an invoice when you have a particular set of vendors or customers in mind. For example, if one set of customers always requires overnight shipping, create an invoice with special UPS or Federal Express fields; or, if certain customers always order large quantities from you at a discount, design a form with unique quantity fields.

Determining Which Template to Change

Follow these steps to customize an invoice:

1. From the Activities menu, choose Create Invoices (or press Ctrl+I).
2. From the Custom Template drop-down list at the upper right, choose the type of invoice you want to customize. This can be your starting point for customizing. You'll see the fields of the invoice change to reflect the type of template you choose for customizing.
3. Again, click the drop-down menu. You'll notice that a check appears by the name of the template you are customizing.
4. Select Customize, and you'll see the Customize Template screen pictured in Figure 20.1.

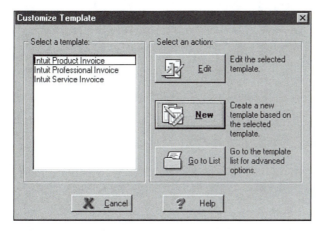

Figure 20.1
Customize a template to create a reusable form.

> **Note**
>
> If you choose to customize a template that has the word Intuit in front of it, you'll be prompted to duplicate this template before proceeding. QuickBooks protects these default templates from being edited by prompting you to create a duplicate before you begin. First, close the two dialog boxes that just opened and, from the Lists menu, choose Templates. The Templates window appears. Highlight the template you want to duplicate and click the Templates drop-down menu. Choose Duplicate. A new version of this template appears along with the others. The word DUP appears in front of the name of the template copy. You can now edit this duplicate knowing that you have a backup of the original, if you ever want to use that form.

> **Note**
>
> You might notice that the form you are working with now is being referred to as a template. This means that you are creating a document that you can open and reuse later in many instances, applying it in more than one circumstance.

5. Select Customize to display the Customize Template dialog box. When it appears, click Edit to make changes to the current template, New to start from scratch, and Go to List to open the Template window.

From the Template window, you can duplicate, delete, and import templates, as well as make them inactive and find templates used in specific transactions (see Figure 20.2). The Select a Template panel on the left is one other way to choose which template you want to edit.

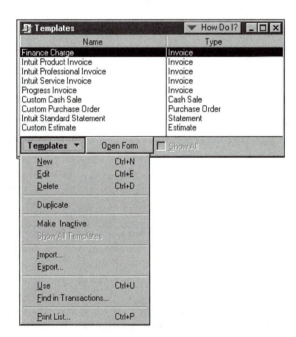

Figure 20.2
The Templates drop-down menu, available in the Templates List window, enables you to duplicate, delete, and import templates.

If you are trying to find a form that closely resembles something you are trying to create, use the Find feature (Edit, Find). With it, you can scroll through every type of QuickBooks form, searching for a certain transaction type or payment method, or even for a particular template. When the form you want appears in the Find list, click Go To, and the form appears, ready for editing.

ADDING AND REMOVING FIELDS

Click Edit to open the Customize Invoice dialog box (see Figure 20.3). You'll see five or six tabs (if you choose to edit an Intuit standard template, some of the options described here are not available to you). Each tab controls a specific area of the form. For example, to specify if a date or invoice number is to appear at the top of your form, click the Header tab. To include a special message, memo, or grand total figure at the bottom of your form, click the Footer tab. To turn fields on and off or to change their titles, click the Fields tab.

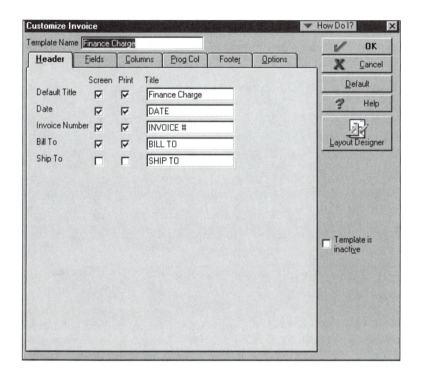

Figure 20.3
Click a check box in the Screen column to view a field onscreen, and check the Print column to specify which fields are to print.

Change the name of your template by typing something new in the Template Name area at the top of the template. After renaming, this new template appears with the others in the Template window. If you save it without renaming, the template on which you based your new invoice is changed.

Each of the tabs in this dialog box enables you to change different aspects of the form and specify whether a certain field or data area is to appear. You can determine, for example, that the shipping number or customer's email address is to appear on your computer screen, but is not to be printed out on the paper form itself. You can change the title of the form or any field. For example, you can change REP to a more explanatory Sales Rep, or change FOB to Goods Liability. Or perhaps you want to change the title, Invoice, to Bill of Sale.

Tip #57 from

Gail Perry

You cannot change a field's basic type by simply renaming it. For example, if you change the Shipping Date field title to Estimated Arrival Date, it still appears with the shipping date. Likewise, changing the title of a column or header area does not cause that field to suddenly appear with different data. Data in an invoice is populated from the Customer:Jobs

> List, and any numbers you type in by hand. To change the type of data available to Invoice fields, work with the Customer:Jobs List.

CUSTOMIZING A FORM HEADER

At the top of the customize screen is the Template Name. This name appears on the form. The name can contain up to 41 characters; therefore, if you want to, you can be much more descriptive than "Invoice."

On the Header tab, you can specify features that are to appear at the top of the form. For example, you can specify if the Invoice Number is to appear onscreen, printed, both, or neither. Although you can change the title "Invoice #," the invoice number itself is generated by the number on the actual invoice.

CUSTOMIZING INDIVIDUAL FIELDS

As an example for editing field titles and visibility, here's a closer look at the Fields tab (see Figure 20.4):

- Each line of this tab represents an area of information on the form. The type of data that appears on the form is shown at the left.
- To make any field visible on your screen, place a check in the Screen column next to that field's title. The fields you check here are available to you when you fill in the form, but do not necessarily appear on the printed form.
- To make any field visible on your printed form, place a check in the Print column next to that field's name.
- For visibility both onscreen and in print, check both the Print and Screen boxes.
- To the right of each field is the Title. You can change the title simply by typing in this area. Click OK, and your changes appear on the form.

ADDING, REMOVING, AND REORDERING COLUMNS

The Columns tab introduces another control (see Figure 20.5): the Order box.

The Order box enables you to sequence the order in which your columns are to appear. Type 1 in the Order box to make a column appear farthest to the left, type 2 for a column to appear to the right of column 1, and so forth. Only columns you have checked can be ordered.

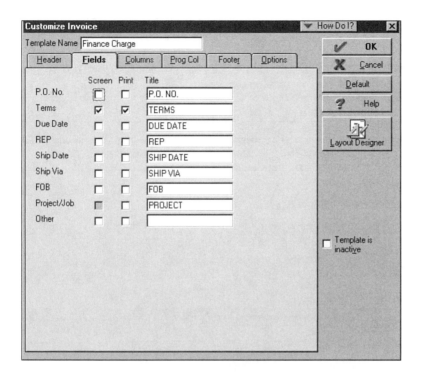

Figure 20.4
Use the Fields tab to add or remove any field from your form.

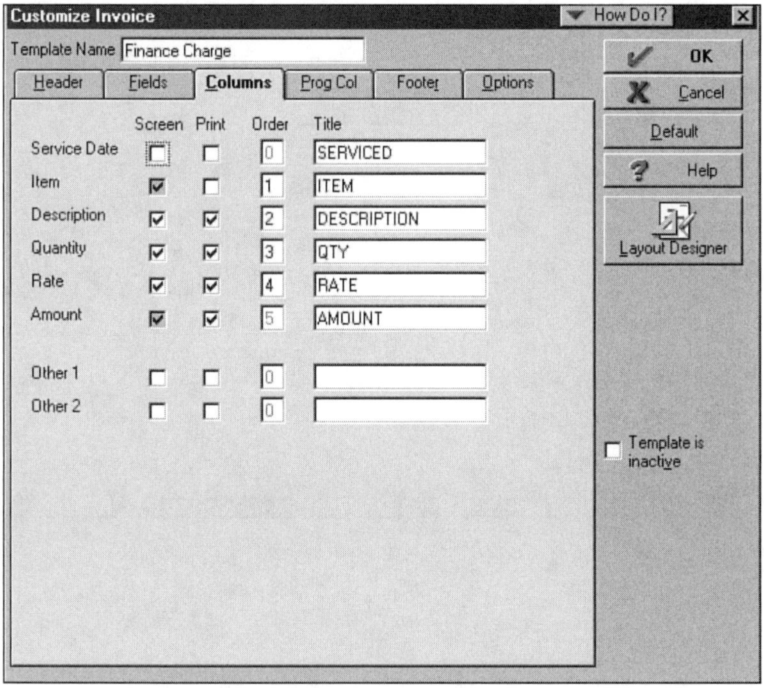

Figure 20.5
Change the columns sequence by using the Columns tab.

Tip #58 from
Gail Perry

If you remove a field or column that has data in it, the data is not gone. By using the controls found here, you've merely chosen not to view it at this time. QuickBooks continues to save it. If you make that field or column visible again, the data it contained is visible as well.

Tip #59 from
Gail Perry

If your experimentation takes a turn for the worse, restore the template to its original state by clicking Default on the far right of the Customize Invoice dialog box.

CUSTOMIZING A PROGRESSIVE ESTIMATE INVOICE

Earlier you learned that the Customize Template dialog box might show five or six tabs. Not all invoice templates show the Prog Col tab (see Figure 20.6).

→ To find more information about progress billing, see "Turning on the Progress Billing Feature," on **p. 176**

Figure 20.6
The Progressive Invoice Columns tab.

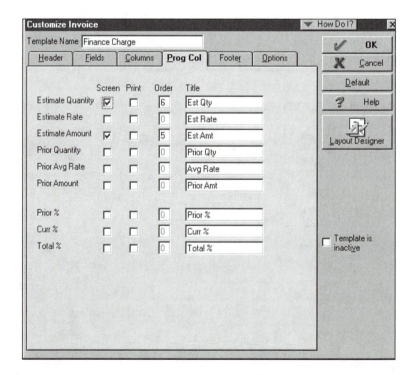

This tab appears if Progress Invoicing is turned on. Progress Invoicing is important if you bill customers for partially completed work. Following are two examples of when partial billing is important:

- Contracting or construction jobs that require partial payment at different intervals
- Billing a client on a monthly basis for legal work that will take several months to complete

→ To find more information about progress billing and billing from estimates, **see p. 169**

The Prog Col tab creates a special set of columns for Progressive Estimate Invoices. This tab creates fields for specifying the percentage of work that is completed and comparisons between prior estimates and actual dollar amounts, billed as labor or supplies.

Tip #60 from

Together with Progress Invoicing, Job Status Descriptions help you keep track of how far along you are in any work you are doing. You can, for example, use the Customer:Jobs List to call up all jobs with pending contracts or all jobs that were eventually awarded to other businesses. Job Status Descriptions are covered in Chapter 10, "Job-cost Estimating and Tracking."

Tip #61 from

Some invoices are set up to bill for various items, and not all items are applicable each time you bill. For example, sometimes you'll perform labor, but not use billable parts. By default, though, QuickBooks includes that non-billable item on the invoice, showing a charge of $0.00. To make this non-billable item not appear on your invoice, choose File, Preferences, Jobs & Estimates, and select the Don't print items that have a zero amount check box.

Like the Columns tab, the number in the Order box determines the sequence of columns. Type 1 to make a column appear first from the left, with each number moving progressively rightward.

CUSTOMIZING A FORM FOOTER

The Footer tab contains two special text areas (see Figure 20.7). In the Message area, type in a message 41 characters in length or less (long enough for "Your bill is 3 months overdue," or "For $10 off, reorder this month," for example). You can type beyond the visible field, if you want, up to a total of 41 characters.

In addition, there is an area for long text, up to 960 characters. This is ideal for warranty information and legal disclaimers. This text block does not show up on your screen—but it does show up on your printed invoice.

Figure 20.7
Enter a message that will appear at the bottom of each of your customized forms.

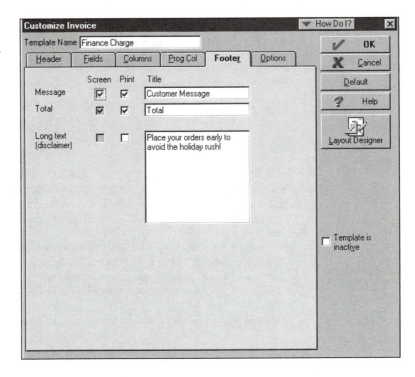

CUSTOMIZING COMPANY INFO AND ADDING A LOGO

To place the company name and address on your form, select the tOptions tab. Place a check by Print Company name, Print Company address, or both. The invoice prints the company name and address as it is found in Company Info (File, Company Info).

To include a company logo, click Use Logo, and then click the Specify button, and the Logo dialog box appears (see Figure 20.8). Click File to open a Browse menu to search your hard drive for a logo. It must be a .BMP file. After the file is located and selected, QuickBooks automatically resizes it appropriately and copies the logo to the QuickBooks folder.

> **Note**
>
> You can use a logo for checks and paychecks by choosing Printer Setup from the File menu. From the Form name drop-down menu, choose Check/Paycheck. You'll notice a Logo button off to the right. Click it to choose a logo for your company's checks and paychecks. The logo you choose need not be the same as the one used on invoices, or sale or purchase forms.

CUSTOMIZING A FORM | 347

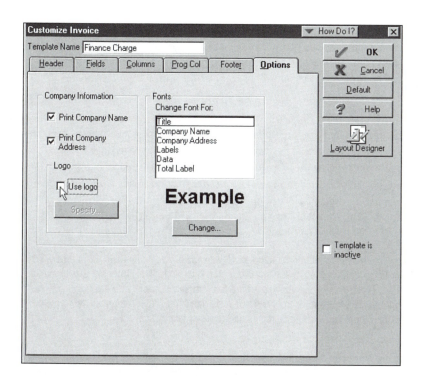

Figure 20.8
To place a logo on your form, from the Options tab, check Use Logo and click the Specify button.

Tip #62 from Gail Perry

If the artwork you want to use for your logo is not saved as a .BMP file, use any photo editing program such as Microsoft Paint to open the logo and resave it in the .BMP format.

Follow these steps to change fonts:

1. In the Fonts section of the Options tab, click any item in the Font box (see Figure 20.9), and see the font size and type that QuickBooks has selected. The following is displayed: AaBbYyZz. You might notice that the font for Title is very large, whereas the font for Labels is quite small.

2. With any Change Font For item selected, click the Change button. A Font dialog box appears, enabling you to choose a new font, font style, and size for each item. Click OK to finalize your choice.

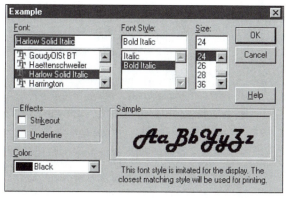

Any font settings that you change here apply to all items of that same type of business form. (Change the font for Labels, for example, and every label printed from that type of form uses that same font setting.) If you want to use a unique font style to set a particular word or two apart from the rest of the items (for example, have the company name utilize two types of fonts), you have to use the QuickBooks Layout Designer, which provides many more customization options for your forms.

Making a Template Inactive

To make a template inactive, click the Template is inactive check box, near the bottom right of the Customize Invoice dialog box. There are several reasons why you might want to make a template inactive. For example, if you decide that only one version of a particular invoice is to be used, you might want to deactivate a particular template with the same or similar name. An inactive template does not appear in the list of available templates. Deactivating a template places it off limits to employees until you activate it again.

> **Note**
>
> If you have made a number of templates inactive, you can locate them again for editing or use. To view all your templates, inactive or not, select Templates from the Lists menu and place a check in the Show All box. An inactive template appears with a very small "hand" symbol to its left when the Show All box is checked. To make this template active, select it, click the Templates drop-down menu, and choose Make Active.
>
> You can also open the original template and uncheck the Template Is Inactive check box.

Moving and Resizing Fields

You can use the Layout Designer to rearrange form elements, aligning them horizontally or vertically, either giving your form a whole new look or perhaps just making key elements stand out a bit more. In the Layout Designer, you can easily change the location and size of fields that appear on your form.

In Layout Designer, your form appears as clusters of rectangular boxes. Each box is an element of your form, such as the Address data field or the Due Date label. Click any box and look at the bottom left of the screen. The form element on which you've clicked is identified. Each element appears as a rectangle and is easy to resize or move. The rectangles are not printed on the final form.

Here's how to work with form elements in Layout Designer. When you click any form element, black handles appear on the corners and sides of the rectangle. Try the following:

- Select an element by clicking on it.
- Select multiple elements by dragging your mouse pointer over several adjacent elements, or by holding down the Shift key while you click on individual elements.
- To move a selected form element anywhere on the page, click inside the rectangle and drag to a new location.

- To center an element or group of elements horizontally between the margins of the form, make your selection, and then click the Center Horz button at the top of the screen.
- To resize a form element, click and drag the handles inward or outward.

Follow these steps to move and resize fields:

1. Open any form from the Activities menu (Estimates, Invoices, Cash Sales, Credit Memos, Purchase Orders, or Statements, for example), and then choose Customize from the Custom Template drop-down menu.
2. Choose the type of template you want to change, or choose the Custom option to create an entirely new template from scratch. Then click on Edit or New. The Customize window appears.
3. Click the Layout Designer button. You'll see the Layout Designer, as shown in Figure 20.10.

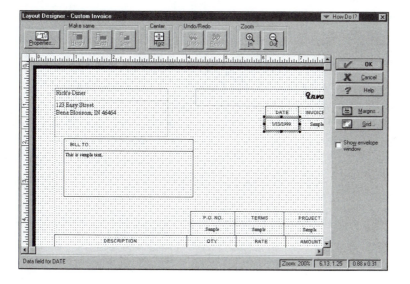

Figure 20.10
The Layout Designer.

Tip #63 from Gail Perry

If you want to create a new field, you need to return to the Customize dialog box. Click OK, select the Fields tab, and choose Other. Create a title for this field, and it appears on the form. You can then return to the Layout Designer where you can resize and move your field as you want.

CREATING A COMMON HEIGHT OR WIDTH

In Layout Designer, you can select two or more elements, and then make them the same height or width (see Figure 20.11).

CHAPTER 20 CUSTOMIZING QUICKBOOKS FORMS

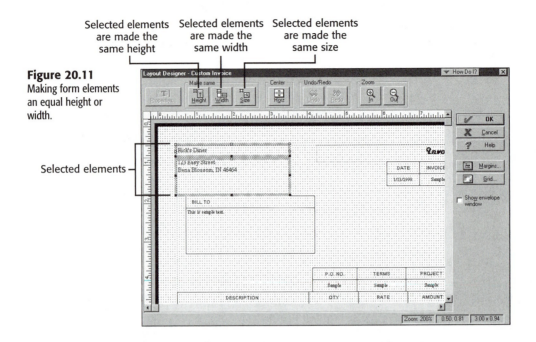

Figure 20.11
Making form elements an equal height or width.

Follow these steps to modify form elements uniformly:

1. Select the form elements that you want to make uniform. Perform the selection by clicking on one element, and then holding down the Shift key while you click on additional form elements. Handles appear around each form element that you click.
2. The features for all selected form elements match those of the last element selected.
3. To make your selected elements have a common height, click the Make Same...Height button.
4. To make your selected elements have a common width, click the Make Same...Width button.
5. To make all selected elements the same size, click the Make Same...Size button.

RESIZING AND CHANGING TEXT IN A FORM

If you want to make a form element larger, drag the handles to increase its size. You can make the font inside the element larger too. To change the font, font style, or font size in any form element, double-click the element, which opens the Properties dialog box, and then select the Font button on the Text tab.

The Properties dialog box enables you change justification of text, as well as create a border or partial border around your form elements. There are two tabs in the Properties dialog box. To justify text horizontally or vertically, click the appropriate button in either the Horizontal or Vertical Justification panel.

You can also edit text by selecting a field and clicking the Properties button on the upper left of the Layout Designer toolbar.

Tip #64 from *Gail Perry*	You might have discovered that, in Layout Designer, you cannot change the text message inside any form element. You can change the size, font style, and font, but not the content. To change content, return to the Customize screen by clicking OK, and make your changes using the tabbed menus, as described previously. Then return to Layout Designer to rearrange and resize your objects.

ADDING A BORDER TO A FORM ELEMENT

Click the Border tab in the Properties window to perform the following tasks:

- Add a visible rectangular border around a form element.
- Add a partial border, or half a rectangle, as shown in Figure 20.12. This border has a 3-dimensional appearance.
- Add a single underline.

For example, click the Left check box to add a visible line on the left side of the form element, click the Bottom checkbox to add an underline, and so forth.

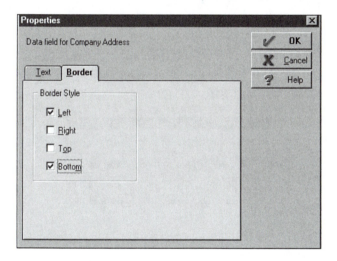

Figure 20.12
Creating a half rectangle border around a form element provides a 3D appearance.

Changing Your View of Your Form

Layout Designer provides Zoom In and Zoom Out buttons at the top of the screen, enabling you to view your form close up or from farther away. Using these buttons, you can do the following:

- Click the Zoom In button to make form elements appear larger on the screen. You might have to use the scroll buttons at the right and bottom of the screen to see the element.
- Click the Zoom Out button to see more of your form at once.

These views do not change the actual size of the form.

The Layout Designer Grid

The Layout Designer shows your form against a non-printing grid. For some people, this series of dots makes it easier to visualize how to evenly align and position form elements. You can do the following:

- To change grid settings, or to turn the grid off entirely, click the Grid button on the middle right of the Layout Designer. The Grid and Snap Settings dialog box appears (see Figure 20.13).
- To turn the grid off, remove the check from Show grid.
- If you prefer the grid dots closer together or farther apart, choose from various options on the Grid Spacing drop-down list box.
- If you are repositioning form elements and want them in just the right position, turn on the Snap to grid feature. With Snap to grid on, your elements snap into place, aligning with a common grid boundary.

Figure 20.13
Changing grid settings and visibility with the Grid and Snap Settings dialog box.

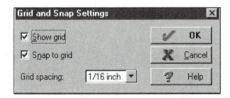

Layout Designer Margins

Layout Designer provides a lightly dashed margin around your form. The dashes do not print. Layout Designer's margin does not correspond to your printer's set margin. It's merely a visual reminder to help you keep all your form elements inside the boundary that you specify.

You can change the margin by clicking the Margins button on the right side Layout Designer. The Margins dialog box appears (see Figure 20.14). Notice that you can set separate measurements for each margin, allowing a bigger margin at the bottom than at the top, for example. However, you might never need to alter these margins at all because they default to fairly universal settings that work well with most printers and conventional form sizes.

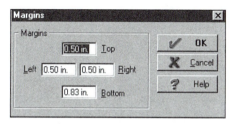

Figure 20.14
Changing margins in Layout Designer.

Note the following when using the margins dialog box:

- The unit of measurement used by the Margin controls defaults to inches, but several other units of measurement can be employed, including millimeters and picas. To change the unit of measurement, type a new abbreviation into the margin data area. For example, rather than the default .5 in., type 13 mm., or 3 pi.

- Notice that if you click inside the Top margin data area, the QuickBooks QCard reminds you of the allowable measurement abbreviations.

> **Note**
> A more comprehensive list of allowable abbreviations is available by clicking the Help button and selecting the Changing the unit of measure topic.

SHOW ENVELOPE WINDOW

Intuit sells envelopes with viewing windows, as do office supply stores. These envelopes enable you to put a form in the envelope with prewritten address and return address areas, which show through the windows. If you use window envelopes, click the Show envelope window option in the Layout Designer, and non-printing gray shaded areas appear where the windowed areas of the envelope would be. You can then position a form's address and return address so that they are visible in the windows.

PREVIEWING YOUR FORM

Follow these steps to preview your form:

1. Click OK to close the Layout Designer dialog box.
2. Click OK to close the Customize dialog box.
3. Click the Preview button on the actual form window to see a full-screen version of your form as it will appear if you print it.

To do further editing, you must return the way you came, back to the Layout Designer.

There are apparently no shortcuts for obtaining a quick preview while the Layout Designer is still open. For this reason, you might try to do most of your editing all at once, and then preview it.

CREATING CUSTOM FIELDS

You can create custom fields that can appear in invoices, job orders, sales receipts, statements, and credit memos. These fields can be prefilled with your information from an estimate or other source from a QuickBooks file. Custom fields can appear onscreen, can be printed, or both, just like all other fields. Curiously, though, when you use the Create dialog box to add these custom fields to your forms (as described earlier), they appear in the Columns tab, and not the Fields tab, as you might expect.

WHEN TO USE CUSTOM FIELDS

The process described here is rather complex, and is significant if you are creating a new field that you want to apply to many receipts or invoices, setting up a criterion for tracking or billing many customers or clients. Short of this, you might find it easier to use one of the extra fields provided by QuickBooks in the Fields tab (called Other), and title it anything you want. Adding a field using the method described in this section is valuable if you are planning to add a data source to go along with it.

REVIEWING A CUSTOM FIELD EXAMPLE

The following example creates two fields, one called Referred By and the other called 10% Discount. These two fields enable you to track how a particular client was referred to you, and to track those who are eligible for a 10 percent discount that you are offering for repeat customers. After these fields are added, you can add them to your invoices and other forms and use the Find in Transactions feature to look at all customers who fit these new categories.

Follow these steps to create custom fields:

1. Select Items from the Lists menu.
2. Click the Item drop-down menu.
3. Select New (or press Ctrl+N), and the New Item dialog box appears (see Figure 20.15). For purposes of this exercise, you don't need to fill in any of the fields in this window.

Figure 20.15
The New Item dialog box, where Custom Fields are created.

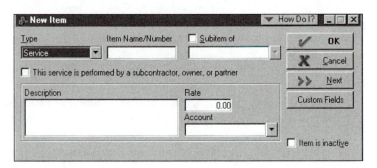

4. Click the Custom Fields button and click past the warning that no custom fields have been created yet (if you have created a custom field previously, you do not see this warning).

5. Select Define Fields. As you can tell, you are allowed to create up to five custom fields. You are going to create two. (If you are experimenting with the sample company, notice that two custom fields have already been created: Color and Material.)

6. In the first blank field, enter Referred By and 10% Discount (see Figure 20.16). To make these fields available to forms, you must check the Use box.

7. Click OK and you'll see these new fields appear in a dialog box called Custom Fields for unnamed item. They are now available for use, but have not yet been applied or assigned to any existing forms. Click OK to close that dialog box, and click OK to close the New Item dialog box as well.

APPLYING YOUR NEW FIELDS

This example illustrates how to add a newly-created field to an invoice form.

Follow these steps to add new custom fields to a form:

1. Select Create Invoices (or press Ctrl+I) from the Activities menu. The Create Invoice window appears.

2. Select Customize from the Custom Template drop-down menu.

3. Click on the style of invoice to which you want to add a custom field.

4. Click Edit and select the Columns tab in the Customize Invoice window that appears. You'll see your two new categories: Referred By and 10% Discount (see Figure 20.17).

5. In the Referred By field, place a check under Screen but not Print because it's not important for the customer to see who referred him to you; it's just good information for you.

6. In the 10% Discount field, place a check by both Screen and Print because you do want your customer to know he's getting special treatment for his repeat business.

CREATING FORMS THAT USE YOUR NEW FIELD

After you've added these new fields to a number of customers' documents, you might want to see where your referrals are coming from and how much repeat business your 10 percent discount offer is generating. Using the Find in Transactions command, as described here, you can view all the invoices, sales receipts, credit slips, and estimates that use these fields; thus, you can compare your data.

Figure 20.17
The two newly created fields appear in the Columns tab of the Customize Invoice dialog box.

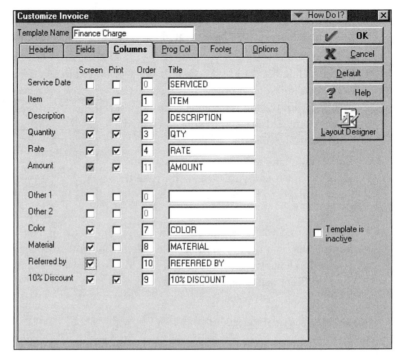

Follow these steps to determine if your fields are being used:

1. Select Items from the Lists menu and the list of all items appears. Click the Item drop-down menu.
2. Select Find in Transactions from the Item drop-down menu. You'll see the dialog box shown in Figure 20.18.

Figure 20.18
Click Find in Transaction to open the Find dialog box.

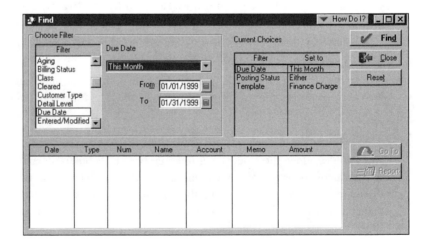

3. In the Filter column, select which field you want to use as a search criterion.
4. Click the Fin<u>d</u> button, and you'll see all the transactions that have used this field at the bottom of the dialog box. The matches are noted on the bottom right of the dialog box.

Customizing Tips

Although you've used invoices as your customizing forms example, all sales forms, such as cash receipts, credit memos, and statements, are customized the same way. Let's look briefly at a few examples of how and why you might customize specific types of forms.

For credit memos, it might be helpful to have a field indicating if an item was returned because of customer dissatisfaction, was exchanged because of defective merchandise, or if there was an overpayment. If an item was returned, did the customer accept credit toward another purchase or demand a refund? These are things you might want to know at a glance, just by looking at the credit memo. Also, with such data, you can use Find in Transaction to view trends in your customers' satisfaction, or to generate reports from these fields.

In this example, you'll use a Cash Sales form to create a quick record of all sales over a given period, for example a Weekly Sales Summary or something similar. A Cash Sales form is used to receive payment for any item that is not ordered on a regular basis (for example, invoiced). It can be used to record payments with checks and credit cards as well.

Follow these steps to create a summary of sales activities:

1. Select Enter Cash <u>S</u>ales from the <u>A</u>ctivities menu, at the top of the screen.
2. Select a payment method.
3. In the Item area, use the drop-down menus to make a list of items you sell most regularly. You can always add new items on-the-fly.
4. Don't type anything in the Quantity column because you'll be using this form on a regular basis to summarize sales activity. Also, don't type anything in the Customer:Job area.
5. Select <u>E</u>dit, <u>M</u>emorize Cash Sale (or press Ctrl+M). This adds your custom form to the Memorized Transactions List.
6. In the <u>N</u>ame area, type in a descriptive title for this form, such as Cash Sales Summary.
7. Click OK, and when you are back at the Enter Cash Sales dialog box, click the <u>C</u>ancel button. Do not click OK because you don't want to record the transaction.

You might also want to customize a sales form if you plan to sell on consignment; you need a form with a service item that debits your account with your percentage of each sale and a standard sales item that pays the remainder to the consignor.

Follow these steps to summarize your sales activities:

1. Click the Mem Tx icon on your Iconbar or select Memorized Transactions from the Lists menu (or press Ctrl+T).
2. From the Memorized Transaction List that appears, double-click on the cash sale transaction you saved, type in Quantities for the period in question, and fill in any sale items that were not included in the item list you originally saved with this file.
3. Click OK to save the new file for that particular month or week with a new name. That way, you won't overwrite the form you created for regular use.

Special Considerations for Statements

For monthly statements, you might want to create a Bounced Check, Stop Payment, and Bank Fee field, or a field that indicates if a particular statement has been printed or mailed yet. This information is available from reports, but it can be convenient to have it right on the statement itself.

Don't forget that many charges can be applied to a statement automatically, such as regular membership fees or monthly rents. Consider automating any recurring charges.

Additionally, you might want to bypass entering charges to each customer's register and, instead, enter statement charges all at once directly into your Accounts Receivable Register. This can save you lots of time. Furthermore, you can create a Memorized Transaction for an entire group of regular statements—for example, if you bill all regular customers at the same time of the month.

Adding a Form to the Iconbar

QuickBooks offers a way to quickly produce a regularly used report by enabling you to add an icon to the iconbar for any window that you can display onscreen. To add an icon for a form or report, follow these steps:

1. Open the report to which you want fast access and then select Window, Add Window to Iconbar.
2. You'll see a dialog box prompting you to name your icon as it will appear on the bar and to add a brief description, which will not appear. Type in a name and a description.
3. On the left side of the dialog box, scroll through the list of icon possibilities, picking one that seems appropriate for your form.
4. Click OK to close the dialog box, and the button is included with the others on the iconbar. From now on, clicking the icon once opens that report.
5. If your iconbar is not yet visible, select Preferences from the File menu.
6. On the far left, scroll down to click the Iconbar button.
7. On the My Preferences tab, click which version of the iconbar you want to view (icons and text, icons only, or text only).

8. Click OK to close the Preferences dialog box and save your changes. The iconbar remains on your screen until you change your preferences.

The My Preferences tab reveals options to make your iconbar visible, showing only the pictures, only the text, or both. To choose icon visibility, click one of the buttons.

Notice here that you can also add, remove, and edit icons, as well as place a space in between them if you want your icons to appear in logical groupings.

→ To find more information on customizing your iconbar, see "Iconbar Preferences," on **p. 390**

Click OK to save your customized settings. To change the Iconbar back to the way it was before you altered it, click <u>D</u>efault.

Troubleshooting

Custom Fields

There are only five custom fields available in the Define Custom Fields window, but I want to have more than five custom fields. Can the limit of five be overridden?

Although it's true there are only five custom fields available for use with your items, there are an additional 15 custom fields available for use with vendors, customers, and employees (the same 15 fields for all three lists). You cannot add to the number of custom fields provided by QuickBooks, so if you have lots of information you want to track, choose your fields wisely.

Sizing Forms

Am I limited to the full-size, 8 1/2 by 11 sheet of paper on which the standard forms are set up, or can I change the size of a form I am customizing?

You acan change the size of any form to match that of the actual forms on which you print. You are not limited to the full size sheet of paper as displayed in the Layout Designer. Click the <u>M</u>argins button while in the Layout Designer and set your own margins. Just be sure to move all your form elements inside the new margins you designate.

CHAPTER 21

QUICKBOOKS REPORTS AND GRAPHS

In this chapter

Standard Reports   363

Commonly Used QuickBooks Reports   363

Customizing Reports   368

Printing Reports   374

QuickBooks's Graphs   376

After you have taken the time to enter all your business transactions in QuickBooks, it would be a shame not to reap the benefits of that work by producing reports that summarize your business activity.

You can produce many types of reports in QuickBooks. You can create the following, for example:

- Profit and loss reports that show you how much revenue your company is producing
- Balance sheet reports that show you how much your company is worth
- Comparative reports that display current year numbers with prior year numbers so that you can see how performance has changed
- Forecast reports that help you predict your financial future
- Trial balance reports that show the balance in every account
- Transaction reports that display every transaction in every account for a specified time period
- Audit trail reports that show all changes and adjustments that have been made
- Budget reports that tell you how close you're coming to meeting your goals
- Accounts receivable reports that provide you with information on how much is owed to your company
- Sales reports that tell you how sales of particular items are going, or how much business particular customers give you
- Job costing reports (available in QuickBooks Pro) that give you the details on how each job is doing and how estimates compare to actual performance
- Accounts payable reports that tell you how much your company owes others
- Purchase reports that give you breakdowns of how your money is being spent
- Inventory reports that tell you what items are in stock and what items are on order
- Tax reports that help you prepare your tax forms
- Payroll reports that give you updates on how much you are spending on payroll and payroll taxes

Many of the reports that QuickBooks prepares are discussed throughout this book in the appropriate chapters. Payroll reports, for example, are described in the chapters on payroll and payroll taxes; inventory reports are described in the inventory chapters, and so on.

In this chapter you'll find an overview of QuickBooks reports, information on how to find and request them, and instructions on customizing and memorizing reports.

Standard Reports

QuickBooks comes with many standard reports that you can display and print. You can access the Reports menu in QuickBooks and examine the list of standard reports, which are organized by topic (see Figure 21.1).

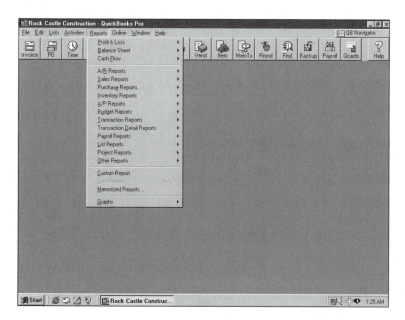

Figure 21.1
The main Reports menu. Clicking a topic provides a side menu of additional reports.

You can create any of the standard reports by selecting the report that you want from the Reports menu. Choose Reports, and then click the general type of report you want to view. When a side menu appears, click the report that you want and QuickBooks displays the report onscreen.

Many reports are also available from the List window and the Items window. For example, choose Lists, Chart of Accounts. Click the Reports button in the Chart of Accounts list window, and choose Reports on All Accounts; a menu of standard reports appears.

Commonly Used QuickBooks Reports

You'll find, as you experiment with the QuickBooks reports, that some reports don't provide you with information that you find useful to your business, but that other reports are so useful you can't function without them.

In this section, you'll get an introduction to some of the most commonly used reports. Later in this chapter (see the section "Customizing Reports") you'll learn how to customize your reports; that way, if the standard report is close to providing what you need but needs a little tweaking, you can alter the report to conform to your needs. Maybe you need to have things sorted differently, for example, or maybe one of the columns on the report is not of use to you.

PROFIT AND LOSS STATEMENT

The Profit and Loss Standard report lists all your income and expense accounts and shows the current total in each account; the result is a net income figure derived from reducing your total income by the total of your expenses. Individual transactions are not shown on this report—only the balance for each account.

From the Chart of Accounts list window, select the Reports drop-down menu. Then click Reports on all Accounts, Profit & Loss, and choose from a variety of ways to view Profit and Loss Reports. Each report enables you to choose which time frame to view, from an entire year to a single day. Choose Standard Report, Year to Date Comparison, Previous Year Comparison, or an itemized, highly detailed look.

Follow these steps to create a standard Profit and Loss statement:

1. Choose Reports, Profit & Loss. The Profit & Loss side menu appears.
2. Choose Standard. The Profit and Loss report appears onscreen and displays a balance for each income and expense account (see Figure 21.2).

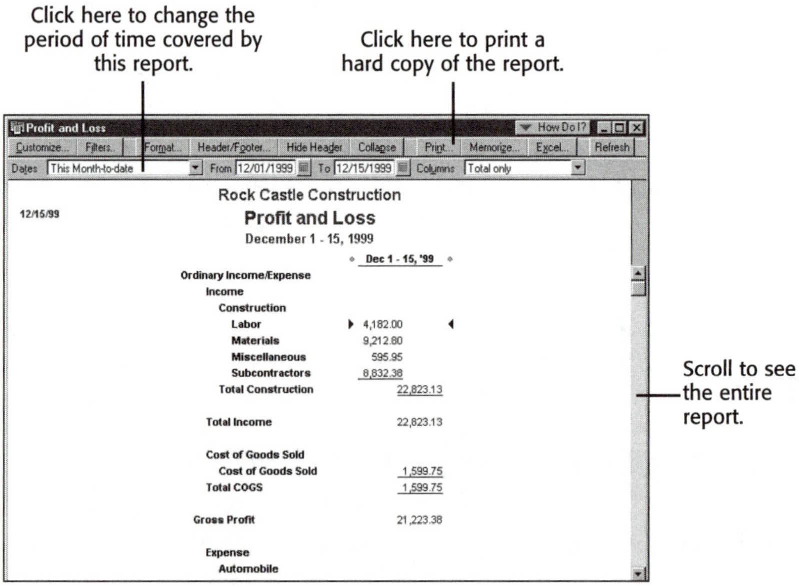

Figure 21.2
The standard Profit and Loss statement summarizes your company's net income (or loss) for the designated period.

3. QuickBooks has selected the period of time that this report covers. The period of time is shown in the Dates area at the top of the report. Click the arrow to the right of the Dates area to choose a different time period, or indicate specific dates in the From and To areas at the top of the report.

4. Print a hard copy of the report by clicking the Print button, and then clicking the Print button located on the Print Reports window that appears.

> **Tip #65 from**
>
> The Profit and Loss Statement is one of the most commonly produced reports—and one of the most useful. The report gives you an up-to-the-minute view of the income and expenses of the company. Potential lenders and investors will want to see this statement. Produce this statement at least monthly and keep the reports on file so that you can refer back to them for budgeting and forecasting purposes.

With the Profit and Loss Statement displayed, you can double-click on any dollar amount to display a secondary report showing the details of all the transactions that make up that amount on the Profit and Loss Statement. On the secondary report, double-click on any item to open and view the original document from which the amount was created.

Balance Sheet

The Balance Sheet goes hand in hand with the Profit and Loss Statement; together they give a clear view of how a business is performing. The Profit and Loss Statement shows how much money a company has made for a selected period of time, and the Balance Sheet shows what the company is worth at a particular point in time.

Like the Profit and Loss reports described previously, QuickBooks's Balance Sheet reports present a *global* view of their topic and enable you to double-click any amount to open a supporting report that shows the details behind the amount.

The Standard and Summary balance sheet reports provide simple balance information; the Comparison report compares the current year with the previous year, showing the percentage of difference between the two. The Itemized report includes Memo, Split Transaction information, and the amounts of individual transactions.

Follow these steps to create a standard Balance Sheet report:

1. Choose Reports, Balance Sheet. The Balance Sheet side menu appears.
2. Choose Standard. The Balance Sheet appears onscreen, displaying a value your company's asset, liability, and equity accounts (see Figure 21.3).

Figure 21.3
The standard Balance Sheet displays your company's net worth (assets minus liabilities) as of the specified date.

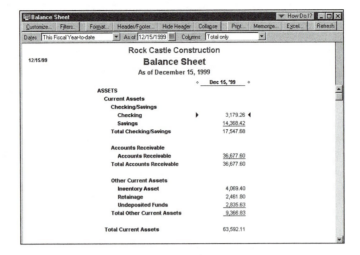

3. Typically, the Balance Sheet is displayed as of today's date. You can change the date, however, by clicking the arrow next to the Dates area and choosing the date that you want.

ACCOUNTS RECEIVABLE AGING REPORTS

The Accounts Receivable Aging Reports will give you insight into the timeliness of your customers' payments. The Aging Summary report shows outstanding balances arranged by customer name and divided into time periods: amounts due currently, 1–30 days overdue, 31–60 days overdue, 61–90 days overdue, and more than 90 days overdue. The Aging Detail report provides the same information for each invoice that is overdue.

Follow these steps to create an Aging Summary report:

1. Choose Reports, A/R Reports. The Accounts Receivable side menu appears.
2. Choose Aging Summary. The A/R Aging Summary appears onscreen, displaying all customers with outstanding balances and the time period into which each balance falls (see Figure 21.4).

The Aging Report is an essential tool of good business management. Use this report to discover which accounts require special attention due to the age of the overdue accounts. This report is also useful in exploring the effectiveness of the credit terms that you assign to your customers. Customers who are notoriously past due might need to be placed on a prepayment or COD status. Sometimes an incentive, such as a discount for timely payments, might stimulate customers to pay on time.

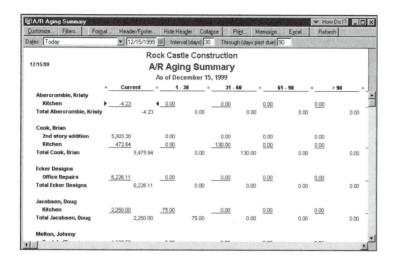

Figure 21.4
The Aging Summary report displays amounts that are overdue, and the amount of time for which they are overdue.

COLLECTIONS REPORT

Another useful report, the Collection Report, lists all customers with balances that are more than 30 days overdue, along with phone number information so that you can easily follow up on the collection with phone calls.

Follow these steps to produce the Collections report:

1. Choose Reports, A/R Reports. The Accounts Receivable side menu appears.
2. Choose Collections Report. The report appears, displaying customer and outstanding balance information. This report includes information as of today's date (see Figure 21.5).

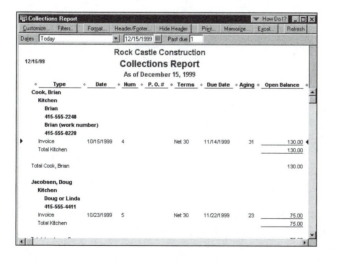

Figure 21.5
Use the Collections Report as a guide for tracking customers with overdue balances.

General Ledger

Use the General Ledger as a guide to finding any transaction that has occurred in your company. The General Ledger is a collection of all company accounts—asset, liability, equity, income, and expense accounts—and the transactions that occur in those accounts.

Many companies print a General Ledger report on a monthly basis to provide a hard copy reference for activity in all the company accounts.

Follow these steps to create a General Ledger report:

1. Choose Reports, Other Reports. The Other Reports side menu appears.
2. Choose General Ledger. The General Ledger report appears (see Figure 21.6). The report lists each account alphabetically within these groups and in the following order: assets, liabilities, equity, income, and expense. If you use account numbers, the accounts appear in numerical order within each group.

Figure 21.6
Use the General Ledger as a master reference to all company transactions.

3. By default, the report displays the transactions for the current month up to today's date. You can change the date (you might want to display the prior month's activity, for example, or the current year to date rather than month to date) by clicking the arrow in the Dates area and choosing the appropriate time period.

Customizing Reports

You have learned that QuickBooks provides many standard reports that can help you understand the progress and performance of your business. Sometimes, however, the standard reports don't give you exactly the information that you need. You might need to display information for dates that differ from those shown on the standard report, for example; or perhaps you want to display a report of receivables, but only those receivables of more than a certain dollar amount.

You can customize reports to display the exact information that you need. The buttons at the top of the report window provide you with options for customizing. You can also click the Customize or the Filters buttons at the top of the window to provide more fine-tuning for your report.

CHANGING THE REPORT DATE

Each report you create is either for a specified period (such as a Profit and Loss Statement for the year to date) or as of a specific date (such as a Balance Sheet showing balances as of today).

You can change the dates on reports by either clicking the Dates button and choosing a specific time period, or by entering exact dates in the From and To areas (see Figure 21.7).

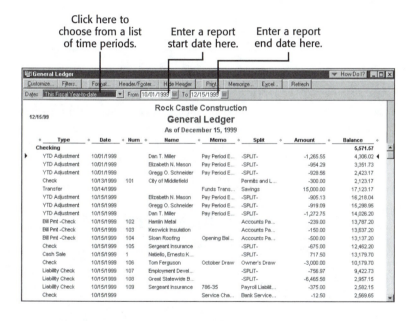

Figure 21.7
Change report dates so that the reporting period fits your needs.

CHANGING THE REPORT COLUMNS

Some reports include a Columns area at the top of the report. You can use this feature to determine how a report is subtotaled. If you use class tracking, for example, you can choose to subtotal a report by class, such as the Profit and Loss report, and see the income and expense activity for each division of your company (see Figure 21.8).

One column appears for each type of choice that you make from the Columns list. For example, if you choose Vendor from the Columns list, you see a separate column for each vendor.

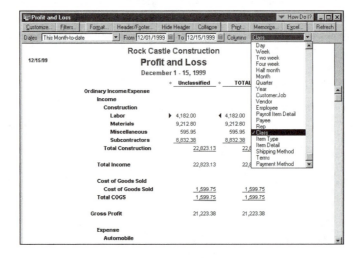

Figure 21.8
Click here to display a drop-down list of choices for subtotaling your report.

Changing Report Headers and Footers

Click the Header/Footer button at the top of a report to customize the header information (see Figure 21.9), including the wording of the Company Name, the Report Title and Subtitle, and the Date Prepared (which appears in the upper-left corner of the report). You can select from a group of date styles by clicking the arrow in the Date Prepared area. In addition, you can choose to exclude any of these header features.

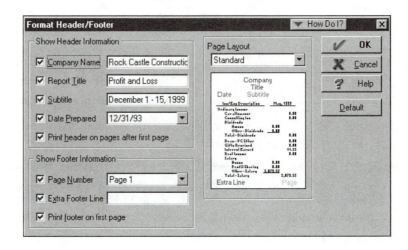

Figure 21.9
Click Header/Footer to choose your own header and footer information, or choose to exclude this information by unchecking the boxes.

Indicate whether you want to display a Page Number in a footer at the bottom of each page of a report, or in an Extra Footer Line.

You can choose to exclude the header in all but the first page of your report, and you can choose to exclude the footer from the first page. You can also select an alignment option for the header and footer information on your report by clicking the Page Layout button and making a selection from the drop-down menu.

A Hide Header button on the report screen enables you to turn off the display of the header altogether. On reports for internal use, you might not need to display the header because you already know what company this report is for; you can thereby save space on your report page.

Collapsing Subaccounts

When you click the Collapse button on the report screen, the balances of any subaccounts are combined with their parent accounts, and are removed from the report.

The Collapse button becomes an Expand button when you click it. Clicking the Expand button returns the subaccounts to the report.

Using the Customize Button

Click Customize to determine what information is to be included with the report, as shown in Figure 21.10. Each parameter you include (Previous Period, and % of Column, for example) requires a column, so keep space limitations in mind as you add these fields.

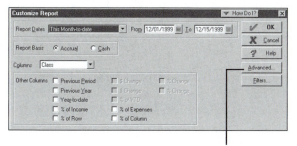

Figure 21.10
Customize, one of the options available at the top of every report, enables you to determine the scope and content of your report.

Click here to select additional parameters to include on your report.

You can indicate if this report is to be prepared on the Cash or Accrual basis. Typically, you won't have to change this field because you have already told QuickBooks whether your company is a cash basis or an accrual basis company.

→ To find more information about the selection of cash or accrual basis, **see p. 384**

Click the Advanced button and indicate whether you want rows and columns to appear on your report only if they are active (have had transactions), and if you want to display accounts that have zero balances. Also, choose the reporting year if you use different years for your fiscal year and your tax year (the years are entered when you set up your QuickBooks company).

APPLYING FILTERS

Click Filters, either from the Customize window or from the main report screen, to narrow the scope of each parameter you've selected to view. You can create a report that displays merchandise shipped on a specific date, for example, or you can choose to display accounts only if the balance exceeds a certain amount.

Follow these steps to set filtering options:

1. Click the Filters button from either the main report screen or from within the Customize window. The Report Filters window appears (see Figure 21.11).

Figure 21.11
Set filters to limit the information in your report to meet specific criteria.

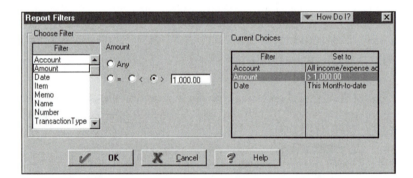

2. From the choices in the Filter list, click the type of item that you want to filter. You can choose more than one item, but choose one item at a time. To limit the accounts that appear on your report to those with a balance of more than $1,000, for example, choose the Amount filter.

3. In the area to the right of the filter list, set your filter criteria. To limit the accounts that appear on your report to those with a balance of more than $1,000, for example, click the > symbol, and then enter *1000* in the box provided. After you click another item to filter or click the Amount filter in the Current Choices list at the right of the window, your filter will be added to the list and applied to the report the next time you view it.

> **Note**
> Depending on the filter choice that you make at the left side of the Filter window, the options available to you for setting the filter criteria will change.

4. After you have made all the selections you want, click OK to save your filtering choices and close this window.

Change your mind? You can delete a filter by clicking the Filter button. In the Report Filters window that appears, all filters pertaining to the current report are listed at the right side of the window in the Current Choices column. Click the filter that you want to remove and press the Delete key on your keyboard. Click OK to save your changes and close the Report Filters window. Your report is rewritten to include the change.

Formatting a Report

Click the Format button at the top of your report window to choose how negative numbers are shown, the font for column labels, and whether numbers are to be shown divided by 1000 or without cents.

Memorizing the Report Format and Setting

Now that you've customized your report, you might want to use this report again without having to start from scratch with customizing.

Updated data on memorized reports is displayed according to the way in which the form is saved. Memorizing a report is important—if you go to all the trouble to customize a form to make it look a certain way, you'll probably want to use this same report format at a later date, as well.

To save your report for future uses, click the Memorize button at the top of the Report window. You are asked to give this report a name (see Figure 21.12).

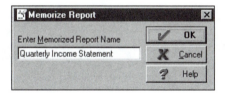

Figure 21.12
Give your memorized report a unique name so that you can use the report in the future without having to re-create it.

The next time you want to use this report, choose Reports, Memorized Reports; this report name appears on the list of memorized reports. From the names on the list, click the report that you want to view and click the Generate Report button. The report appears as you created it, with updated information.

Editing and Deleting Memorized Reports

You can change the name of a memorized report, or delete it if you no longer plan to use the report.

To change the name of a memorized report, choose Reports, Memorized Reports. The Memorized Reports List window appears. Click the name of the report that you want to change, and then click the Memorized Report button at the bottom of the window. Click Edit (Ctrl+E). Enter a new name in the box that appears, and then click OK.

To delete an existing memorized report, choose Reports, Memorized Reports. Click the name of the report that you want to delete, and then click the Memorized Report button at the bottom of the window. Click Delete (Ctrl+D). You are asked to confirm that you want to delete this report.

Printing Reports

Viewing a report on the screen is helpful, but often you'll want to have a copy of the report to file, pore over, or give to someone else. QuickBooks enables you to print reports to your printer or to a file so that you can open the report in a word processing or spreadsheet program.

Follow these steps to print reports to your printer:

1. Create the report you want to print.
2. Click the Print button at the top of the report window (or choose File, Print Report). The Print Reports window appears (see Figure 21.13).

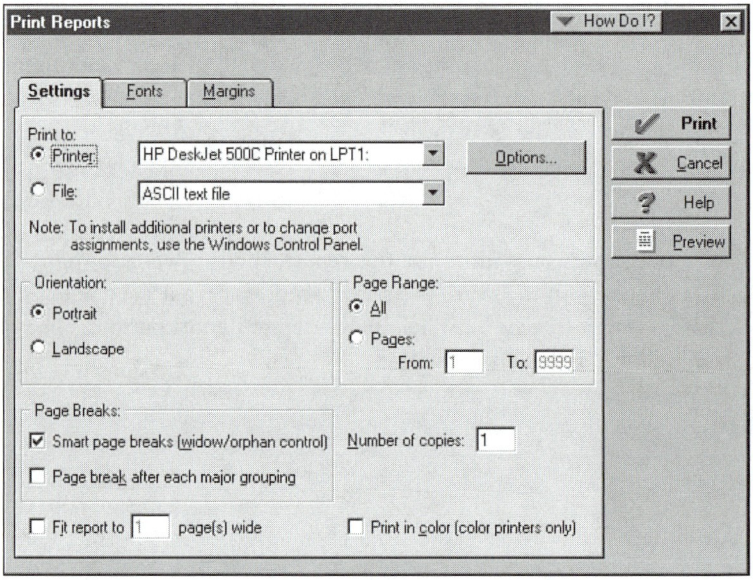

Figure 21.13
Choose from among several print options to produce a lasting copy of your report.

3. Choose either Printer or File for your output. Then click the down arrow across from your selection, if necessary, to choose the printer that you plan to use or to choose the type of file to which you plan to print.

> **Note**
>
> If you choose to print your report to a file, you can easily retrieve the file into a spreadsheet or word processing program for further calculations or enhancements. When you print to a file, you can choose from three options: ASCII text file, which can be read by word processing programs; Excel/Lotus 123 spreadsheet, which can be read by spreadsheet programs; and Tab delimited file, which can be read by either word processing or spreadsheet programs.
>
> For more information about using QuickBooks in conjunction with other programs, see Appendix C, "Transferring Data Between QuickBooks and Other Applications."

4. Choose Portrait or Landscape orientation. If you're not sure which orientation works better for this report, click the Preview button to display your report onscreen.
5. If you need to print only a portion of your report, enter the page numbers that you need to print in the Page Range area. Otherwise, leave the page range set to All.
6. Check the Print in color box if you want this report to be printed in color. (You must have a color printer to take advantage of this option.)
7. Check the Fit report to one page wide box if you want to force QuickBooks to print this report on a single page width. This might result in a smaller typeface for your report.
8. Indicate the Number of copies that you want to print.
9. If you want to change the typeface or other formatting options used in the report, click the Fonts tab at the top of the screen, and then click the Fonts button. The Format Report window appears (see Figure 21.14). Select from various methods of displaying negative numbers and choose whether you want your report numbers divided by 1,000 and displayed with or without cents. Choose one of the report labels in the Change Font For list, and then click the Change Font button to open a window in which you can change the font for the selected item. Choose from a list of fonts, font styles, and font sizes, and indicate whether you want to print in color. Click OK, and then answer Yes or No to the Change all related fonts question, and you return to the Report Format window. Click OK to save your changes and return to the Print Reports window.
10. If you want to change font settings for all future reports, click the Default Fonts button. The Report Format Preferences window appears (this window contains the same information as the Format Report window discussed in step 9); here you can set report appearance choices that will carry forward to future reports.
11. You can set specific margins for your report by clicking the Margins tab in the Print Reports window (see Figure 21.15). Enter the measurement for each margin—the default is 1/2" on each side—keeping in mind that the smaller your margin, the more difficulty your printer might have in printing the information close to the edge of the paper.

Figure 21.14
In the Format Report window, you can set specific report formatting options, including changing the typeface of headings.

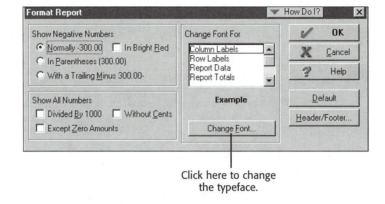

Click here to change the typeface.

Figure 21.15
Enter new report margins on this screen.

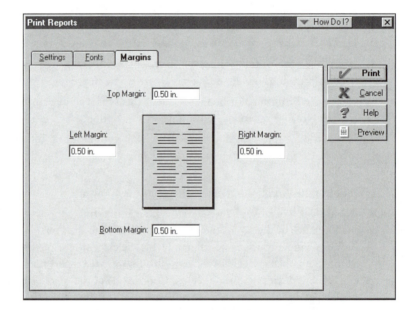

12. Click the Preview button to verify that the report looks the way you intended. Click Close to close the preview.
13. Click Print when you have finished making your changes, or click Cancel if you decide you don't want to print at this time.

QuickBooks's Graphs

You can create graphical representations of the information in your reports. The graphs provide illustrations that are often easier to understand and embrace than all those gray numbers on the reports.

QuickBooks offers six standard graphs, which are found at the bottom of the Reports menu. Each time you choose a graph, you actually get two graphs for the price of one. You can double-click any piece of either graph to see an additional graph of just that item. Then double-click the secondary graph to see a report of all the transactions that make up that graph piece.

You can change the period of time that the graphs represent by changing the dates at the top of the screen. You can also right-click any bar or pie piece to see the actual dollar amount represented by the graph.

The graphs from which you can choose are as follows:

- **Income and Expenses**—The Income and Expense Graphs (see Figure 21.16) show how much income your company has earned—and how much you have spent—for a selected period of time. The bar graph displays total income and total expenses, and the accompanying pie graph shows a piece of the pie for each income or expense account (your choice).

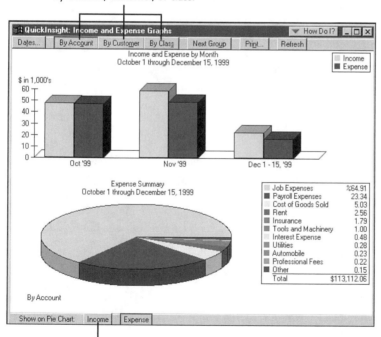

Figure 21.16
The Income and Expense Graphs show your company's earnings and expenditures.

- **Sales**—The Sales Graphs (see Figure 21.17) show sales income for the selected period of time. The bar graph shows sales by month; the pie graph shows sales by item, customer, or sales rep (click your choice from the buttons at the top of the graph).

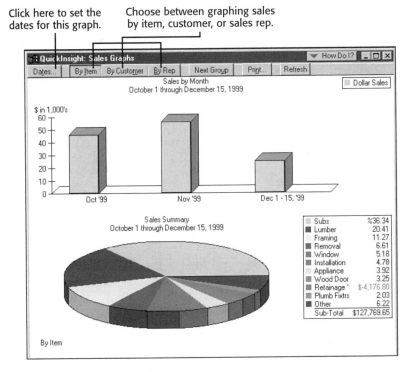

Figure 21.17
The Sales Graphs show sales income for your company.

- **Accounts Receivable**—The Accounts Receivable Graphs (see Figure 21.18) show how much your customers owe. The bar graph is an aging graph, showing how much is overdue in 30 day intervals. The pie graph shows a piece of the pie for each customer who owes you money. This graph is incredibly useful for giving you a complete image of your outstanding receivables by showing which customers make up the bulk of the outstanding amounts, and how overdue your receivables really are.

- **Accounts Payable**—The Accounts Payable Graphs (see Figure 21.19) are similar to the accounts receivable graphs, but they show how much you owe rather than how much is owed to you. The bar graph shows an aging schedule of how overdue your bills are. The pie graph breaks out a piece of the pie for each creditor so you can easily see to whom you owe the most money.

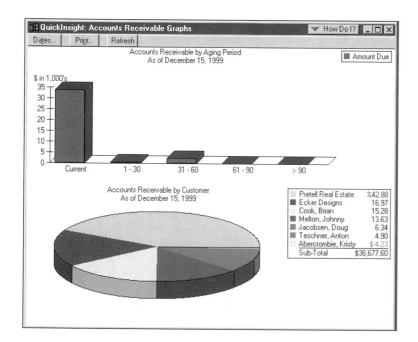

Figure 21.18
The Accounts Receivable Graphs present an A/R aging schedule and a breakdown of receivables per customer.

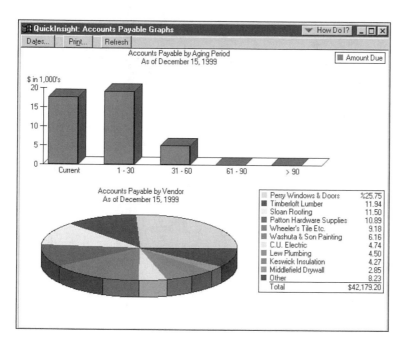

Figure 21.19
The Accounts Payable Graphs show how much your company owes and to whom.

- **Net Worth**—The New Worth Graph (see Figure 21.20) is a little different from the others. It is a bar graph with a bar for each month, and it shows assets above the zero line and liabilities below the zero line. A line graph connecting each bar shows your actual net worth for each month (assets minus liabilities). Double-click any asset or liability part of the graph to see a pie graph that details the accounts that make up the bar. Double-click any net worth point (shown as small squares within the bars) to see a pie depicting the breakdown of assets, liabilities, and net worth.

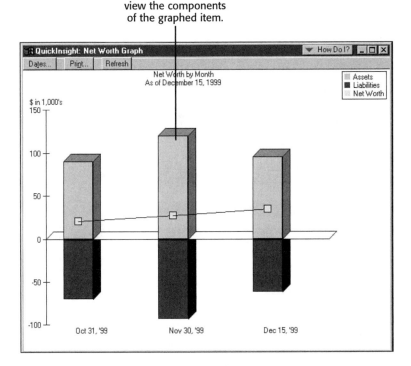

Figure 21.20
Use Net Worth Graphs to visualize the value of your company.

- **Budget vs. Actual**—Two bar graphs (see Figure 21.21) display the difference between your budget and your company's actual performance. The top graph shows actual net income compared to budgeted net income for the month. The bottom graph shows the individual accounts and how far they are off the budget.

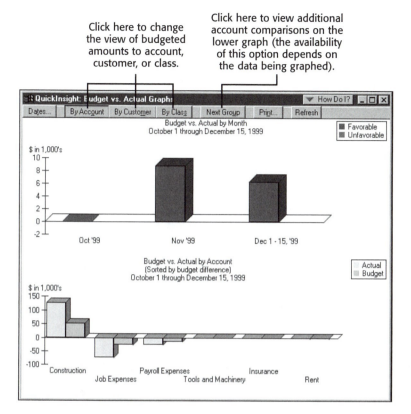

Figure 21.21
Use the Budget vs. Actual Graphs to visualize how close you are coming to meeting your budget.

TROUBLESHOOTING

CUSTOMIZING REPORTS

The QuickBooks standard reports just don't meet my needs. Is there any way to customize these reports other than using the Customize and Filter options?

Refer to Appendix C, where you will find information about exporting reports to word-processing and spreadsheet programs so that you can have more flexibility in organizing and analyzing your data.

DISPLAYING REPORTS

I've customized a report and plan to use this report frequently. Other than memorizing the report, is there a quick way to display this report on a regular basis?

Add your report to your QuickBooks iconbar and you can click a button each time you want to view the report. Display the report that you want to recall quickly, and then choose Window, Add Window to Iconbar. In the window that appears, give your new iconbar button a name and description, and choose an image for the button. Click OK and you see your new button appear on the iconbar. (If your iconbar is not visible, choose File, Preferences, Iconbar; then make a choice as to how you want to display the iconbar.)

CHAPTER 22

SETTING PREFERENCES

In this chapter

Accounting Preferences   384

Checking Preferences   385

Finance Charge Preferences   386

General Preferences   388

Iconbar Preferences   390

Jobs & Estimates Preferences   392

Menus Preferences   393

Payroll and Employees Preferences   394

Purchases & Vendors Preferences   396

Reminders Preferences   398

Reports and Graphs Preferences   399

Sales & Customers Preferences   402

Sales Tax Preferences   403

Tax 1099 Preferences   404

Time Tracking Preferences   405

When you begin using QuickBooks, there are procedures and options already in place that control the way you enter information and the way QuickBooks performs.

You can change many of the program options so that QuickBooks behaves the way you want it to and offers the options that suit the needs of your company.

Many of the preferences can only be changed by your QuickBooks program administrator. If you have established security and password settings, as described in Chapter 28, "Security," you might need to rely on your administrator to adjust the settings as described in this chapter.

The sections in this chapter provide guidance for changing and setting all the performance options in QuickBooks. All these options are accessed by choosing Preferences from the File menu.

Accounting Preferences

When you click the Accounting icon in the Preferences window, you see that there are no options available on the My Preferences tab. On the Company Preferences tab (see Figure 22.1), you can turn on or off the following preferences:

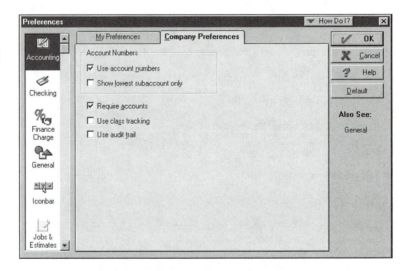

Figure 22.1
Click the check boxes to indicate which accounting preferences apply to your company.

- **Use account numbers**—You can turn the account numbers preference on and QuickBooks automatically assigns account numbers to all existing accounts. In the future, when you create new accounts, an account number field appears so that you can assign account numbers to your accounts. The account number becomes part of the account name so that reports sorted by account name are listed in account number order. To override the QuickBooks automatic account numbers, you have to edit each account individually by choosing Accounts, Edit from the Chart of Accounts List window.

> **Tip #66 from Gail Perry**
>
> The choice to use account numbers is yours. QuickBooks doesn't require the numbers and, in fact, won't assign account numbers unless you request it in this preference window. For companies with a small quantity of accounts (fewer than 50, for example), account numbers might not be necessary. A company that has many accounts might appreciate the fact that using account numbers enables you to control the organization of accounts as they appear in reports. Accounts that are numbered are grouped in order of their numbers. Without account numbers, QuickBooks groups accounts in alphabetical order on reports.

- **Show lowest subaccount only**—If you don't use account numbers, choosing this option has no effect. If you use account numbers, and you choose an account on a form or register transaction, the parent account name is displayed with the subaccount name unless you turn on this feature. Check this box and the subaccount name that you choose appears without its parent's name.

- **Require accounts**—If this box is checked, you can't exit a transaction if an account hasn't been indicated in any area that requests an account. This box is checked by default when you start using QuickBooks, and it is recommended that you keep it checked. Having the capability to enter transactions without account numbers causes QuickBooks to assign transactions to accounts with names such as "Uncategorized Expense"—and that might cause confusion on your financial statements.

- **Use class tracking**—If you want to use the class tracking feature offered by QuickBooks, you must check this box. QuickBooks provides a field for entering a class on all your transactions. See Chapter 9, "Separating Your Company Into Logical Divisions," for more information about class tracking.

- **Use audit trail**—The audit trail is a record of all transactions and changes made to transactions in QuickBooks. Although you might find that using the audit trail slows the performance of your QuickBooks program, this is a beneficial feature for tracing activity and changes that have been entered in the program. The audit trail is particularly useful if more than one person has access to your QuickBooks file.

If you are finished entering or changing preferences, be sure to click the OK button so that your selections are saved and implemented.

Checking Preferences

Consider changing checking preferences if you use the check-writing feature of QuickBooks. When you click the Checking icon in the Preferences window, you see that the only options available are on the Company Preferences tab (see Figure 22.2). On this tab you can turn the following preferences on or off:

- **Print account names on voucher**—If this selection is turned on, QuickBooks includes the name of the account with the detailed information that prints on the voucher that accompanies your check.

- **Change check date when check is printed**—When you create a check, a date appears on the check form. If you want to use the date from the check form on your printed check, leave this option unchecked. Check this box if you want QuickBooks to use today's date when it prints checks.
- **Start with payee field on check**—Rather than positioning your cursor at the top of a check, bill, or credit card charge form, checking this option forces QuickBooks to position your cursor in the Payee or Vendor field as soon as you open one of these forms.
- **Warn about duplicate check numbers**—As a reminder to you, QuickBooks issues an audible warning if you are about to write a check with a number that duplicates a check that was previously written. If this box is unchecked (it is checked by default), you get no warning when a check number is about to be duplicated.

Figure 22.2
Customize some of the checking preferences if you use the check-writing feature in QuickBooks.

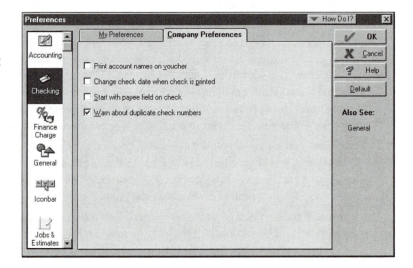

→ To find more information about using QuickBooks to write checks, **see p. 233**

FINANCE CHARGE PREFERENCES

If your company regularly assesses finance charges—and does so in a consistent manner—it can be useful to you to set standard finance charges that apply to all customers. This way, you won't have to determine a separate charge for each customer—you can rely on QuickBooks to assess finance charges for you.

Click the Finance Charge icon on the left side of the Preferences window to access these options that appear on the Company Preferences tab (see Figure 22.3). On this tab you can see the following preferences:

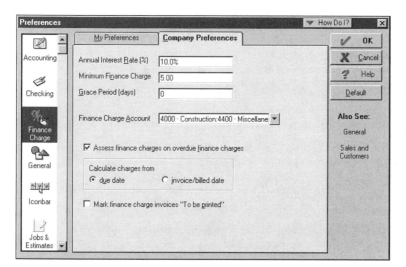

Figure 22.3
Does your company apply finance charges when customers don't pay on time? If so, set your standard rate and minimum amount of charge on this screen.

- **Annual Interest Rate (%)**—The annual interest rate is the standard rate that applies to all or most of your customers. The rate is entered here as an annual rate (enter 12 for 12 percent, 9.5 for 9.5 percent, and so on); QuickBooks calculates the rate as a monthly charge on overdue invoices.

- **Minimum Finance Charge**—This is an amount—the smallest amount you want QuickBooks to charge to a customer. For example, you might want QuickBooks to round a small finance charge up to $1 if the assessed charge is less than $1. If that is the case, you enter 1.00 for the minimum finance charge.

- **Grace Period (days)**—You can designate a grace period before finance charges are assessed. Giving customers a few extra days after a payment is due allows for delays in mail delivery, or for delays due to customer emergencies.

- **Finance Charge Account**—Indicate the income account to which finance charges are to be added. This might be an account called Finance Charges, Late Payment Fees, or Interest Income.

- **Assess finance charges on overdue finance charges**—If a customer owes you $1,000 and has already been assessed a finance charge of $12, is the next month's finance charge based on $1,000 or the full balance due of $1,012? Check this box if you want to include the finance charge that is already due (in this case, $12) when calculating the next month's finance charge.

- **Calculate charges from: due date or invoice/billed date**—If your finance charge is to be assessed if payment is not received within 30 days, does the 30 days start with the date the invoice is due or the date the invoice is issued? After you have established this company policy, check the appropriate box.

- **Mark finance charge invoices "To be printed"**—If you want to send an invoice to your customers when finance charges are assessed, QuickBooks automatically generates invoices and places them in your list of statements that are waiting to be printed. Check this box if you want QuickBooks to set these forms up for printing.

General Preferences

When you click the General icon on the left side of the Preferences window, you see that you have both personal preferences (My Preferences) and Company Preferences available to you.

The general preferences include options for changing the way that your QuickBooks program performs and responds to you. The preferences are listed as follows:

- **Hide QCards for all windows**—If the pop-up QCards seem to frequently get in your way, or if you are familiar enough with the program that you don't need constant reminders about how each feature works, you can uncheck this box and the QCards leave you alone. Check the box again and QCards come running back to greet you.

- **Pressing Enter moves between fields**—When entering transactions on forms or in a register, pressing Enter normally finishes the transaction and moves you to the next form or the next register entry. If you prefer to have Enter move you from field to field, check this box. Then, instead of pressing Enter to complete the transaction, press Ctrl+Enter, or click the OK or Next button.

- **Beep when recording a transaction**—Each time you finish a transaction and either close the window or move to the next transaction, a "beep" sounds if this box is checked.

- **Automatically place decimal point**—If most of the entries you make include numbers that have two decimal places (such as 12.75 or 1978.55), you might want to consider having QuickBooks type the decimal place for you. You enter all the digits of the number (197855, for example), and QuickBooks inserts the decimal place before the last two digits (1978.55). Be careful, however, that when you enter a number with zeros in the decimal places (345.00, for example), you type the zeros.

- **Warn when editing a transaction**—If this option is checked, and you have made changes to a previously-saved transaction, QuickBooks presents you with a pop-up warning if you try to close the transaction without saving it.

- **Warn when deleting a transaction or unused list item**—If this option is checked and you attempt to delete a transaction, or if you attempt to delete an item that hasn't been used, QuickBooks presents you with a pop-up warning, asking you to verify that you want to continue with the deletion.

- **Bring back all one time messages**—Sometimes you see messages in QuickBooks that are accompanied by a check box that enables you to request that the message not be viewed again. If you checked all those boxes and now the one-time-only messages are only a fond memory, you can check this box and bring them all back.

- **Automatically recall last transaction for this name**—If this option is turned on, QuickBooks automatically fills in a bill, check, or credit card with the same information you used the last time you issued such a form with the same vendor name. For example, if you wrote a check last month to Electric Power Co. for $212.50 for utilities expense, and this month you begin writing another check to Electric Power Co., QuickBooks fills in the rest of the check with the same amount and account that you used the last time. You always have the option of overriding this information.

- **Desktop options**—Choose one of the desktop options (as shown in Figure 22.4). If you select Save when closing company, all the windows you were displaying when you closed the company file appear the next time you open QuickBooks. If you pick Save current desktop, all the windows that are visible on the desktop at the moment you choose this option, with the exception of the Preferences window, appear each time you open QuickBooks. (Note that if you choose Save current desktop, the next time you open this screen in the preferences window, a fourth choice appears—Keep previously saved desktop. Choose this setting if you want to return to the desktop you saved the last time you set this preference.) If you pick Don't save the desktop, your desktop is always cleared each time you open the program.

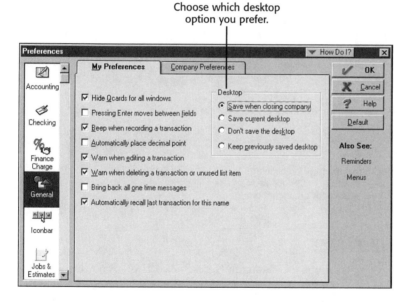

Figure 22.4
The General preferences include several miscellaneous items that control how your QuickBooks program performs.

- **Time format**—On the Company Preferences tab (see Figure 22.5), choose a format for displaying time, either with a period or a colon separating hours and minutes. The time format is used when tracking time for payroll or billing time to customers.

- **Four-digit years**—Beginning with QuickBooks 99, all dates appear with four-digit years to accommodate the switch to Year 2000. If you prefer not to see your years displayed with four digits, you can uncheck the box on this tab. Your dates appear with two-digit years.

- **Never update name information when saving transactions**—If you change the address or other information about a vendor or customer while creating a form such as an invoice or purchase order, a box pops up onscreen asking you whether you want to update the name information in your customer or vendor list. Checking this box in the Company Preferences prevents QuickBooks from asking whether you want to update the name information.

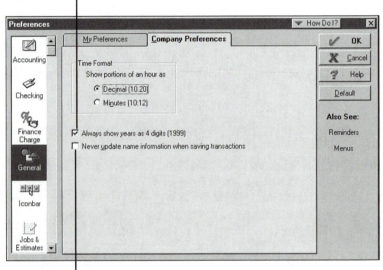

Figure 22.5
When the lower checkbox is unchecked, QuickBooks updates your vendor and customer lists whenever there is a change of address or similar change on a form.

Deselect this box if you prefer to see your years displayed with two digits.

Check this box only if you don't want QuickBooks to update your customer and vendor information.

Iconbar Preferences

Are you wondering where the iconbar is hiding in QuickBooks? If you want to see the iconbar, you have to ask for it in the Preferences window. In addition to choosing whether to display the iconbar, there are some steps you can take to customize the bar. Click the Iconbar icon on the left of the Preferences window to explore the following options:

- **Displaying the iconbar**—Choose from one of four display options (see Figure 22.6). Show icons and text displays the iconbar with both pictures and text on the buttons. Show icons displays the iconbar with only the pictures. Show text displays the iconbar with words but no pictures. Don't show iconbar turns off the display of the iconbar.

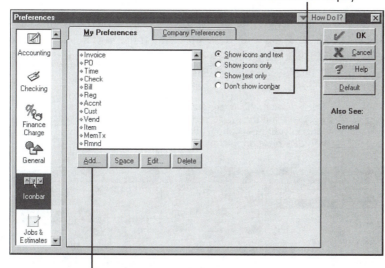

Figure 22.6
Choose how you want your iconbar to be displayed.

- **Add**—Add a button to the iconbar by clicking Add and choosing from a list of additional buttons available in QuickBooks. The Add Iconbar Item window appears and you are expected to click the name of a button that you want to add, click an image for the button from a list of available pictures, enter a name that will appear on the button, and enter an optional description. Personally, I like adding the Calculator button to the Iconbar so that I can pop up a calculator onscreen just by clicking a button.

> **Tip #67 from**
> *Gail Perry*
>
> If you find that there is a particular window, such as a favorite report, that you display frequently, turn that window into a button on your iconbar and save yourself the time of searching through the menus every time you want to open the window. To add a button to the iconbar that displays a window, open the window on your screen, and then choose Window, Add Window to Iconbar. In the window that appears (see Figure 22.7), choose an image for the button by clicking a picture in the available list, and then add a name that will appear as text on the button and a description that will appear when your mouse hovers over the button. Click OK to add the button to your iconbar.

- **Space**—To place a separating space between the buttons on your iconbar, click the name of the button after which you want to place a space, and then click the Space button. When you close the Preferences window, a space appears after the button you indicated on your iconbar.

- **Edit**—To change the picture that appears on an iconbar button, or its accompanying text, click the name of the malfeasant button on the list of iconbar buttons, and then click Edit. In the window that appears, make your choices for a fresh face for this button. Click OK to save your changes.

- **Delete**—One problem with the QuickBooks iconbar is that the buttons seem awfully large, and it's hard to fit additional buttons on the bar. But maybe there are some buttons that you don't ever use, and you want to bump them off the bar to make room for other, more useful buttons. Click the name of a button you don't want, and then click the Delete button. Presto! The button is off the list.

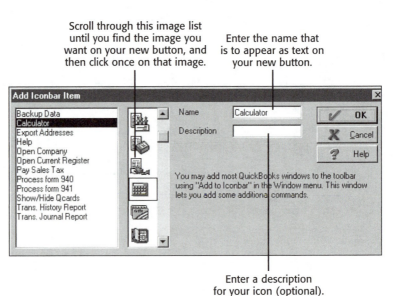

Figure 22.7
It's a quick process to add a button to your iconbar that displays a favorite window. Display the window, and then choose Window, Add Window to Iconbar.

JOBS & ESTIMATES PREFERENCES

If you use QuickBooks Pro, you have a Jobs & Estimates icon in your Preferences window (see Figure 22.8). The options presented in this category include the right to reword the choices for job status and some general questions about whether your company prepares estimates and does progress billing. You can skip this section if you use the regular QuickBooks program.

The preferences are listed as follows:

- **Job status descriptions**—QuickBooks uses the descriptions of Pending, Awarded, In progress, Closed, and Not awarded to describe the status of jobs you perform. If other descriptions fit your business better (a writer, for example, might use descriptions such as Proposal, Outline, Manuscript, Edit, and Completed to describe the stages of his work), you can enter your own descriptions in the spaces provided on the Company Preferences tab.

- **Do You Create Estimates?**—Indicate whether your company uses QuickBooks to create estimates. Choose No if you create estimates on paper but don't record them in QuickBooks.
- **Do You Do Progress Invoicing?**—Indicate whether you want to use the progress billing option for partial billing of jobs in progress. Choosing Yes doesn't mean that you have to bill a job in pieces; choosing No prevents you from ever doing so—you probably want to choose Yes just so you have the option.
- **Warn about duplicate estimates numbers**—Leave this option blank if you do not create estimates in QuickBooks. Check this box if you want QuickBooks to give you a reminder that you're about to issue the same estimate number to a second estimate.
- **Don't print items that have zero amount**—Leave this option blank if you chose No for the progress invoicing question. If you plan to use progress invoicing and some items on your invoice have been paid, leaving a zero balance, check this box if you want to leave the zero-balance items off of future invoices.

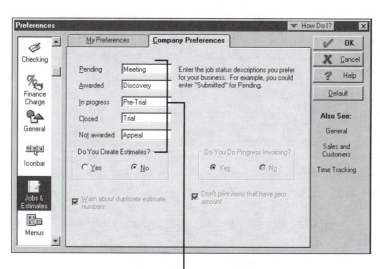

Figure 22.8
Update the preferences that apply to job status, estimates, and progress billing on this screen.

You can choose your own job status descriptions and enter them in these boxes.

Menus Preferences

After you get used to finding your way around QuickBooks, you might find that some of the menu choices you use frequently are hidden away on side menus such as Other Activities and Other Lists. To bring those shy items into the spotlight of the main Activities and Lists menus, click the Menus icon in your Preferences window and check off the items that you want to free from the Other side menus.

The items listed under Activities Menu (see Figure 22.9) normally appear on the Activities menu. Check the box next to any item you want to move off of the main Activities menu and on to the Other Activities side menu.

Figure 22.9
Check off all the items that are to appear in the Other section of your main Activities and Lists menus.

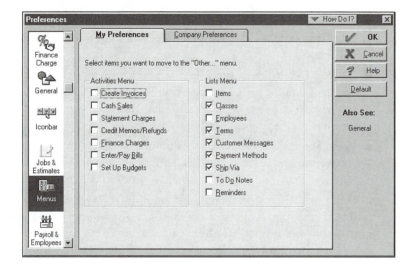

Likewise, the items shown under Lists Menu normally reside on the Lists menu. Check any of these boxes, and these lists slide over to the Other Lists side menu off the main Lists menu.

PAYROLL AND EMPLOYEES PREFERENCES

If you use QuickBooks to track your payroll, you might be interested in the preferences that apply specifically to employees and payroll. These are only available on the Company Preferences tab; choose from several options to help customize the performance of QuickBooks in this area (see Figure 22.10). The preferences are listed as follows:

Figure 22.10
Choose from several preferences relating to your QuickBooks payroll.

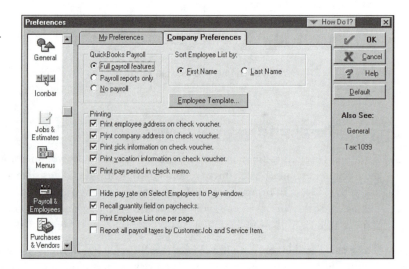

- **QuickBooks Payroll**—Tell QuickBooks whether you plan to use the program to track all your payroll, only to produce payroll reports, or if you don't use QuickBooks at all for payroll.

- **Sort Employees List**—You can sort your employees list (available on the Lists menu) by first name or last name.

- **Printing options**—If you plan to use QuickBooks to print paychecks, choose which items you want to have print on the check voucher form. See Chapter 18, "Paying Employees and Contractors," for more information about using QuickBooks for processing your payroll.

- **Hide pay rate on Select Employees to Pay window**—Depending on who has access to your QuickBooks file, you might want to make the Select Employees to Pay window available to other users, but without the pay rate displayed. Check this box to prevent display of the pay rate.

- **Recall quantity field on paychecks**—Check this box if you want to have QuickBooks carry forward information from prior paychecks relating to amounts based on quantities. For example, amounts based on the number of hours an employee works, where the employee works the same number of hours in each pay period, can be repeated on future pay checks without your having to enter the information again.

- **Print Employee List one per page**—When you print an employee list in QuickBooks, you have the option of printing one employee per page with all that employee's related information. That option, however, is available only if you check this box in the Preferences window.

- **Report all payroll taxes by Customer:Job, Service Item, and Class**—Some, none, or all the options might be presented to you, depending on what QuickBooks features your company uses. Checking this item enables you to print reports that break down payroll taxes by the features listed (job, item, class).

- **Assign one class per paycheck/earnings item**—This item is available only if you use the QuickBooks class tracking feature. Choose to assign a class to an entire paycheck or break out separate service items and assign each item to a class.

In addition to the preceding preferences, you can click the Employee Template button (see Figure 22.11) to open a window that enables you to set payroll information that all employees have in common. The information that you enter in the employee template window appears on the payroll record for each employee. Then, when you create a paycheck for an employee, you can use this information. You can also remove or overwrite this information for individual employees.

The following payroll information can be entered on the employee template:

- **Type of earnings**—Enter regular pay, vacation pay, overtime pay, and so on, and a standard rate for these earnings. This option is particularly useful for a company that employs a lot of hourly employees who all work at the same pay rate.

- **Pay period**—Choose the frequency with which you issue paychecks.
- **Use time data to create paychecks**—If you use the QuickBooks Timer, check this box to instruct QuickBooks to use data from the Timer program when creating paychecks.
- **Additions, deductions, and company contributions**—Indicate items that appear on all or most paychecks, such as deductions for health insurance, expense reimbursements, or bonuses. If the amount is the same for all employees, include an amount here in addition to the item name. If there is a maximum amount that applies to all or most employees (for example, bonuses cannot exceed $500), enter that maximum amount in the Limit column.
- **Taxes**—Click the Taxes button to indicate which taxes apply to all or most employees (such as federal withholding, social security, state income tax, and so on).
- **Sick/Vacation Pay**—Click the Sick/Vacation button to set company standards for issuing and tracking sick time and vacation pay. Indicate the total number of hours per year or pay period that is to be issued to employees, and whether sick and vacation hours start over with zero at the beginning of each year (check the Reset hours each new year box to start over again).

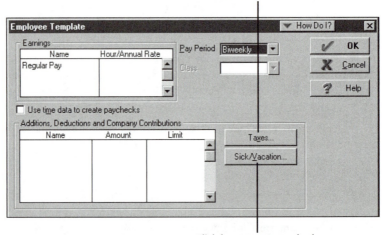

Figure 22.11
Choose payroll preferences that appear on each employee's payroll record.

Purchases & Vendors Preferences

There are a few company preference items that affect the treatment of purchase orders and inventory. If you don't use the QuickBooks inventory feature and don't use purchase orders, these items won't apply to you. The preferences are listed as follows:

- **Inventory and purchase orders are active**—Check this box if you use the inventory and purchase order features in QuickBooks. This box is automatically set if you indicated an interest in using these features during the EasyStep Interview.
- **Warn if not enough inventory to sell**—QuickBooks keeps track of the quantity of inventory items you have on hand. If you prepare an invoice or a cash sale form for a quantity of inventory items that exceeds the amount you have on hand, QuickBooks pops up with a message telling you about the potential problem. Uncheck this box and QuickBooks won't bother you with information about inventory shortages.

Tip #68 from

When you issue an invoice, if you get a warning indicating there is not enough inventory on hand to fill the quantity shown on the invoice, you are not prevented from issuing the invoice for the quantity requested. When you see a warning that the quantity of inventory items you are selling exceeds the amount you have on hand, make a note to yourself to check inventory items on order, or to order more items so that you won't run short.

- **Warn about duplicate purchase order numbers**—Check this box if you want QuickBooks to present you with a warning that you are issuing a purchase order with a number that duplicates another order.
- **Bills are due**—When you enter bills in QuickBooks, a reminder appears in the Reminders list to indicate that the bill payment is due. Set the number of days here (see Figure 22.12) so that QuickBooks knows how long to wait before getting after you to pay your bills.

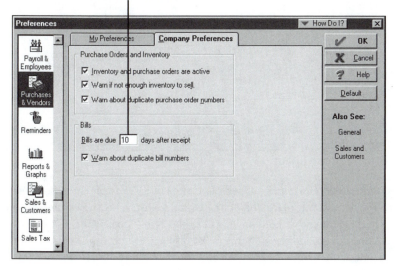

Figure 22.12
Set up preferences that apply to your inventory and other purchases.

- **Warn about duplicate bill numbers**—This check box is quite handy. Suppose you get a bill from Acme Supply Company and you enter it in QuickBooks. Two weeks later you get another bill from Acme Supply Co. and you enter it in QuickBooks. If the second bill has the same number as the first, you've probably gotten a duplicate bill. Check this box and QuickBooks tells you that you've got a duplicate.

REMINDERS PREFERENCES

The QuickBooks Reminders list gives you a summary of everything that needs to be done. It's your master to-do list—with reminders about checks and forms that need to be printed, bills that need to be paid, invoice payments that are late, and money that is waiting to be deposited.

When you use the Reminders list, you can easily stay on top of all the day-to-day tasks that help keep your company running. Click the Reminders icon in the Preferences window to access the following options:

- **Show Reminders List when opening a Company file**—Check this box on the My Preferences tab and QuickBooks displays your Reminders list every time you open the program (see Figure 22.13).

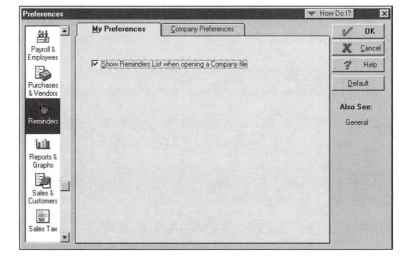

Figure 22.13
Check this box and you see your Reminders list each time you open QuickBooks.

- **Reminders: Company Preferences**—Click the Company Preferences tab and choose which items you want to see displayed on your Reminders list. The Show Summary option displays a total amount without any detail of the actual items. Click Show List next to any item on the list, and the Reminders list displays the details of what makes up the total amount. Click Don't Remind Me and the item won't appear on your Reminders list. For all items that include a Remind Me option, indicate the number of days before the item is due that you want to start seeing this type of item in your

Reminders list. For example, in Figure 22.14, a reminder to print paychecks appears in the Reminders list five days before the paychecks are due.

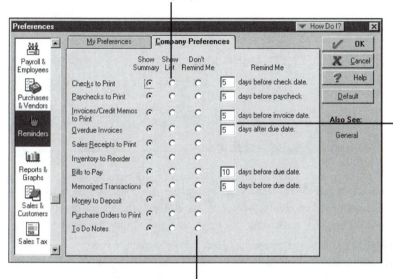

Figure 22.14
Customize your Reminders list in this window.

Reports and Graphs Preferences

If you make some basic decisions about how you want your reports to print, you save lots of time when you actually create the reports. The options in this section apply to all reports in QuickBooks. Click the Reports & Graphs icon in the Preferences window, and then choose the options that will be helpful to you:

- **Refreshing Reports and Graphs**—If you make changes to a report or to the underlying data that makes up a report, you might want QuickBooks to update the report immediately, or perhaps you don't. On the My Preferences tab (see Figure 22.15), Choose Prompt me to refresh if you want QuickBooks to ask you whether you want a report refreshed to reflect your changes. Choose Refresh automatically to have QuickBooks take care of refreshing your reports every time you make a change. Choose Don't refresh if you want to take charge of refreshing your reports yourself (by clicking the Refresh button that appears on each report).

Figure 22.15
Enter report preferences on this screen.

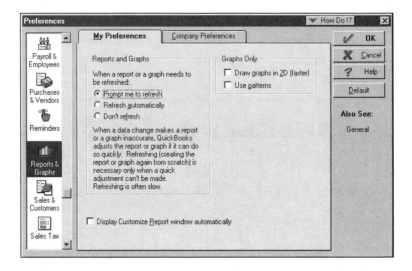

- **Draw graphs in 2D (faster)**—Two dimensional graphs work just as well as the fancy 3D kind, and QuickBooks can create them a bit faster. Click this check box if you find that your 3D graphs are taking too long to create, or if you simply prefer the 2D style.
- **Use patterns**—Click this box if you want QuickBooks to display your graphs in designs made up entirely of black, gray, and white. The color graphs are nice, but the effect can be lost if you don't have a color printer.
- **Display Customize Report window automatically**—If you spend a lot of time customizing your reports, and are a regular customer of the Customize Reports window, you can check this box and QuickBooks automatically displays that window each time you open a report.
- **Summary Reports Basis**—Is your company a cash-basis company or an accrual-basis company? Do you typically like to see your company reports on the cash basis or the accrual basis? Generally, the answer is the same to both of these questions. If your company tracks accounts receivable and accounts payable, you want accrual-basis reports. If you report income when you receive it rather than when it is earned, and expenses when they are paid rather than when they are incurred, it sounds like you are a cash basis company. On the Company Preferences tab, indicate which basis applies to your company (see Figure 22.16).
- **Reports—Show Accounts by**—Another option for displaying information on reports. Choose Name only if you need to see only the name of your accounts on your company reports. Remember that if you use account numbers, the account number is part of the name and is displayed along with the name. Choose Description only if you prefer to show account descriptions rather than names. If you display your reports with account descriptions, be sure to fill in the description field every time you create a new account. Choose Name and Description if you want your reports to display both types of information for your accounts.

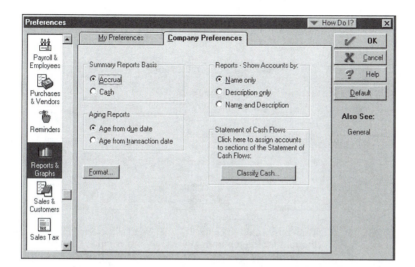

Figure 22.16
Choose from several options that determine how your reports are prepared and displayed.

- **Aging Reports**—Accounts Receivable Aging Reports show how much is owed to your company and for how long the amounts have been owed. Choose whether aging is determined from the due date of the invoice or the date of the actual transaction. If you create invoices on the same day of your transactions, it doesn't matter which option you choose here.

- **Statement of Cash Flows**—QuickBooks gives you the opportunity to customize your Statement of Cash Flows report. Click the Classify Cash button to display a list of all your accounts followed by three columns, labeled Operating, Investing, and Financing. Check off each account that you want to appear on your Statement of Cash Flows, and in which of the three categories on the report the account is to appear.

- **Format**—Click the Format button to display the Report Format Preferences window (see Figure 22.17). Choose items in this window that apply to all reports you create. Choose whether negative numbers are to be displayed with a minus sign to the left of the number, in red, in parentheses, or with a minus sign to the right of the number. Choose to display all numbers divided by 1000 (1,000,000 is then displayed as 1,000), not to display accounts with zero amounts, and whether to display cents. Choose font options, and choose a standard header or footer for your reports. Click OK to close the format window when you have made all your choices.

→ To find more information about creating and customizing reports in QuickBooks, **see p. 361**.

Figure 22.17
Choose standard format options that apply to all your reports.

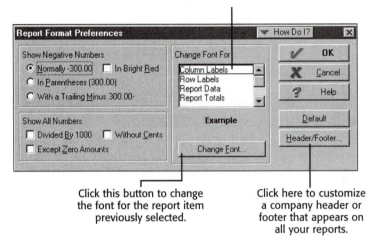

Click a report item for which you want to change the font.

Click this button to change the font for the report item previously selected.

Click here to customize a company header or footer that appears on all your reports.

SALES & CUSTOMERS PREFERENCES

Click the Sales & Customers icon in the Preferences window to set some standard sales options that apply to all your invoices. You can always override these options on the actual invoice form. The preferences are listed as follows:

- **Usual Shipping Method**—Is there one method of shipping you use time and again? Choose the carrier that you prefer, and your entry appears on all your sales forms (see Figure 22.18).

Figure 22.18
Choose sales options that apply to all the invoices that your company issues.

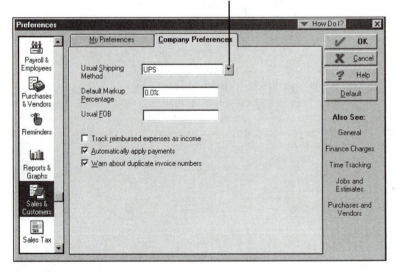

Click this arrow to display a choice of shipping methods.

- **Default Markup Percentage**—Enter an amount for standard markup. Any items that you purchase and resell are affected by this amount. To enter a 20 percent markup, enter 20 in the space provided. A 10.5 percent markup needs to be entered as 10.5. QuickBooks fills in the percent (%) sign.

- **Usual FOB**—Choose the normal FOB status that applies on your sales. Enter Destination if your company pays to ship the order to its destination and retains ownership of the item until it reaches its final destination. Enter Our warehouse if the customer pays to ship the item from your warehouse and takes over ownership at the time of shipment. This status is for your information only, can be overridden on the actual invoice, and has no accounting implications.

→ To find more information on the meaning of FOB (Free on Board) and its importance to your company, **see p. 186**.

- **Track reimbursed expenses as income**—When you make a purchase and expect reimbursement from your customer, does that reimbursement offset the purchase price, or do you report it as income? If you report reimbursements as income, check this box. If you don't use this option, QuickBooks relieves the expense account by the amount of the reimbursement, and the result on your income statement is as if no transaction had occurred.

- **Automatically apply payments**—If this box is checked, payments you receive are applied to outstanding invoices, the oldest invoice first. If you leave this box unchecked, when you receive a payment and open the Receive Payments window, QuickBooks lists the outstanding invoices for the customer but makes no attempt to apply the payment to any particular invoices.

- **Warn about duplicate invoice numbers**—Check this box if you want QuickBooks to indicate that you are about to issue an invoice with a number that has already been used.

Sales Tax Preferences

If your company doesn't charge sales tax, you can skip this section. If you do charge sales tax, click the Sales Tax icon in the Preferences window, and choose Yes as an answer to the Do You Charge Sales Tax? question on the Company Preferences tab (see Figure 22.19). The other options on this tab are only available if the first question is answered Yes.

The preferences are listed as follows:

- **Owe Sales Tax**—When do you charge sales tax to your customers? At the time that you issue the invoice or when you receive payments? Cash basis taxpayers don't charge sales tax until they actually receive money from the customer. Accrual basis taxpayers charge sales tax on their invoices and owe sales tax to authorities based on invoiced sales rather than cash received.

- **Pay Sales Tax**—Do you report and pay your sales tax monthly, every three months (quarterly), or once a year (annually)? Choose the option that applies to your company.

- **Most common sales tax**—Click the arrow and choose the sales tax item that you most frequently charge to customers. You have probably already set up items for your sales tax rates, but if you haven't, choose Add New from the list that appears when you click the arrow. If you only charge one type of sales tax, that is what appears in this area. Some companies charge both a state and local sales tax. Only one item can appear here. The sales tax you indicate here automatically appears on your invoices. You can override that amount on the invoice form, or add another sales tax, if necessary.

- **Mark taxable amounts with "T" when printing**—If you sell both taxable and nontaxable items (you might charge sales tax on sales of merchandise, but not on services you provide), QuickBooks marks the taxable items with a capital letter "T" if you check this box. You probably don't need to bother with this if the items you sell are either all taxable or all nontaxable.

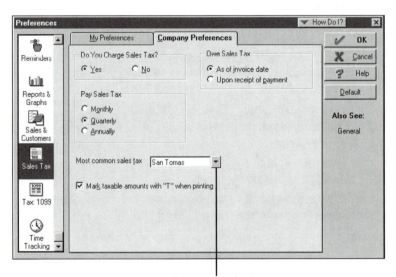

Figure 22.19
These sales tax preferences automate the process of charging sales tax to customers.

Click here to display the sales tax items.

TAX 1099 PREFERENCES

There are guidelines set out by the IRS indicating when a 1099 form must be issued. For example, if you pay a contractor more than $600 in a calendar year, you are supposed to present him with a 1099 form showing his earnings for the year.

You probably won't need to change the threshold amounts that are already listed in the Tax 1099 Company Preferences window (see Figure 22.20) because these amounts comply with the federal guidelines.

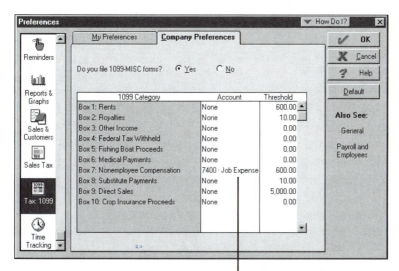

Figure 22.20
You probably won't need to change the thresholds listed in this window.

Enter the accounts where the 1099 category items are recorded.

You do, however, need to indicate the accounts in which these types of amounts are tracked. For example, if you pay rent, you probably have a Rent Expense account. That is the account you choose for the 1099 category of Rents. If you pay subcontractors, you probably have an account called Contract Labor or Subcontractors. That is the account you choose for the 1099 category of Nonemployee Compensation.

→ To find more information about 1099 filing requirements, **see p. 301**.

Time Tracking Preferences

If you don't use the QuickBooks Time Tracking feature, you can skip this section. If you do use this feature, your preference choices here are simple.

Click the Time Tracking icon in the Preferences window, and then choose Yes on the Company Preferences tab to indicate that you use the time tracking feature (see Figure 22.21).

Indicate the day that represents the first day of your work week. This is the day on which your company time sheets begin.

Figure 22.21
Click Yes if you use the QuickBooks Time Tracking feature.

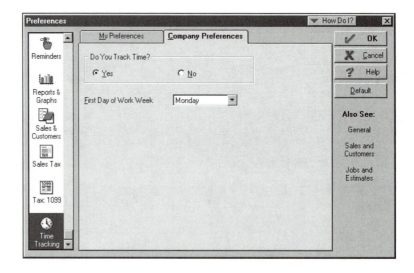

Troubleshooting

The Account Numbering Feature

I turned on the account numbering feature and assigned account numbers, but now I've decided that I don't want to use account numbers. What effect does turning this feature off have on my reports and account names?

Turning off the account numbering feature, by choosing File, Preferences, and then unchecking the Use account numbers checkbox under Company Preferences, has the effect of removing account numbers from your file names. This might change the order in which accounts appear on your reports. By default, accounts appear alphabetically by account name on many reports. Because account numbers are considered to be part of the name, accounts that formerly appeared in numerical order might not have been in alphabetical order.

The Iconbar

My iconbar wraps around on my screen, taking up two lines and using up so much screen space that some of my windows don't appear in full. Is there a way to make the iconbar smaller?

You can either remove some buttons from the iconbar, in order to make it fit on one screen (see the process for deleting an icon under Iconbar Preferences, earlier in this chapter), or you can change the screen area settings on your Windows desktop. Right-click on your Windows desktop, and then choose Properties from the pop-up menu. Click the Settings tab, and then experiment with the Screen area settings by increasing the screen area to the "More" side of the sliding bar. The higher the resolution under Screen area, the more you can view on your desktop. Note that your programs appear smaller as more of the program screen is visible.

PART V

QUICKBOOKS MEETS THE 21ST CENTURY

23 Going Online with QuickBooks 409

24 Online Web Information 431

CHAPTER 23

GOING ONLINE WITH QUICKBOOKS

In this chapter

Common Questions About QuickBooks and Online Banking   410

Preliminary and Precautionary Steps   411

After Your Account is Activated   412

Setting Up QuickBooks's Internet Connection   413

Using QuickBooks Online Interview   414

Going Online with A New Account   418

Making an Online Payment   422

Sending an Online Message   423

Sending a Payment Inquiry   425

Transferring Money Between Accounts Online   425

Obtaining a Report on Online Transactions   426

QuickBooks Online Payroll Service   427

QuickBooks's Online Resources   427

Some business owners love online banking and swear by its convenience. Others question the safety of its transactions, and prefer to stick to paper checks. In this chapter, you explore online banking and online payments, and look at some of the online resources that QuickBooks provides. Even if you decide not to do your banking or bill-paying online, there's a wealth of relevant and frequently updated information on the Web to which QuickBooks provides links.

Common Questions About QuickBooks and Online Banking

For the moment, let me cut to the chase and answer a handful of questions that many people have about online banking and bill payment:

- To begin with, QuickBooks does not conduct financial transactions over the Internet. A private secure line is used. If you log on through and fill out any bank's online application, it's highly doubtful that anyone can see what you are doing.

- Most of the complaints people have with online banking are not issues of security, but of convenience never realized. Although it's true that with online banking you visit your lending institution much less frequently, the time spent handling initial glitches can add up to a good deal of frustration. Others point out that after you take the time to work out the kinks, you truly save time and money. Most complaints do not revolve around money unaccounted for or payments made late; rather, they concern the usual technological muddle of PIN code errors and the occasional inability to properly access your account because of some software problem.

> **Note**
>
> To read some articles about what others think of online banking, check out the following Web sites:
>
> http://techweb.cmp.com/hpc/Jan97/31BANK01.HTM
>
> http://www.investorlinks.com/service-bank-us.html
>
> http://www.idg.net/idg_frames/english/content.cgi?vc=docid_9-39612.html
>
> http://www.exis.net/umbrella/onlinbnk.htm

- Even if your bank does not support online banking, you can sign up through Intuit for online bill payment.

- Online bill payment is almost never instantaneous. Very few institutions are set up to receive online regular customer remittance. Most often, when you pay bills online, you are simply empowering a company to write checks on your behalf, which are sent through standard mail to your designated payee. The entire process for a bill to be noted as paid and the check to clear your account takes longer than if you mailed the payment yourself. Online bill payment does not mean saying goodbye to paper. It means that you are paying someone else to manage the paper for you.

- Transferring money between your own accounts is somewhat instantaneous. If you are the type to snoop around your accounts and transfer extra dollars to the accounts that are earning the highest interest, you can transfer these funds with a click of the mouse.

- When we go to the bank, most of us take the opportunity to ask questions about our accounts while we conduct regular bank business. It's true, though, that when you do online banking, you can send an email along with your transaction, and perhaps someone will get back to you. Understand, however, that the capability to raise a real response from your bank via email truly varies from institution to institution. Some banks are simply going to be more in tune with their online clients' needs than others.

Preliminary and Precautionary Steps

You'll find that the nuts and bolts of carrying out online banking are pretty easy. Before going into detail about setting up accounts and conducting online transactions, the following are some preliminary and precautionary steps to keep in mind. This bird's-eye view is just to show you, at a glance, what's involved:

1. First, determine whether your existing bank provides online services. You can do this by calling the bank or by viewing the QuickBooks list of QuickBooks-friendly online institutions.

2. To see what your options are, begin walking through the QuickBooks Online Banking Interview (From the QuickBooks Navigator, select Online Banking from the Checking and Credit Card tab). Be prepared to deal with the following choices:

   - If your bank is one of the couple dozen that provides online services directly through QuickBooks, you've won half the battle. You can simply continue the interview, make your lending institution aware that you are now taking advantage of their online service, and begin banking and bill paying through QuickBooks.

   - If your bank provides online services, but is not working directly with QuickBooks, you can still use the software that your bank provides for an online connection to pay bills through QuickBooks, but you cannot do full online banking through QuickBooks. Stop the Interview, consult your lending institution, and get them to send you their software package for going online. It might not be difficult to convince them to begin working with Intuit to provide online service through QuickBooks.

> **Note**
>
> The following are Web page links to other banks that do online banking, but might not yet be set up to bank directly through QuickBooks. This status can change quickly, though.
>
> http://www.netbanker.com/index.shtml
> http://www.keybank.com/educate/
>
> As with many Internet links, content gets rearranged and sent to different pages within a site. If you find one of the preceding links to be invalid, simply lop off the final segment of the URL. For example, remove the /educate segment from the www.keybank.com address, and try again.

- If your bank does not provide online banking, you can change your bank to a QuickBooks-friendly lending institution or simply sign up for Intuit's online bill paying service. You can continue the interview, exploring the options that are offered.
- If you decide to switch banks to one that works online with QuickBooks, submit your online application as mentioned previously and wait for account information to appear in the mail. (Check out the accompanying CPA Tip about what to consider when switching banks.) Expect the process of getting set up with a new bank and its online services to take 2–4 weeks.

3. After you've received your bank info through the mail, return to the QuickBooks Online Banking Interview. You can then set up online accounts.

Tip #69 from

Gail Perry

If you are considering changing banks simply for online access, think twice. Even in this electronic age, some important banking and lending decisions are still based on rapport. If you've taken the time to get to know your banking officer, loan managers, and so on, give a little thought to severing those relationships just to do things electronically. It's very true, however, that online banking can diminish much of the drudgery of licking those stamps and envelopes and filling out all those checks yourself, month after month.

After Your Account is Activated

What follows is a synopsis of what you must do after your account is activated and before you can really start making online transactions. This can help you decide whether online banking is really for you.

After you establish an online bank account, go online and download the most recent transactions that have cleared at your financial institution. It's important to know what transactions are outstanding before you generate new transactions. If you find discrepancies between the downloaded account information and what you think is correct, call your bank and clarify. If you have to perform a reconciliation adjustment, do so before you do any transacting. Before you move on, your information in QuickBooks must match what your lending institution says about your account.

Finally, from the Chart of Account list, click your online account and choose Edit. You see an Online Info tab. Make sure that the account information shown here (routing number, account number, federal tax ID) matches what your bank sends you on paper. These precautions cut down on missing transactions. You can then begin transferring money between accounts online, paying bills, and occasionally matching transactions and reconciling accounts.

Go to the beginning and take a close look at what's involved with QuickBooks online banking and bill paying. At the end of the chapter, you look at QuickBooks online information resources that are valuable for any small business, even if you decide that online banking is not for you.

Setting Up QuickBooks's Internet Connection

When QuickBooks takes you online, it does so using an Internet connection that you must specify in advance. QuickBooks does not walk you through setting up Internet access as part of the Online Banking Interview. You might have taken the time to set this up when you first installed QuickBooks, but if not, you have to do it now before you can even begin investigating online banking. Before you start the Online Banking Interview, choose your Internet connection as follows. From the Online menu (at the top of the QuickBooks screen), select Internet Connection Setup, and the dialog box shown in Figure 23.1 appears. You have the three following choices:

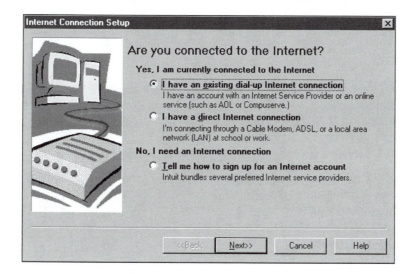

Figure 23.1
You must tell QuickBooks what kind of Internet connection you'll be using.

- If you use a dial-up connection through an Internet service provider, or have AOL 4.0 for Windows 95 (or higher), check the first option: I have an existing dial-up Internet connection. Click Next, and you see a list of the valid Internet dial-up connections on your computer. Select one, and each time you begin a QuickBooks online session, QuickBooks dials this connection for you. If you are already online when you start your next QuickBooks online session, QuickBooks simply uses the existing connection. If you change your Internet connection, QuickBooks tries to dial it up the old way, and your connection won't work (see the accompanying note about changing your dialup Internet connection).

> **Note**
> If you change your dialup Internet connection (for example, if you cancel AOL and choose a new ISP), you have to tell QuickBooks that you've done this. Select Internet Connection Setup from the Online menu, choose I have an existing dial-up Internet connection, and choose your new connection from the list.

- If you connect to the Internet through a LAN, or some other continuous access that does not require a dial-up connection, check the I have a direct Internet connection option. You're asked to identify your Internet browser (Microsoft Explorer version 4.0 is recommended, but not necessary), HTTP Proxy, and Security Proxy. Use the Next button to click through the rest of the setup windows to provide this information.
- If you have no Internet access and want to give Intuit's preferred Internet service provider a spin, check Tell me how to sign up for an Internet account. Interestingly, the following screen doesn't tell you how to sign up for an Internet account, it just tells you to come back after you have accomplished this task. In other words, you can't use the QuickBooks online features until you have signed up with an outside Internet provider.

After you have finished entering all applicable information, click Finish to complete the setup process.

> **Caution**
> Only the most recent version of AOL provides the type of Internet access that QuickBooks can use. Unless you have AOL 4, you have to invest in an Internet service provider that can set up a more standard type of dial-up connection.

> **Note**
> If you want to use your browser to learn more about banks that offer online banking through QuickBooks, point your browser to the following URL: http://www.intuit.com/banking/filist.html. Please note that this page includes banks that use Quicken files as well as QuickBooks.

USING QUICKBOOKS ONLINE INTERVIEW

Start learning about online banking and bill paying by walking through the Online Interview.

To start the setup interview, follow these steps:

1. Click the Online Banking icon from the Checking and Credit Card tab of the QuickBooks Navigator. You're informed that no accounts are set up for online service, and you're prompted to set them up (see Figure 23.2).

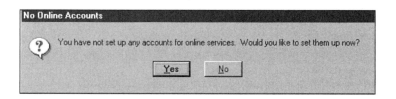

Figure 23.2
When exploring online banking, QuickBooks wants to sign you up with accounts first.

2. Click past the prompts, and the Getting Started with Online Banking window appears. You notice five buttons: Tell Me More, Set up Internet Access, Financial Institutions, Application Information, and Enable Accounts.
3. To see what QuickBooks has to say about online banking, click the Tell Me More button and read the help screens that appear. There is also a video that you can view if you install your QuickBooks CD and click the Show Me button in Help. After you close Help, you're ready to explore your online banking account options with the Application Information button.
4. You're asked whether you want to apply now over the Internet, or have already received online banking information from a lending institution (see Figure 23.3). What follows are two sets of instructions, depending on how you answer this question.

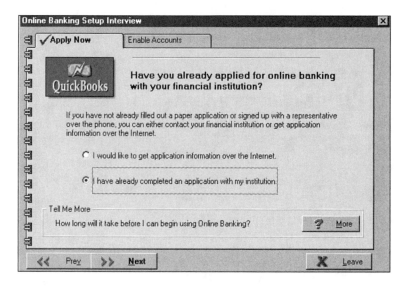

Figure 23.3
Here you can continue to set up your account from paperwork you've received, or you can apply online.

If You've Received Your Bank Info Through The Mail

If you've received a startup kit from your online banking service, you are ready to make your account active. If you've been following along from the previous section and have not closed any dialog boxes, proceed to the step-by-step that follows. If you haven't been following along from the previous section, select the Online Banking icon of the Checking and Credit Card tab of the QuickBooks Navigator (or choose Online, Online Banking, Getting Started, and then click the Enable Accounts button).

To activate your online account, follow these steps:

1. On the Apply Now tab, click the Next button. You're prompted with the following question: Have you already applied for online banking with your financial institution?
2. Choose the second option, I have already completed an application with my institution, and be prepared to enter your federal tax ID and a routing number provided by your bank.
3. You can either create a totally new QuickBooks account for your online banking or select an existing one.
4. Complete the account setup options, providing an account type and account number (see Figure 23.4).

Figure 23.4
After choosing a bank and entering an account routing number, set up a QuickBooks account for that bank account.

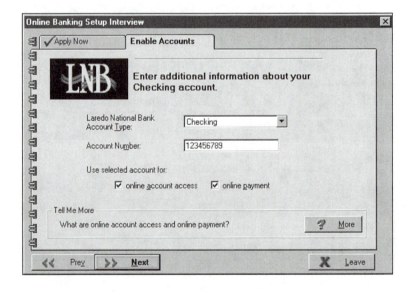

5. Click Next to move through each window. Pay special attention to the distinction between online access, which simply enables you to check balances and transfer funds online, and online bill payment. Check both, if you want both enabled.
6. You can set up more than one online account at this time, or you can set up only one and return later to set up others.

IF YOU ARE STILL EXPLORING YOUR OPTIONS

If you are just now gathering information about applying over the Internet, you can explore the online banking options by following these steps while viewing the screen (refer to Figure 23.3):

1. Check I would like to get application information over the Internet, and click Next.
2. A new window appears. Click the Apply Now button (see Figure 23.5).
3. You see the Financial Institutions Directory. It takes a moment for this screen to appear because an open Internet connection is required. If you are not currently online, QuickBooks logs on and opens the page (see Figure 23.6).

Figure 23.5

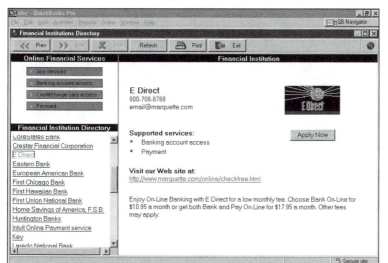

Figure 23.6
Click a name on the left side, and an application for that lending institution appears on the right.

4. The left side of the screen is a scrolling menu, listing banks that offer online services in conjunction with QuickBooks. Click one, and the right side of the screen fills with information about that particular bank. Most banks offer online applications right there on the spot. Determine the following:

   - If you want to apply, fill out an application and click the Submit button. After you've filled out an application, or perhaps found a bank that requires you to call first, back out of the Financial Institutions Directory by clicking the Exit button at the upper right.

   - If you did not apply, feel free to return to this screen at some later time and explore some more. Back out now by selecting the Exit button. Later, just click the Apply Now tab of the Online Banking Interview, and you can search through

more banking selections. When you return to the Online Banking Interview, you find yourself just where you left off. QuickBooks does not make you go back to step one again.

5. Before closing the private connection, QuickBooks automatically searches each bank's data for updates (see Figure 23.7). Be patient while QuickBooks downloads newer information and returns you to the opening Apply Now screen.

6. After submitting your application, wait for a few days for a packet to arrive in the mail with your account information. This usually includes a PIN number, Routing number, clarifying provisos, and other legalese that you need to take the time to read (see the sidebar "What Am I Getting Into?").

7. With your account number, routing number, and additional online info handy, you're ready to move on to "Going Online with a New Account," later in this chapter.

What Am I Getting Into?
What sort of guarantees do banks make regarding online transactions? When you fill out an online application, each bank spells out how much responsibility they assume regarding your online transactions. Sometimes, a bank views an online transaction similarly to an ATM withdrawal. Read very carefully what kind of recourse you have if there's a disagreement.

If you are going to use this account to pay bills online, get a clear picture of how much responsibility the bank takes if a payment arrives late to the payee, even though you sent the payment online in plenty of time. Please keep in mind that most banks do not consider an email notice of a disagreement to be as binding as a written letter.

Note

When you conduct the QuickBooks Online Interview, you have to go online through QuickBooks. You can't simply log on to the Internet without opening QuickBooks and begin selecting QuickBooks online options because QuickBooks conducts online business through a secure connection.

GOING ONLINE WITH A NEW ACCOUNT

After setting up your account (see "If You've Received Your Bank Info Through the Mail," earlier in this chapter), leave the interview and click the Online Banking icon again (from the Checking and Credit Card tab of the Navigator). You see the Online Banking Center window. Click here to send and receive online transactions. The top panel shows your pending outgoing transactions, and the bottom panel shows incoming notices from your bank.

> **Note**
>
> If you create a new online account, or convert an existing account to an online one, a small lightning bolt appears next to its name in your Chart of Accounts.

Retrieving your QuickStatements

You have a handful of chores to take care of when your account is finally active.

Retrieve and verify account balances online by following these steps:

1. Your first order of business is to retrieve your statement from your bank. Click Online Banking in the Checking and Credit Cards section of the Navigator. In the Items to Send panel, highlight the entry Get New QuickStatement for account, and select Send. You've just sent a request to your bank to receive a statement on your most recent transactions. Electronic statements usually cover the last three months of transactions. If you've set up more than one account, you notice two Get New Statement entries. Before doing anything else, view these.

2. When your QuickStatement for that particular account arrives, it appears in the Items Received from Financial Institution panel, the lower half of the Online Banking Center. A QuickStatement tells you about transactions that have cleared the bank, not only those that have been conducted online.

3. Click View and you can compare this downloaded statement with what QuickBooks says about your accounts. You'll see a window with information on the number of matched and unmatched transactions. Click OK and the Match QuickStatement transactions to those already in QuickBooks dialog box appears.

> **Tip #70 from** *Gail Perry*
>
> After you've chosen a bank through QuickBooks and have set up an account, QuickBooks does not make it easy to explore other banks. When you click the Online Banking icon, you're opening your own account. You won't see that screen (discussed earlier) that enabled you to tour through all the different available banks.
>
> If you want to go back again and look at what other banks have to offer, select Online Banking from the Online menu (at the top of the QuickBooks screen), and choose Getting Started. When the Getting Started with Online Banking screen appears, select Apply Now. Click Next a few times, and you can review other banks' options again.

Matching QuickBooks Accounts with Online Bank Statements

To match your bank's QuickStatement with your QuickBooks numbers, select a QuickStatement from the Items Received From Financial Institution window of the Online Banking Center and click View. The Match QuickStatement transactions to those already in QuickBooks dialog box appears (see Figure 23.8).

Figure 23.8
You must regularly match your downloaded statements with your QuickBooks account records.

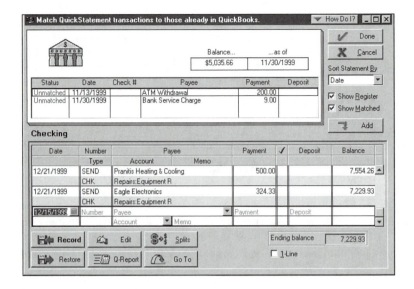

Tip #71 from

Gail Perry

The QuickStatement items in the upper window of the Online Banking Center are *requests* for QuickStatements. To view and match your account balance numbers, click the QuickStatement itself in the lower window: the Items Received From Financial Institution.

Follow these steps to match QuickBooks numbers with your online statement:

1. Your account balance is located at the top of the Match QuickStatement dialog box, as of a particular date. Please note that this date might not be as recent as you think. Some transactions might be missing.

2. At the bottom is your register for that account. Scroll through to see the most current QuickBooks data on this account.

3. In the middle is the Matching window. You see a list of all transactions since the previous QuickStatement was sent to you. Determine the following:
   - If a transaction appears in your bank's records and in QuickBooks, it is said to be matched.
   - If a transaction appears in your bank's records, but not in QuickBooks, it is labeled unmatched.

4. If the transaction is unmatched, click the transaction, and then click Add, and QuickBooks creates a transaction in your account register that matches the one in your bank records. Be sure to read the accompanying note about what to do if a transaction appears unmatched.

Tip #72 from

A transaction can be unmatched because you have yet to record it in QuickBooks, or it is made out to a slightly different name, or the check number is different. To match QuickBooks with the QuickStatement, scroll through the check register and try to find an entry that records the same dollar amount, but perhaps with a different payee or check number. This way, you can make an adjustment without the risk of creating a duplicate entry in QuickBooks that represents the same transaction.

If you've explored the check register a bit and are ready to chalk this one up to a forgotten entry, click Add, and the downloaded transaction is recreated and recorded in your QuickBooks account register.

5. When you are finished matching transactions, click Done, and the Online Banking Center screen appears again. Remember that if you have more than one online account, you have to check each QuickStatement for unmatched entries. Highlight the other account's QuickStatement, select View, and repeat the matching process with each online account.

6. After matching QuickBooks with your online statement, you are ready to conduct banking business online.

Note

Transactions that appear in QuickBooks but have not yet cleared your bank (are not yet part of your downloaded statement) are not counted as unmatched. The Online Banker simply assumes that the transaction has not yet cleared. Only transactions that are part of the bank's record but not found in QuickBooks are called unmatched.

Looking Up An Account's Identification

Sometimes you want to quickly track down an online account's routing and account number. This can be especially important if a transaction never appeared on a QuickStatement and you want to find out what happened to it.

Each online account has an Online Info tab (shown in Figure 23.9). Locate vital account numbers by following these steps:

1. Open the Chart of Accounts from the QuickBooks Lists menu (press Ctrl+A).
2. Click once on the account that you want to view, and select Edit from the Account drop-down menu (or press Ctrl+E). An online account has a lightning bolt next to its name.
3. You see two tabs: General Info and Online Info. Click Online Info to view the account's Routing Number, Account Number, Account Type, and your Federal Tax ID number.
4. Please note that you cannot edit these numbers. Your financial institution or the IRS assigns them to you. You can, however, change the type of access for which your account is enabled.

Figure 23.9
When you make an account into an online account, QuickBooks creates a special tab for online information.

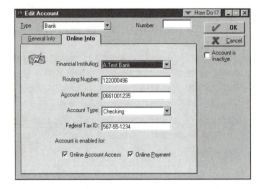

Tip #73 from

If you decide that you want to pay bills from your online account and discover that you are not allowed to, you simply have to enable your account to perform this task. To do so, open the Chart of Accounts (Ctrl+A) and click once on the account from which you want to enable bill-paying. Select Edit from the drop-down Accounts menu (or press Ctrl+E). On the Online Info tab, check Online Payment.

MAKING AN ONLINE PAYMENT

If you have online banking through QuickBooks, or have set up an online bill-paying service (such as Intuit's Online Payment Service), you can make online payments in the same way as you normally do with QuickBooks.

To review, the following are three ways in which you can write checks or pay bills in QuickBooks. Also noted are the things that you do differently to make this into an online transaction:

1. Click the Checks icon in the Checking and Credit Card tab of the Navigator. For online payment, fill out an amount, specify a payee, assign the payment to an account as you normally do, and check the Online Payment box (see Figure 23.10). Select OK to close the checkbook, or click Next to move on to another payment.

2. Select Pay Bills from the QuickBooks Activities menu. The Pay Bills dialog box appears. Check any upcoming bill that you want to pay, as you normally do; if you want to see pending bills due by another date, rather than the date that is shown, select a new date using the calendar that is provided. To make this an online payment, check the Online Payment box in the Pay By panel.

Figure 23.10

3. Select the Check Register from the Checking and Credit Cards tab of the Navigator. Specify the account from which you want to write a check. Fill out a payment as you normally do in the register, using the drop-down menus to choose a vendor, and assign this expense to a particular account. To make this an online payment, type the word SEND in the Number (No.) field (see Figure 23.11).

Figure 23.11

SENDING AND EDITING A PAYMENT

After creating a payment, that payment item appears in the Items to Send window of the Online Banking Center the next time you open the window. This is what happens next:

- To send the payment, highlight that item, making sure that a check appears next to its name, and click Send.
- To edit the payment, highlight the item and click the Edit button. The payment appears as a check, ready to be edited. Following are the changes you can make:
  - The amount
  - The payee
  - The account to which the payment is assigned
  - The date on which you send the payment out

All changes you make are noted in the QuickBooks register, and are not recorded as a second payment. Rather, QuickBooks understands that you mean to edit the first one. Please note that most online financial institutions recommend that you send your payment to them about ten days before you actually want the payment to clear your account. Keep in mind that you are not sending your payment online to the payee; rather, you are sending it to your bank or online financial institution, who then assumes some responsibility for making sure that money gets to its intended destination.

HIGHLIGHTING ITEMS YOU WANT TO SEND

Many items can appear in the Items to Send window in the Online Banking Center at one time. It is not assumed that you want to send every item simultaneously.

Send the correct online items by following these steps:

1. When you click the Send button, only those items with a check by them are sent.
2. If a check mark does not appear next to an item's name, click the item once, and the check mark appears. The next time you click the Send button, that item is sent.
3. To remove the check mark, click the item again.

SENDING AN ONLINE MESSAGE

When you send an online message to your bank, the message appears as an email on your online account manager's computer. To increase the odds that your message gets the attention it deserves, do the following:

- Send your message separately from your other transactions (fund transfers and bill payments). That way it appears as a separate item on your bank's list of incoming messages and transactions. Someone is more apt to see what is written in the Subject field, and perhaps to take a moment to look at the message.

- The Subject field is the first thing your online account manager sees when he views your message. Therefore, use the Subject field to your advantage, quickly summarizing the message contents and emphasizing its urgency.
- Keep in mind that, at times, an email is no substitute for a phone call. Do not assume that just because you've sent an email, a request has been acted upon. At least until you get acquainted with how your bank responds to email, and until you've become a familiar name to your online banking people, you might have to follow up your initial inquiries with an old fashioned trip to the phone.

To send a message to your bank, do the following:

1. From the Online menu, select Online Banking, Create Message, and Online Banking Message. The Banking Message dialog box appears (see Figure 23.12).

Figure 23.12
Send a Message to your bank, separate from a payment.

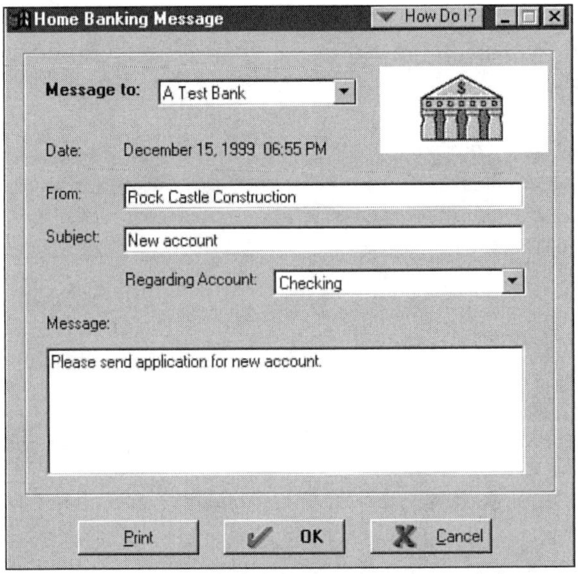

2. If you have more than one bank with which you do online business, select a bank in the Message to field. Also, in the From field, identify yourself in such a way that the reader knows who you are.
3. Include a subject, remembering that what you type here is seen first. Use the Regarding Account drop-down menu to choose the account to which this message is relevant.
4. Finally, in the Message field, type a message. Don't be fooled by the size of the message box. You can type in a message many times larger than the visible field (eighteen lines of 60 characters each). Use the QuickBooks Edit menu to Cut, Copy, and Paste message content as well.

5. Click OK, and the message appears, ready to send, in the Items to Send window of the Online Banking Center dialog box.

> **Caution**
> Many banks still require complaints to be sent to them in writing. An email message might not be regarded as an official word from you. The liability to which a bank holds itself regarding an email message varies from bank to bank.

Sending a Payment Inquiry

A payment inquiry is treated with more urgency than a message by the receiving financial institution. This sort of important message is flagged differently.

To send a payment inquiry, you must have already sent the payment to the bank and have the payment highlighted in the Online Banking Center. (That simply means opening the Online Banking Center by clicking the Online Banking icon and clicking once on the payment about which you are inquiring.) After the payment is highlighted, do the following:

1. From the Online menu (at the top of the QuickBooks screen) select Online Banking, and then Create Message.
2. From the side menu that appears, select Online Payment Inquiry.
3. You're prompted to answer some questions about the payment.
4. When you are finished, click OK to close the dialog box and send your inquiry.

Transferring Money Between Accounts Online

To transfer money between accounts, both the source and destination account must have online access. Please note that transferring money between accounts online is somewhat instantaneous, but might still require the intervention of an account manager at the other end of the transaction. For this reason, do not assume that your transfer is immediately effective until you've experienced a track record with this particular institution.

To transfer funds between two online accounts, follow these steps:

1. Click the Transfer Money icon in the Checking and Credit Card tab of the Navigator. The Transfer Funds Between Accounts dialog box appears (see Figure 23.13).

Figure 23.13
You can transfer funds between any two online accounts at the same bank.

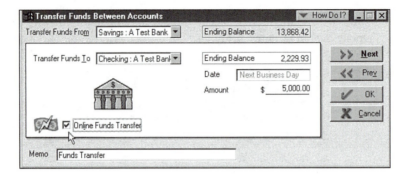

2. To select a source account, use the Transfer Funds From drop-down menu.
3. To select a destination account, use the Transfer Funds To drop-down menu.
4. Enter an amount.
5. Check the Online Funds Transfer option.
6. Click OK; your transfer is now waiting to be sent.
7. Click the Online Banking icon in the Checking and Credit tab of the Navigator, and your transfer appears as an Item To Send.
8. At this time you can go back and edit your transfer transaction, or click Send to really send the transfer instructions to your bank.

OBTAINING A REPORT ON ONLINE TRANSACTIONS

To create a report of any group of transactions you've conducted online, use the filter option on any transaction report to create any grouping you want.

Create an online transactions report by following these steps:

1. From the Reports menu at the top of the QuickBooks screen, select Transaction Detail Reports, and then By Date.
2. When the report appears, change the dates covered by the report, if you want to.
3. Select Filters, scroll through the Choose Filter menu, and locate Online Status (see Figure 23.14).
4. The drop-down menu to the right of Choose Filters enables you to pick the online status by which to filter your reports. You can, for example, view only those transactions you have yet to send, or those you've already sent.
5. When you are finished choosing filters for your report, click OK, and the report appears. (Figure 23.15 shows a report of all transactions conducted online during the previous quarter.)

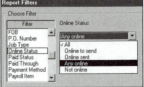

Figure 23.14

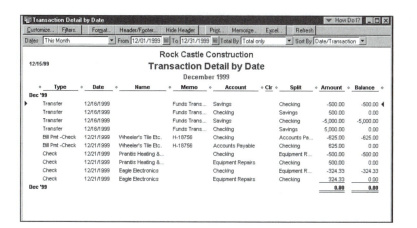

Figure 23.15
A report based on online transactions.

QuickBooks Online Payroll Service

QuickBooks provides an online payroll service. The type of service offered varies greatly depending on your business and payroll needs. To learn more, select Payroll Service from the Online menu (at the top of the QuickBooks screen), and click About QuickBooks Online Payroll. Select Help to view the video that provides a general overview of what's available. At the present time, QuickBooks Payroll Online Service cannot work with some businesses. Because this is a very new feature, however, expect more services to be added in QuickBooks maintenance updates.

QuickBooks's Online Resources

QuickBooks has a number of online business resources, available from the Business Resources tab of the Navigator. These include product and technical support, including a very thorough FAQ site as well as a site for locating a QuickBooks expert advisor in your community. A link is provided to Cashfinder.com, which is a one-stop application center for obtaining a business loan. You can also visit Quicken's Small Business site, which provides frequently updated articles related to every aspect of running a small business. The following sections briefly look at each of these resources.

QuickBooks.com

To access this site, click the QuickBooks.com icon in the Business Resources tab of the Navigator. This opens the QuickBooks home Web site (see Figure 23.16). This site contains links to updated tax tables and maintenance upgrades, tax preparation software offers, and user-to-user forums, among other things. You can also order Intuit's checks and other forms from this site. The QuickBooks Frequently Asked Questions link, however, is worth a special look.

Figure 23.16
The QuickBooks Web site.

Click the Frequently Asked Questions link under the heading Support Resources or, if QuickBooks rearranges its page, point your browser to www.intuit.com/support/quickbooks. Here you can type in keywords regarding any QuickBooks topic and retrieve the most recent and thorough answers. Many points that are not really fleshed out in the manual, as well as highly specialized instructions for specific industries, can be found here. You can print out or save any information found here as well.

FIND AN ADVISOR

If you like the security of having a QuickBooks expert in your community, click the Find an Advisor icon in the Business Resources tab of the Navigator. When the page opens, type your city, state, and area code, and you see a list of accountants and consultants who are especially knowledgeable about QuickBooks in your community. This page can be especially helpful when choosing an accountant. If your accountant is set up to work with QuickBooks, both her job and yours are much easier. If the QuickBooks internal browser can't access the site for some reason, just point your browser to www.quickbooks.com, and select Professional Advisors.

www.cashfinder.com

At www.cashfinder.com, you can apply through QuickBooks for a business loan or line of credit to a number of lending institutions. You do not send an online application. Rather, after answering a number of general questions about your business type, you can download a software wizard that builds a highly detailed application for you. This application is printed out and mailed. cashfinder.com's role is to help choose a lending institution that is likely to do business with you.

The major benefit that you derive from this service is speed of response. cashfinder.com claims that you'll know about your loan 48 hours from your submission.

cashfinder.com is free, but you must still pay loan application fees to the companies to which you ultimately end up applying. Currently, ten lending institutions do business through cashfinder.com, although this number is likely to grow. If you have trouble with the internal QuickBooks link to cashfinder, simply open your own Internet connection, and point your browser to www.cashfinder.com.

SMALL BUSINESS BY Quicken.com

From your Internet browser, go to http://www.quicken.com/small_business/ and you'll find yourself at a Web site filled with information and useful links about operating a small business (see Figure 23.17). The site has general articles and, by following links, you can obtain very specific advice pertaining to your end of the marketplace. You find thousands of answers to many small business questions, as well as discussion boards where you can post questions and answers. At the top of the page is a drop-down menu that links you to a page dealing with your concerns. Some of these are investments, taxes, insurance, banking & borrowing, and home & mortgage.

Figure 23.17
The Small Business by Quicken Web site.

Troubleshooting

Getting a Response from Your Bank

My bank is not responding to inquiries I send via email. How can I get a better response?

There are some things that are not within the control of QuickBooks, and the response of your bank is one of these things. Contact your bank and find out what their policy is regarding responding to email.

Online Bill Payment

I need to send an online payment today, but when I try to enter the payment I'm told the bill won't be paid for three days. What do I do?

Online bill payment is sometimes frustrating. It seems that your payment ought to be able to travel at the speed of light, or at least at the speed of your Internet connection. Unfortunately, some time is required for the processing of the payment. If you don't think the payment will be made in time to meet your deadline, you might need to resort to alternative measures. Try calling the intended recipient and ask for a few days' leeway. If that won't work, you might have to write a check manually and send the payment via overnight mail.

CHAPTER 24

ONLINE WEB INFORMATION

In this chapter

Poking Around on the Web   432

Visiting the QuickBooks Home Page on the Web   432

Useful Business Resources   433

Taxes and Accounting   435

Laws and Regulations   435

What's in the News?   436

A wealth of information is available on the Internet, including many links from the QuickBooks Web site and other financial resources. This chapter provides an introduction to finding financial and business information on the Internet.

Use these locations as a starting point when you begin your exploration. The Internet changes constantly, and some of the links provided in this chapter, as well as the illustrations you see here, might vanish into Internet obscurity before you get a chance to sample them. Rest assured that something comparable will take the place of the information that is retired. A little sleuthing can no doubt provide you with the information you seek.

This chapter assumes that you have access to a modem and an Internet connection.

> **Note** For more information on the Internet, refer to *Using the Internet, Fourth Edition* from Que Publishing, written by Barbara Kasser, or *Special Edition Using the Internet, Fourth Edition* from Que Publishing, written by Jerry Honeycutt.

Poking Around on the Web

Several search engines are available for digging into the Internet. Following are some of the major search addresses:

Excite: http://www.excite.com

Yahoo: http://www.yahoo.com

Lycos: http://www.lycos.com

Infoseek: http://www.infoseek.com

HotBot: http://www.hotbot.com

LookSmart: http://www.looksmart.com/

AltaVista: http://www.altavista.digital.com

When you search, enter a key word or a string of words. If you enter more than one word, enclose the words in quotation marks. Most search engines also respond to Boolian searches using "AND" or "OR" in the search criteria. If you are searching for tax sites, for example, you might search for the word "tax", or the phrase "income tax" (in quotes), or the combination "tax AND property".

Visiting the QuickBooks Home Page on the Web

You can go to www.quickbooks.com and visit the QuickBooks home page, where you can find information about the program, technical support options, industry tips, an online store for ordering forms, an update service for payroll tax tables, and links to other Intuit sites (see Figure 24.1).

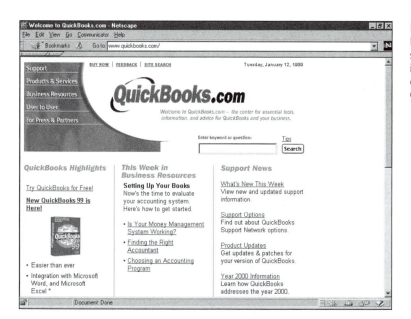

Figure 24.1
Find links to technical support and financial institutions, among other things, on the QuickBooks Web site.

→ To find more information about QuickBooks online resources, **see p. 409.**

Useful Business Resources

The U.S. Small Business Administration has a Web site at www.sba.gov where you can find, among other things, information about starting a business and information about finding financing. You can download a business plan workbook or an application for an SBA loan, or you can browse their online library for tax information and the text of the Small Business Act and information about the Freedom of Information Act.

You can find links to insurance calculators for determining the cost versus benefit of your insurance, and you can find insurance companies that provide services on the Web at www.insuremarket.com (sponsored by Intuit). You can also get price comparisons from major insurance companies at this site.

Follow up on the latest business news at the Business Week site, http://www.businessweek.com (see Figure 24.2).

If you're looking for investment information and stock quotes, plenty of sites can provide

Figure 24.2
View the latest copy of Business Week online at `www.businessweek.com`.

you with the latest news and price information. Try CNN Financial Network at `www.cnnfn.com/markets/quotes.html` or `www.stockpoint.com`.

There are several online resources for stock trading at deep discounts, such as Charles Schwab at `www.schwab.com`, Datek at `www.datek.com`, and etrade at `www.etrade.com`. Or keep up with the financial gurus at Money Magazine by signing up for an online subscription at `http://www.pathfinder.com/money/plus/index.oft.?null` (see Figure 24.3).

Figure 24.3
Subscribe to Money Magazine, or use their free stock quote service, at `http://jcgi.pathfinder.com/money/plus/index.oft`.

Looking for a loan? Several Web sites provide you with loan calculators for determining potential loan payments, as well as links to financial institutions that provide online loan applications. Try `www.financenter.com` for personal finance advice and online calculators for determining monthly payments, tax savings, and refinancing (see Figure 24.4).

Figure 24.4
Calculate loans or figure out how much money you'll need for retirement at www.financenter.com.

Taxes and Accounting

Nothing can clear up a tax headache faster than having tax information at your fingertips. Visit the IRS's own Web site at `http://www.irs.ustreas.gov/cover.html`, where you can download federal tax forms and publications.

Visit the American Institute of Certified Public Accountants (AICPA) at `http://aicpa.org/` and find links to tax and accounting sites all over the Internet.

Confused about that new Roth IRA? The Roth has its own Web page, where you can have all your questions answered: `http://www.rothira.com/`.

Check out the TaxWeb for links to federal government tax sites, all the state governments, and a lot more: `http://www.taxweb.com/`. If that site doesn't get you where you want to go, another equally well-stocked Web page, called Tax Professionals.com, contains links to income-tax related information on the Internet: `http://www.taxprofessionals.com`.

Laws and Regulations

Search for the government document of your choice—the one that's sure to put you to sleep at night—at the U.S. House of Representatives' Internet Law Library, at http://law.house.gov/109.htm. If you're still counting sheep after browsing the law library documents, try reading the full text of the U.S. Tax Code at http://www.fourmilab.ch/ustax/ustax.html or check out

http://www.ed.gov/EdRes/EdFed/GenGuide.html, the General Guides to Government Internet Resources.

What's in the News?

Every good businessperson stays on top of the news. It's easy to keep up with current events with the aid of the Internet. Most metropolitan newspapers are available online either in full or in an excerpted form, and many offer "home delivery" right to your emailbox. Following is a sample of where you can go for the breaking stories:

The Boston Globe: http://www.globe.com/globe/ (see Figure 24.5)

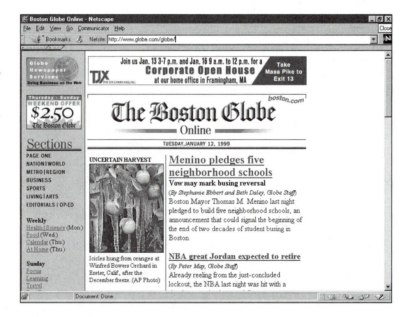

Figure 24.5
The news of the world at your fingertips: The Boston Globe is one of many papers that offer online services, including the capability to search the paper for a specific topic.

Cable News Network: http://www.cnn.com/

The Detroit Free Press: http://www.freep.com/

The Chicago Tribune: http://www.chicago.tribune.com/

The Economist: http://www.economist.com/ (see Figure 24.6)

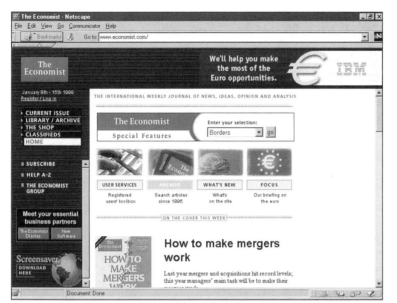

Figure 24.6
Get in-depth news summaries with the *Economist*.

The New York Times: http://www.nytimes.com/

The Seattle Times: http://www.seattletimes.com/

The Washington Post: http://www.washingtonpost.com/ (see Figure 24.7)

Figure 24.7
Stay on top of the next Watergate when you read the *Washington Post* online.

The Baltimore Sun: http://www.sunspot.net/

Christian Science Monitor: http://www.csmonitor.com/

The Miami Herald: http://www.herald.com

The Philadelphia Enquirer: http://www.phillynews.com/

The St. Petersburg Times: http://www.sptimes.com/

USA Today: http://www.usatoday.com/

ODDS AND ENDS

Test your financial knowledge at a fascinating Web site—the Financial Players Center—at http://fpc.net66.com (see Figure 24.8). You can do loan calculations, learn about how the value of money changes over time, and take financial trivia quizzes.

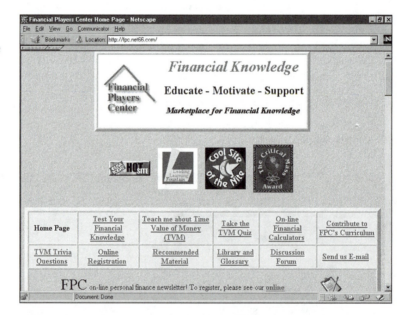

Figure 24.8
The Financial Players Center delves into the meaning of money.

Check the ratings of mutual funds with the Morningstar service, or check up on the markets of the world at http://www.quicken.com/investments/.

This brief summary only highlights a few of the interesting business and financial sites available for you on the Internet. Start searching, and you'll find that you have information coming out your ears!

Troubleshooting

Error Message

One of the links you provided in this chapter returns an error message when I try to access the site.

It seems that Internet Web sites change addresses frequently—and sometimes disappear completely. Also, sites can be made unavailable while the information is being changed. If you have trouble accessing a site, try using a search engine such as Alta Vista at `http://www.altavista.com` or Excite at `http://www.excite.com` to search for the name of a Web site. If the site location appears to be correct, but you continue to get an error message, try accessing the site a little later, or even the next day.

The Acrobat Reader

I'm trying to download tax forms and I keep getting a message saying I need something called an Acrobat Reader. Do I really need this, and if so, what do I do to get it?

If you are told you need the Adobe Acrobat Reader, you might also be given an opportunity to click on a link, which causes this little graphics reader program to download onto your computer. If you aren't linked right to the Adobe site, you can go there yourself by entering the following site location: `http://www.adobe.com/prodindex/acrobat/readstep.html`. The Acrobat software is available for free. Follow the downloading instructions on the screen at the site listed previously, and then return to the location where you want to download tax forms. You should have no trouble getting the tax forms now.

PART VI

GETTING THE MOST FROM QUICKBOOKS

25 QuickBooks Pro and Time Tracking 443

26 Budgeting 463

27 Forecasting Your Financial Future with QuickBooks 471

28 Security 480

29 Income Taxes 489

CHAPTER 25

QUICKBOOKS PRO AND TIME TRACKING

In this chapter

QuickBooks Timer Overview   444

What You Need To Run the QuickBooks Timer   446

Getting Ready to Use the Timer   446

Exporting Timer Data To QuickBooks   454

Opening Timer Data in QuickBooks   455

Creating Install Disks for the Timer   457

Getting Your Employees Up to Speed With the Timer   458

Backed Up and Condensed Timer Data   458

Viewing and Editing Timer Data in Detail   460

This chapter starts out by saying that the QuickBooks Timer is a feature available only in QuickBooks Pro. Nothing in this chapter really applies to QuickBooks Standard Edition.

The QuickBooks Timer (see Figure 25.1) is a portable extension of QuickBooks. Employees, subcontractors, and vendors can install it on their own computers, where it runs as a digital stopwatch that tracks how much time is spent on a particular job.

Figure 25.1
This is how the Timer usually looks when you are working with it.

Following are some uses for the Timer:

- With the Timer, your employees can work offsite and still have an accurate record of how much time is spent on a particular project. Timer data can be returned to you, and when it is entered into QuickBooks, each customer's account can be properly billed and hours can be credited to the employee for payroll. A Timer user can type a memo. Later, QuickBooks imports this memo along with the other Time, Employee, and Customer:Job data.

- Give the Timer to a vendor who does work for you, such as a graphics designer or proofreader. They can install the Timer in a few minutes. When they are finished, they can send you the data, and you have all the information that QuickBooks needs to properly account for and pay the vendor.

- Give the Timer to several subcontractors who are working for you on a job. They can each keep track of their time, job type, and customer, and when they are finished, QuickBooks instantly recognizes and processes the information just as if you had typed it into QuickBooks "the long way."

QUICKBOOKS TIMER OVERVIEW

Before you explore the Timer in detail, here's a brief tour of how it works, and how data is shared between the Timer and QuickBooks:

- The QuickBooks Timer is more than just a stopwatch; it tracks time on behalf of an employee or vendor, and notes which customer and job that time is to be credited to. So before you really think about working with the Timer, your QuickBooks company needs to have a least one employee, as well as some customers and jobs that you are in the habit of billing.

- Save QuickBooks data in a form that the Timer can use (File, Timed Activities, Export Lists for Timer). This Timer data contains all your company's current employees, employee pay rates, vendors, customers, and jobs.
- Note the name of the file you save because your employee or vendor will need to know it.
- Create Timer Install disks to give to your employee or vendor.
- Give the Timer Install disks to your employee or vendor, as well as the QuickBooks file you saved.
- Instruct your employee or vendor to install the Timer on his computer and copy the QuickBooks Timer data onto his hard drive.
- The employee or vendor is prompted to import a list from QuickBooks. They need to locate the QuickBooks file you gave to them. The Timer is then set up to work with your company data.
- The employee or vendor then clicks the Timer's New Activity button, and uses the Your Name drop-down menu (see Figure 25.2) to select his name. (After all, you gave this Timer to one of your employees, or a vendor, so his name appears on the list, not yours.)

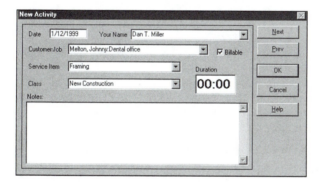

Figure 25.2
When using the Timer, Your Name refers to the employee or vendor's name, not the company owner or administrator.

- The employee or vendor needs to use the other drop-down menus to choose a customer and a job for which to charge.
- Finally, after clicking OK and Start, the clock is ticking, and all the time spent on a project is accounted for.

> **Note**
>
> The idea might seem a bit odd at first, asking someone who works for you to let a computer clock run while they do a job for you. What if the work they do has nothing to do with a computer? One of the special benefits is how the Timer associates an employee's hours with specific customers and jobs. They can manually type the hours they've spent on a job, even if they do not use the actual "stopwatch" feature. Just the fact that they enter the hours for various jobs and save those as a single file makes it much easier for you to enter employee data into QuickBooks.

What You Need To Run the QuickBooks Timer

The QuickBooks Timer is a standalone program and, therefore, does not have the same system requirements as QuickBooks does. Consequently, you can run it on Windows 3.1, as well as Windows 95, 98, and NT. You need only 8MB of RAM—although 16 is better—and 8MB of free disk space. Also, a user can get by with a VGA monitor—SVGA is not necessary.

Getting Ready to Use the Timer

To understand what exactly the Timer does for you, here's a look at what it imports from QuickBooks and what it sends back to QuickBooks after an employee or vendor has used it.

The following list is data from QuickBooks that the Timer uses. When you export a file from QuickBooks to the Timer, this is what is exported:

- Employee Names
- Employee Payroll Items (salary, hourly, overtime, and so on)
- Customer:Job data.
- Classes, if you have created any
- Memos

After an employee or vendor uses the Timer, the following data is imported back into QuickBooks:

- The number of hours an employee or vendor spends on a job. These hours are broken into regular time, salary, and overtime, depending on how you regularly pay that employee or vendor.
- The number of jobs an employee worked on.
- The number of timed sessions (called Activities by the Timer) on which an employee worked. These sessions can be on behalf of one customer or many.
- Any memos generated by the employee or vendor, to help you keep track of where all this offsite time is being spent.

When Timer data is brought back into QuickBooks, QuickBooks accounts for the time in the following ways:

- Payroll keeps track of the hours spent by the employee and generates paychecks accordingly.
- The QuickBooks weekly timesheet shows the employee hours.
- Every timed activity in from the Timer appears as a single activity in the QuickBooks Enter Single Activity screen.
- When Timer data is imported, you can immediately view a detailed report of how much this offsite work has cost you.

Exporting a List for the Timer

Your first task in preparation for using the Timer does not involve the Timer at all. The Timer does not read QuickBooks files directly. QuickBooks converts necessary files in a few simple steps. After this is done, you can begin working with the Timer.

> **Note**
>
> The link between QuickBooks and the Timer is the .IIF file type. QuickBooks exports its necessary files in this .IIF format, and they are read by the Timer. Likewise, when the Timer exports files for QuickBooks to use, they are converted to an .IIF file, which QuickBooks can read and import appropriately.

To export QuickBooks files for the Timer, follow these steps:

1. Open QuickBooks and select Timer Activities from the File menu. Choose Export Lists For Timer (see Figure 25.3).

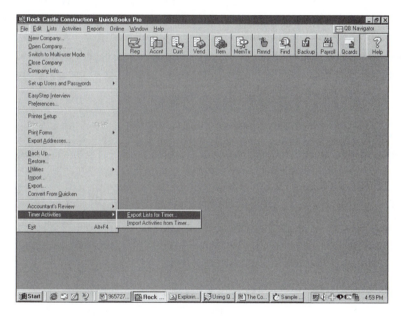

Figure 25.3
This is the only menu item in QuickBooks that deals with Timer data.

2. Click past the confirmation screen, and you see the Export dialog box (see Figure 25.4), which prompts you to type a filename and save it.
3. Make a note of the save location (the folder in which you are saving) because you'll have to locate this file and copy it to a floppy disk shortly.
4. Type a name for this export file. It must end with a .IIF file extension. Do not simply overwrite one of the existing files; instead, type a new name.
5. You see a confirmation that your file has been successfully exported.

Figure 25.4
Exporting an .IIF file is the first step toward using the Timer.

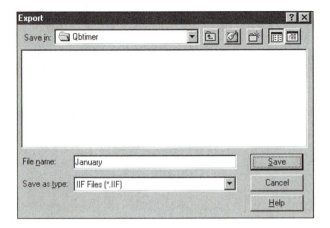

6. Locate this .IIF file and copy it onto a floppy disk. This is done so that you can give it to your employees when you give them the Timer Install disks. It does them no good to have the Timer up and running unless you give them the company data as well.

7. Create as many copies of the .IIF file as you have employees or vendors who need to use it. The file size is not large, usually, so if they have email access, you can perhaps email them the file as an attachment.

INSTALLING THE TIMER

Technically speaking, you don't even have to install the Timer on your own computer (unless you are an employee in your company, and you are tracking your own time spent on a project). On a day-to-day basis, you are only working with data returned to you from your employees and vendors, and not with the Timer itself.

However, if you're going to instruct your employees and vendors on how to use it, it's a good idea for you to be familiar with it; so now you'll explore how to install the Timer and learn your way around the interface.

Install the Timer by following these steps:

1. Insert the QuickBooks CD into your CD-ROM drive, and select Install Timer (see Figure 25.5).

2. Follow the onscreen instructions, accepting the default choices for file location and options. There's nothing to customize here.

3. Make a note of the name of the folder into which the Timer is installed (the default is QBTIMER); to make the lives of your Timer users easier, tell them what folder to import and export Timer data to and from.

4. At the end of installation, QuickBooks Timer asks to restart your computer. Allow it to do so before proceeding.

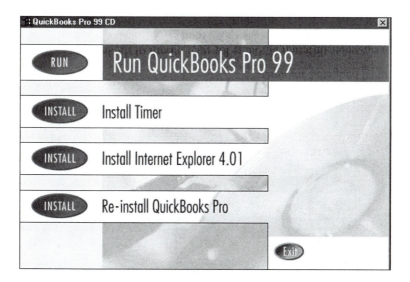

Figure 25.5
Install the QuickBooks Timer as a separate program.

LEARNING YOUR WAY AROUND THE TIMER

When you first install the Timer, it tries to open a Timer data file, and can't find one, so you are prompted to create a Timer data file. Following are several points that need to be clarified from the start:

- In the QuickBooks Timer program, you name a file at the time you create it, rather than saving and naming it later. This is confusing because the Timer shows you a screen that makes it look as if you are supposed to select an existing file and open it—but that is not the case.

- You are supposed to type any name you want—that is your new file. You are not being told to pick an existing file.

Follow these steps to get started with the QuickBooks Timer:

1. Start the Timer program by selecting the QuickBooks Pro Timer icon from the QuickBooks Pro group of the Windows Start menu. The Timer is not started automatically when you open QuickBooks.

2. You are prompted to create a new Timer file (see Figure 25.6). To do so, click past the prompts and select New Time File from the File menu. In the dialog box that is provided, type a name similar to the name of your company. Click OK.

3. You are prompted to import a QuickBooks list (see Figure 25.7). Import the .IFF file you created, as directed in the preceding section "Exporting A List for the Timer." Do this by selecting Import QuickBooks Lists from the Timer File menu.

Figure 25.6
To create a new Timer file, type a name—and don't try to overwrite an old one.

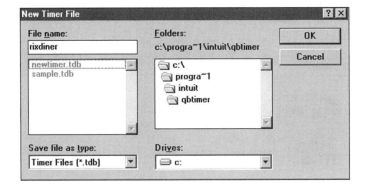

Figure 25.7
Before you can start timing, you need to import your first .IIF file from QuickBooks.

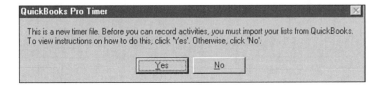

- If, when you exported the list from QuickBooks, you saved the file in the QBTIMER folder, the file you need is right there.
- If you saved the export file in the QuickBooks folder itself, change the folder to your QuickBooks folder and locate the .IFF file that has your QuickBooks company Timer data. (If this data was saved to a floppy disk, put the floppy in drive A and locate the file there.)
4. After importing the QuickBooks lists, you can begin time tracking sessions. Whether you are simply experimenting right now, or explaining to employees and vendors how to use the Timer, the next step is to create a new activity for which to track time. Proceed to the next section.

This is how to create a new activity in the Timer:

1. Click the New Activity button, and the dialog box shown in Figure 25.8 appears.
2. The Your Name drop-down menu contains the names of all employees and vendors. It doesn't have the company owner's name because the Timer is used for tracking employee and vendor hours spent on customer jobs, not the owner's time. Whoever is doing the work for this session needs to locate his name in the Your Name field.
3. Use the Customer:Job drop-down menu to select a job and customer associated with this activity. If the activity is going to be billed, check the Billable box.
4. Every employee or vendor has a type of task that she performs. You set these up as service items when you started your QuickBooks company. The employee or vendor selects a task from the Service Item drop-down menu.

Getting Ready to Use the Timer

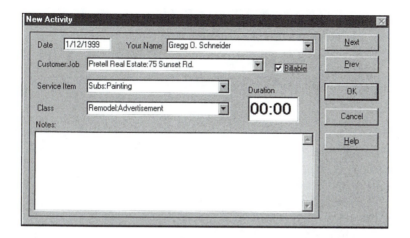

Figure 25.8
Use the New Activity dialog box to set up customers and jobs, and to identify yourself.

5. The employee or vendor can type a memo to help identify this activity after it's been exported to QuickBooks. This is highly recommended because offsite work can easily get expensive if untracked.

6. When the New Activity windows and fields have been filled out, click OK, and the Timer is ready to track activities. Please proceed to the next section.

> **Note**
> A Timer activity is a task that an employee or vendor performs on behalf of a customer. A Timer activity consists of an employee or vendor, a customer, a job related to that customer, and a date on which the activity in question is carried out. A Timer activity correlates directly to the Enter Single Activity feature in QuickBooks.

Using the Timer

After creating an activity, click OK, and the Timer is ready for use.

Follow these steps when timing an activity:

1. Click the Start button to begin timing. The following list tells you how you know that your time is being tracked:
   - You see the digital readout begin to advance, one minute at a time. The colon between the two numbers (00:01) blinks to confirm that time is being tracked. See Figure 25.9.
   - Also, while time is elapsing, the activity displayed in the Current Activity line shows the word "Timing."

Figure 25.9
The Timer button can start, stop, or resume timed activities.

2. Stop the clock by clicking the Stop button. Resume activity by clicking the same button, which now shows the word "Resume". To minimize the Timer so that it takes up less room on your computer screen, click the Space Saver button at the far right of the Timer (it shows two windows). You can also minimize the Timer by clicking the standard Windows Minimize button.

3. To edit an activity while you are working on it, click the Edit Activity button. While an activity is in progress, your editing is limited to the memo area. At this time, you can alter the memo and type anything new that you want to add. Time is still elapsing while you are editing.

4. When you are finally finished with this activity, there is no saving the file that has to be done. Close the Timer by selecting Exit from the File menu, or export the activity to QuickBooks.

CREATING A NEW TIMED ACTIVITY

At any time, you can start a new activity, such as a new job for the same customer, or a job for another customer altogether.

Follow these steps to set up a new activity:

1. Click the New Activity button (see Figure 25.10), and the New Activity dialog box appears.

2. Fill out the fields as previously indicated in the "Timing an Activity" section.

3. When you are done, click OK; the Timer appears again.

4. As previously discussed, click the Start button to begin time tracking this activity.

5. Now, however, you can use the Current Activity drop-down menu to choose the activity with which you want to work at the moment (see Figure 25.11).

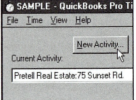

Figure 25.10

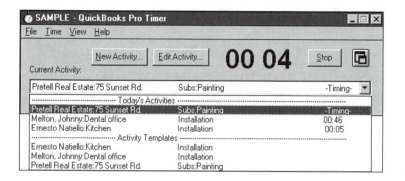

Figure 25.11
Change to a new activity with the Current Activity drop-down menu.

6. Switching between activities using the drop-down menu automatically starts the New Activity time tracking and stops the previous activity.

7. Click Stop when you are finished with the tasks; again, there are no files to save. Just exit the Timer when you are through, or prepare to export activities to QuickBooks for accounting, which is covered next.

> **Caution**
> If you are distributing the Timer to employees to obtain some sort of immutable record of time spent, the QuickBooks Timer doesn't really work that way. The Timer's digital time counter can be changed simply by clicking any activity in the Current Activity drop-down list, choosing Edit Activity, and typing a new number in the Duration window.

USING AN ACTIVITY TEMPLATE

When you stop the clock on a Timer activity and begin a new one, that first activity remains available for you to make current and begin timing it again at any time, until you export it. However, the activity is also stored down below, near the bottom of the Current Activity list (see Figure 25.12). It is saved as an Activity Template.

An Activity Template saves everything about the current activity except the hours. It enables you to start from scratch with an activity that is identical to the one you are working on, but with the hours set to zero. Use the Activity Template to begin a new project that is similar to the first one, perhaps changing only one or two items.

Figure 25.12
Activity Templates are found at the bottom of the Current Activities list.

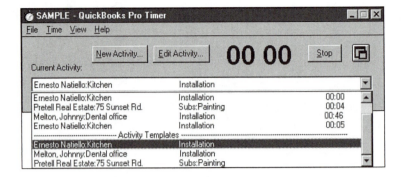

Exporting Timer Data To QuickBooks

When you export Timer data, create a new file by typing a name for it. Take care to note the folder in which you save that file so that you can retrieve it quickly, when you are inside QuickBooks.

To simply export all timed activities, select Export Time Activities from the File menu, and then follow these steps to export Timer data to QuickBooks:

1. Click past the confirmation boxes; the Create Export File dialog box appears (see Figure 25.13).

Figure 25.13
When the Timer exports data, it creates an .IIF file.

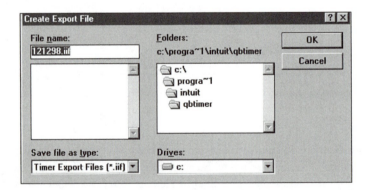

2. Make a note of the folder into which you are saving your file because after you open QuickBooks, you're going to have to locate this file again.
3. Type a name into the File name field, rather than choose an existing one. Make sure you use the .IIF file extension.
4. Click OK. You see a confirmation that your file has been converted. The data is now available to be imported into QuickBooks.

How is this data retrieved in QuickBooks, and how is it used? It's time to move on to the next section.

Opening Timer Data in QuickBooks

QuickBooks imports Timer data into payroll, the Enter Single Activity feature, the timesheet, and related reports. Here's how to import the data and verify that it's where you want it to be.

When you created the .IIF file in the Timer, you made Timer data available for QuickBooks to import, but QuickBooks must still import the file itself before it can be used.

Follow these steps to import and verify data from the QuickBooks Timer:

1. With QuickBooks open, choose Timer Activities from the File menu, and click Import Activities from Timer.
2. Click past the confirmation screen; an Import menu appears (see Figure 25.14). Chose the .IIF file that you exported from your Timer, and click Open.

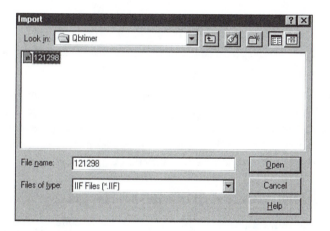

Figure 25.14
The Timer exports .IIF files, which QuickBooks can understand.

3. You hear a reassuring clang of the cash register, one for each activity that your faithful employees carried out, and see the QuickBooks Pro Timer Import Summary dialog box, as shown in Figure 25.15. The dialog box confirms the number of activities that were imported.
4. To learn more about your data, click View Report; the Timer Import Detail report appears, as shown in Figure 25.16.

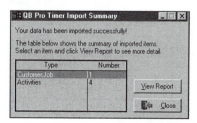

Figure 25.15

Figure 25.16
Immediately after importing Timer data, you can view a report on that data.

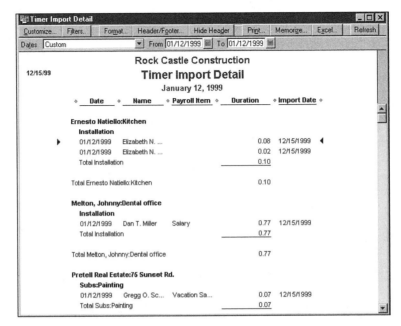

5. Each line of the report represents an activity that was carried out by an employee or vendor. Double-click one, and the same activity appears in the Enter Single Activity window (see Figure 25.17). You see all the fields filled in, except Payroll Item. Use the Prev or Next arrow to view other activities carried out by this employee, or click the Name drop-down menu to view work done by a different employee or vendor.

Figure 25.17
Timer data activities import directly as QuickBooks single activities.

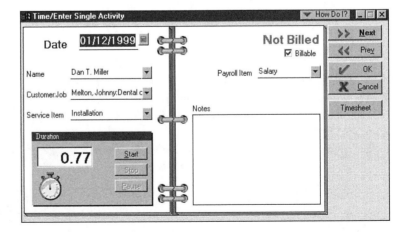

Tip #74 from

> The first time a Timer activity is imported and appears in the Enter Single Activity window, you are prompted to associate that activity with a payroll item. That's because when your employee set up the Timer and carried out the tasks, she did not have access to payroll item data. The Timer does not deal with salary, wages, hourly rate, overtime rate, and so on. You have to add that here, after you import the Timer data back into QuickBooks.

6. After you've viewed this line of the Timer data in the Enter Single Activity window, click the Timesheet button; you see a whole week's worth of that employee's work displayed on the timesheet (see Figure 25.18), including the data you just imported from the Timer.

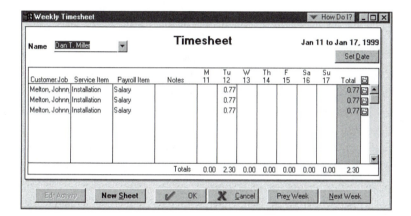

Figure 25.18
Data from the Timer is also available for the timesheet.

7. To see how the Timer data affected payroll, select Create Paychecks from the Payroll and Time tab of the Navigator. The Select Employees to be Paid dialog box appears. All the hours reported by the Timer for each employee are included in the list.

8. If the jobs carried out on the Timer were done by subcontractors (vendors), select Pay Bills from the QuickBooks Activities menu, and you see all the time reported by the Timer on behalf of each vendor.

CREATING INSTALL DISKS FOR THE TIMER

A huge question remains: How do you get the QuickBooks Timer to someone else's computer? Do you loan them your QuickBooks CD? That can be a bit cumbersome, especially when there are multiple users. Here's the solution: The QuickBooks Timer includes a program for creating *install disks* that you can distribute to the Timer users in your company. You can create one set of disks and pass them around—or you can create as many sets as you want.

Follow these steps to run the Timer Install disk program:

1. Prepare three blank high-density floppy disks by labeling them Disk 1, Disk 2, and Disk 3.
2. Put Disk 1 into your floppy disk drive.
3. Make sure that the QuickBooks CD-ROM is in your CD-ROM drive. Click My Computer, and right-click on the QuickBooks CDRom icon. Select Open, and locate the folder QB_tc.
4. Inside the QB_tc folder, click the Create icon, and follow the onscreen instructions.
5. Set aside those disks and give them to your employees or to vendors who need to use the Timer.

Getting Your Employees Up to Speed With the Timer

Installing the Timer onto a computer from floppies is not a big chore: Simply have your employees put Disk 1 into their floppy drive and follow the onscreen directions. You can help them get started with the Timer, however, by explaining to them the points that were outlined in the section "Learning Your Way Around the Timer." Specifically, keep the following points in mind:

- Remember that you are providing them with data from QuickBooks, the Customers:Jobs list that they need to import before they can start time tracking. Point out that this data is in the form of an .IIF file, and direct them to install it in the same directory (or folder) as the QuickBooks Timer. The default Timer folder is C:\QBTIMER.
- Tell them that first they have to name and create a QuickBooks Timer file, just as soon as they start the program, before they do anything else.
- After the file is created, they have to import the .IIF file, as was previously pointed out. They can then start activities.
- Acquaint them with the drop-down menu system of setting up their own name, customer, and job before actually clicking the Start button to begin time tracking.
- After they've worked through all this, your employees and vendors might come to appreciate the convenience of using the QuickBooks Timer.

Backed Up and Condensed Timer Data

To facilitate faster transport and to diminish transmission problems, the QuickBooks Timer enables you to condense and back up your data in one step. When you condense Timer data, the program automatically creates a backup of your file as well. After condensing a QuickBooks Timer file, it takes up less room on a floppy disk.

Condensing and Backing Up Timer Data

This section discusses how to condense and back up Timer data. If you simply want to make a backup of Timer data, select Back Up Timer File from the File menu, and you are prompted to provide a filename for your backed up data. Following are three points to remember about backed up Timer files:

- After performing a backup, your original Timer data is untouched.
- Timer backup files have a .BDB file extension, whereas Timer files are .TDB
- Backed up Timer files must be restored with the Timer's Restore feature before they can be used.

Follow these steps to condense QuickBooks Timer data:

1. With the Timer open, select Condense Timer File from the File menu (see Figure 25.19).

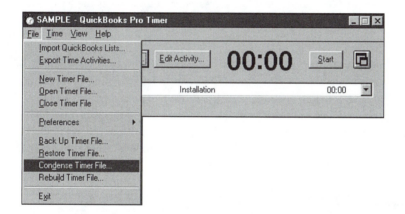

Figure 25.19
Condensing a file does not affect its usability.

2. You are informed that the Timer performs a backup as well. Click OK.
3. The name of the backup file is selected for you. It is the same as your Timer file, except the file extension is .BDB, rather than .TDB. Click OK to confirm.
4. You receive no more messages. Your original QuickBooks Timer file is now condensed and has not been renamed. You also now have a new backup file, as explained in step 3.
5. As a result, your condensed file takes up a bit less room and is as usable as ever. There is no notable performance degradation.

Tip #75 from
Gail Perry

Because any type of file compression can potentially lead to problems, make sure that you really need to condense your file before doing so. For example, if your Timer data is far less than the capacity of a floppy disk, there's really no need to condense it. However, if the Timer file is getting up around 900K or so, condensing is a good idea because floppies do fail; the more data you put on them, the more apt they are to fail.

Restoring Backed Up Timer Data

When you restore Timer data, you are asked to create a new file to restore to. That means you'll end up with a new Timer data file on your hard drive at the end of the process. The program does not allow you to overwrite the old one. This is kind of nice from the viewpoint of protecting your data, but you can end up with "file clutter" if you carry out this process more than once or twice.

Follow these steps to restore Timer data:

1. From the File menu, select Restore Timer File.
2. You are prompted to select which file to restore from. Select it from the list provided.
3. You are then asked to type a name for your new Timer file. This is a bit confusing because the directions say "Select A file to Restore TO." Well, you are not really selecting an existing file, you're creating a new one. So just type a name.
4. After a moment, your New Timer data file is created, and it becomes the currently open Timer file.

Viewing and Editing Timer Data in Detail

To view a list of all Timer activities, even ones that have been exported, select Time Activity Log from the View menu. Click the Date drop-down menu at the upper left to select a date range. You'll see a list as shown in Figure 25.20. What can you view here that you can't view just by clicking the Current Activities list on the Timer? Following are some special features of this list:

Figure 25.20
You have more control over managing activities in the Time Activity Log.

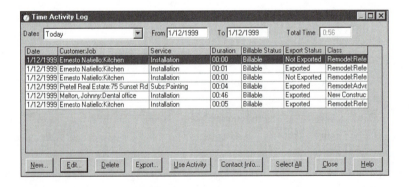

- You can see whether an activity has been exported yet.
- You can choose a date range for this list. If you want to see all the activities you did a week ago, or over a span of two or three days, use the Dates, From and To windows to create a custom date range for viewing activities.
- Double-click any activity in the list to edit it.

- To turn any activity into a template, click it once and select Use Activity.
- View any customer's contact info by clicking the Contact Info button at the bottom of the screen. (Contact info must have been provided from QuickBooks—you cannot add customer contact info in the Timer program.)
- Use the Control key and the mouse to select any combination of activities you want, and then use the Export button to export only those you selected.

TROUBLESHOOTING

THE JOB LIST

My employee tried to use the Timer, but the job on which he was working was not among the choices in his Timer program. What does he need to do?

If the job list is not complete in the employee's version of the Timer file, you have probably added jobs since you exported the job list for your employee's Timer. See the section "Exporting a List for the Timer" in this chapter for instructions on getting the current job information to your employee's Timer program.

THE SERVICE ITEM LIST

Having the employee's time is great, but how can I keep track of what kind of work the employee performed?

Your employee needs to choose a service item when entering his time. There is a service item drop-down menu in the Timer from which he can make his choice. In addition, you can recommend that your employees enter information in the memo area of the Timer. In this area, he can provide explicit details about the work he is performing.

CHAPTER 26

BUDGETING

In this chapter

What is a Budget?   464

Creating a Budget   464

The First Year of Business   465

Creating Budget Reports   467

Few things are as important—and as overlooked—as budgeting. Many businesses either don't take the time to make a budget or, after they create a budget, they stick it in a file folder and forget to look at it again.

Creating a working budget helps you keep an eye on the performance of your business and its relationship to your expectations. Using a budget helps you plan for the future, not just do business today.

QuickBooks provides you with everything you need to create a budget. It's up to you to take advantage of this powerful tool and to make it work for you.

What is a Budget?

A *budget* is a financial plan. It looks similar to a financial statement—just like the ones you produce for your company—but the numbers on the budget are based on goals, past performance, and consideration of future trends, rather than the actual transactions that make up your standard financial statements.

Often, you use the income and expense numbers of the prior year as the starting point for a budget. Then you must consider your knowledge of the future expectations and anticipated trends of your industry and adjust the budget numbers to embrace those trends. In addition, you'll want to throw in a dose of your personal experience with the way your business operates and the way you expect it to operate so that you can build a budget that accurately reflects your goals and reasonable expectations for the year or years ahead.

For example, if you are in the new home construction industry and you know that the new factory in town will bring hundreds of new employees, you can probably reasonably expect your business to increase next year. Or, if your landlord has been raising the rent on other buildings he owns and your lease is due for renewal, you can safely expect your rent expense to increase in the near future.

Creating a Budget

The QuickBooks budgeting feature enables you to set up a budget amount for each income and expense account in your chart of accounts.

Traditionally, a budget is created for an entire year at a time, with amounts shown for each month of the year. The monthly amounts are often the same, using an average of annual amounts from the prior year as a starting point.

You enter the monthly amount that you expect to earn or spend in the next year, and QuickBooks automatically extends that amount to each month of the coming year. You can then revise individual budgeted amounts.

Alternatively, you can enter different amounts for each month of the budgeted year, or you can enter an initial monthly amount and ask QuickBooks to increase or decrease that amount by a particular percentage each month.

Before you begin the budget process in QuickBooks, print a copy of your prior year's (or several prior years') Profit and Loss Statement. This statement can be a guide for you as you create the budget. You might also want to schedule a session with other members of your company to discuss plans and expectations for the future and to rough out a budget on paper before committing it to QuickBooks.

THE FIRST YEAR OF BUSINESS

Sometimes it's difficult to know where to begin in creating a budget when you have no prior experience on which to draw. That doesn't preclude you from creating a budget, however. Some suggestions for resources when trying to project your first year of business follow:

- Contact financial advisors in the community who work with businesses of your type—accountants and bankers, for example—who might have some insight into what you can expect your first year.

- Try to meet with other members of your profession, either through professional societies, local business clubs, or direct contact with owners of similar companies, and explain that you are looking for guidance and helpful hints about determining the financial expectations of a company such as yours.

- Use the library and the Internet to research your field. You can probably locate an Internet group of people who are in the same field as you, and who can lend advice and insight.

- Draw on your own understanding of the industry or profession. Your company might be new, but you have knowledge of the business. Sometimes a gut feeling based on experience and wisdom provides the best guidance.

Use the following steps to create a budget in QuickBooks:

1. Choose Activities, Set Up Budgets. The Set Up Budgets window appears (see Figure 26.1).

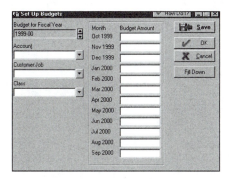

Figure 26.1
Create a budget in this window by choosing the individual accounts, and then designating budgeted amounts for the coming year.

2. Determine the year for which you want to set up a budget. By default, QuickBooks assumes that you want to create a budget for the next fiscal year. You can choose a year beyond the next fiscal year, or, to view budgets that you have created in the past, you can choose a previous year; the prior budget information appears.

3. Choose the account for which you want to enter a budgeted amount. Budgeting in QuickBooks is an account-by-account task. The drop-down arrow in the Account field provides you with a complete list of your entire chart of accounts. Typically, you will choose to budget for income and expense accounts only.

4. If applicable, choose either a Customer:Job or a Class for this budgeted amount.

5. QuickBooks automatically fills in budget amounts based on an average of your prior year's activity, rounded to the nearest $100. You can accept these amounts and go on to the next account or you can enter your own budgeted amounts in each monthly block.

6. To enter your own budgeted amounts, in the first block of the Budget Amount column enter the amount that you want to budget for the account that you have selected.

7. To copy this amount down through the rest of the monthly blocks, click the Fill Down button. After you click this button, QuickBooks asks you to specify a percentage or an amount by which you want this amount to increase each month throughout the budgeted year (see Figure 26.2). You can enter 0, which provides you with the same budgeted amount for each month of the year, or you can enter a positive or negative number to cause QuickBooks to increase or decrease the number on a monthly basis. If my monthly budgeted amount for a particular account is $1,000, for example, and I enter a 4 percent increase, the budget shows $1,000 for the first month, $1,040 for the second month, $1,081.60 for the third month, $1,124.86 for the fourth month, and so on.

8. Repeat steps 3–7 for each account in your budget.

9. After you have finished entering all your budget information, be sure to click the Save button. Your budget is not saved if you don't click this button!

10. Click OK to close the budget window.

Figure 26.2

You can go back to the budget at any time and revise budget amounts. Choose Activities, Set Up Budgets to access your budget and make revisions.

Tip #76 from

> Although it is important to revise budgets when changes occur in the economic climate or when unexpected situations that affect your plans occur, it is just as important to keep your budget intact as much as possible. One of the main reasons to have a budget is to compare budgeted performance with actual performance so that you can better understand the areas of your business that are not performing as planned.

CREATING BUDGET REPORTS

You can choose from several budget reports. You can view the actual budget, see a comparison between the budget and actual performance, prepare budget reports based on your various jobs, or create a budget report for balance sheet accounts.

THE BUDGET OVERVIEW REPORT

Take a look at your finished budget by preparing a Budget Overview report. This report, presented in the form of a profit and loss statement, shows all amounts budgeted for all accounts, with one column for each month of the year.

Print a copy of this handy report at the beginning of the year and keep it close, using it as a reference as you plan your expenditures and record your income.

Follow these steps to prepare the Budget Overview report:

1. Choose Reports, Budget Reports. The Budget side menu appears.
2. Choose Overview. The Budget Overview report appears.
3. Change the Dates if you want to display a report for a time period other than the current fiscal year (the default report).
4. Choose how you want the Columns displayed on the report. By default the report appears with one column for each month. If you prefer to have quarterly, weekly, or some other calculation of budgeted amounts, click the Columns indicator and choose from the drop-down list.

THE BUDGET VERSUS ACTUAL REPORT

After you have created a budget and have begun entering transactions for the period covered by the budget, you can produce a report that shows how you are performing in comparison with your plans. The Budget vs. Actual report displays all your income and expense accounts for a selected time period and shows you the following:

- The actual total of transactions in those accounts
- The budgeted amount for the same time period
- The dollar amount over or under budget
- The percent over or under budget

Figure 26.3 shows a sample of the Budget vs. Actual report.

Figure 26.3
The Budget vs. Actual report shows you how your company is performing compared to the budget expectations.

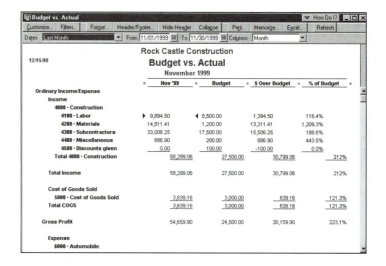

Use the following steps to create a Budget vs. Actual report:

1. Choose Reports, Budget Reports. The Budget side menu appears.
2. Choose Budget vs. Actual. The report appears.
3. Select dates to indicate the time period for which you want to display this report. By default, the report shows each month of your current year, with four columns for each month, as described in the preceding bulleted points. If the dates that you choose include a partial month (such as the current month to date), QuickBooks prorates the monthly budget amounts for the number of days in the month.
4. Alternatively, you can choose a different method (other than monthly) for reporting your budget by clicking the Columns drop-down list and selecting a budget; for example, by Quarter, by Customer:Job, or by Class.

Note that you can also select customizing and filtering options to deviate from the standard report format. You learned about these options in Chapter 21, "QuickBooks Reports and Graphs."

THE BUDGET BY JOB OVERVIEW REPORT

If you track income and expenses by jobs, and you have prepared a budget based on anticipated job activity, the Budget by Job reports can be useful to you. The Budget by Job Overview report displays all budgeted amounts in a profit and loss statement format, with one column for each job.

To prepare the Budget by Job Overview report, follow these steps:

1. Choose Reports, Budget Reports. The Budget side menu appears.
2. Choose By Job Overview. The report appears.

3. Change the Dates if you want to display a report for a time period other than the current fiscal year (the default report).

4. If you prefer to see this report broken out by a particular time period instead of by job, click the Columns button and choose from weekly, monthly, quarterly, and several other time periods. You can also choose to display this report by Class, if you use class tracking.

The Budget by Job Comparison Report

The Budget by Job Comparison report compares actual job performance to budgeted amounts. Each job occupies four columns: the actual activity, the budgeted amount, the amount over or under budget, and the percentage over or under budget.

Here's how to prepare the Budget by Job Comparison report:

1. Choose Reports, Budget Reports. The Budget side menu appears.

2. Choose By Job Comparison. The report appears.

3. Change the Dates if you want to display a report for a time period other than the current fiscal year (the default report).

4. If you prefer to see this report broken out by a particular time period instead of by job, click the Columns button and choose from weekly, monthly, quarterly, and several other time periods. You can also choose to display this report by Class, if you use class tracking.

The Budget Balance Sheet Overview Report

Many companies only budget for income and expense items, rather than for balance sheet items, thinking that they only have control over these revenue-producing accounts. A balance sheet budget can be particularly useful if you plan major asset or liability changes during the year, such as equipment purchases or large loans. Remember, it is your balance sheet that tells you how much your company is worth. Budgeting for changes in assets and liabilities will ultimately tell you how the expected value of your company will change.

The Balance Sheet Overview report shows the amounts that have been budgeted for balance sheet accounts. Follow these steps to prepare it:

1. Choose Reports, Budget Reports. The Budget side menu appears.

2. Choose Balance Sheet Overview. The report appears.

3. Change the Dates if you want to display a report for a time period other than the current fiscal year (the default report).

4. The report shows budgeted amounts by month. If you prefer to view budgeted amounts by some other time period (such as weekly or quarterly), click the Columns button and select a different time period.

The Budget Balance Sheet Comparison Report

The Balance Sheet Overview report shows the actual balance sheet amounts for each month of the current year, the amounts that have been budgeted for balance sheet accounts, the amount over or under budget, and the percentage over or under budget. Follow these steps to produce the Balance Sheet Overview report:

1. Choose Reports, Budget Reports. The Budget side menu appears.
2. Choose Balance Sheet Comparison. The report appears.
3. Change the Dates if you want to display a report for a time period other than the current fiscal year (the default report).
4. The report shows budgeted amounts by month. If you prefer to view budgeted amounts by some other time period (such as weekly or quarterly), click the Columns button and select a different time period.

Troubleshooting

Earnings versus Budget

My company earned more than I budgeted for last month. Do I change the budget to reflect the additional earnings?

You don't have to change the budget every time there is a difference between the budgeted amounts and the real life amounts. The budget, in fact, provides you with an opportunity to see how you thought the company would perform and to compare that with how it actually performed. If you change the budget, you lose the opportunity to note the difference between the two. On the other hand, if you think the net increase in revenue marks the beginning of a trend, you might want to consider revising your budgeted revenue for future months, so that you can better plan how the rest of the year will proceed economically.

CHAPTER 27

Forecasting Your Financial Future with QuickBooks

In this chapter

Understanding the Types of Forecasting   472

Utilizing a Sales Forecast   472

Preparing Forecasts   475

No successful business operates in the dark. You never want to get into a position where your company's available cash is not adequate to meet required expenditures.

In order to grow, there must be plans for the future, and expectations of how those plans will be implemented. Forecasting techniques enable you to meet your short-term needs as well as to prepare for the future.

You can use QuickBooks to help you prepare financial forecasts and thus project your business profitability into the years ahead.

Understanding the Types of Forecasting

There are several areas of your business in which forecasting can be useful. Try to envision how knowledge of the future can help you plan for the years ahead as you read through this list:

- **Sales Forecast**—Project future sales for your company, taking into consideration inflation, competition, and the economy as a whole.
- **Cash Receipts Forecast**—An offshoot of the Sales Forecast, this forecast includes expected receipts from all sources.
- **Cash Outflow for Inventory Forecast**—How much inventory do you need to supply the sales that you predict in your sales forecast, and what will it cost?
- **Cash Outflow Forecast**—Starting with the Cash Outflow for Inventory forecast, Cash Flow Forecast projects all other anticipated outflows.
- **Cash Flow Forecast**—Both as a monthly report and a glimpse into the long-range future, predicting your cash flow is a must for determining your ability to meet your business's obligations.

The Cash Flow Forecast is a standard report in QuickBooks. The others are not. The following sections describe how you can create the various forecasting reports, so you can look to the future with some expectation of what to expect from your business.

Utilizing a Sales Forecast

A forecast of your company's sales provides you with a sense of what kind of revenue can be expected in the future. By predicting revenue, you can then determine several important factors, including

- The quantity of inventory you need to meet the revenue demands
- The excess of revenue over cost of inventory to meet other expenses
- The availability of excess revenue to fund future expansion
- The need for additional sources of revenue

Preparing a Sales Forecast

To prepare a sales forecast, start with your current sales. In addition, you want to look at some other past activity. The farther into the future you want to predict, the deeper into the past you want to explore.

For example, if you are trying to forecast sales for next month, you want to examine last month's sales as well as last year's sales for the same time period.

Follow these steps to prepare a sales report:

1. Choose Reports, Custom Report. The Customize Report window appears (see Figure 27.1).

Select a date here.

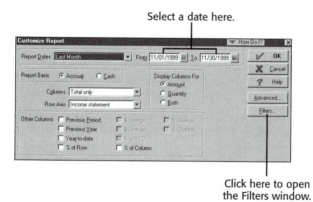

Figure 27.1
Change the Report Dates to reflect the month for which you want to display income figures.

Click here to open the Filters window.

2. Change the Report Dates to Last Month. This causes your income report to show the activity for the prior month.
3. Click the Filters button. The Report Filters window appears (see Figure 27.2).

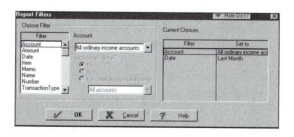

Figure 27.2
Filter out all accounts except for income by choosing Account in the Filter column, and then choosing All ordinary income accounts in the Account field.

4. Set the Account filter to All ordinary income accounts. This causes your report to show only your company's income accounts.
5. Click OK to close each window. The custom report that shows your company's income for last month appears. Change the heading by clicking the Header/Footer button at the top of the report and entering a new Report Title.

Printing a Sales Report

You can print a hard copy of this report by clicking the Print button at the top of the report. Alternatively, you can transfer this report to a spreadsheet or other program by printing the report to a file.

Follow these steps to print to a file:

1. Click the Print button, or choose File, Print Report. The print window appears.

2. Indicate that you want to print to a file by clicking the File option button.

3. Click the drop-down arrow across from File to display your choices: ASCII text file, Excel/Lotus 123 spreadsheet, or Tab delimited file (see Figure 27.3). Make a choice from among these three, depending on the program where you open this file. If you're not certain which to choose, see the accompanying sidebar.

Figure 27.3

4. Click OK to save your report to a file.

You can change the appearance of the report in another program and create a new column for projected income for the future period that you are forecasting for. Open the program in which you want to view the report, and then open the report.

Printing to a File
QuickBooks provides three types of files to which you can print. Use the following descriptions for guidance, but you might find that you need to experiment with your own software to see which choice is best for you:

- **ASCII text file**—Use this type of file if you plan to open your report in a word processing program. Spaces appear between the columns when you open the file, so you might have to work with the appearance to make it look the way you want it to.

- **Excel/Lotus 123 spreadsheet**—Use this type of file if you plan to open your report in a spreadsheet program. When I open this type of file in Excel, I receive a message that this is a delimited file, meaning that a character takes the place of tabs. In this case, the character is a comma. You see a window in which you can indicate the delimiting character; then the program separates the information into columns, breaking it at the delimiting character. In other words, for every comma, a new column starts.

- **Tab delimited file**—This type of file can be opened in either a spreadsheet program or a word processing program. Tab characters appear between the columns of text.

If you want to examine a report of sales for another period (such as last year's sales for the month that you are forecasting), follow the same steps, indicating a time period other than Last Month.

Preparing Forecasts

After you have gathered information from which you can make a forecast, consider the trends of your business, the business environment as a whole, and any economic conditions that might affect your sales; then prepare a forecast of future sales.

Cash Receipts Forecast

A cash receipts forecast is somewhat different from a sales forecast, unless your business operates on a *cash basis*. A cash basis business is one in which all revenue is reported as income only when it is received, and all expenses are reported only when the bills are actually paid. A retail store, where income is recorded as it is received in the cash register, is an example of a cash basis business.

The alternative is an *accrual basis* business, one in which revenue is reported when it is earned and expenses when they are incurred, regardless of the actual dates on which money is received or payments are made. When revenue is earned, an accounts receivable is recorded. The accounts receivable is reduced on the day that cash is actually received, but the income was reported back on the day when it was originally earned. Expenses are recorded when you receive a bill and an accounts payable is recorded. When the bill is actually paid, the accounts payable is reduced, but the expense was reported on the day when the bill was originally received.

Many small businesses operate on a cash basis, simply because it is easier and involves fewer steps. Taxable corporations and many S corporations and partnerships use accrual basis accounting because it is considered a truer representation of a business's financial position.

If yours is a cash basis business, you don't need to read about a cash receipts forecast because your sales forecast accomplishes the same thing. For an accrual basis business, a cash receipts forecast provides a projection of when cash will actually be received.

For example, your business might earn money evenly throughout the year, but perhaps it only sends bills to customers on a quarterly basis. Cash receipts, therefore, tend to bunch up around the months when bills are received by customers, and generally dwindle as the quarter cycle comes to an end.

Creating a cash receipts report in QuickBooks, if yours is an accrual basis business, is a bit tricky—but it can be done. Following is one way to create a cash receipts report. This example is for the prior month, but you can choose any time period that helps with your forecasting.

Create a previous month cash receipts report by following these steps:

1. Choose Reports, Custom Report. The Customize Report window appears.
2. Select Last Month for the Report Dates. This causes your report to show activity only for last month.
3. Select Cash for the report basis.
4. Click the Filters button. The Report Filters window appears.

5. With Account selected as the first filter, click the arrow in the Account field to the right of the filter list, and choose Selected Accounts. A window appears, showing all your company's accounts. Click each bank account (Checking, Payroll, Savings, for example), and a check mark appears next to the account name. Click OK when you have selected all bank accounts.

6. Click Amount in the filter list. In the amount field, which appears to the right of the filter list, indicate that amounts must be greater than zero (see Figure 27.4). This ensures that only deposits to your bank accounts are included in this report.

7. Click OK to close the Report Filters window, and OK to close the Customize Report window. Your custom report appears onscreen.

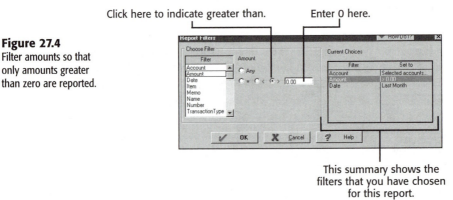

Figure 27.4
Filter amounts so that only amounts greater than zero are reported.

You can choose to print a hard copy of this report, or print it to a file and open it in another program, as discussed in the previous section.

When determining a forecast for future cash receipts, consider factors such as your company's collection pattern for receiving payments from customers, your sales forecast (which you determined earlier), prior payment record of the customers who currently owe you money, time of year, and any other factors that might influence the timing of payments.

You might find it useful to print out a copy of your current accounts receivable report (choose Reports, A/R Reports, Customer Balance Detail)—or any other report that might be helpful—when projecting future cash receipts.

Cash Outflow for Inventory Forecast

If your business is a service business, such as a law firm or a consulting business, you might have only very little or no inventory. The Cash Outflow for Inventory Forecast might be completely inapplicable in helping you determine the future performance of your business.

If, however, you do maintain an inventory, this forecast can be useful to you in helping determine what is probably the single largest expense item of your business.

The best way to determine a forecast for the cost of inventory is to start with the sales forecast that you determined in the section "Cash Receipts Forecast." In order to meet the sales that you have predicted, you need to produce or acquire a corresponding amount of inventory to fulfill those projected sales obligations.

Using your sales figures and cost of inventory figures for prior time periods, express your cost of goods sold as a percentage of your sales. Then use this percentage as a starting point for projecting future inventory costs.

Keep in mind fluctuations in the marketplace for the inventory or parts that you must purchase. Also consider the cost and quantity of goods that you have on hand.

Cash Outflow Forecast

How much does your business spend? How much can you expect your business to spend in the future? Knowing how much you can expect to spend helps you determine whether the projected income and cash receipts will be enough to meet those expenditures. Determining this information early can help you plan and make adjustments, if necessary, in your business performance.

Cash outflow includes payments for all business-related purposes, including cost of inventory (as projected earlier), cost of maintaining the business (utilities, rent, repairs, and so on), payroll, expenditures for loan payments, and tax payments. Also consider anticipated purchases of equipment and other large payments that occur infrequently.

Prepare the QuickBooks report that helps you calculate a Cash Outflow Forecast in exactly the same way that you prepared the report for your Cash Receipts Forecast—with one exception. When filtering the Amount information from your bank account, click the less than button (<)—the second button rather than the third button (see Figure 27.4, where the third button has been selected). Leave the amount at zero.

Changing from greater than zero to less than zero results in a report that displays all cash outlays from your bank account(s) for the selected period, rather than all cash deposits.

From there, you can print the report or open it in another program, and make your Cash Outflow Forecast using these amounts as a starting point.

Cash Flow Forecast

A Cash Flow Forecast puts all the other reports together into one scenario—a prediction of when your business will receive and disburse cash, and what the cash balances will be at certain points in time.

There are many advantages to creating a Cash Flow Forecast, some of which are itemized here:

- The forecast helps predict whether there will be enough cash throughout the projected period to meet the financial needs of the company.
- The forecast helps you determine how much cash will be available, and how much you might need to borrow in order to realize the plans of the company.
- A cash flow forecast that is well thought out and thorough attracts investors because it creates a favorable impression of your management capabilities.

You've already done all the work necessary to produce this report yourself, and if you use the reports that you worked up earlier in this chapter, your report is probably much more accurate than anything QuickBooks can create for you.

However, a Cash Flow Forecast report is included in QuickBooks; it is one of the standard reports on the Report menu. Keep in mind that no thought goes into the preparation of this standard report—it is based solely on the past performance of your company. Therefore, no outside factors, such as the ones you probably considered when making your own reports, are taken into consideration.

It is recommended that you print a copy of the QuickBooks Cash Flow Forecast and analyze it. If your business is steady and totally predictable, this report will probably be a fairly accurate rendition of what you have to expect in the future.

If your business is subject to market trends, changes in the weather, seasonal buying habits, drastic changes in inventory costs, or other variations from any outside sources, this report will be minimally helpful. It might provide you with a steady path to follow, but it won't take into account any obstacles that might fall in your way.

To view and print the Cash Flow Forecast report as produced by QuickBooks, choose Reports, Cash Flow, Forecast. Select any time period for which you want the report to be prepared. By default, the report projects cash flow on a weekly basis (see Figure 27.5). If you prefer to see the cash flow reported on some other basis (daily, monthly, and so on), click the Customize button and change the Reporting Periods to the period that is most useful to you.

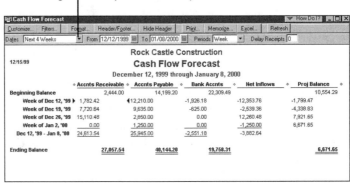

Figure 27.5
The QuickBooks standard Cash Flow Forecast report is an interesting starting point for analyzing the future based on past transactions.

Click the Print button and you can print a hard copy of this report, or choose to print it to a file whereby you can open it in another program as discussed earlier in this chapter.

Troubleshooting

Projected Cash Versus Future Expenses

I've prepared a cash flow forecast, and the resulting information tells me my projected cash won't meet my future expenses. Now what?

Having this knowledge at hand is the first step in solving the problems of your business. You must analyze your business situation to determine if this is a temporary or permanent problem, and then you can consider alternatives for improving your cash flow, decreasing your expenses, or changing the timing of cash inflows and outflows. Some methods for improving cash inflow include borrowing money, stiffening your credit procedures, and raising prices. You can possibly decrease expenses by exploring relationships with other suppliers, changing your manufacturing methods, or cutting back in certain areas. Timing of inflows and outflows can be controlled by offering incentives for customers to pay sooner, and working out longer payment arrangements with your suppliers and lenders. The cash flow forecast itself doesn't solve your business problems, but it can give you advance notice of what you can expect from your business so that you can plan and act to circumvent potential problems.

CHAPTER 28

SECURITY

In this chapter

Backing Up Your Company Files   482

Working With Passwords and User Access   482

Year-End Protection: Closing Your Books   487

You don't need to be reminded about how sensitive and confidential your financial data is. Not only can your company be crippled by the loss of financial information, but much of this information is not intended for the eyes of the casual observer.

You might not want your competition knowing how your business is doing, and you might not want some of your employees to know either. Furthermore, your customers don't need to know the details of your business performance.

This chapter addresses many ways that you can protect your QuickBooks data and make sensitive information available only to those who have a right to see it.

Backing Up Your Company Files

The first issue of security is making backup copies of your QuickBooks data.

→ To find detailed information about backing up data, **see p. 14**.

There is no excuse for not backing up your company QuickBooks file. The amount of work you put into setting up the file alone is work that you don't want to have to repeat, and the quantity of data that you can lose, after you've been using QuickBooks for awhile, can be staggering.

Additionally, after a company begins using QuickBooks to record all its financial transactions, the amount of paper and documents stored can generally be reduced because the company can so easily create reports for any time period using QuickBooks. The potential downside of this trend toward a "paperless office" is that a computer crash or the loss of data on a disk can wipe out months—even years—of work with no easy method of reconstruction.

Working With Passwords and User Access

If more than one person uses the computer on which your company data is stored, you might want to use passwords to prevent unauthorized access to your data, and to restrict the activities that users can perform with your company file.

When you use the passwords feature in QuickBooks, the person who opens QuickBooks is asked to enter a password before the company file ever opens (see Figure 28.1). QuickBooks provides different levels of password protection, so each user of your company file can have access to different areas of the program.

WORKING WITH PASSWORDS AND USER ACCESS | 483

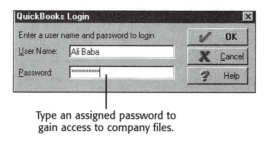

Figure 28.1
"So he called out aloud, 'Open, Sesame!' And no sooner had he spoken than straightaway the portal flew open and he entered within."

Type an assigned password to gain access to company files.

If you choose to activate the password feature in QuickBooks, one person has unlimited access to the entire QuickBooks company file—this person is known to QuickBooks as the administrator. (Technically, however, more than one person can know the password and access the program as the administrator.) The administrator has the right to change how much of the program other users have access to, to import data from other financial software programs, to export data to other software programs, and to change information about the company, such as the name and address or the fiscal year. The administrator is also the only person with access to the EasyStep Interview.

> **Note**
> Using passwords in QuickBooks is entirely optional. If you don't need this level of protection, you can skip this part of the book.

SETTING UP THE ADMINISTRATOR FIRST

After you have set up the administrator, you can establish other users and passwords so that you can control the access that other people have to the file. Only the person designated as the administrator can set up new users and establish how much of the program these users can access.

> **Tip #77 from**
> *Gail Perry*
>
> When deciding what to use as your password, try to think of something that is easy for you to remember—but not so easy that others figure it out—and then remember it! If you've given up all hope of remembering your password, and you are not the administrator, the administrator can assign a new username and rights for you. If you are the administrator, you're out of luck. You can start your company file all over again (ouch!), or call Intuit at 888-320-7276 and they can help you—for a fee. Obviously, the best remedy is to remember your password!

Follow these steps to set up the administrator:

1. Choose <u>F</u>ile, Set up Users and Pass<u>w</u>ords, <u>S</u>et up Users. The Set up QuickBooks Administrator dialog box appears (see Figure 28.2).

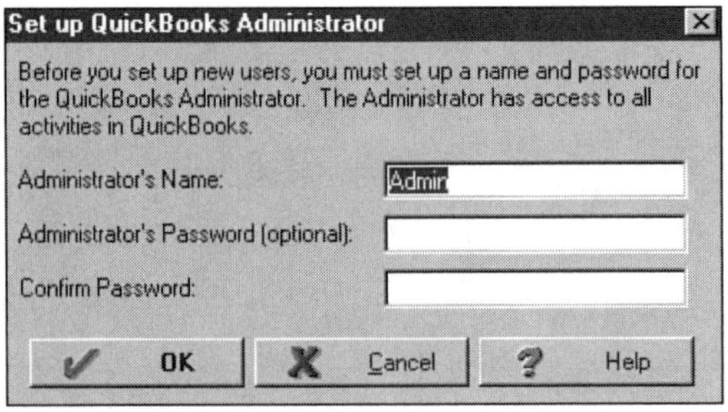

Figure 28.2
Enter the name that you plan to use for the administrator, and then enter the password of your choice on each of the password lines.

2. QuickBooks supplies a suggested name for your administrator—Admin—in the Administrator's Name field. You can use this, or you can enter another name here.

3. Enter the password that you want to use for the administrator. You have the option of not using a password at all (in which case anyone can sign on as the administrator), or you can enter any combination of letters, spaces, and numerals, from 1 to 16 characters. The password is not case sensitive, so it doesn't matter if you type upper- or lowercase.

4. Enter your password again on the Confirm Password line.

5. Click the OK button.

6. A Set Up User List box appears (see Figure 28.3), from which you can choose to change your password, add new users, edit information for existing users, remove users (except the administrator), view the rights issued to any user, and set a closing date. All these options are explained in this chapter. Note that the administrator is the only person with access to this window.

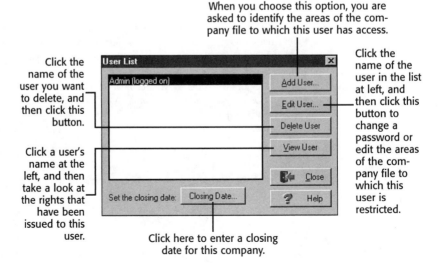

Figure 28.3
The administrator can perform a variety of security tasks from the User List window.

7. Click Close when you have finished with this window.

From now on, each time anyone tries to open your company's QuickBooks file, the person accessing the program is asked to log in by entering the correct Username and Password (as described earlier in this chapter, and as shown in Figure 28.1).

Setting Up Access for Other Users

After your company administrator has been set up, you can begin setting up access for other users of the company QuickBooks file. Part of the setup process includes determining which areas of the company file the users can access—and which areas they are prohibited to access.

Follow these steps to set up a new user:

1. Choose File, Set up Users and Passwords, Set up Users. The User List appears.
2. Click Add User. The Set up user password and access box appears.
3. Enter the username with which this user logs in. See Figure 28.4. The name must be no longer than 29 characters and can include any combination of letters, spaces, and numerals. Case does not matter.

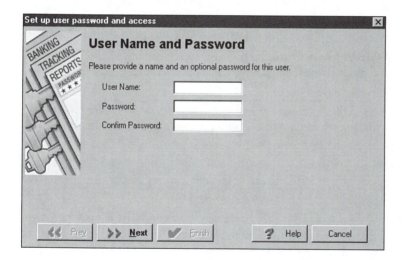

Figure 28.4
Enter the name and password for the new user. The password is optional.

4. Enter a password (optional) for this user. You might want to have the user sit down at the terminal and enter the password, which appears on the screen as asterisks. The password is limited to 16 characters and can include any combination of letters, spaces, and numerals. Case does not matter. Enter the password a second time to confirm.

5. Click Next to proceed to the next screen. You are given the choice of assigning access for this user to All areas of QuickBooks or to Selected areas. All areas of QuickBooks includes all areas except those specifically mentioned previously as being restricted to

just the administrator. Click Next to continue. If you choose All areas, you are asked to confirm your selection.

6. If you choose Selected areas and click Next, you are given a chance to designate the areas to which the user has access. See the following section regarding access to different areas of QuickBooks before making choices on the screens that follow.

Assigning Access to Areas of QuickBooks

When you set up a new user with selected access to QuickBooks, you are given a choice to issue Full, Selective, or No access to the areas of the company's QuickBooks file. For each area, if you choose Selective access, you must then choose either the capability to create transactions only, create and print transactions, or create transactions and print reports. The areas are as follows:

- **Sales and Accounts Receivable**—Provides the right to enter and print information regarding company income, to bill customers, to create and edit customer, job, payment method, and ship via lists, and to customize sales forms. This area also includes the capability to create and print reports regarding sales, accounts receivable, and customers.

- **Purchases and Accounts Payable**—Provides the right to enter and print information regarding company purchase orders, bills, and credit card charges, to enter payment for bills and sales tax, and to customize sales and purchase forms. Also includes the capability to create and print reports regarding purchases, accounts payable, and vendors.

- **Checking and Credit Cards**—Provides the right to write and void checks for expenses, make deposits, edit credit memos, enter credit card charges, and print checks and deposit slips.

- **Inventory**—Provides the right to write and print purchase orders, enter receipts of inventory, adjust inventory totals, edit items on inventory list, enter bills, and create and print inventory, purchase, and vendor reports.

- **Time Tracking**—If your company uses time tracking in QuickBooks Pro, this provides the right to prepare and print timesheets, enter time, import and export data to the Timer program, and create and print timesheets and time reports.

- **Payroll**—Provides the right to write and print paychecks and payroll tax forms, pay payroll taxes, enter year-to-date payroll amounts for employees, edit the employee and payroll lists, create and print payroll reports.

- **Sensitive Accounting Areas**—Provides the right to use online banking, edit the chart of accounts, enter transactions in the register of any asset, liability, or equity account, reconcile accounts, create budgets, make general journal entries, use the Accountant's Review, and print registers.

- **Sensitive Financial Reporting**—Provides the right to create and print reports and graphs for all areas of QuickBooks except inventory and payroll.

- **Changing or Deleting Transactions**—Provides the right to edit and delete transactions in any areas in which the user has rights, as previously described. Includes a special provision to enable the user to edit or delete transactions prior to the closing date.

After choosing the areas of access, you see a screen similar to the one shown in Figure 28.5. Click Pre_v_ to go back to any screen and make a change. Click _F_inish to accept your entries and close the window. Your new user is added to the User List. Click _C_lose to close the User List box.

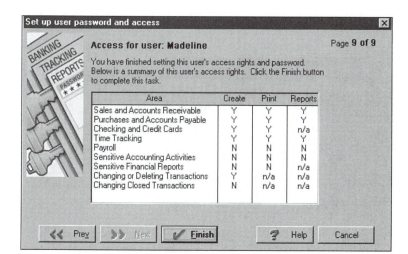

Figure 28.5
Look over this screen to make sure that you have assigned rights to all the appropriate areas for this user. Click Pre_v_ if you need to go to a previous screen to make changes.

Tip #78 from *Gail Perry*

Protecting sensitive company information doesn't end with employee passwords. Customers can be nosy too. If your computer sits on a counter in your place of business, consider acquiring a glare screen that keeps everyone but the person directly in front of the monitor from seeing what is being displayed.

YEAR-END PROTECTION: CLOSING YOUR BOOKS

With many accounting programs, you are required to "close the books" as of the last day of each year. After this closing process has been completed, there can be no changes made to transactions prior to the date of closing.

This is not the case with QuickBooks. The transactions in your QuickBooks file go on and on and can be changed even years after they occurred. Accountants cringe at the idea of their clients having the capability to go back to the prior year and change the numbers after the year has closed. For better or worse, it can be done, unless you protect the prior year.

The administrator always has the right to go back to a prior year and change something. No other users have that right unless it is assigned.

488 | CHAPTER 28 SECURITY

Any user who has been given full access to the company files has the right to go back to a prior year and change information.

Follow these steps to prevent a user from changing prior year information:

1. Set a closing date by going to the User List.
2. Click the Closing Date button.
3. Enter a date.
4. Edit a user's profile (click the username, and then click <u>E</u>dit User) and choose the user's post-year-end access to company records on the Changing and Deleting Transactions screen (see Figure 28.6).

Figure 28.6
Click Next to get through each of the Change user password and access screens until you reach this one. Then choose Yes or No in the bottom half of the screen to enable or prevent user access to last year's company records.

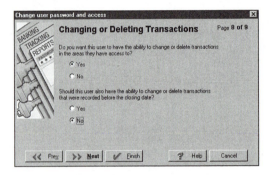

TROUBLESHOOTING

CHANGING COMPANY RECORDS

Is there a way to prevent the person with administrative security clearance from going back to a prior year and changing the company records?

The administrator always has complete rights to change the information stored in the company file. If this is a problem, you can consider assigning the administrative rights to your outside accountant rather than to someone who works at your company. You can also keep separate QuickBooks files for each year, and not make the prior year file available to the administrator. The downside of this procedure, of course, is that it is more difficult (although not impossible) to prepare comparative statements. You can pull information from each year of QuickBooks records into a spreadsheet program, and create your comparative statements there instead of within QuickBooks.

TECHNICAL SUPPORT

QuickBooks is unable to open my company file. My backup doesn't include the latest information. Do I have to go back to the backup and re-enter everything that has occurred since I last backed up?

Before making extra work for yourself, contact Intuit at 888-320-7276. The technical support representatives can possibly help you access your data without your having to restore from your old backup.

CHAPTER **29**

Income Taxes

In this chapter

Preparing Quarterly Estimated Taxes   490

Assigning Tax Lines   491

Tax Reports   492

Tax Forms   495

Tax Software Programs   496

Non–Tax-Related Transactions   497

Hiring a Pro   498

As a user of QuickBooks, you will find that your income tax return preparation time is shortened considerably and made substantially easier. Although QuickBooks doesn't actually prepare income returns for you, you can prepare tax reports that give you all the information that you need to prepare the tax returns yourself.

In addition, QuickBooks communicates with TurboTax, Intuit's tax software program, so if you are a TurboTax user, you can export your QuickBooks company file to TurboTax and create a tax return right on your computer screen (see "Tax Software Programs" later in the chapter for instructions on how to communicate with TurboTax).

Preparing Quarterly Estimated Taxes

If your business is a taxable corporation, or if you are the owner of the business and the business income is reported on your personal income tax return, you have a responsibility to estimate and pay quarterly income taxes.

The IRS requires quarterly payments as an alternative to withholding. Penalties are imposed if quarterly tax obligations are not met, so don't discount the importance of these payments, thinking you can catch up at the end of the year. Your company might also be liable for state and local taxes, so check the rules of your state to determine due dates for quarterly payments.

The dates that quarterly payments are due and the rules for calculating those payments vary, depending on whether your business is a corporation or you are paying taxes individually.

Estimated Payments for Corporations

If your business is a taxable corporation (as opposed to an S corporation that passes its income through to its shareholders), the business itself is required to make quarterly payments if its income tax for the year is expected to exceed $500.

→ To find a description of various types of corporate and business structures, **see p. 111.**

Each quarterly payment needs to equal at least 25 percent of the lesser of 100 percent of the estimated income tax for the current year, or of 100 percent of the tax shown on the corporation's tax return for the preceding year (unless no tax return was filed in the preceding year, or if that tax return was for fewer than 12 months).

Use form 8109, available from the IRS, to make payments on or before the following dates:

First Quarter	April 15
Second Quarter	June 15
Third Quarter	September 15
Fourth Quarter	December 15

If the 15th of the month in which a tax payment is due falls on a Saturday, Sunday, or federal holiday, the tax payment is due on the next business day.

Estimated Payments for Individuals

Individuals are required to make quarterly estimated payments when the income tax they expect to owe for the year (after any withholding) exceeds $1,000.

Each quarterly payment needs to equal at least 90 percent of the tax for the current year or 100 percent of the tax shown on the prior year's tax return (110 percent if the taxpayer's adjusted gross income for the previous year exceeds $150,000).

Use Form 1040-EasyStep Interview (available from the IRS) to make payments on or before the following dates:

First Quarter	April 15
Second Quarter	June 15
Third Quarter	September 15
Fourth Quarter	January 15

If the 15th of the month in which a tax payment is due falls on a Saturday, Sunday, or federal holiday, the tax payment is due on the next business day.

→ To find information about downloading tax forms directly from the IRS, **see p. 435**.

Assigning Tax Lines

If you plan to use QuickBooks to help create your income tax return, you want to assign tax lines to each of your company's accounts. When you assign tax lines, you enable QuickBooks to print tax reports that summarize how all your company's financial activity needs to appear on your tax return.

→ To find information about setting up new accounts, **see p. 113**.

Assign a tax line to an existing account by following these steps:

1. Choose Lists, Chart of Accounts (or press Ctrl+A). The Chart of Accounts window appears.
2. Click the name of the account to which you want to assign a tax line.
3. Click the Account button, and then click Edit (or press Ctrl+E). The Edit Account window appears.
4. Click the arrow to the right of the Tax Line area (see Figure 29.1). A list of possible tax lines appears. The tax lines that are displayed in this list are a result of the tax return you selected when the business was set up.

Figure 29.1
Choose a tax line from this pop-up list.

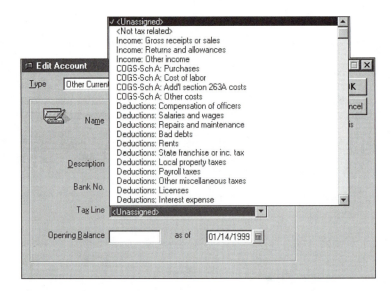

Tip #79 from

You will find that it is extremely helpful if you have a copy of your company's tax return from the prior year by your side while assigning tax lines (or your personal tax return from the prior year, if the income and expenses of this company flow through to your personal tax return). If this is the first year that this company has been in business and there is no tax return from last year to which you can refer, get a blank tax return and use it as a guide.

5. Scroll through the list until you find the tax line that is appropriate for this account, and then click that tax line; the line you have chosen appears in the Tax Line area of the Edit Account screen.
6. Click OK to save the tax line assignment for this account.

TAX REPORTS

Three income tax reports can be produced with QuickBooks: the Income Tax Preparation Report, the Income Tax Summary Report, and the Income Tax Detail Report. Each of these reports provides you with a different type of information that can be useful in the preparation of your tax return.

INCOME TAX PREPARATION REPORT

The income tax preparation report lists every account and the tax line to which it has been assigned.

If you need to know if and where your company's accounts have been assigned to tax lines, view or print this report; you can see at a glance the tax line location of every account, rather than looking up each account individually.

To view the Income Tax Preparation Report, choose Reports from the menu bar at the top of the screen, and then choose List Reports, Accounts, Income Tax Preparation. The Income Tax Preparation Report appears (see Figure 29.2).

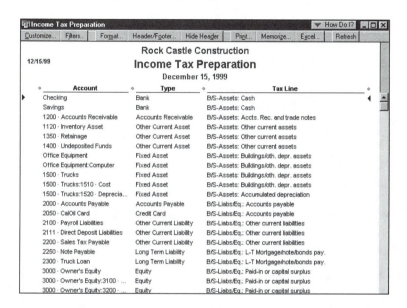

Figure 29.2
Each of your company's accounts is listed at the left, and the tax line (if one has been assigned) appears at the right.

You can print this report by clicking the Print button at the top of the report.

INCOME TAX SUMMARY REPORT

Use the Income Tax Summary Report to gain an overview of your company's taxable income at any point in time. This report is excellent to use as a planning tool for preparing quarterly estimated payments.

All the income and expense accounts that have been assigned to tax lines are summarized on this short report. The net income—the amount on which you pay income tax—is shown at the bottom of the report on a somewhat vaguely-described line: Tax Line Unassigned (balance sheet).

To prepare an Income Tax Summary report, choose Reports, Other Reports, Income Tax Summary. The report appears onscreen (see Figure 29.3), and you can click the Print button at the top of the report if you need a hard copy of this report.

Figure 29.3
Double-click any number on this report to see the details of the transactions that add up to the summary number.

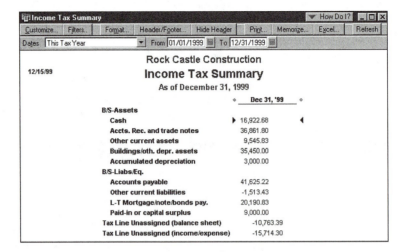

To see the details of the transactions and subaccounts that make up any of the amounts on this report, double click the amount for which you want details. A report showing all the transactions that make up the number that you clicked appears.

The dates at the top of the report indicate the time period being covered by this report. If you are interested in an income tax summary for a particular time period (the first three months of the year, for example), change the dates, and then click the Refresh button to rewrite the report to the new dates.

> **Note**
> Don't forget to click the Refresh button whenever you make a change in the dates of a report. Otherwise, the dates at the top change, but the numbers on the report do not!

You can close this report by clicking the *X* button in the upper-right corner of the report window.

INCOME TAX DETAIL REPORT

The largest and most thorough of all the tax reports, the Income Tax Detail Report, gives you comprehensive details of all the transactions for the selected time period, listed in order of tax lines.

Always print a copy of the Income Tax Detail report before preparing an annual income tax return. Prepare to set aside some time to analyze this report, considering all the transactions for the year and where they fall in your tax return.

To create the Income Tax Detail Report, choose Reports, Other Reports, Income Tax Detail. Print a copy of the report by clicking the Print button at the top of the window.

With the Income Tax Detail Report onscreen (see Figure 29.4), you can double-click any transaction shown on the report and pull up the original document that created the transaction.

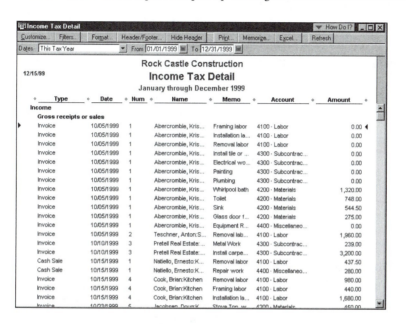

Figure 29.4
Double-click any number on this report and you are transported to the original document (for example, invoice, check, bill) where this transaction was created.

The dates at the top of the report indicate the time period being covered by this report. If you want to see an income tax report for a particular time period (for example, the first six months of the year or last year's report), change the dates, and then click the Refresh button to rewrite the report to the new dates.

TAX FORMS

Depending on the type of business that was indicated at setup, your company files its annual income tax return on one of a variety of tax forms (such as 1120, 1120S, 1040, and so on). For a complete breakdown of the various types of business income tax returns, see "Choose a Tax Return" in Chapter 4, "Setting Up a Company in QuickBooks."

Tax forms are available from a variety of sources. If your company has filed a tax return in the past, you will probably receive a tax return form in the mail. If you don't, or if you can't find the one you received, here is a checklist of several places where you can seek out tax forms and instructions:

- **The IRS**—This might seem like an obvious place to start, but you'd be surprised at how many people are reluctant to set foot in an IRS office. You can, however, reach the

IRS by phone at 1-800-TAX-FORM, and you can download tax forms from their Web site on the Internet at www.irs.ustreas.gov/prod/forms_pubs/forms.html.

- **Public Library**—Although it is generally a better place to look for individual tax forms rather than business tax forms, the library can be a lifesaver if it's the day before the filing deadline and you still don't have any forms.
- **Post Office**—Post offices are notorious hangouts for tax forms.
- **Law Library**—If you live near a law library, you can probably persuade a friendly librarian to lead you to the tax form books and point you in the direction of a copy machine.
- **CPAs and Lawyers**—They're not just for hiring. If you know a friendly CPA or lawyer, you can probably persuade him or her to bring home a few tax forms for you.

Don't forget to pick up state forms as well. Your state revenue department can supply you with forms, and the preceding sources probably have state forms as well as federal. All states are now making tax forms available over the Internet.

→ To find more information on state tax forms, **see p. 513**.

Tax Software Programs

There are a handful of tax software programs that can greatly simplify the process of preparing your tax return on the market. Intuit, the maker of QuickBooks, is also the maker of TurboTax. One advantage to using TurboTax for tax return preparation is that you can directly import your QuickBooks data into the TurboTax program.

To send information to TurboTax, you must first assign tax lines to every account that will ultimately provide a number for your tax return.

Start your TurboTax program. As soon as the program begins, you are asked if you want to import information from QuickBooks. When you answer positively, you are taken to a screen (see Figure 29.5) on which you can review and revise tax lines by clicking the Change Links button; then click the Import button to perform the transfer of information.

QuickBooks data can be imported into TurboTax, TurboTax for Business, and TurboTax Pro Series; so no matter which version of TurboTax you own, it communicates with QuickBooks.

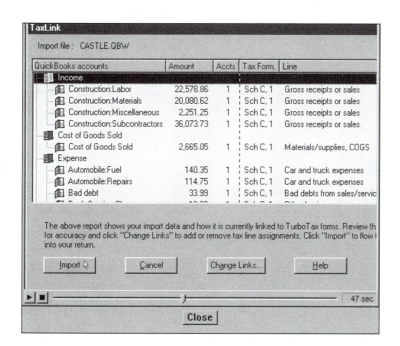

Figure 29.5
The TaxLink screen appears when you begin importing QuickBooks data into TurboTax.

Non–Tax-Related Transactions

From time to time, transactions occur in your business that have no business on your tax return. Following is a checklist of typical business transactions that you do not include as income or deductions on your tax return:

- **Penalties you pay the IRS and state revenue agencies**—If you make a late tax payment, the interest portion is deductible, but the penalty is not.
- **Costs of tickets for traffic violations**—The cost of breaking the law is not deductible.
- **Startup costs of beginning a new business**—The legal fees, corporate filing fees, research costs, market surveys, and other expenses that you incur to help get your business rolling can be amortized over a period of five years, but not deducted all in the first year.
- **Charitable contributions**—Unless you are incorporated, charitable contributions belong on a business-owner's Schedule A with other itemized deductions, even if the business paid the contribution.
- **Lobbying costs**—Even if lobbying results in a direct benefit to your business, the costs are not deductible.
- **Dues to entertainment facilities**—The cost of specific entertainment events can qualify as a business deduction, but the country club dues are not deductible.
- **Appreciation in property**—Assets owned by your company might increase in value over the years, but you are not taxed on that increase (at least not until you sell the assets for a profit).

Hiring a Pro

If you are considering hiring a professional to help with your tax return preparation or to advise you on tax issues, be aware of both the benefits and the consequences. This can be a money-saving expenditure, if the professional helps you cut your taxes. It can cost you more in the long run, however, if the professional steers you the wrong way. Following are some points to keep in mind when looking for professional help:

- How long has the professional worked in the tax field?
- What is the education and experience of the professional?
- Will the professional provide you with referrals?
- How much experience has the professional had at representing clients before the IRS?
- Has the professional ever been fined or penalized with respect to tax work he or she has performed?
- Does this professional plan to be in the same line of business five years from now?
- What is the fee and how is it determined?
- What is the cost to you for representation if your tax return is audited?

Troubleshooting

Quarterly Income Taxes

My company owes quarterly income taxes but there's no extra money in the till. Can't we just wait and pay up at the end of the year?

The payment of quarterly income taxes is a legal liability, not an option. You must plan ahead and prepare for timely income tax payments. If you do miss a payment, make the payment as soon after the due date as possible. A late payment is subject to a penalty and interest, but the interest stops accumulating as soon as the payment is made.

Assigning Tax Lines

Is there a quick way to assign tax lines to all my accounts?

Here's one shortcut: Open an Account Listing report (press Ctrl+A to open the Chart of Accounts List, and then click the Reports button in the Chart of Accounts List window and choose Account Listing). The right-most column on this report is for tax lines. Double-click on the name of any account in need of a tax line assignment; the Edit Account window opens for that account. Enter your tax line assignment and click OK. Repeat this process for each account that is in need of a tax line.

PART VII

APPENDIXES

A Installation of QuickBooks 501

B Sharing QuickBooks on a Network 505

C Transferring Data Between QuickBooks and Other Applications 507

D State Revenue Agencies 513

Glossary 521

APPENDIX A

INSTALLATION OF QUICKBOOKS

You need to install QuickBooks on your hard drive to use the program. This appendix gives you the information you need to perform that installation.

HARDWARE AND SOFTWARE REQUIREMENTS

QuickBooks installs on most computers without any problem. If you have an older machine, however, or if you are concerned that there might be problems with installation, review the requirements listed in the following sections to ensure that you can use this program.

The following hardware items are required for you to properly install QuickBooks version 6.0 and QuickBooks 99:

- **QuickBooks 6.0**—IBM 486/66 (or higher) or compatible computer. Pentium is recommended.

  QuickBooks 99—Same as version 6.0.

- **QuickBooks 6.0**—16MB RAM. 32MB is recommended.

  QuickBooks 99—Same as for version 6.0.

- **Hard Disk Space**—Hard disk with at least 35MB available space for QuickBooks 6.0; 45MB available space for QuickBooks99 and QuickBooks Pro, Version 6.0; 55MB available space for QuickBooks Pro 99. Add an additional 9MB available space if you are installing the QuickBooks Timer.

- **CD-ROM drive**—A CD-ROM drive is necessary. However, you can request disks from Intuit if you don't have a CD-ROM drive.

- **Sound Card**—8-bit or 16-bit sound card if you are using the CD-ROM version and want to use the program's sound features.

- **Monitor**—A monitor capable of displaying at least 256 colors.

Monitor Resolution
You might have to adjust the resolution of your monitor if you find that some QuickBooks screens do not fit on the screen. For example, you might need to change from 640×480 to 800×600. Click the Start button at the bottom of your screen, choose Settings, Control Panel, double-click the Display icon, click on the Settings tab, and adjust the desktop resolution. The less screen area you request, the more space your program takes up on the screen; the more screen area you use, the less onscreen space your program occupies.

- **Printer**—A printer, if you plan to print reports, forms, lists, or mailing labels.

Obviously, you must own a copy of QuickBooks or QuickBooks Pro. In addition, you need to have Windows 95 or higher, or Windows NT 4.0 or higher with Service Pack 3.

Performing the Installation

1. Close all the programs that are currently running on your computer.
2. If you are installing from the CD-ROM, insert the CD-ROM in your computer's CD-ROM drive. The installation starts automatically, and you see the screen pictured in Figure A.1.

→ To find information on installing QuickBooks from diskettes, see "Installing from Floppy Disks" later in this appendix.

Installation Doesn't Begin Automatically
If the installation doesn't begin automatically, click the Start button, choose Run, enter D:\Autorun.exe, and click OK (assuming D: is the CD-ROM drive).

Figure A.1
Click on the Install button to install QuickBooks onto your hard drive.

3. Follow the onscreen prompts to proceed to the next screen, agree to the license agreement, and enter the key registration code for your copy of the software. The key registration code appears on an orange sticker on your CD case.

4. In the Choose Destination Location window, verify the correct location at which you want QuickBooks to reside on your hard drive. Then click Next.

5. On the Accept Program Group screen, you are asked if you want to add the QuickBooks programs to your Start menu. Click Next to accept this option and proceed.

6. Look over the choices you've made. If you need to make any changes, click Back to return to previous screens. Otherwise, click Next to proceed.

7. You see a message asking if you want to add a QuickBooks shortcut to your screen. Clicking Yes adds an icon for your QuickBooks program to your main Windows desktop.

8. Click the Finish button, and you have completed the QuickBooks installation.

9. You are then asked if you want to upgrade to the Internet Explorer version 4.0. Click Yes if you need to add this browser to your computer. If you already have an Internet browser installed, you can use your own Internet browser for connecting to the QuickBooks site.

10. If you choose to install the Internet Explorer, follow the onscreen instructions for installation.

11. If you are installing QuickBooks Pro, you are given an option to install the Timer, which is a time-tracking program (for more information about this program, see Chapter 25, "QuickBooks Pro and Time Tracking"). If you want to install this program, click Next through the three installation screens. Before you use the Timer, you are told that you must restart your computer. Choose whether or not you want to restart at this time, and then click Finish.

The installation process is complete! When you have finished installing QuickBooks, put your CD-ROM or disks in a safe place.

Installing from Floppy Disks

You can request floppy disks from Intuit if your computer does not support a CD-ROM drive.

If you are installing from disks, insert Disk 1 in your computer's disk drive, click on the Start button, choose Control Panel, and double-click on Add/Remove Programs. Click the Install button, and then click Next, and you see the Run Installation Program window depicted in Figure A.2. If you don't see this window, make sure that the disk is seated properly in the disk drive and try again.

Figure A.2
Click on Finish, and then follow the onscreen prompts to complete the installation of QuickBooks onto your hard drive.

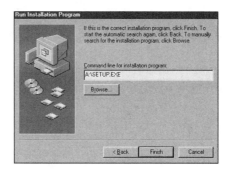

APPENDIX B

Sharing QuickBooks on a Network

If you use QuickBooks Pro, you have the option of installing the program on a network and having up to five simultaneous users. Without the Pro version of QuickBooks, you can use QuickBooks on a network, but only one person can have access to the company file at a time.

This appendix discusses the installation and use of QuickBooks Pro in a multiuser environment.

Network Requirements

Before installing your software, make sure that the following items are in place:

- Windows NT 4.0 or NetWare Network File Server
- Peer-to-Peer File Server using Windows 95, Windows 98, or Windows NT 4.0 with Service Pack 3 file sharing
- A separate copy of the QuickBooks program for each user

Performing the Installation

The QuickBooks program needs to be installed separately on each computer. You must purchase separate QuickBooks programs for each user. (You can purchase QuickBooks in a five-pack if you plan to have five users.)

→ To find more information on the installation of QuickBooks, **see p. 501.**

The company file, which is shared by all users, resides on a shared network directory.

Setting Up Your Users

QuickBooks comes with a New User Setup Wizard that can guide you through the process of making your QuickBooks company file accessible to more than one user. While setting up user accessibility, you can indicate how much access each user is entitled to have. The access options are as follows:

- **Full access**—The user has access to all areas of the company file.
- **Selective access**—The user has access to certain parts of an area of the company file (for example, maybe he can produce reports, but cannot write checks).
- **No access**—The user has no access to certain areas of the company file (for example, the payroll person might be the only one who has access to the payroll area).

Each user you set up has a unique username and password. When a user opens the program and identifies himself or herself, only the designated areas of the program are accessible.

To access the New User Setup Wizard, choose File, Set Up Users & Passwords, Set Up Users. The first user is the administrator, or Admin (see Figure B.1); this user sets up the priorities for all the other users on the system. Remember that a maximum of five people can be set up to use the company file at one time.

Figure B.1

For more information about setting up passwords and giving other users access to selected parts of the program, see Chapter 28, "Security."

Multiuser and Single-User Mode

To make your QuickBooks program accessible to multiple users, you must place the program in multiuser mode. This is done by choosing File, Switch to multiuser mode (Figure B.2). You receive a message indicating that the file can be used by multiple users.

To go back to single-user mode, choose File, Switch to single-user mode.

Figure B.2

APPENDIX C

TRANSFERRING DATA BETWEEN QUICKBOOKS AND OTHER APPLICATIONS

This appendix provides information for Quicken users who want to transfer their Quicken data to QuickBooks rather than re-entering information in QuickBooks or losing valuable historical information.

This appendix also includes instructions for exporting information from QuickBooks to any spreadsheet, database, or word processing program. You are freed from some of the reporting limitations in QuickBooks when you can take the QuickBooks data and use it in another program.

USING QUICKBOOKS WITH QUICKEN

If you have been a Quicken user, you will be pleased to know that QuickBooks communicates directly with Quicken. You can transfer files from Quicken into QuickBooks without having to re-enter information.

When you transfer information from Quicken into QuickBooks, your Quicken files remain intact, so you can continue using Quicken while you make the complete transition into QuickBooks.

In addition, if you've been using Quicken for a combination of personal and business finances, you can move the financial portion of the file into QuickBooks and continue using Quicken for your personal finances.

Note QuickBooks automatically converts files from Quicken for Windows versions 5, 6, 98, and 99, and versions 5–8 of Quicken for DOS. If you're using Quicken for Macintosh, or earlier versions of Quicken for DOS or Windows, you can call Intuit at 1-888-320-7276 to request free software that will enable you to perform the conversion.

Before you convert from Quicken to QuickBooks, you want to perform a few tasks to get your Quicken files in order for the transition:

- Clear any to-do's that are pending in your Quicken file.
- Turn off the option for memorizing transactions in your Quicken file. With this option turned off, QuickBooks converts all your existing memorized transactions.
- Delete any accounts in Quicken that you do not plan to use in QuickBooks.
- Record any overdue scheduled transactions in Quicken.
- Delete any memorized transactions in Quicken that you don't want to convert to QuickBooks.

To convert Quicken files to QuickBooks, follow these steps:

1. Close Quicken so the program is not running.
2. Open QuickBooks. From the File menu, choose Convert From Quicken. An Important Documentation window appears, giving you the option to view detailed information about converting from Quicken. This information is useful; read it before you continue the conversion.
3. Click OK when you are ready to proceed with the conversion. The Convert a Quicken File window appears. Select a Quicken file to convert.
4. Click the Open button to open the Create a new QuickBooks for Windows file window. Enter the name that you want to give to the new QuickBooks file.
5. Click the Save button. QuickBooks begins the process of setting up your new data file.
6. You are asked if there is an accounts receivable account in Quicken. If you answer Yes, you are asked to indicate which account is used for accounts receivable.

> **Caution**
> Because of the nature of the Quicken data you are converting, you might encounter a number of different prompt boxes during the conversion of files from Quicken, for example `unable to convert online data` (because the data is in a format that QuickBooks cannot recognize). Click Yes to continue converting, or click OK (the appropriate response varies depending on the prompt).

7. You are told that your data has been converted successfully. Click OK to leave this screen. One more screen appears, giving you the option to read industry data. Choose Yes if you want to read this material (also available from the Help menu in the QuickBooks program), or click No to open your new QuickBooks file.

Using QuickBooks with Your Favorite Program

You can create reports in QuickBooks and transfer them to your favorite spreadsheet, word processing, or database program. You can also transfer lists and registers, write letters, prepare labels, and create Rolodex cards.

You can send a report from QuickBooks to Excel with the click of a mouse. Open the report that you want to use, and click the Excel button at the top of the report. In the box that appears, indicate if you want the report to appear in a new Excel spreadsheet or an existing spreadsheet, and then click OK. Excel opens and the report appears (see Figure C.1).

> **Caution**
>
> Notice to Microsoft Excel Users: You must use Microsoft Excel version 97 or higher in order to use the Excel button that appears on QuickBooks reports.

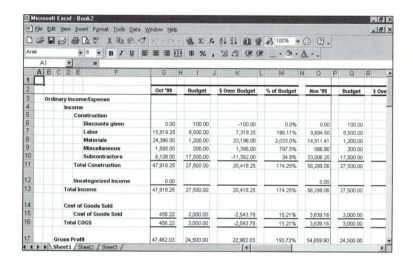

Figure C.1
The Budget vs. Actual Report has been transferred to an Excel spreadsheet.

To transfer a report from QuickBooks to a program other than Excel, follow these steps:

1. Open the report in QuickBooks.
2. From the File menu, choose Print Report (or click the Print button at the top of the report). The Print Reports window appears.
3. On the Settings tab, indicate that you want to print to a File.
4. Click the drop-down arrow to indicate the type of file to which you want to print. Choose from ASCII text file, Excel/Lotus 123 Spreadsheet, or Tab delimited file. Depending on the program to which you want to send the report, you might have to experiment with these choices.

> **Caution**
>
> If you plan to export a QuickBooks file to Quattro Pro, save the file as a tab-delimited file. The file opens in Quattro Pro with the information separated into the proper columns.

5. Choose which pages of the report you want to print (the default is All pages).
6. Click the Print button, give a name to the file you are creating, and indicate the folder in which it is to be stored (be sure to remember this folder so it is easy to find the file in the other program). Click Save when you have entered the file name information. The file is saved and you are returned to the QuickBooks screen.

Exporting Lists

You can send any of your lists from QuickBooks to another program by creating a special text file that can be read by spreadsheet or word-processing programs. The file you create has an IIF extension.

Create a list file for export by following these steps:

1. Choose File, Export. The Export window appears (see Figure C.2).

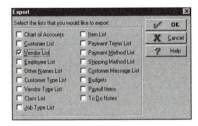

Figure C.2
Check off the list or lists that you want to export to another program.

2. Check all the lists that you want to export. Only one file is created by this procedure, so if you want to export two lists in two separate files, you must go through these steps separately for each list.
3. Click the OK button. Another Export window appears (see Figure C.3).

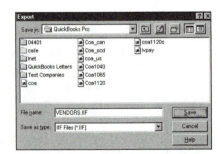

Figure C.3
Give your list file a name, and remember the location of the file so you can find it later.

4. Enter a filename for the file you are about to create. There will be an IIF extension at the end of the filename (for example: VENDORS.IIF).
 5. Click the Save button, noting the folder in which this file has been saved.
 6. A prompt box appears, indicating that the data has been exported successfully. Click OK.

At this point you are ready to open the program in which you want to view the file. Depending on the program in which you want to view this file, you might be asked some preliminary questions about the nature of the file, or the way in which data is to be separated into logical groups or columns (by commas, for example).

Tip #80 from Gail Perry

Here's a quick method for exporting lists to Excel: Open the list window in QuickBooks. Click the Reports button in the list window, and choose a report that displays all members of the list. For example, from the Vendor List window, you might choose to prepare a Contact List. Then filter the report or customize it so that only the information that you need is showing. Click the Excel button in the report window; your list is immediately transferred over to Excel.

USING MICROSOFT WORD WITH QUICKBOOKS

You can easily prepare business letters and other types of correspondence by combining your QuickBooks data with the power of the Microsoft Word program. Follow these steps to create a Word letter from your QuickBooks program:

Caution

Notice to Microsoft Word Users: You must use Microsoft Word version 97 or higher in order to use the features described here.

 1. Choose Activities, Write Letters; the Write Letters window appears (see Figure C.4).

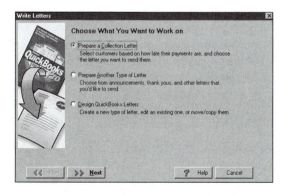

Figure C.4
QuickBooks provides several choices of form letters.

2. Choose from any of several types of predefined letters, or choose to create your own custom letter. If you decide to create your own letter, you will give the letter a name; that document will then be available to you for future use.

3. Proceed through the various Write Letters screens, making selections to fit the correspondence needs of your business. As you make letter choices, you are asked to indicate from which list you want to draw information, and which members of the list are to receive the letter (which customers, for example, or which vendors).

4. After you've entered all the appropriate information for your letters, click the Create Letters button. Microsoft Word opens and your letters are displayed, one per page. At this point you can choose to print the letters, or you can edit them to make changes.

TROUBLESHOOTING

EDITING A FORM LETTER

I created form letters in QuickBooks, but now I want to make a change. How can I go back and edit a form letter?

You can edit an existing letter in QuickBooks by choosing Activities, Write Letters. On the first screen in the Write Letters window that appears, choose Design QuickBooks Letters. Then click the Next button. On the next screen choose View or Edit Existing Letters, click Next, and then click the Edit Letter button. On the following screen, choose the letter that you want to edit. Microsoft Word opens, and the form letter appears; you can make your changes, and then save the revised form letter.

IMPORTING INFORMATION INTO QUICKBOOKS

My list of vendors is saved in an Excel spreadsheet. How can I import this information into QuickBooks so that I don't have to enter all the vendor names and addresses again?

Any list, such as your vendor list or your chart of accounts, can be imported into QuickBooks. The process is time-consuming, but if your list is large enough the time it takes to set up the file for import can be time well spent. You must redesign your Excel spreadsheet so that it meets certain requirements for importing into QuickBooks. The requirements are detailed and very precise, and they vary depending on the type of list you want to import. It is recommended that you search for Importing Data in the QuickBooks Help Index, and then choose Creating an import file from the available options. Print out the resulting help screens to use as a guide in setting up your import file.

CHAPTER D

STATE REVENUE AGENCIES

If you are interested in being set up to collect and pay payroll taxes, sales taxes, or income taxes, contact your state revenue department. Following is a list of all state taxing agencies, with phone numbers, addresses, and Internet addresses:

Alabama—334-242-1000

Department of Revenue
P.O. Box 327410
Montgomery, AL 36132-7410
http://www.ador.state.al.us/

Alaska—907-465-2320

Department of Revenue
State Office Building
P.O. Box 110420
Juneau, AK 99811-0420
http://www.revenue.state.ak.us

Arizona—602-542-4260

Department of Revenue
1600 W. Monroe St.
Phoenix, AZ 85007-2650
http://www.revenue.state.az.us/

Arkansas—501-682-1100

Department of Finance & Administration—Revenue Division
P.O. Box 8055
Little Rock, AR 72203
http://www.state.ar.us/revenue/rev1.html

California—800-852-5711

Franchise Tax Board
P.O. Box 942840
Sacramento, CA 94140-0070
http://www.ftb.ca.gov

Colorado—303-232-2416

Department of Revenue
1375 Sherman St.
Denver, CO 80261
http://www.state.co.us

Connecticut—203-297-4753

Department of Revenue Services
State Tax Department
25 Sigourney St.
Hartford, CT 06106
http://www.state.ct.us/drs/

Delaware—302-577-3300

Department of Finance
Division of Revenue
Delaware State Building
820 N. French St.
Wilmington, DE 19801
http://www.state.de.us/govern/agencies/revenue/revenue.html

District of Columbia—202-727-6170

Department of Finance & Revenue
Room 1046
300 Indiana Ave., N.W.
Washington, D.C. 20001
http://www.dccfo.com/taxpmain.html

Florida—904-922-9645

Department of Revenue
Supply Department
168-A Blounstown Highway
Tallahassee, FL 32304
http://sun6.dms.state.fl.us/dor/

Georgia—404-656-4293

Department of Revenue
P.O. Box 38007
Atlanta, GA 30334
http://www.state.ga.us/departments/dor

Hawaii—800-222-3229

First Taxation District
830 Punchbowl St.
P.O. Box 259
Honolulu, HI 96809
http://www.hawaii.gov/icsd/tax/tax.htm

Idaho—208-334-7789

State Tax Commission
P.O. Box 36
Boise, ID 83722
http://www.idwr.state.id.us/apa/idapa35/taxindex.htm

Illinois—800-356-6302

Department of Revenue
101 W. Jefferson
Springfield, IL 26794
http://www.revenue.state.il.us

Indiana—317-232-2240

Department of Revenue
100 North Senate Avenue
Indianapolis, IN 46204
http://www.ai.org/dor/

Iowa—515-281-3114

Department of Revenue & Finance
P.O. Box 10457
Des Moines, IA 50306
http://www.state.ia.us/government/drf/index.html

Kansas—913-296-4937

Department of Revenue
Division of Taxation
Taxpayer Assistance Bureau
P.O. Box 12001
Topeka, KS 66612-2001
http://www.ink.org/public/kdor

Kentucky—502-564-3658

Revenue Cabinet
200 Fair Oaks Lane, Bldg. 2
Frankfort, KY 40602
Revweb@mail.state.ky.us

Louisiana—504-925-7532

Department of Revenue
P.O. Box 201
Baton Rouge, LA 70821
http://www.rev.state.la.us

Maine—207-624-7894

Bureau of Taxation
State Office Bldg., Station 24
Augusta, ME 04332
http://www.state.me.us/taxation

Maryland—410-974-3951

Comptroller of the Treasury
Revenue Administration
110 Carroll St.
Annapolis, MD 21411
http://www.comp.state.md.us

Massachusetts—617-887-6367

Department of Revenue
Customer Service Bureau
P.O. Box 7010
Boston, MA 02204
http://www.magnet.state.ma.us/dor/dorpg.htm

Michigan—800-367-6263

Department of the Treasury
Revenue Administrative Services
The Treasury Building
430 W. Allegan St.
Lansing, MI 48922
http://www.treas.state.mi.us/

Minnesota—800-652-9094

Department of Revenue
Mail Station 4450
St. Paul, MN 55146-4450
http://www.taxes.state.mn.us

Mississippi—601-354-6247

State Tax Commission
750 South Galatin
Jackson, MS 39204
http://www.treasury.state.ms.us/

Missouri—800-877-6881

Department of Revenue
P.O. Box 3022
Jefferson City, MO 65105-3022
http://www.state.mo.us/dor/tax

Montana—406-444-2837

Department of Revenue
P.O. Box 5805
Helena, MT 59604
http://www.mt.gov/revenue/rev.htm

Nebraska—800-747-8177

Department of Revenue
P.O. Box 94818
Lincoln, NE 68509-4818
http://www.nol.org/revenue

Nevada—702-687-4892

Department of Taxation
Capitol Complex
Carson City, NV 89710-0003
http://www.state.nv.us/taxation/

New Hampshire—603-271-2191

Department of Revenue Administration
State of New Hampshire
61 S. Spring St.
Concord, NH 03301
http://www.state.nh.us/

New Jersey—609-292-7613

Division of Taxation
CN 269
Trenton, NJ 08646
http://www.state.nj.us/treasury/taxation/

New Mexico—505-827-0700

Taxation and Revenue Department
P.O. Box 630
Santa Fe, NM 87504-0630
http://www.state.nm.us/tax

New York—800-462-8100

Department of Taxation & Finance
Taxpayer Service Bureau
W. Averell Harriman Campus
Albany, NY 12227
http://www.tax.state.ny.us/

North Carolina—919-715-0397

Department of Revenue
P.O. Box 25000
Raleigh, NC 27640
http://www.dor.state.nc.us/DOR/

North Dakota—701-328-3017

Office of State Tax Commissioner
State Capitol
600 E. Boulevard Ave.
Bismarck, ND 58505-0599
http://www.state.nd.us/taxdpt/

Ohio—614-433-7750

Department of Taxation
P.O. Box 2476
Columbus, OH 43266-0076
http://www.state.oh.us/tax/

Oklahoma—405-521-3108

Tax Commission
2501 Lincoln Blvd.
Oklahoma City, OK 73194
http://www.oktax.state.ok.us/

Oregon—503-378-4988

Department of Revenue
955 Center St., N.E.
Salem, OR 97310
http://www.dor.state.or.us

Pennsylvania—717-787-8201

Department of Revenue
Strawberry Square
Harrisburg, PA 17128
http://www.revenue.state.pa.us

State Revenue Agencies

Rhode Island—401-277-3934

Division of Taxation
One Capitol Hill
Providence, RI 02908-5800
http://www.tax.state.ri.us

South Carolina—803-737-5000

Tax Commission
P.O. Box 125
Columbia, SC 29214
http://www.state.sc.us/dor/dor.html

South Dakota—605-773-3311

Department of Revenue
700 Governors Dr.
Pierre, SD 57501
http://www.state.sd.us/state/executive/revenue/revenue.html

Tennessee—615-741-4465

Department of Revenue
Andrew Jackson State Office Bldg.
500 Deaderick St., 4th Floor
Nashville, TN 37242
http://www.state.tn.us/revenue

Texas—512-463-4600

Comptroller of Public Accounts
State of Texas
111 West 6th
Starr Building
Austin, TX 78701
http://www.window.state.tx.us

Utah—801-297-2200

State Tax Commission
210 North 1950 West
Salt Lake City, UT 84134
http://www.tax.ex.state.ut.us

Vermont—802-828-2515

Department of Taxes
109 State St.
Montpelier, VT 05609
http://www.state.vt.us/tax/

Virginia—804-367-8031

Department of Taxation
Taxpayers Assistance
P.O. Box 1880
Richmond, VA 23282-1880
http://www.state.va.us/tax/tax.html

Washington—360-786-6100

Department of Revenue
General Administration Bldg.
P.O. Box 47478
Olympia, WA 98504-7478
http://www.ga.gov/dor/wador.htm

West Virginia—304-558-3333

State Tax Department
Taxpayer Service Division
P.O. Box 3784
Charleston, WV 25337-3784
http://www.state.wv.us/taxrev/

Wisconsin—608-266-1961

Department of Revenue
P.O. Box 8903
Madison, WI 53708-8903
http://www.dor.state.wi.us

Wyoming—307-777-7378

The State of Wyoming
Revenue Department
Herschler Building
122 W. 25th
Cheyenne, WY 82002
http://www.state.wy.us

Glossary

account A record for maintaining financial information. A separate record, or account, is used for each type of information, such as cash, sales revenue, repairs expense, and so on.

accounts payable An account that tracks the amounts you owe for items or services you purchase.

accounts receivable An account that keeps a running balance of the amounts that your customers owe you.

accrual basis A system of accounting in which revenue is reported when it is earned and expenses are reported when they are incurred, regardless of the actual dates on which money is received or payments are made. Contrast to *cash basis*.

accumulated depreciation An account comprised of the total of depreciation expense deducted.

aging The process of tracking due dates of unpaid bills.

amortization schedule A report that shows the balance of the loan after each payment is made and a breakdown of the interest and principal portion of payments on the loan.

asset Rights and resources that belong to your company and have future value.

balance sheet A report showing the value of a business based on assets (items and resources owned), liabilities (amounts owed), and equity (the difference between assets and liabilities).

base pay rate The rate for working standard hours, as distinct from a rate for overtime or holiday hours.

book value The value of the company's assets (items that the company owns), minus what the company owes (amounts due to others). Also called *equity*.

capital Amounts invested in a company by its owners.

cash basis An accounting system under which revenue is reported as income only when it is received, and expenses are reported only when the bills are actually paid. A retail store, where income is recorded as it is received in the cash register, is an example of a cash basis business. Compare to *accrual basis*.

chart of accounts A group of categories into which you categorize your company's income, expenses, debts, and assets so that you can make sense of all your business transactions in the form of professional-looking financial statements.

contra asset A type of asset account whose purpose is to offset the value of the assets. An example is an Accumulated Depreciation account which offsets the account containing the cost of an asset by the amount of the accumulating depreciation.

cost of goods sold The cost of goods held in inventory and then sold.

credit Depending on the type of account, either an increase or a decrease to the balance of the account. Liability, equity, and income accounts are increased with credits. Asset and expense accounts are decreased with credits.

credit memo A statement that reduces the balance due on a purchase. It is usually a result of a return of merchandise or a defect in merchandise.

customer type Categorizations of different kinds of customers, such as wholesale, commercial, and retail customers.

daily activities QuickBooks activities that need to be performed daily, such as entering bills, checks, deposits, sales, and employee time.

debit Depending on the type of account, either an increase or a decrease to the balance of the account. Liability, equity, and income accounts are decreased with debits. Asset and expense accounts are increased with debits.

equity The net worth of the company, or the total assets reduced by the total liabilities.

equity account An account that reflects the value of the company. Included are accounts such as Capital Stock, Preferred Stock, Retained Earnings, Owner Draw, and Additional Paid-In Capital.

expenses Costs incurred in an attempt to obtain revenue.

FOB Free On Board. Refers to the transfer of ownership of merchandise from seller to buyer and is based on where the merchandise is in the shipping process.

general journal entry Adjustments that are made to the balances in your accounts without the use of forms, such as invoices, bills, and checks. A general journal entry must always have two sides—a debit and a credit.

income The result when expenses are subtracted from revenues.

inventory The items you sell to earn money in your business. You might sell machine parts, books, or groceries that you purchase somewhere and offer for sale to others. Or you might produce your own inventory, such as clothing that you make, ships that you build, or pottery that you create.

job A project that has a beginning and an end. You might have multiple jobs for the same customer. QuickBooks can track the income and expenses for each job separately.

job type A categorization of the types of jobs you perform. For example, as a wedding photographer, you might offer a standard and a deluxe picture package.

liability Obligations that you must satisfy by the disbursement of assets (such as payment of cash) or by the performance of services.

line of credit A type of loan, usually a bank loan, from which you can draw money when needed and pay it back on a predetermined schedule.

maintenance releases Downloadable updates to the QuickBooks software that fix small problems and offer the latest information.

net income The result when total expenses are deducted from total income.

net worth The term applied to the sum of a company's *equity* accounts. If you add the value of the company's assets (items that the company owns) and subtract what the company owes (amounts due to others), the resulting amount is the *book value* of the company, or equity.

parent account In QuickBooks, the major category of an account. You can provide more details of the components of a parent account by creating subaccounts. The total value of all the subaccounts of one parent make up the total amount in the parent account.

principal The face value, otherwise known as the original amount, of a loan.

profit and loss statement A statement covering a specific time period and listing income earned for the period and expenses incurred during the period.

service items A job that you perform for which you charge a customer.

start date The date on which you want to begin tracking information in QuickBooks. When you set up a company in QuickBooks, you need to enter all transactions that have occurred in the company from the start date to today.

subaccount In QuickBooks, the subsidiary category of an account. You can provide more details of the components of a parent account by creating subaccounts. The total value of the subaccounts of one parent make up the total amount in the parent account.

type lists In a submenu of the Lists menu, you'll find Other Lists. Of particular interest here are the *Type* Lists. Types enable you to further break down your lists into subgroups that make sense for your business.

vendor type A categorization of types of vendors that you work with. For example, as a restaurateur, perhaps you purchase consultation and marketing services to come up with plans to bring in more customers. You would not group these transactions in the same expense category with ordering paper cups and food inventory. In this case, you'd set up two vendor types.

weighted average A method of valuing the inventory that you have on hand. As each new item is added to the total inventory, the cost of the new item is added to the cost of all pieces of the same item on hand to provide a total. When an item is sold, the total cost of all inventory items is divided by the number of pieces on hand to determine an average cost. This cost is reflected at the time of sale as the cost of sales for the item sold.

INDEX

Symbols

2D (two dimensional) graphs, 400

5-year assets, depreciation deductions, 257

7-year assets, depreciation deductions, 257

1000-1999 account numbers, 118

2000-2999 account numbers, 118

3000-3999 account numbers, 118

4000-4999 account numbers, 118

5000-5999 account numbers, 118

6000-6999 account numbers, 118

A

A/P Reports menu commands
Customer Balance Detail, 92
Vendor Balance Detail, 90

A/R Reports command (Reports menu), 366

A/R (accounts receivable)
defined, 67, 522
graphs, 194, 378
register
  displaying, 191
  opening, 191
  searching, 192
reports
  Aging Detail, 193
  Aging Summary, 192, 366
  Collections, 193, 367
  Customer Balance Detail, 193
  Customer Balance Summary, 193
  Open Invoices, 193
  Unbilled Costs by Job, 193

About QuickBooks (Pro) command (Help menu), 29

Access databases, inventory tracking, 231

access rights, 486-487, 506

account numbers, assigning
automatically, 384
manually, 118
QuickBooks numbering system, 117-118

accounting (overview), 106
accrual basis system, 475, 522
cash basis system, 522
record maintenance
  annual activities, 37-38
  corrections, 38
  daily activities, 32-33
  monthly activities, 35-36
  payroll issues, 35
  quarterly activities, 36-37
  task checklists, 33-34
  weekly activities, 34

accounting preferences
account numbers, 384
audit trails, 385
class tracking, 385

accounts
account numbers, assigning
  automatically, 384
  manually, 118
  QuickBooks numbering system, 117-118
activating, 116
bank accounts
  creating, 78
  deposits, 201-203
asset accounts, 107-109
  creating, 78
  defined, 107-108
  depreciation, 78
  examples, 108
cash transactions
  cash over/short, 266-268
  Cash Sales form, 199-201, 264
  credit card payments, 268
  daily cash summaries, 265-266
  deposits, 268
  troubleshooting discrepancies, 269
chart of accounts, 51
  defined, 522
  displaying, 113
  printing, 119

ACCOUNTS

checks
- *forms, 251*
- *printing, 245-246*
- *register, 247-248*
- *voiding, 248, 251*
- *writing, 243-245*

creating, 113-114

credit card accounts
- *creating, 75*
- *lines of credit, 76*

deactivating, 115-116
debit accounts, 523
defined, 106-107, 522
deleting, 114
deposits, 201-203
editing, 86

equity accounts, 523
- *capital accounts, 110*
- *capital stock, 110*
- *creating, 79-80*
- *defined, 79, 107, 109*
- *opening balance equity accounts, 110*
- *paid-in capital, 110*

expense accounts
- *creating, 66*
- *defined, 52, 107, 112*

general journal entries
- *creating, 259-260*
- *defined, 258, 523*

hierarchical level, changing, 116

historical transactions
- *bills paid, 99*
- *bills received, 90-92*
- *cash payments, 97-98*
- *checks, 102*
- *credits/refunds, 96-97*
- *deposits, 99-100*
- *discounts, 95-96*
- *invoices, 92-94*
- *payments against invoices, 94-95*
- *payroll, 100-102*

- *required documents/information, 88-90*
- *start dates, changing, 88*

income accounts
- *creating, 64-65*
- *defined, 52, 64, 107, 112*

liabilities
- *defined, 107, 109*
- *examples, 109*

merging, 116-117

online accounts
- *activating, 416*
- *application information, downloading, 417-418*
- *matching with QuickStatements, 419-421*
- *payments, 422-423, 430*
- *routing/account numbers, 421*
- *Transaction Detail reports, 426*
- *transferring funds, 425-426*

opening balances
- *customer information, 74*
- *entering, 72-73*
- *vendor information, 74-75*

parent accounts, 524

payable
- *defined, 522*
- *graphs, 378*

payments against, *see* payments

Payroll Expense, 278-279
Payroll Liability, 278-279
preference settings, 384-385

receivable
- *defined, 67, 522*
- *graphs, 194, 378*
- *register, 191-192*
- *reports, 192-193, 366-367*

reconciling, 248-250
Sales Tax Payable, 206-207
subaccounts, 65, 524

user accounts, 482-483
- *access rights, 486-487*
- *administrator accounts, 483-485*
- *passwords, 485-486*

year-end protection, 487-488

Accounts menu, Enter Bills command, 90

accounts payable
defined, 522
graphs, 378

Accounts Payable graphs, 378

accounts receivable. See A/R

Accounts Receivable Aging Summary reports, 366

Accounts Receivable graphs, 378

accrual basis accounting system, 522

accrual basis businesses, 475

accumulated depreciation, 254-255, 522

Acrobat Reader, 439

activating
accounts, 116
online accounts, 416
templates, 348

activities (Timer)
creating, 450-452
defined, 451
exporting, 454
opening in QuickBooks, 455-457
switching between, 453
templates, 453
timing, 451-452
viewing, 460-461

Activities menu commands
Adjust Quantity/Value on Hand, 140
Change Prices, 135-136

Create Credit Memos/Refunds, 96
Create Estimates, 175
Create Invoices, 92, 185
Create Purchase Orders, 234
Create Statements, 188
Enter Bills, 139
Enter Cash Sales, 97, 199, 265
Inventory, 224
Make Deposits, 99, 201, 203
Make Journal Entry, 259
Pay Bills, 99, 242
Pay Sales Tax, 214
Receive Payments, 94, 198
Reconcile, 249
Set Up Budgets, 465
Write Checks, 102, 243
Write Letters, 511

Add New Payroll Item window, 317

Add Window to Iconbar command (Window menu), 358

additional first year depreciation, 262

Additional Info tab (New Customer window), 151

Address Info tab (New Customer window), 150

Adjust Quantity/Value on Hand command (Activities menu), 140

Adjust Quantity/Value on Hand window, 140, 228-229

adjustment periods, 286-287

administrator accounts, 483-485

Adobe Acrobat Reader, 439

advances, 203-204

advisors, 428

aging, 522
Aging Detail reports, 193
Aging Summary reports, 192, 366

AICPA (American Institute of Certified Public Accountants) Web site, 435

Alabama Department of Revenue, 513

Alaska Department of Revenue, 513

All Customers option (monthly statements), 189

AltaVista Web site, 432

American Institute of Certified Public Accountants (AICPA) Web site, 435

amortization schedules, 77, 522

Annotate command (Options menu), 24

annotating Help index, 24

annual activities (record maintenance), 37-38

Arizona Department of Revenue, 513

Arkansas Department of Finance and Administration, 513

ASCII text files, printing to, 474

Assess Finance Charges window, 189

asset accounts, 107-109
creating, 78
defined, 107-108
depreciation, 78
examples, 108

assets
defined, 522
depreciation
accumulated depreciation, 254-255, 522
additional first year depreciation, 262
calculating, 255-258, 261-262
contra asset accounts, 254, 522
depreciatiable assets, selling, 260-261
general journal entries, 258-260
equity, 522-523
fixed, 254
inventory
activating, 226
adding items to, 221-223
adjusting quantity/value, 140-142, 228-229
counting, 227-228
defined, 218
editing, 224
manufactured goods, 218-219
purchase orders, 234-238
receipt of items, 139, 224, 226, 239-241
reorder feature, 220
reports, 226-228
theft, 232
third-party software, 229-232
troubleshooting, 232
valuing, 218-220, 524
net values, 254, 380

assigning account numbers
automatically, 384
manually, 118
QuickBooks numbering system, 117-118

audit trails, 260, 385

Auto Insert Notification feature (CD-ROMs), 13

Automated Expert (Intuit technical support), 28

automatic payment feature, 204

average-costing method (inventory valuation), 218-220

Awarded job status, 172

B

Back Up command (File menu), 15

Back Up Company To window, 15

backups, 14-15, 482
   creating, 15-16
   online backups, 16
   restoring from
     disk backups, 16
     tape backups, 16
     troubleshooting, 19
   Timer files, 459

Balance Sheet command (Reports menu), 365

Balance Sheet Comparison reports, 470

Balance Sheet Itemized command (Reports menu), 163

Balance Sheet Overview reports, 469

Balance Sheet reports, 365-366

balances
   balance sheets
     defined, 522
     reports, 163, 365-366, 470
   opening account balances
     asset accounts, 78
     bank accounts, 78
     credit card accounts, 75
     customer information, 74
     entering, 72-73
     equity accounts, 79-80
     lines of credit, 76
     loans/liabilities, 76-78
     payroll, 83, 85
     vendor information, 74-75

Baltimore Sun Web site, 438

bank accounts. See also **accounts**
   creating, 78
   deposits, 201-203

banking (online). See **online banking**

Banking Message window, 424

base pay rates, 522

bills. See also **invoices**
   aging, 522
   entering, 137-138
   paying, 99, 241-243
   received
     historical transactions, 90-92
     printing list of, 90

book value, 109-110, 522-523. See also **equity accounts**

bookkeeping. See **accounting**

borders, 351

Boston Globe Web site, 436

Budget by Job Comparison reports, 469

Budget by Job Overview reports, 468-469

Budget Overview reports, 467

Budget Reports command (Reports menu), 467

Budget vs. Actual graphs, 380

Budget vs. Actual reports, 467-468

budgets
   creating, 464-466
   defined, 464
   graphs, 380
   projecting, 465
   reports
     Balance Sheet Comparison, 470
     Balance Sheet Overview, 469
     Budget by Job Overview, 468-469
     Budget Overview, 467
     Budget vs. Actual, 467-468
   troubleshooting, 470

Business Week Web site, 433

buttons
   EasyStep interview
     Leave, 44-45
     Next, 45
     Prev, 45
     Skip Interview, 45
   How Do I?, 26

buttons (iconbar)
   adding, 391
   deleting, 392
   editing, 391
   separating spaces, 391

C

Cable News Network Web site, 436

calculating
   depreciation, 255-256
     MACRS (Modified Accelerated Cost Recovery System), 256-258
     straight-line method, 256
     third-party software, 261-262
   prices, 136-137

California Francise Tax Board, 514

capital accounts, 110, 522

capital stock, 110

cards (QCards)
    displaying, 25
    hiding, 25, 30
    moving, 25

cash basis accounting system, 475, 522

cash flow forecasts, 472
    advantages, 477
    displaying, 478
    printing, 478

cash outflow for inventory forecasts, 472, 476-477

cash outflow forecasts, 472

Cash Sales form, 199-201, 264

cash transactions, 264
    cash over/short, 266-268
    cash receipts forecasts
        creating, 475-476
        defined, 472
    Cash Sales form, 199-201, 264
    credit card payments, 268
    daily cash summaries, 265-266
    deposits, 268
    historical transactions, 97-98
    sales tax, 206
        applying to purchases, 211
        enabling collection, 209-210
        items, 207-208
        liability reports, 213-215
        paying, 214-215
        Sales Tax Payable accounts, 206-207
        tax-exempt sales, 212-213
    troubleshooting discrepancies, 269

Cashfinder Web site, 428-429

CD-ROMs
    Auto Insert Notification feature, 13
    installing QuickBooks from, 502-503
    Introduction to QuickBooks videos, 26-27
    running QuickBooks from, 13-14

Change Prices command (Activities menu), 135-136

Change Prices window, 135-136

changing. See editing

Charles Schwab Web site, 434
    defined, 522
    displaying, 113
    printing, 119

Chart of Accounts command (Lists menu), 113

checking preferences, 385-386

checklists (record-keeping tasks), 33-34

checks
    forms, 251
    historical transactions, 102
    paychecks
        creating, 291-292
        deleting, 294
        displaying, 293
        editing, 292-293
        previewing, 292
        printing, 295-296
        voiding, 294
    payroll tax payments, 309-311
    preference settings, 385-386
    printing, 245-246
    register
        opening, 247
        searching, 247-248
    voiding, 248, 251
    writing, 243-245

Chicago Tribune Web site, 436

choosing
    passwords, 483
    QuickBooks versus QuickBooks Pro, 10-11
    start dates, 40-41

Christian Science Monitor Web site, 438

city payroll taxes, 314-315. See also taxes

Class List window, 161
    Class menu commands, 162
    Reports menu commands, 162-163

Class menu commands
    Delete, 162
    Edit, 162
    Find in Transactions Inactive, 162
    Make Inactive, 162
    Print List, 162

classes
    changing, 165
    creating
        Class List window, 161
        on-the-fly, 163
    deactivating, 162
    defined, 160
    deleting, 162
    editing, 162
    enabling, 160-161
    finding in transactions, 162
    printing list of, 162
    reports, 162
        graphs, 163
        itemized balance sheets, 163
        profit/loss, 162, 164
        purchase, 164
        sales, 164
    subclasses, 160
    tracking feature, 385
    troubleshooting, 165

clock. See Timer

CLOSED JOB STATUS

Closed job status, 172

closing Timer, 452

"closing the books" (year-end protection), 487-488

CNN Financial Network Web site, 434

collapsing subaccounts, 371

Collections report, 193, 367

Colorado Department of Revenue, 514

columns (report)
- changing, 369-370
- reordering, 342

Columns tab (Customize Invoice window), 342-343

commands
- A/P Reports menu
  - *Customer Balance Detail, 92*
  - *Vendor Balance Detail, 90*
- Activities menu
  - *Adjust Quantity/Value on Hand, 140*
  - *Change Prices, 135-136*
  - *Create Credit Memos/Refunds, 96*
  - *Create Estimates, 175*
  - *Create Purchase Orders, 234*
  - *Create Statements, 188*
  - *Enter Bills, 139*
  - *Enter Cash Sales, 97, 199, 265*
  - *Inventory, 224*
  - *Make Deposits, 99, 201, 203*
  - *Make Journal Entry, 259*
  - *Pay Bills, 99, 242*
  - *Pay Sales Tax, 214*
  - *Receive Payments, 94, 198*
  - *Reconcile, 249*
  - *Set Up Budgets, 465*
  - *Write Checks, 102, 243*
  - *Write Letters, 511*
- Class menu
  - *Delete, 162*
  - *Edit, 162*
  - *Find in Transactions, 162*
  - *Make Inactive, 162*
  - *Print List, 162*
- Edit menu
  - *Delete Estimate, 181*
  - *Find, 131*
- File menu (QuickBooks)
  - *Back Up, 15*
  - *Convert From Quicken, 508*
  - *Export, 510*
  - *New Company, 42*
  - *Open Company, 19*
  - *Preferences, 17*
  - *Print Report, 474, 509*
  - *Resort, 16*
  - *Set up Users & Passwords, 506*
  - *Switch, 506*
- File menu (Timer)
  - *Condense Timer File, 459*
  - *Export Time Activities, 454*
  - *Import QuickBooks Lists, 449*
  - *New Time File, 449*
  - *Restore Timer File, 460*
- Help menu
  - *About QuickBooks (Pro), 29*
  - *Help Index, 23*
  - *Hide/Show QCards, 25, 30*
  - *QuickBooks and Your Industry, 29*
- Lists menu
  - *Chart of Accounts, 113*
  - *Customer:Job, 170*
  - *Items, 267*
  - *Reminders, 18*
- Online menu, Internet Connection Setup, 413
- Options menu
  - *Annotate, 24*
  - *Keep Help on Top, 23*
- Payroll menu, Pay Employees, 100
- Print Forms menu, Print Checks, 245
- Reports menu
  - *A/R Reports, 366*
  - *Balance Sheet, 365*
  - *Balance Sheet Itemized, 163*
  - *Budget Reports, 467*
  - *Custom Reports, 473*
  - *Graphs, 163*
  - *Memorized Reports, 373*
  - *Other Reports, 368*
  - *Quick Report, 162*
  - *Profit & Loss, 164, 364*
  - *Purchase Reports, 164*
  - *Reports on All Classes, 162*
  - *Sales Reports, 164*
- Reports on All Items menu
  - *Graphs, 147*
  - *Inventory Reports, 147*
  - *Project, 147*
  - *Purchase Reports, 145*
  - *Sales Reports, 145*
- Window menu, Add Window to Iconbar, 358

company contributions, 283

company information, setting up, 41-42
- access control, 52
- addresses, 47-48
- bill-paying preferences, 60
- business types
  - *changing, 61*
  - *specifying, 50*
- chart of accounts, 51-52
- classes feature, 59
- company name, 46-47
- customizing, 346
- FEIN (Federal Identification Number), 48

filenames, 51
fiscal year, 48-49
inventory preferences, 53-54
invoice styles, 56
job estimates, 58
legal name, 46-47
multiple companies, 47
multiple locations, 47
payroll information, 57
reminders preferences, 60
sales tax items, 54-55
start dates, 524
  changing, 61, 88
  choosing, 40-41
tax return forms, 49-50
time-tracking feature, 59

completion dates (jobs), 173

Condense Timer File command (Timer File menu), 459

condensing Timer files, 459

configuring
accounts
  asset accounts, 78
  bank accounts, 78
  credit card accounts, 75
  customer balances, 74
  equity accounts, 79-80
  expense accounts, 66
  income accounts, 64-65
  lines of credit, 76
  loans/liabilities, 76-78
  opening balances, 72-73
  parent accounts, 65
  subaccounts, 65
  vendor balances, 74-75
company information, 41-42
  access control, 52
  addresses, 47-48
  bill-paying preferences, 60
  business types, 50
  chart of accounts, 51-52
  classes feature, 59
  company name, 46-47

FEIN (Federal Identification Number), 48
filenames, 51
fiscal year, 48-49
inventory preferences, 53-54
invoice styles, 56
job estimates, 58
legal name, 46-47
multiple companies, 47
multiple locations, 47
payrolll information, 57
reminders preferences, 60
sales tax items, 54-55
start dates, 40
tax return forms, 49-50
time-tracking feature, 59
Internet connections, 413-414
user accounts
  access rights, 486-487
  administrators, 483-485
  passwords, 485-486

Connecticut Department of Revenue Services, 514

contra assets, 522

contractors. See also employees
paying, 301-302
setting up, 303-304

Convert From Quicken command (File menu), 508

converting Quicken files to QuickBooks, 507-508

corporations
defined, 111
PSCs (personal service corporations), 111
S corporations, 49, 111

correcting mistakes
deposits, 103
records, 38

cost of goods sold, 522

costing inventory
  FIFO (first in, first out), 220
  LIFO (last in, first out), 220
  specific identification method, 220
  weighted average method, 218-220, 524

counting inventory, 227-228

county payroll taxes, 314-315. *See also* **taxes**

Create Credit Memos/Refunds command (Activities menu), 96

Create Credit Memos/Refunds window, 96

Create Estimates command (Activities menu), 175

Create Estimates window
Customer Job field, 175
Description field, 175
Markup column, 176
Memo field, 176
Template field, 175

Create Export File window, 454

Create Invoices command (Activities menu), 92, 185

Create Invoices window, 92
Bill To address field, 186
Customer Message field, 187
Customer:Job area, 185
Item column, 187
Memo field, 187
Rep field, 186
Ship field, 186
Ship To address field, 186
Tax field, 187
Terms field, 186

Create Item Receipts window, 224-225, 239-241

Create Progress Invoice Based On Estimate window, 177

Create Purchase Orders command (Activities menu), 234
Create Purchase Orders window, 234
Create Statements command (Activities menu), 188
credit
   defined, 79, 523
   entering, 140
credit card transactions, 75, 268
credits, 107-108
   credit memos, 523
   historical transactions, 96-97
current liabilities, 77
custom forms, 338-339
   borders, 351
   colummn order, 342
   company information, 346
   examples, 357-358
   fields
      adding, 340-341, 355
      creating, 354-355
      deleting, 340-341
      maximum number of, 359
      monitoring use of, 355, 357
      moving, 348-349
      sizing, 348-350
      visibility, 342
      when to use, 354
   fonts, 347-348
   footers, 345
   grid settings, 352
   headers, 342
   logos, 346-347
   margins, 352-353
   progressive estimate invoices, 344-345
   sizing, 359
   statements, 358
   templates
      activating, 348
      deactivating, 348
      duplicating, 339
      selecting, 339-340
   text justification, 350
   zooming in/out, 352
custom invoices, 56
Custom Report command (Reports menu), 473
Customer Balance Detail command (A/P Reports menu), 92
Customer Balance Detail report, 193
Customer Balance Summary report, 193
Customer field (New Customer window), 150
Customer list, 157
Customer Messages list, 156
Customer:Job command (Lists menu), 170
Customer:Job field (Cash Sales form), 200
Customer:Job list, 149, 151
customers
   account balances, 74
   Customer:Job list, 149, 151
   inactive, 157
   invoicing, *see* invoices
   job estimates
      advantages, 174
      creating, 175-176
      defined, 174
      deleting, 181
      displaying, 176
      invoicing against, 176-178
      overriding, 181
      previewing, 176
      printing, 176
      reports, 180-181
      revising, 179-180
   jobs
      creating, 170-171
      defined, 523
      descriptions, 173
      preference settings, 392-393
      service items, 524
      start/completion dates, 173
      status, 171-173
      types, 174, 523
   messages, 156
   monthly statements
      creating, 188-190
      printing, 190
   New Customer window
      Additional Info tab, 151
      Address Info tab, 150
      Customer field, 150
      Job Info tab, 151
   outstanding transactions, 194
   payments, 195
   preference settings, 402-403
   tax-exempt, 238-239
   types, 523
Customers of Type option (monthly statements), 190
Customize Invoice window, 340-341
   Columns tab, 342-343
   Fields tab, 342-343
   Footer tab, 345
   Header tab, 342
   Options tab, 346
   Prog Col tab, 344
Customize Report window, 473
customizing. See editing

D

daily activities (record maintenance), 32-33, 523
daily cash summaries, 265-266
databases, inventory tracking, 231

date-driven terms, 155

dates
  jobs, 173
  preference settings, 389
  report dates, 369
  start dates
    changing, 88
    defined, 524

deactivating. See disabling

debits, 79, 107-108, 523

deductions, 258. See also depreciation

Delaware Department of Finance, 514

Delete command (Class menu), 162

Delete Estimate command (Edit menu), 181

deleting
  accounts, 114
  classes, 162
  estimates, 181
  form fields, 340-341
  invoice items, 187
  memorized reports, 374
  paychecks, 294
  transactions, 388

departments. See classes

deposits
  cash transactions
    cash over/short, 266-268
    Cash Sales form, 199-201, 264
    daily cash summaries, 265-266
    troubleshooting discrepancies, 269
  correcting, 103
  historical transactions, 99-100
  recording, 201-203

depreciation
  accumulated depreciation accounts, 254-255
  additional first year depreciation, 262
  calculating, 255-256
    MACRS (Modified Accelerated Cost Recovery System), 256-258
    straight-line method, 256
    third-party software, 261-262
  contra asset accounts, 254
  defined, 522
  depreciable assets, selling, 260-261
  general journal entries
    creating, 259-260
    defined, 258
  tracking, 78

desktop preference settings, 389

Detroit Free Press Web site, 436

dialog boxes. See windows

disabling
  accounts, 115-116
  automatic payment feature, 204
  CD-ROM notification feature, 13
  classes, 162
  QCards, 388
  templates, 348
  terms, 156

discounts
  historical transactions, 95-96
  items, 125

disks, floppy
  installing QuickBooks from, 503
  Timer install disks, 457-458

displaying
  accounts receivable register, 191
  cash flow forecasts, 478
  chart of accounts, 113
  estimates, 176
  iconbar, 381, 390
  inactive accounts, 116
  inactive customers, 157
  job status, 173
  list entry details, 129
  outstanding transactions, 194
  paychecks, 293
  payment details, 204
  QCards, 25
  QuickStatements, 419
  Reminders list, 18, 398
  reports, 381
  Timer activities, 460-461
  W-2 forms, 299
  warning messages
    deleted transactions, 388
    duplicate bill numbers, 398
    duplicate check numbers, 386
    duplicate invoice numbers, 403
    duplicated estimate numbers, 393
    edited transactions, 388
    inventory shortage, 397

District of Columbia Department of Finance and Revenue, 514

divisions. See classes

double-entry accounting, 79

down payments, 203-204

downloading
  Acrobat Reader, 439
  online banking information, 417-418
  QuickStatements, 419

drill-down techniques (QuickReports)
  date ranges, 327
  double-clicking transactions, 328-329
  filters, 328

duplicating templates, 339

E

earned income credit, 332-333

Earned Income Credit Advance Payment Certificate, 332

EasyStep interview, 42
  buttons
    Leave, 44-45
    Next, 45
    Prev, 45
    Skip Interview, 45
  General information
    access control, 52
    addresses, 47
    bill-paying preferences, 60
    business types, 50
    chart of accounts, 51-52
    Classes feature, 59
    company names, 46-47
    FEIN (Federal Identification Number), 48
    filenames, 51
    fiscal year, 48-49
    inventory preferences, 53-54
    invoice styles, 56
    job estimates, 58
    legal names, 46-47
    multiple companies, 47
    multiple locations, 47
    payroll information, 57
    reminders preferences, 60
    sales tax items, 54-55
    tax agencies, 54
    tax return forms, 49-50
    time-tracking feature, 59
  Income & Expenses section, 43
    income accounts, 64-65
    parent accounts, 65
    subaccounts, 65-66
  Income Details section, 43
    income information, 66-67
    inventory items, creating, 71-72
    non-inventory part items, creating, 69-70
    other charge items, creating, 70-71
    defined, 67
    service items, creating, 67-69
    defined, 67
  Menu Items section, 43, 85
  mistakes, correcting, 46
  navigating, 43-44
  Opening Balances section, 43, 72-73
    asset accounts, 78
    bank accounts, 78
    credit card accounts, 75
    customer information, 74
    equity accounts, 79-80
    lines of credit, 76
    loans/liabilities, 76-78
    vendor information, 74-75
  Payroll section, 43
    payroll items, 80-83
    starting balances, 83, 85
  restarting, 43
  skipping, 45
  stopping, 43
  What's Next section, 43, 85

Economist Web site, 436

Edit Account window, 117

Edit command (Class menu), 162

Edit Item window, 132-133, 224

Edit menu commands
  Delete Estimate, 181
  Find, 131

editing
  accounts, 86, 116
  business type information, 61
  classes, 162, 165
  form text, 347-348, 351
  inventory list, 224
  invoices, 185
  items, 132-133
  job estimates, 179-180
  job status, 172-173
  letters, 512
  memorized reports, 374
  online payments, 423
  paychecks, 292-293
  prices, 135-136
  start dates, 61, 88
  reports, 368-369, 381
    columns, 369-370
    dates, 369
    fields, 371-372
    footers, 370-371
    format, 373
    headers, 370-371
  terms, 154-156
  Timer activities, 452-453
  transactions, 388
  W-2 forms, 300-301

electronic statements. *See* **QuickStatements**

email, online banking messages
  creating, 423-425
  payment inquiries, 425

Employee Earnings Summary reports, 320-321, 326-327

Employee list, 153

employees. *See also* **independent contractors; payroll**
  adding, 279-280
  Employee list, 153
  preference settings, 394-396

reports, 320-321, 326-327
tax status
city/county taxes, 314-315
earned income credits, 332-333
federal taxes, 312-313
state taxes, 313-314
wage base information, 315-316, 522

enabling
Audit Trail feature, 260
CD-ROM notification feature, 13
class tracking, 160-161
class tracking feature, 385
Classes feature, 59
online payments, 422
Progress Billing feature, 177
purchase orders, 234
QCards, 388
sales tax collection, 209-210
time-tracking feature, 59

Enter Bills command
Accounts menu, 90
Activities menu, 139

Enter Bills window, 90, 138, 241

Enter Cash Sales command (Activities menu), 97, 199, 265

Enter Cash Sales window, 97

Enter key, 134

equity, 109-110, 522-523

equity accounts
capital accounts, 110
capital stock, 110
creating, 79-80
defined, 79, 107, 523
opening balance equity accounts, 110
paid-in capital, 110
retained earnings, 110

estimated income taxes
corporations, 490-491
individuals, 491

estimates
advantages, 174
creating, 175-176
defined, 174
deleting, 181
displaying, 176
invoicing against
entire estimate, 176-177
partial estimate, 177-178
overriding, 181
preference settings, 392-393
previewing, 176
printing, 176
reports
invoices vs. estimates, 181
Open Balance, 180
profit/loss, 181
QuickReports, 180
unbilled costs, 181
revising, 179-180

etrade Web site, 434

Excel
files, importing, 512
inventory tracking, 230-231
QuickBooks files, importing, 509
spreadsheets, printing to, 474

Excite Web site, 432

exempt organizations, 49

expanding subaccounts, 371

expense accounts, 523
creating, 66
defined, 52, 107, 112

experience rates, 81

Export command (File menu), 510

Export window, 447

Export Time Activities command (Timer File menu), 454

Export window, 510

exporting
lists, 447-448, 510-511
reports, 509-510
Timer data, 454

F

FAQs (frequently asked questions), 27

Federal Identification Number (FEIN), 48

federal taxes. See also taxes
income tax
forms, 495-496
non-tax-related transactions, 497
professional preparation, 498
quarterly estimates, 490-491
reports, 492-495
tax lines, 491-492, 498
TurboTax software, 496
payroll, 308
earned income credits, 332-333
employee tax status, 312-313
federal umemployment tax, 329-330
Form 940, 323-325
Form 941, 322-323
paying, 309-311
payroll items, 317-319
reports, 326-329
troubleshooting, 330-332
wage base information, 315-316

FEIN (Federal Identification Number), 48

FICA. See payroll taxes

fields

fields
  adding, 340-341
  custom fields, 371-372
    adding, 355
    creating, 354-355
    maximum number of, 359
    monitoring use of, 355, 357
    when to use, 354
  deleting, 340-341
  moving, 348-349
  sizing, 348-350
  visibility, 342

Fields tab (Customize Invoice window), 342-343

FIFO (first in, first out), 220

File menu commands (QuickBooks)
  Back Up, 15
  Convert From Quicken, 508
  Export, 510
  New Company, 42
  Open Company, 19
  Preferences, 17
  Print Report, 474, 509
  Restore, 16
  Set up Users & Passwords, 506
  Switch, 506

File menu commands (Timer)
  Condense Timer File, 459
  Export Time Activities, 454
  Import QuickBooks Lists, 449
  New Time File, 449
  Restore Timer File, 460

filenames, 51

files
  ASCII, printing to, 474
  company files
    opening, 19
    importing, 512
  Excel/Lotus 123 spreadsheets, printing to, 474
  IIF format, 447
  Quicken files, converting to QuickBooks, 507-508
  tab delimited, printing to, 474
  Timer files
    activity log, 460-461
    condensing/backing up, 459
    creating, 449
    exporting, 454
    naming, 449
    opening in QuickBooks, 455-457
    restoring, 460

filters, 328, 372-373

finance charge preferences
  account information, 386-387
  annual interest rates, 387
  assessment method, 387
  grace period, 387
  invoices, 388
  minimum charges, 387

Financenter Web site, 435

financial forecasts. See forecasts

Financial Institutions Directory (Online Interview), 417

financial plans. See budgets

Find command (Edit menu), 131

Find feature, 24-25

Find in Transactions command (Class menu), 162

finding
  classes, 162
  list entries, 131-132
  terms, 156

first in, first out (FIFO), 220

fiscal year, 40, 48-49

fixed assets
  defined, 254
  depreciation
    acculumated depreciation accounts, 254-255
    additional first year depreciation, 262
    calculating, 255-258, 261-262
    contra asset accounts, 254
    depreciable assets, selling, 260-261
    general journal entries, 258-260

floppy disks
  installing QuickBooks from, 503
  Timer install disks, 457-458

Florida Department of Revenue, 514

FOB (Free on Board), 186, 403, 523

fonts, 347-348

Footer tab (Customize Invoice window), 345

footers, 345, 370-371

forecasts
  cash flow
    advantages, 477
    defined, 472
    displaying, 478
    printing, 478
  cash outflow, 472, 476-477
  cash receipts
    creating, 475-476
    defined, 472
  sales
    creating, 473
    defined, 472
    printing, 474

forms. See also invoices
  adding to iconbar, 358-359
  custom, 338-340

borders, 351
column order, 342
company information, 346
examples, 357-358
fields, 340-342, 348-350, 354-355, 357, 359
fonts, 347-348
footers, 345
grid settings, 352
headers, 342
logos, 346-347
margins, 352-353
progressive estimate invoices, 344-345
sizing, 359
statements, 358
templates, 339-340, 348
text justification, 350
previewing, 353-354
tax forms
Form 940, 323-325
Form 941, 322-323, 333
Form 990, 49
Form 990-PF, 50
Form 990-T, 50
Form 1040, 49
Form 1065, 49
Form 1099, 404-405
Form 1120, 49
Form 1120S, 49
statements
monthly statements, 188-190
QuickStatements, 419-421
zooming in/out, 352

Free on Board (FOB), 186, 403, 523

frequently asked questions (FAQs), 27

full access, 506

FUTA (federal unemployment tax), 81, 329-330

G

general journal entries
creating, 259-260
defined, 258, 523

General Journal Entry window, 259-260

General Ledger reports, 368

general preferences, 388-390
date format, 389
decimal point placement, 388
desktop options, 389
pop-up warnings, 388
QCards, 388
sounds, 388
time format, 389

General section (EasyStep interview), 42
access control, 52
addresses, 47
bill-paying preferences, 60
business types, 50
chart of accounts, 51-52
Classes feature, 59
company names, 46-47
FEIN (Federal Identification Number), 48
filenames, 51
fiscal year, 48-49
inventory preferences, 53-54
invoice styles, 56
job estimates, 58
legal names, 46-47
multiple companies, 47
multiple locations, 47
payroll information, 57
reminders preferences, 60
sales tax items, 54-55
tax agencies, 54
tax return forms, 49-50
time-tracking feature, 59

Georgia Department of Revenue, 514

Getting Started with Online Banking window, 415

goods. See inventory

grace periods, 387

graphics
logos, 296, 346-347
graphs, 147-149, 163, 376-377
2D (two-dimensional), 400
Accounts Payable, 378
accounts receivable, 194, 378
Budget vs. Actual, 380
Income and Expenses, 377
Net Worth, 380
preference settings, 399-401
refreshing, 399
Sales, 378

Graphs command
Reports menu, 163
Reports on All Items menu, 147

Grid and Snap Settings window, 352

grid settings (Layout Designer), 352

group items, 124

H

hard drive, running QuickBooks from, 14

hardware
monitor resolution, 502
QuickBooks requirements, 501-502

Hawaii First Taxation District offices, 515

headers (report), 342, 370-371

Help index
annotating, 24
keeping on top, 23
opening, 23

HELP INDEX

searching, 23
topics, printing, 23

Help Index command (Help menu), 23

Help menu commands
About QuickBooks (Pro), 29
Help Index, 23
Hide/Show QCards, 25, 30
QuickBooks and Your Industry, 29

help systems
Find feature, 24-25
Help index
annotating, 24
keeping on top, 23
opening, 23
searching, 23
topics, printing, 23
How Do I? button, 26
Introduction to QuickBooks videos, 26-27
Intuit technical support
Automated Expert, 28
industry-specific information, 29
QuickFax system, 29
telephone service, 28-29
QCards
displaying, 25
hiding, 25, 30
moving, 25
QuickBooks Web site
FAQs (frequently asked questions), 27
User-to-User Forums, 28

Hide/Show QCards command (Help menu), 25, 30

hiding QCards, 25, 30

historical transactions
bills paid, 99
bills received, 90-92
checks, 102
deposits, 99-100
invoices, 92-94

payments
cash payments, 97-98
credits/refunds, 96-97
discounts, 95-96
payments against invoices, 94-95
payroll, 100-102
required documents/information, 88-90
start dates, changing, 88

HotBot Web site, 432

How Do I? button, 26

How to Depreciate Property, 256

I

iconbar
buttons
adding, 391
deleting, 392
editing, 391
separating spaces, 391
displaying, 381, 390
forms/reports, 358-359
preference settings, 390-392

Idaho State Tax Commission, 515

IIF file type, 447

Illinois Department of Revenue, 515

Import QuickBooks Lists command (Timer File menu), 449

importing
Excel files, 512
lists, 449-450

In Process job status, 172

inactive accounts
creating, 115-116
displaying, 116
reactivating, 116

income. *See also* **payments**
company information, entering, 66-67
defined, 523
net income, 112, 524

Income & Expenses section (EasyStep interview), 43
income accounts
creating, 64-65
defined, 64
parent accounts, 65
subaccounts, 65-66

income accounts
creating, 64-65
defined, 52, 64, 107, 112

Income and Expenses graphs, 377

Income Details section (EasyStep interview), 43
income information, 66-67
inventory items, 71-72
non-inventory part items, 69-70
other charge items
creating, 70-71
defined, 67
service items
creating, 67-69
defined, 67

income statements. *See* **profit & loss reports**

Income Tax Detail reports, 494-495

Income Tax Preparation reports, 492-493

Income Tax Summary reports, 493-494

income taxes
forms, 495-496
non-tax-related transactions, 497
professional preparation, 498

quarterly estimates
corporations, 490-491
individuals, 491
reports
Income Tax Detail, 494-495
Income Tax Preparation, 492-493
Income Tax Summary, 493-494
state revenue agencies, 513-520
tax lines, 491-492, 498
TurboTax software, 496

independent contractors
employees, compared, 274-275, 277-278, 305
setting up, 303-304

indexes, Help
annotating, 24
keeping on top, 23
opening, 23
searching, 23
topics, printing, 23

Indiana Department of Revenue, 515

industry-specific technical support (Intuit), 29

Infoseek Web site, 432

install disks (Timer), 457-458

installing QuickBooks, 501
from CD-ROM, 502-503
from floppy disks, 503
system requirements, 501-502
Timer, 448

InsureMarket Web site, 433

Internal Revenue Service. *See* **IRS**

Internet Connection Setup command (Online menu), 413

Internet connections, 413-414

Internet Web sites. See **Web sites**

interviews
EasyStep, *see* EasyStep interview
Online Interview, 414-415
account activation, 416
application information, downloading, 417-418
starting, 414

Introduction to QuickBooks videos, 26-27

Intuit technical support, 488
Automated Expert, 28
industry-specific information, 29
QuickFax system, 29
telephone service, 28-29

inventory
activating, 226
adding items to
multiple items, 223
on-the-fly, 221-223
adjusting quantity/value, 140-142, 228-229
cash outflow for inventory forecasts, 472, 476-477
cost of goods sold, 522
counting, 227-228
defined, 53-54, 218, 523
editing, 224
items, 67, 71-72, 124
manufactured goods, 218-219
purchase orders
creating, 234-237
enabling, 234
previewing, 238
printing, 237-238
saving, 237
tracking, 238
raw materials, 218
receipt of items, 139
with bill, 226, 241
without bill, 224, 226, 239-241

reorder feature, 220
reports
Inventory Stock Status by Item, 226
Inventory Stock Status by Vendor, 226
Inventory Valuation Detail, 226
Inventory Valuation Summary, 226
Item Price List, 227
Physical Inventory Worksheet, 147, 227-228
Stock Status by Item, 147
Valuation Summary, 147
shortage pop-up warnings, 397
theft, accounting for, 232
third-party software, 229-230
database programs, 231
dedicated inventory-tracking programs, 231-232
spreadsheet programs, 230-231
tracking, 53-54
troubleshooting, 232
valuing
FIFO (first in, first out), 220
LIFO (last in, first out), 220
specific identification method, 220
weighted average method, 218-220, 524

Inventory command (Activities menu), 224

Inventory Reports command (Reports on All Items menu), 147

Inventory Stock Status by Item report, 226

Inventory Stock Status by Vendor report, 226

Inventory Valuation Detail report, 226

invoices
   creating, 185-187
   customizing, *see* custom forms
   historical transactions, 92-94
   items
      adding, 122-124
      deleting, 187
   job estimates, 176-178
   payments
      advances/prepayments, 203-204
      down payments, 203-204
      entering, 198-199
      historical payments, 94-95
   previewing, 187
   printing, 187
   printing list of, 92
   product, 184
   professional, 184
   progressive estimate invoices, 344-345
   sales tax
      applying to purchases, 211
      enabling collection, 209-210
      items, 207-208
      liability reports, 213-215
      paying, 214-215
      Sales Tax Payable accounts, 206-207
      tax-exempt sales, 212-213
   service, 184
   styles, 56

Iowa Department of Revenue and Finance, 515

IRS (Internal Revenue Service), 256, 495. See also taxes
   payroll forms
      W-2 forms, 298-301
      W-3 forms, 301
   publications
      How to Depreciate Property, 256
      Sales and Other Dispositions of Assets, 261
      Sales of Business Property, 261
   tax return forms
      Form 940, 323-325
      Form 941, 322-323, 333
      Form 990, 49
      Form 990-PF, 50
      Form 990-T, 50
      Form 1065, 49
      Form 1040, 491
      Form 1099, 302-305, 404-405
      Form 1120, 49
      Form 1120S, 49
      Form 8109, 490
   Web site, 256, 435

Item Estimates vs. Actuals report, 147

Item Not Found window, 221

Item Price List report, 227

Item Profitability report, 147

itemized balance sheet report, 163

items
   applying, 122-124
   creating, 133
   defined, 67, 122
   editing, 132-133
   Items list, 134
   prices
      calculating, 136-137
      changing, 135-136
   reports, 142
   subitems
      benefits of, 126-127
      creating, 126
   types
      discount, 125
      group, 124
      inventory part, 67, 71-72, 124
      noninventory part, 69-70, 124
      other charge, 70-71, 125
      payment, 124
      payroll, 80-83, 281-282, 305, 316-319
      sales tax, 125, 207-208
      sales tax group, 125
      service, 67, 122, 124, 524
      subtotal, 125

Items command (List menu), 267

Items list, 134

J

job estimates, 58

Job Info tab (New Customer window), 151

Job Profitability Summary reports, 181

Job Progress Invoices vs. Estimates reports, 181

jobs
   creating, 170-171
   Customer:Job list, 149, 151
   defined, 523
   descriptions, 173
   estimates
      advantages, 174
      creating, 175-176
      defined, 174
      deleting, 181
      displaying, 176
      invoicing against, 176-178
      overriding, 181
      previewing, 176
      printing, 176
      reports, 180-181
      revising, 179-180
   preference settings, 392-393

reports
- *Budget by Job Comparison, 469*
- *Budget by Job Overview, 468-469*
- *invoices vs. estimates, 181*
- *profit/loss statements, 181*
- *profitability summaries, 181*
- *unbilled costs, 181*

service items, 524
start/completion dates, 173
status, 171
- *Awarded, 172*
- *changing, 172-173*
- *Closed, 172*
- *displaying, 173*
- *In Process, 172*
- *Not Awarded, 172*
- *Pending, 172*

types, 174, 523

journal entries
creating, 259-260
defined, 258, 523

justified text, 350

K-L

Kansas Department of Revenue, 515

Keep Help on Top command (Options menu), 23

Kentucky Revenue Cabinet, 515

last in, first out (LIFO), 220

launching. See starting

Layout Designer
fields, moving/sizing, 348-350
grid settings, 352
margins, 352-353
Show Envelope Window option, 353
zooming in/out, 352

Leave button (EasyStep interview), 44-45

legal business names, 46-47

letters
editing, 512
writing, 511-512

liabilities
current, 77
defined, 77, 107, 109, 523
examples, 109
long-term, 77
payroll
- *Payroll Liability account, 278-279*
- *year-to-date amounts, 287-288*

short-term, 77
year-to-date, 298

limited liability companies, 111

lines of credit
creating, 76
defined, 76, 523

List menu, Items command, 267

lists, 127-130. See also items
common features, 130
Customer, 157
Customer Messages, 156
Customer:Job, 149
Customer:notes, 151
Employee, 153
entries
- *adding, 128-129*
- *displaying details, 129*
- *finding, 131-132*
- *merging, 129*
- *moving, 130*
- *subitems, 131*

exporting, 447-448, 510-511
importing into Timer, 449-450
Items, 134

Payment Method, 156-157
Reminders list, 16-17
- *creating, 17-18*
- *displaying, 18*
- *launching at startup, 60*
- *preference settings, 398-399*
- *troubleshooting, 19*

Terms
- *creating terms, 154-156*
- *deactivating terms, 156*
- *editing terms, 154-156*
- *finding terms, 156*
- *printing terms, 156*

Type, 154, 524
Vendors, 151-152
- *adding vendors, 152*
- *editing vendors, 153*

Lists menu commands
Chart of Accounts, 113
Customer:Job, 170
Reminders, 18

loans
amortization schedules, 77, 522
calculators, 435
Cashfinder service, 428-429
lines of credit
- *creating, 76*
- *defined, 76, 523*

principal, 524
setting up, 76-78

logos
adding to forms, 346-347
adding to paychecks, 296

long-term liabilities, 77

LookSmart Web site, 432

Lotus 123 spreadsheets
inventory tracking, 230-231
printing to, 474

Louisiana Department of Revenue, 516

Lycos Web site, 432

M

MACRS (Modified Accelerated Cost Recovery System), 256-258
   advantages/disadvantages, 256
   depreciation tables, 257-258

magazines
   Business Week, 433
   Money Magazine, 434

Maine Bureau of Taxation, 516

maintaining records
   annual activities, 37-38
   daily activities, 32-33
   monthly activities, 35-36
   payroll issues, 35
   quarterly activities, 36-37
   task checklists, 33-34
   weekly activities, 34

maintenance releases, 288-290, 524

Make Deposits command (Activities menu), 99, 201, 203

Make Inactive command (Class menu), 162

Make Journal Entry command (Activities menu), 259

manufactured goods, inventory records of, 218-219

margins (forms), 352-353

Margins window, 352

markup percentages, 403

Maryland Comptroller of the Treasury, 516

Massachusetts Department of Revenue, 516

matching QuickStatements with QuickBooks accounts, 419-421

members, 111

memorized reports
   creating, 373
   deleting, 374
   editing, 374

Memorized Reports command (Reports menu), 373

memos
   Cash Sales form, 201
   credit memos, 523
   estimates, 176

Menu Items section (EasyStep interview), 43, 85

menu preferences, 393-394

merchandise. See inventory

merging
   accounts, 116-117
   list entries, 129

messages (online)
   creating, 423-425
   payment inquiries, 425

Miami Herald Web site, 438

Michigan Department of Revenue, 516

Microsoft Excel, importing QuickBooks files into, 509

Microsoft Word letters
   editing, 512
   writing, 511-512

Minnesota Department of Revenue, 516

Mississippi State Tax Commission, 516

Missouri Department of Revenue, 517

modes, multiuser, 506

Modified Accelerated Cost Recovery System. See MACRS

Money Magazine Web site, 434

monitor resolution, 502

Montana Department of Revenue, 517

monthly activities (record maintenance), 35-36

monthly statements
   creating, 188-190
   printing, 190

moving
   form fields, 348-349
   QCards, 25

multiuser environments
   access options, 506
   multiuser mode, 506
   network requirements, 505
   software installation, 505

multiuser mode, 506

N

names
   company names, 46-47
   file names
      company information files, 51
      Timer files, 449
   legal names, 46-47

navigating EasyStep interview, 43-44

Nebraska Department of Revenue, 517

net income, 112, 524

net values, 254

net worth (equity), 109-110, 522-524. See also equity accounts

Net Worth graphs, 380

net worth statements. See balance sheet reports

networks, sharing QuickBooks over
  access options, 506
  multiuser mode, 506
  network requirements, 505
  software installation, 505

Nevada Department of Taxation, 517

New Account window, 113-114, 267

New Activity window, 451

New Company command (File menu), 42

New Customer window
  Additional Info tab, 151
  Address Info tab, 150
  Customer field, 150
  Job Info tab, 151

New Employee window, 280

new features (QuickBooks), 11-12

New Hampshire Department of Revenue Administration, 517

New Item window, 133, 221

New Jersey Division of Taxation, 517

New Mexico Taxation and Revenue Department, 517

New Time File command (Timer File menu), 449

New User Setup Wizard, 506

New York Department of Taxation and Finance, 518

New York Times Web site, 437

newspaper Web sites, 436, 438

Next button (EasyStep interview), 45

no access option, 506

non-inventory part items, 124
  creating, 69-70
  defined, 67

North Carolina Department of Revenue, 518

North Dakota Office of State Tax Commissioner, 518

Not Awarded job status, 172

numbers (account), assigning
  automatically, 384
  manually, 118
  QuickBooks numbering system, 117-118

O

Ohio Department of Taxation, 518

Oklahoma Tax Commission, 518

One Customer option (monthly statements), 190

online banking, 410-411
  accounts
    activating, 416
    routing/account numbers, 421
  application information, downloading, 417-418
  Internet connections, 413-414
  messages
    creating, 423-425
    payment inquiries, 425
  Online Banking Center window, 418
  Online Interview, 414-415
  payments
    creating, 422
    editing, 423
    enabling, 422
    limitations, 430
    sending, 423
  payroll service, 427
  preliminary steps, 411-413

QuickStatements
  displaying, 419
  downloading, 419
  matching with QuickBooks accounts, 419-421
  resources
    advisors, 428
    articles, 410
    bank pages, 411
    Cashfinder Web site, 428-429
    QuickBooks Web site, 427-428
    Small Business by Quicken Web site, 429
  Transaction Detail reports, 426
  transferring funds, 425-426

Online Banking Center window, 418

online help (QuickBooks Web site)
  FAQs (frequently asked questions), 27
  User-to-User Forums, 28

Online Interview, 414-415
  account activation, 416
  application information, downloading, 417-418
  starting, 414

Online menu, Internet Connection Setup command, 413

online resources. See Web sites

open balance reports, 180

Open Company command (File menu), 19

Open Invoices report (accounts receivable), 193

Open Purchase Orders By Job report, 146

Open Purchase Orders report, 146

opening
accounts receivable register, 191
check register, 247
company files, 19
Help index, 23
Timer files, 455-457

opening balance equity accounts, 110

opening balances, 72-73, 83, 85
asset accounts, 78
bank accounts, 78
credit card accounts, 75
customer information, 74
equity accounts, 79-80
lines of credit, 76
loans/liabilities, 76-78
vendor information, 74-75

Opening Balances section (EasyStep interview), 43, 72-73
asset accounts, 78
bank accounts, 78
credit card accounts, 75
customer information, 74
equity accounts, 79-80
lines of credit, 76
loans/liabilities, 76-78
vendor information, 74-75

Options menu commands
Annotate, 24
Keep Help on Top, 23

Options tab (Customize Invoice window), 346

options. See preferences

ordering lists, 130

orders. See purchase orders

Oregon Department of Revenue, 518

Other Charge items, 125
creating, 70-71
defined, 67

Other Reports command (Reports menu), 368

outstanding transactions, 194

overriding estimates, 181

overtime summary reports, 297

P

paid-in capital, 110

par value, 110

parent accounts, 524

partnerships, 49, 111

passwords
choosing, 483
configuring, 485-486

Pay Bills command (Activities menu), 99, 242

Pay Bills window, 99, 242

Pay Employees command (Payroll menu), 100

Pay Liabilities window, 310

Pay Sales Tax command (Activities menu), 214

Pay Sales Tax window, 214

paychecks
creating, 291-292
deleting, 294
displaying, 293
editing, 292-293
previewing, 292
printing, 295-296
voiding, 294
year-to-date amounts
adjustment periods, 286-287
updating, 285-287

Payment Method list, 156-157

payments
advances/prepayments, 203-204
automatic payment feature, 204
bills, 99, 241-243
cash transactions
cash over/short, 266-268
Cash Sales form, 199-201, 264
daily cash summaries, 265-266
deposits, 268
troubleshooting discrepancies, 269
credit cards, 268
details, displaying, 204
down payments, 203-204
employee salaries, *see* payroll
historical transactions
cash payments, 97-98
credits/refunds, 96-97
discounts, 95-96
payments against invoices, 94-95
invoice payments, 198-199
items, 124
online payments
creating, 422
editing, 423
enabling, 422
limitations, 430
payment inquiries, 425
sending, 423
sales tax, 214-215
tax liabilities
multiple check, 311
single check, 309-311
terms
creating, 154-156
deactivating, 156
editing, 154-156
finding, 156
printing, 156
reports, 156
tracking, 195

Payments to Deposit window, 99, 201-202

payroll, 80, 274-276. *See also* payroll taxes
  employee information, 279-280
    additions, 283
    base pay rates, 280-281
    company contributions, 283
    deductions, 283
    pay rates, 281
    shift differentials, 282
    sick time, 284
    taxes, 283
    vacation time, 284
    weekend pay, 282
  Expense accounts, 278-279
  historical transactions, 100-102
  independent contractors
    paying, 301-302
    setting up, 303-304
  items
    applying, 281
    creating, 80-83, 281-282, 305
  Liability accounts, 278-279
  online banking, 427
  opening balances, 83, 85
  paychecks
    creating, 291-292
    deleting, 294
    displaying, 293
    editing, 292-293
    previewing, 292
    printing, 295-296
    voiding, 294
  planning, 276-277
  preference settings, 394-396
  record maintenance, 35
  reports
    Payroll Summary by Item, 296-297
    YTD Liabilities, 298
  setting up, 86
  year-to-date amounts, 284
    adjustment periods, 286-287
    paychecks, 285-287
    taxes/liabilities, 287-288

Payroll Expense accounts, 278-279

Payroll Liability accounts, 278-279

Payroll menu, Pay Employees command, 100

Payroll section (EasyStep interview), 43
  payroll items, 80-83
  starting balances, 83, 85

Payroll Summary by Item report, 296-297

Payroll Summary report, 327

payroll taxes, 308
  advanced earned income credit, 332-333
  employee tax status
    city/county taxes, 314-315
    federal taxes, 312-313
    state taxes, 313-314
  federal unemployment tax, 329-330
  Form 940, 323-325
  Form 941
    adjusting, 322-323
    preparing, 322
    Schedule B, 333
  paying
    multiple check, 311
    single check, 309-311
    creating, 316-319
  reports
    Employee Earnings Summary, 320-321, 326-327
    Payroll Summary, 327
    Quick Reports, 327-329
  state revenue agencies, 513-520
  tax tables, 288-290
  troubleshooting
    county taxes, 333
    incorrect liability amounts, 330-332
    state taxes, 333
  W-2 forms, 298-299
    editing, 300-301
    printing, 299, 301
    reviewing, 299
  W-3 forms, 301
  wage base information, 315-316

Pending job status, 172

Pennsylvania Department of Revenue, 518

periodic recordkeeping activities
  annual activities, 37-38
  daily activities, 32-33
  monthly activities, 35-36
  payroll issues, 35
  quarterly activities, 36-37
  task checklists, 33-34
  weekly activities, 34

personal service corporations (PSCs), 111

Philadelphia Enquirer Web site, 438

Physical Inventory Worksheet, 147, 227-228

pop-up warnings, displaying
  deleted transactions, 388
  duplicate bill numbers, 398
  duplicate check numbers, 386
  duplicate estimate numbers, 393
  duplicate invoice numbers, 403
  duplicate purchase order numbers, 397
  edited transactions, 388
  inventory shortage, 397

preferences
  accounting
    account numbers, 384
    audit trails, 385
    class tracking, 385
  checking, 385-386
  customers, 402-403
  employees, 394-396
  finance charges, 386
    account information, 387
    annual interest rates, 387
    assessment method, 387
    grace period, 387
    invoices, 388
    minimum charges, 387
  general, 388-390
    date format, 389
    decimal point placement, 388
    desktop options, 389
    pop-up warnings, 388
    QCards, 388
    sounds, 388
    time format, 389
  graphs, 399-401
  iconbar, 390-392
  jobs/estimates, 392-393
  menus, 393-394
  payroll, 394-396
  purchase orders, 396-398
  reminders, 398-399
  reports, 399-401
  sales, 402-403
  sales tax, 403-404
  tax 1099 form, 404-405
  time tracking, 405
  vendors, 396-398
Preferences command (File menu), 17
prepayments, 203-204
Prev button (EasyStep interview), 45
Preview Paycheck window, 101

previewing
  estimates, 176
  forms, 353-354
  invoices, 187
  paychecks, 292
  purchase orders, 238
prices
  calculating, 136-137
  changing, 135-136
principal, 524
Print Checks command (Print Forms menu), 245
Print List command (Class menu), 162
Print Report command (File menu), 474, 509
Print Reports window, 374, 509
Print Statements window, 190
printing
  chart of accounts, 119
  checks, 245-246
  estimates, 176
  Form 1099, 305
  Help topics, 23
  invoices, 187
  lists
    bills received, 90
    classes, 162
    customers, 157
    invoices, 92
  monthly statements, 190
  paychecks, 295-296
  purchase orders, 237-238
  reports, 365, 374-376
  sales forecasts, 474
  terms, 156
  to files
    ASCII text files, 474
    Excel/Lotus 123 spreadsheets, 474
    tab delimited, 474
  W-2 forms, 299, 301
  W-3 forms, 301

Prior Payments of Taxes and Liabilities window, 287
private foundations, 50
product invoices, 56, 184
professional advisors, 428
professional invoices, 56, 184
Profit & Loss command
  Reports menu, 364
  Reports on All Accounts menu, 364
Profit & Loss reports, 162, 164, 181
  creating, 364-365
  defined, 524
  printing, 365
Profit and Loss by Class command (Reports on All Classes menu), 162
Profit and Loss command (Reports menu), 164
Prog Col tab (Customize Invoice window), 344
Progress Billing feature, 177
progressive estimate invoices, 344-345
Project command (Reports on All Items menu), 147
project reports, 147
projecting budgets, 465
proprietors, 111
PSCs (personal service corporations), 111
publications
  Business Week, 433
  Money Magazine, 434
  newspapers, 436-438
purchase orders
  creating, 234-237
  customizing, *see* custom forms

enabling, 234
preference settings, 396-398
previewing, 238
printing, 237-238
reports, 146
saving, 237
tracking, 238

purchase reports, 164
Open Purchase Orders, 146
Open Purchase Orders by Job, 146
Purchases by Item Detail, 146
Purchases by Item Summary, 145
Purchases by Vendor Detail, 146
Purchases by Vendor Summary, 146

Purchase Reports command
Reports menu, 164
Reports on All Items menu, 145

Purchases by Item Detail report, 146

Purchases by Item Summary report, 145

Purchases by Vendor Detail report, 146

Purchases by Vendor Summary report, 146

Q

QCards
disabling, 388
displaying, 25
enabling, 388
hiding, 25, 30
moving, 25

quarterly activities (record maintenance), 36-37

quarterly income tax estimates
corporations, 490-491
individuals, 491

Quattro Pro, exporting files to, 509

QuickBooks and Your Industry command (Help menu), 29

QuickBooks installation
from CD-ROM, 502-503
from floppy disks, 503
system requirements, 501-502

QuickBooks Web site, 427-428, 432-433
FAQs (frequently asked questions), 27
User-to-User Forums, 28

Quicken
files, converting to Quickbooks, 507-508
Web site, 429, 438

QuickFax system (Intuit), 29

QuickReports, 180
drill-down techniques
date ranges, 327
double-clicking transactions, 328-329
filters, 328
generating, 143
payroll information, 327

QuickStatements
displaying, 419
downloading, 419
matching with QuickBooks accounts, 419-421

R

raw materials, 218

reactivating inactive accounts, 116

receipts, 140

Receive Payments command (Activities menu), 94, 198

Receive Payments window, 94, 198

receiving
inventory items, 139
with bill, 226, 241
without bill, 224, 226, 239-241
payments (historical transactions)
cash payments, 97-98
credits, 96-97
discounts, 95-96
payments against invoices, 94-95
refunds, 96-97

Reconcile command (Activities menu), 249

Reconcile window, 249

reconciling accounts, 248-250

records. *See also* **accounts**
company information files, setting up, 41-42
access control, 52
addresses, 47-48
bill-paying preferences, 60
business types, 50
chart of accounts, 51-52
classes feature, 59
company name, 46-47
FEIN (Federal Identification Number), 48
filenames, 51
fiscal year, 48-49
inventory preferences, 53-54
invoice styles, 56
job estimates, 58
legal name, 46-47
multiple companies, 47
multiple locations, 47
payroll information, 57
Reminders preferences, 60
sales tax items, 54-55

RECORDS

    start dates, 40, 88
    tax return forms, 49-50
    time-tracking feature, 59
  correcting, 38
  maintaining
    annual activities, 37-38
    daily activities, 32-33
    monthly activities, 35-36
    payroll issues, 35
    quarterly activities, 36-37
    task checklists, 33-34
    weekly activities, 34
  upgrading to QuickBooks 6.0/7.0, 44-45

refreshing reports/graphs, 399

refunds, 96-97

registers
  accounts receivable
    displaying, 191
    opening, 191
    searching, 192
  check registers, 247

registration number, finding, 29

reimbursed expenses, 403

Reminders command (Lists menu), 18

Reminders windows, 16

Reminders list, 16-17
  creating, 17-18
  displaying, 18
  launching at startup, 60
  preference settings, 398-399
  troubleshooting, 19

reorder feature, 220

reordering lists, 130

Report Filters window, 372, 475

reports, 142-145, 162, 362-364
  accounts receivable,
    Aging Detail, 193
    Aging Summary, 192, 366

    Collections, 193
    Customer Balance Detail, 193
    Customer Balance Summary, 193
    Open Invoices, 193
    Unbilled Costs by Job, 193
  adding to iconbar, 358-359
  amortization schedules, 522
  balance sheets, 365-366, 522
    itemized balance sheets, 163
    open balance, 180
  budget reports
    Balance Sheet Comparison, 470
    Balance Sheet Overview, 469
    Budget by Job Comparison, 469
    Budget by Job Overview, 468-469
    Budget Overview, 467
    Budget vs. Actual, 467-468
  Collections, 367
  customizing, 368-369, 381
    columns, 369-370
    dates, 369
    fields, 371-372
    footers, 370-371
    headers, 370-371
  displaying, 381
  exporting, 509-510
  filters, 372-373
  forecasts
    Cash Flow, 472, 477-478
    Cash Outflow, 472, 477
    Cash Outflow for Inventory, 472, 476-477
    Cash Receipts, 472, 475-476
    Sales, 472-474
  formatting, 373
  General Ledger, 368
  graphs, 147-149, 163, 376-377

    Accounts Payable, 378
    Accounts Receivable, 378
    Budget vs. Actual, 380
    Income and Expenses, 377
    Net Worth, 380
    Sales, 378
  income tax
    Income Tax Detail, 494-495
    Income Tax Preparation, 492-493
    Income Tax Summary, 493-494
  inventory
    Inventory Stock Status by Item, 226
    Inventory Stock Status by Vendor, 226
    Inventory Valuation Detail, 226
    Inventory Valuation Summary, 226
    Item Price List, 227
    Physical Inventory Worksheet, 147, 227-228
    Stock Status by Item, 147
    Valuation Summary, 147
  memorized reports
    creating, 373
    deleting, 374
    editing, 374
  payroll
    Employee Earnings Summary, 320-321, 326-327
    Payroll Summary, 327
    Payroll Summary by Item, 296-297
  preference settings, 399-401
  profit/loss, 162-164, 181
    creating, 364-365
    defined, 524
    printing, 365
  projects
    Item Estimates vs. Actuals, 147, 181
    Item Profitability, 147

job profitability summaries, 181
Time By Item, 147
purchases
  Open Purchase Orders, 146
  Open Purchase Orders By Job, 146
  Purchases by Item Detail, 146
  Purchases by Item Summary, 145
  Purchases by Vendor Detail, 146
  Purchases by Vendor Summary, 146
Quick Reports, 180
  drill-down techniques, 327-329
  generating, 143
  payroll information, 327
refreshing, 399
sales, 164
  Sales by Item Detail, 145
  Sales by Item Summary, 145
  Sales Tax Liability, 213-215
subaccounts, 371
Timer Import Detail, 455
Transaction Detail, 426
unbilled costs, 181
YTD Liabilities, 298

Reports menu commands
  A/R Reports, 366
  Balance Sheet, 365
  Balance Sheet Itemized, 163
  Budget Reports, 467
  Custom Report, 473
  Graphs, 163
  Memorized Reports, 373
  Quick Report, 162
  Other Reports, 368
  Profit & Loss, 164, 364
  Purchase Reports, 164
  Reports on All Classes, 162
  Sales Reports, 164

Reports on All Classes command (Reports menu), 162

Reports on All Classes menu, Profit and Loss by Class command, 162

Reports on All Items menu commands
  Graphs, 147
  Inventory Reports, 147
  Project, 147
  Purchase Reports, 145
  Sales Reports, 145

restarting EasyStep interview, 43

Restore command (File menu), 16

Restore From window, 16

Restore Timer File command (Timer File menu), 460

Restore To window, 16

restoring from backups
  disk backups, 16
  tape backups, 16
  Timer files, 460
  troubleshooting, 19

resuming timing sessions, 452

retained earnings, 110

revenue agencies. See also taxes
  Internal Revenue Service, *see* IRS
  state agencies, 513-520

revising. See editing

Rhode Island Division of Taxation, 519

rights (access), 486-487, 506

Roth IRA Web site, 435

routing numbers (online accounts), 421

running Quickbooks, 12
  from CD-ROM, 13-14
  from hard drive, 14

S

S corporations
salaries. See payroll
sales. See also invoices
  cash transactions
    Cash Sales form, 199-201, 264
    troubleshooting discrepancies, 269
  credit card payments, 268
  depreciable assets, 260-261
  forecasts
    creating, 473
    defined, 472
    printing, 474
  graphs, 378
  preference settings, 402-403
  reports
    Sales by Item Detail, 145
    Sales by Item Summary, 145
  sales tax, 54, 206
    applying to purchases, 211
    enabling collection, 209-210
    items, 125, 207-208
    liability reports, 213-215
    paying, 214-215
    preference settings, 403-404
    Sales Tax Payable accounts, 206-207
    state revenue agencies, 513-520
    tax agencies, 54
    tax-exempt sales, 212-213, 238-239

Sales and Other Dispositions of Assets, 261

Sales by Item Detail reports, 145

Sales by Item Summary reports, 145

Sales graphs, 378

Sales of Business Property, 261

sales reports, 164

Sales Reports command (Reports menu), 164

Sales Reports command (Reports on All Items menu), 145

sales tax, 54, 206
 applying to purchases, 211
 enabling collection, 209-210
 items, 125, 207-208
 liability reports
  creating, 213-214
  printing, 214
  troubleshooting, 215
 paying, 214-215
 preference settings, 403-404
 Sales Tax Payable accounts, 206-207
 state revenue agencies, 513-520
 tax agencies, 54
 tax-exempt sales, 212-213

Sales Tax Payable accounts, 206-207

saving purchase orders, 237

search engines, 432

searching
 accounts receivable register, 192
 check register, 247-248
 help system
  Find feature, 24-25
  Help index, 23
  How Do I? button, 26
 lists, 131-132

Seattle Times Web site, 437

Section 179 depreciation, 262

security
 backups, 482
 company information files, 52

user accounts, 482-483
 access rights, 486-487
 administrator, 483-485
 passwords, 485-486
 year-end protection, 487-488

Select Checks to Print window, 245

Select Employees to Pay window, 100, 291

Select Statements to Print window, 188

Selected Customers option (monthly statements), 189

selective access, 506

selective rights, 506

sending online payments, 423

service invoices, 56, 184

service items, 122-124
 creating, 67-69
 defined, 67, 524

Set Up Budgets command (Activities menu), 465

Set Up Budgets window, 465-466

Set up Users & Passwords command (File menu), 506

Set Up YTD Amounts window, 285

sharing QuickBooks
 access options, 506
 multiuser mode, 506
 software installation, 505

shift differentials, 282

shipping methods, 402

short-term liabilities, 77

Show Envelope Window option (Layout Designer), 353

showing. See displaying

sick bonuses, 284

single-user mode, 506

sites. See Web sites

sizing
 form fields, 348-350
 forms, 359

Skip Interview button (EasyStep interview), 45

skipping EasyStep interview, 45

Small Business Administration Web site, 433

Small Business by Quicken Web site, 429

software
 Acrobat Reader, 439
 TurboTax, 496

sole proprietors, 49, 111

South Carolina Tax Commission, 519

South Dakota Department of Revenue, 519

specific identification method (inventory valuation), 220

spreadsheets
 inventory tracking, 230-231
 printing to, 474

St. Petersburg Times Web site, 438

standard reports. See reports

start dates, 173
 changing, 61, 88
 choosing, 40-41
 defined, 40, 524

starting
 EasyStep interview, 42
 QuickBooks, 12
  from CD-ROM, 13-14
  from hard drive, 14
 Timer, 449

state taxes
  payroll tax
    employee tax status, 313-314
    payroll items, 316-319
    reports, 320-321, 326-329
    wage base information, 315-316
  sales tax, 54, 206
    applying to purchases, 211
    enabling collection, 209-210
    items, 125, 207-208
    liability reports, 213-215
    paying, 214-215
    preference settings, 403-404
    Sales Tax Payable accounts, 206-207
    state revenue agencies, 513-520
    tax agencies, 54
    tax-exempt sales, 212-213, 238-239
  state revenue agencies, 513-520

statements
  customizing, *see* custom forms
  monthly statements
    creating, 188-190
    printing, 190
  QuickStatements
    displaying, 419
    downloading, 419
    matching with QuickBooks accounts, 419-421

status (jobs), 171
  Awarded, 172
  changing, 172-173
  Closed, 172
  displaying, 173
  In Process, 172
  Not Awarded, 172
  Pending, 172

stock (merchandise). See inventory

stocks
  capital stock, 110
  par value, 110
  stock quote Web sites, 434

Stock Status by Item reports, 147

stopping
  EasyStep interview, 43
  timing sessions, 452

stopwatch. See Timer

straight-line depreciation, 256

subaccounts, 65
  collapsing/expanding, 371
  defined, 524

subitems, 131
  benefits of, 126-127
  creating, 126

subtotal items, 125

summary reports
  daily cash summaries, 265-266
  Income Tax Summary, 493-494
  Payroll Summary by Item, 296-297

Switch command (File menu), 506

T

tab delimited files
  printing to, 474
  depreciation tables, 257-258

Tax Professionals.com Web site, 435

tax year (fiscal year), 40, 48-49

tax-exempt sales, 212-213, 238-239

Taxable Compensation window, 318

taxes
  income tax
    forms, 495-496
    non-tax-related transactions, 497
    professional preparation, 498
    quarterly estimates, 490-491
    reports, 492-495
    tax lines, 491-492, 498
    TurboTax software, 496
  online resources, 435-436
  payroll, 308
    advanced earned income credit, 332-333
    employee tax status, 312-315
    federal unemployment tax, 329-330
    Form 940, 323-325
    Form 941, 322-323, 333
    Form 1099, 302-305
    paying, 309-311
    payroll items, 316-319
    QuickBooks tax tables, 288-290
    reports, 320-321, 326-329
    troubleshooting, 330-333
    wage base information, 315-316
    year-to-date amounts, 287-288
  sales tax, 54
    paying, 214-215
    applying to purchases, 211
    enabling collection, 209-210
    items, 207-208
    liability reports, 213-215
    preference settings, 403-404
    Sales Tax Payable accounts, 206-207
    tax agencies, 54
    tax-exempt sales, 212-213
  state revenue agencies, 513-520

tax return forms
  Form 940, 323-325
  Form 941, 322-323, 333
  Form 990, 49
  Form 990-PF, 50
  Form 990-T, 50
  Form 1040, 49
  Form 1065, 49
  Form 1099, 404-405
  Form 1120, 49
  Form 1120S, 49
tax-exempt sales, 238-239
unemployment taxes, 81

TaxWeb Web site, 435

technical support, 28-29, 488

templates
  activating, 348
  customizing, 339-340
    column order, 342
    company information, 346
    fields, 340-342
    fonts, 347-348
    footers, 345
    headers, 342
    logos, 346-347
  deactivating, 348
  duplicating, 339
  Timer, 453

Tennessee Department of Revenue, 519

terms
  creating, 154-156
  deactivating, 156
  editing, 154-156
  finding, 156
  printing, 156
  reports, 156

Terms lists, 154-156

Texas Comptroller of Public Accounts, 519

theft, inventory tracking, 232

Time By Item reports, 147

time display, 389

time tracking feature
  preference settings, 405
  enabling, 59

timed sessions. See activities

Timer, 444-446, 458
  activities
    creating, 450-452
    defined, 451
    editing, 452
    switching between, 453
    templates, 453
    timing, 451-452
    viewing, 460-461
  closing, 452
  counter, changing, 453
  files
    activity log, 460-461
    condensing/backing up, 459
    creating, 449
    exporting, 454
    IIF file type, 447
    naming, 449
    opening in QuickBooks, 455-457
    restoring, 460
  installing, 448, 457-458
  lists, importing, 449-450
  starting, 449
  system requirements, 446
  troubleshooting, 461

Timer Import Detail report, 455

tracking
  classes, 385
  customer payments, 195
  depreciation, 78
  Form 1099 data, 302
  inventory, 53-54
    adding items to, 221-223
    defined, 218
    editing, 224
    manufactured goods, 218-219
    physical count, 227-228
    quantity/value adjustments, 140-142, 228-229
    raw materials, 218
    receipt of items, 224, 226
    reorder feature, 220
    reports, 226-227
    third-party software, 229-232
    troubleshooting, 232
    valuation, 218-220
  purchase orders, 238
  reimbursed expenses, 403
  timesheets, 59

Transaction Detail reports, 426

transactions. See also online banking
  Audit Trails, 260
  cash
    cash over/short, 266-268
    cash receipts forecasts, 472, 475-476
    Cash Sales form, 199-201, 264
    daily cash summaries, 265-266
    deposits, 268
    troubleshooting discrepancies, 269
  classes
    changing, 165
    creating, 161, 163
    deactivating, 162
    defined, 160
    deleting, 162
    editing, 162
    enabling, 160-161
    finding, 162
    printing list of, 162
    reports, 162-164
    subclasses, 160
  credit card payments, 268
  deleting, 388
  editing, 388

historical
  bills paid, 99
  bills received, 90-92
  checks, 102
  deposits, 99-100
  invoices, 92-94
  payments, 94-98
  payroll, 100-102
  required documents/information, 88-90
  start dates, changing, 88
invoices
  creating, 185-187
  custom, 185
  items, deleting, 187
  previewing, 187
  printing, 187
  product, 184
  professional, 184
  service, 184
matching to QuickStatements, 419-421
online payments
  creating, 422
  enabling, 422
  limitations, 430
  sending, 423
outstanding transactions, 194
sales tax
  applying to purchases, 211
  enabling collection, 209-210
  items, 207-208
  liability reports, 213-215
  paying, 214-215
  Sales Tax Payable accounts, 206-207
  tax-exempt sales, 212-213

Transfer Funds Between Accounts window, 425

transferring funds, 425-426

troubleshooting
  account numbering, 406
  budgets, 470
  cash flow difficulties, 479
  cash transactions, 269
  classes, 165
  Customers list, 157
  error messages
    "unable to convert online data", 508
    Web messages, 439
  iconbar, 406
  inventory, 232
  payroll taxes
    county taxes, 333
    incorrect liability amounts, 330-332
    state taxes, 333
  record corrections, 38
  registration numbers, 29
  Reminders, 19
  restore procedures, 19
  sales tax collection, 215
  sales tax liability reports, 215
  Timer, 461

TurboTax software, 496

turning on/off. See disabling; enabling

Type lists, 154, 524

U

U.S. House of Representatives' Internet Law Library Web site, 435

U.S. Small Business Administration Web site, 433

U.S. Tax Code Web site, 436

"unable to convert online data" message, 508

Unbilled Costs by Job reports, 181, 193

unemployment taxes, 81

updating records
  lists, 128-129
  payroll tax tables, 288-290
  scheduling updates
    annual activities, 37-38
    daily activities, 32-33
    monthly activities, 35-36
    payroll issues, 35
    quarterly activities, 36-37
    task checklists, 33-34
    weekly activities, 34
  year-to-date amounts
    adjustment periods, 286-287
    paychecks, 285-287
    taxes/liabilities, 287-288

upgrading QuickBooks versions, 44-45

USA Today Web site, 438

user preferences. See preferences

User-to-User Forums, 28

users
  accounts, 482-483
    access rights, 486-487
    administrator, 483-485
    passwords, 485-486
  shared access
    access options, 506
    multiuser mode, 506
    network requirements, 505
    software installation, 505

Utah State Tax Commission, 519

V

vacation time, 284

Valuation Summary reports, 147

valuing inventory
  FIFO (first in, first out), 220
  LIFO (last in, first out), 220
  specific identification method, 220
  weighted average method, 218-220, 524

Vendor Balance Detail command (A/P Reports menu), 90

vendors. See also contractors
  account balances, entering, 74-75
  adding, 152
  editing, 153
  preference settings, 396-398
  tax issues, 152
  types, 524
  Vendors list, 151-153

Vermont Department of Taxes, 519

viewing. See displaying

Virginia Department of Taxation, 520

visibility (fields), 342

voiding checks, 248, 251, 294

W

W-2 forms, 298-299
  editing, 300-301
  printing, 299, 301
  reviewing, 299

W-3 forms, 301

W-5 forms, 332

wage bases, 315-316

warning messages, displaying
  deleted transactions, 388
  duplicate bill numbers, 398
  duplicate check numbers, 386
  duplicate estimate numbers, 393
  duplicate invoice numbers, 403
  duplicate purchase order numbers, 397
  edited transactions, 388
  inventory shortage, 397

Washington Department of Revenue, 520

Washington Post Web site, 437

Web sites, 432
  Adobe, 439
  American Institute of Certified Public Accountants (AICPA), 435
  Business Week, 433
  Cashfinder, 428-429
  Charles Schwab, 434
  CNN Financial Network, 434
  error messages, 439
  etrade, 434
  Financenter, 435
  General Guides to Government Internet Resources, 436
  InsureMarket, 433
  Internet Law Library, 435
  IRS (Internal Revenue Service), 256, 435, 496
  Money Magazine, 434
  newspapers, 436, 438
  online banking resources
    articles, 410
    bank pages, 411
  QuickBooks, 427-428, 432-433
    FAQs (frequently asked questions), 27
    User-to-User Forums, 28
  Quicken, 438
  Roth IRA, 435
  search engines, 432
  Small Business by Quicken, 429
  state revenue agencies, 513-520
  Tax Professionals.com, 435
  TaxWeb, 435
  U.S. Small Business Administration, 433

U.S. Tax Code, 436

weekly activities (record maintenance), 34

weighted average method (inventory valuation), 218-220, 524

West Virginia State Tax Department, 520

What's Next section (EasyStep interview), 43, 85

Window menu, Add Window to Iconbar command, 358

windows
  Add New Payroll Item, 317
  Adjust Quantity/Value on Hand, 140, 228-229
  Assess Finance Charges, 189
  Back Up Company To, 15
  Banking Message, 424
  Change Prices, 135-136
  Class List, 161-163
  Convert a Quicken File, 508
  Create Credit Memos/Refunds, 96
  Create Estimates, 175-176
  Create Export File, 454
  Create Invoices, 92
    Bill To address field, 186
    Customer Message field, 187
    Customer:Job area, 185
    Item column, 187
    Memo field, 187
    Ship field, 186
    Ship To address field, 186
    Tax field, 187
    Terms field, 186
  Create Item Receipts, 224-225, 239-241
  Create Progress Invoice Based On Estimate, 177
  Create Purchase Orders, 234
  Customer:Job List, 170-171
  Customize Invoice, 340-341
    Columns tab, 342-343

Fields tab, 342-343
Footer tab, 345
Header tab, 342
Options tab, 346
Prog Col tab, 344
Customize Report, 473
Edit Account, 117
Edit Item, 132-133, 224
Enter Bills, 90, 138, 241
Enter Cash Sales, 97
Export, 447, 510
General Journal Entry, 259-260
Getting Started with Online Banking, 415
Grid and Snap Settings, 352
Item Not Found, 221
Make Deposits, 202-203
Margins, 352
New Account, 113-114, 267
New Activity, 451
New Customer, 150-151
New Employee, 280
New Item, 133, 221
Online Banking Center, 418
Pay Bills, 99, 242
Pay Liabilities, 310
Pay Sales Tax, 214
Payments to Deposit, 99, 201-202
Preview Paycheck, 101
Print Reports, 374, 509
Print Statements, 190
Prior Payments of Taxes and Liabilities, 287
Receive Payments, 94, 198
Reconcile, 249
Reminders, 16
Report Filters, 372, 475
Restore From, 16
Restore To, 16
Select Checks to Print, 245
Select Employees to Pay, 100, 291
Select Statements to Print, 188
Set Up Budgets, 465-466
Set Up YTD Amounts, 285
Taxable Compensation, 318
Transfer Funds Between Accounts, 425
Write Checks, 102, 243-245
Write Letters, 511

Wisconsin Department of Revenue, 520

witholding. See payroll taxes

wizards, New User Setup, 506

Word letters
editing, 512
writing, 511-512

worksheets
inventory tracking, 230-231
printing to, 474

Write Checks command (Activities menu), 102, 243

Write Checks window, 102, 243-245

Write Letters command (Activities menu), 511

Write Letters window, 511

writing
checks, 243-245
historical transactions, 102
preference settings, 385-386
letters, 511-512

Wyoming Revenue Department, 520

X-Y-Z

Yahoo Web site, 432
year-end protection, 487-488
year-end tasks (record mainte-
nance), 37-38
year-to-date payroll amounts, 284
adjustment periods, 286-287
paychecks, 285-287
taxes/liabilities, 287-288
year-to-date liabilities, 298

zeroing out sick/vacation time, 280
zooming in/out (forms), 352

Special Edition Using

The One Source for Comprehensive Solutions™

The one stop shop for serious users, *Special Edition Using* offers readers a thorough understanding of software and technologies. Intermediate to advanced users get detailed coverage that is clearly presented and to the point.

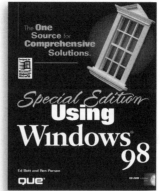

Special Edition Using Windows 98
Ed Bott & Ron Person
ISBN: 0-7897-1488-4
$39.99 US
$56.95 CAN

Other Special Edition Using Titles

Special Edition Using Microsoft Word 97, Bestseller Edition
Bill Carmada
ISBN: 0-7897-1398-5
$34.99 US
$49.95 CAN

Special Edition Using Microsoft Excel 97, Bestseller Edition
Bruce Hallberg
ISBN: 0-7897-1399-3
$39.99 US
$56.95 CAN

Special Edition Using Microsoft PowerPoint 97
Nancy Stevenson
ISBN: 0-7897-0961-9
$34.99 US
$49.95 CAN

Special Edition Using Microsoft Access 97, Second Edition
Roger Jennings
ISBN: 0-7897-1452-3
$49.99 US
$70.95 CAN

Special Edition Using Corel WorkPerfect Suite 8
Bill Bruck, Read Gilgen, and Joyce Nielsen
ISBN: 0-7897-1328-4
$39.99 US
$56.95 CAN

Special Edition Using the Internet, Fourth Edition
Jerry Honeycutt
ISBN: 0-7897-1403-5
$39.99 US
$57.95 CAN

Special Edition Using Microsoft Office 97 Professional, Bestseller Edition
Jim Boyce, et al.
ISBN: 0-7897-1396-9
$39.99 US
$56.95 CAN

Special Edition Using Microsoft Office 97 with Windows 98
Ed Bott, Jim Boyce, and Faithe Wempen
ISBN: 0-7897-1661-5
$39.99 US
$57.95 CAN

www.quecorp.com

All prices are subject to change.